OROKAIVA SOCIETY

An Orokaiva Youth wearing
Head-dress and *Hono*

OROKAIVA SOCIETY

BY

F. E. WILLIAMS

WITH AN INTRODUCTION

BY

SIR HUBERT MURRAY

OXFORD
AT THE CLARENDON PRESS

Oxford University Press, Ely House, London W. 1

GLASGOW NEW YORK TORONTO MELBOURNE WELLINGTON
CAPE TOWN SALISBURY IBADAN NAIROBI LUSAKA ADDIS ABABA
BOMBAY CALCUTTA MADRAS KARACHI LAHORE DACCA
KUALA LUMPUR SINGAPORE HONG KONG TOKYO

This reprint by arrangement with the
Administration of the Territory of Papua
and New Guinea

FIRST PUBLISHED 1930
REPRINTED LITHOGRAPHICALLY IN GREAT BRITAIN
AT THE UNIVERSITY PRESS, OXFORD
BY VIVIAN RIDLER
PRINTER TO THE UNIVERSITY
1969

PREFACE

THE present volume is the tenth published report of the Papuan Government on anthropology. It was also accepted and approved by the University of Adelaide as thesis for the Honours degree of M.A.

The aim of the book is primarily ethnographical. Interpretations of native customs have been essayed only in passing, and no attempt has been made to criticize them from the practical view-point. A Government anthropologist, however, must make some show of being a practical one. If those who have dealings with the Orokaiva—perhaps those also who have dealings with other native peoples— are helped by reading these pages to know their men better, then even pure description is not devoid of practical usefulness. Anthropology, if not necessarily a full-time job, is at least a slow business; and the magistrate, amid a multitude of distractions, cannot always find time for it. But knowledge of native custom is admittedly essential to good government; and books of this kind, in so far as they do something to supply this knowledge, can fairly lay claim to a practical value.

The information presented here was got together during two sojourns in the Northern Division, the first from September 1923 to February 1924, the second from July 1924 to March 1925—a total of about fourteen months. During these two periods I visited most parts of the Orokaiva country. For various reasons I concentrated mainly on the central Aigā tribe, and secondarily on the Binandele and Wasida. But all the other tribes were visited for shorter periods, and as the result of a general survey I found it possible to embrace the whole people in one ethnographic account.

Although the various tribes speak dialects of one and the same language, there are considerable differences between them, and I never gained a fluent speaking knowledge of any one of them. Several very good English-speaking inter-

preters, however, were available—especially one Ihipa, a
man of fine intelligence and character, who had spent his
childhood in the service of white men, at a time when the
Northern Division was a scene of great mining activity;
and another Bapia, who had been one of the best students
of the Anglican Mission. Furthermore there was no lack
of returned labourers, ex-police, and so forth, who spoke
that simplified version of the Motuan tongue which is
something of a Papuan *lingua franca*.

On the plains of the Northern Division working conditions are comparatively favourable, especially by reason of
the general accessibility of the country, and the distribution
of its inhabitants. It was my practice to make camp for
longer or shorter periods in the Government 'rest-houses'
which are erected for the convenience of officers on patrol.
These houses are usually placed in the more important
villages, and actually within the limits of the settlement; so
that one was enabled week in and week out to follow the
course of village life as it went on around one's habitation.

But every ethnographer expects to be able to do this.
The special advantages which one enjoyed in the Northern
Division arose from the fact that the plains were well
populated, and this by tribes who were more or less homo-
geneous in language and culture. Being quartered for some
months in the Aiga village of Korisata, for instance, I found
fifteen villages within easy reach—so easy that, visiting the
most distant of them I could spend several hours at work
there and return to my camp in the afternoon. A good walk
to one's destination; a few hours' work; an *al fresco* lunch
spread out on a banana-leaf table-cloth, and beguiled by
some reading (always, I confess far removed from anthropology and Papua); then a second session; and finally a good
walk home—such was the routine of those little excursions
which have always been the pleasantest part of field-work as
I have attempted to carry it out.

Where this frequent visiting of not-too-distant villages is
possible it carries with it several distinct advantages. In the
first place one is likely to get wind of the social happenings
of the district, near or far. Sometimes through secretive-

ness, but more often perhaps through an exasperating for-
getfulness, those who know of such happenings fail to pass
on the news. But in the course of a fairly constant round of
visits one is likely to pick up the scent somewhere, and then
of course there is only one thing to do, to pack up and
follow it.

Secondly, one is able to hear various views on every new
subject that crops up—and various enough they prove to be;
for how often does the unfortunate ethnographer, with his
ears aprick for verification, sadly jot down the words of
contradiction! Obviously investigation is made none the
easier—far from it; but in such circumstances one is bound
to resist the temptation of a facile reliance on a few eloquent
informants.

Lastly there is this third advantage—by no means to be
despised—that one's welcome does not grow stale. While a
talkative man in our midst may become a bore, the talkative
visitor will at least be tolerated; and among those closely-set
villages of the Orokaiva which I visited from time to time,
but always with intervals, I found not only toleration of the
inquisitive stranger, but an almost flattered anxiety to be
communicative.

Altogether the Orokaiva country was a good one to work
in, especially for these reasons that I have named. Many
other districts of Papua are by no means so kind to the field
worker.

A 'Government' anthropologist may possibly labour
under certain difficulties, but I doubt whether these weigh
against the compensatory advantages. I have always had the
advantage of an Armed Constable as escort. I use the word
'advantage' deliberately; though about the word 'escort' I
feel less confidence. In practice the Armed Constable
usually proves to be a fellow of very good company, and
makes himself useful in a variety of ways, even rising to the
occasion as a cook. But in so far as 'escort' implies protection, it is superfluous in places like the Northern Division.
The policeman's principal duty is to wear his uniform, and
thus to stamp one's retinue, consisting of a cook and one or
two local interpreters, as one of Government importance.

Needless to say this makes a world of difference in the matter
of transport, for without the blue serge and red braid of the
policeman's uniform one might sometimes be left, as they
say, 'in the air'. But it also does much to ensure a welcome;
for the Orokaiva have long been thoroughly under Government control, and a series of intelligent and sympathetic
magistrates have succeeded in developing a general feeling
of confidence and friendliness.

It is certainly true that there are some things which the
native is anxious to conceal from the Government. But he
quickly comes to realize that one is a Government officer
with a difference; that one is not equipped with any authority; and that one has no intention of playing the spy. On
the whole I do not think, when an investigator has been at
work in a district for any length of time, that information
is intentionally withheld because of his connexion with the
Government. Indeed six years' experience has taught me to
think that the ethnographer's most serious obstacle is far
from being deliberate concealment on the part of his informants. Nor is it principally the native's difficulty in
explaining his meaning. The great trouble is, I believe, that
it *does not occur to him* to tell.

A word on the ethics of ethnography. The situation
sometimes arises in which the investigator is favoured with
doubtful confidences. Now no enlightened person thinks
that anthropology, whether under Government or any other
auspices, is to be identified with espionage; and provided
the investigator makes his reports in an impersonal manner,
there is no danger of inculpating his informants. What
subsequent action may be taken, either by Government or
Mission, in the light of his revelations (if he has made any)
cannot be a concern of his, *qua* ethnographer. It is his
business to record in general terms the facts as he finds them,
trusting that those who govern or educate the native will
make the best use of the information. In so far as that
information leads to a fuller understanding of native life
he has done the natives a good turn. If it leads to a harsh,
unsympathetic suppression of customs newly discovered in
his reports, then it will be a bad state of affairs for which he

will be sorry, but not to blame. Happily, however, an anthropologist in Papua need have no fear that those in authority will so misuse the information he gives them.

As a general description the present book should logically have preceded the treatment of certain specific subjects which appeared as 'Orokaiva Magic'; but I have endeavoured not to trespass unduly on the ground of the former work. There remain a collection of fables and legends, some linguistic material, and a quantity of miscellaneous information which I hope may be published in a further report.

It is by courtesy of the Royal Anthropological Institute that the substance of an article, 'Plant Emblems among the Orokaiva', which appeared in *J.R.A.I.*, vol. lv, 1925, is included in chapters VII, VIII, and XIII.

The earlier records of the Orokaiva are embodied mainly in the Annual Reports of Papua, which contain a wealth of information about the exciting early days, and the first-hand observations of men like Sir Wm. MacGregor and Mr. W. E. Armit. Latterly there are three names that stand out: those of the late Wilfred Beaver, of E. W. P. Chinnery, and of L. A. Flint.

F. E. W.

PORT MORESBY

Sept. 1929.

ACKNOWLEDGEMENTS

IT is a great honour to be introduced by Sir Hubert Murray, and my thanks are due not only for the generous foreword to this book, but far more for the continual inspiration of one who has done so much to advance the knowledge of Papua and achieved so much in the field of applied anthropology.

Mr. C. T. Wurth, the Resident Magistrate, together with the other magistrates, Messrs. F. J. Berge, R. L. Dick, and L. E. Ashton, were always ready with their assistance while I was in their Division. So also were the members of the Anglican Mission, Messrs. F. R. Elder, S. R. M. Gill, H. Thompson, C. Saunders, and H. Holland; and Mr. F. Hoyles of Buna Bay Plantation.

I have also to thank my sister, Miss Mabel Williams, for reading the proofs of this book, and my wife for her help in what might have been the boresome task of indexing.

Lastly—and perhaps some day an Orokaiva will open here and read this somewhat unusual acknowledgement—I would thank the natives of the Northern Division for their friendliness and hospitality, and not least for their patience.

F. E. W.

CONTENTS

CONTENTS   xiii

LIST OF FIGURES IN THE TEXT

LIST OF PLATES

INTRODUCTION

THERE has been a great change of late years in the attitude of the civilized world towards what are known as the native races. We find sympathy where we used at the best to find indifference, and a regard for native custom, which threatens at times to become exaggerated, but which is a welcome change from the undisguised contempt which prevailed not so long ago.

One of the results of the change has been an increase in the number of books that are published upon the manners and customs of primitive folk. And especially has this been the case with regard to Papua; anthropologists, missionaries, government officers and others have vied with one another in the production of books on Papua, so that the *terra incognita* of the last generation must now be one of the best known dependencies of the Empire.

Most of the books on Papua are good—some are even first class—but I think that this work of Mr. Williams should be the most successful of all, by reason of the great variety of readers to which it will make appeal. The professional anthropologist may revel to his heart's content among the details which Mr. Williams supplies of the domestic and social organization of the Orokaiva, and the most eager student of what used to be called 'Realien' should be more than satisfied with the information given him on the construction of houses, canoes, and other articles, and with the precise description of the parts of each, and of the names applied to every one of them. Such particularity and precision may deter the general reader, but let him take my advice and persevere, and he will find his reward in much intensely interesting information concerning the daily life of these strange and rather attractive people, and especially in the anecdotes and the personal experiences of the writer which are scattered through the book.

Thus it may be that the Chapters on 'Arts of Life' and 'Individual, Family, and Clan' will appeal only to the scientific investigator, but it is certain that those on 'Marriage', 'Warfare', 'Initiation Ceremonies', 'Dance and Drama', and 'Medicine and Magic' will be full of interest even to those whose scientific equipment is as meagre as my own. To some, Chapters VIII and XV on 'The Plant Emblem', *Heratu*, and the 'Spiritual Substitute', *Asisi*, will be the most interesting of all, for they give a good illustration of the almost insurmountable difficulty there is in getting any real knowledge of these people—a difficulty which is commensurate to their apparent difficulty in forming an appreciation of ourselves. All who have had any experience of native administration must have found how very difficult it is to establish any real contact with the native mind; and how very dangerous those people are who have persuaded themselves that they 'have a thorough knowledge of the native'.

Very interesting as an instance of the great gulf which seems to be fixed between the primitive and ourselves is Mr. Williams's account of the untranslatable *Meh*—a feeling of shame, humiliation, and contrition, which we, of the superior white race, are mercifully spared. The Orokaiva who has been wronged is naturally very sorry for himself, but, according to Mr. Williams, he also 'wants others to be sorry for him, and particularly the man who has wronged him. His attitude is not so much "I'll make you sorry for what you have done" as "I'll make you sorry for me". Accordingly we find a person under a sense of wrong going to extraordinary lengths of self castigation, from merely fasting or running away from home for a while, to delivering himself up to an enemy tribe or hanging himself from a tree.' And Mr. Williams gives a case that he knew where a dozen water melons were hacked to pieces by the owner because one had been stolen, in order to create a feeling of *Meh* in the man who had stolen it. With us the thief would regard the destruction of the other dozen with complete indifference; but with the Orokaiva he would be overwhelmed with shame and remorse. All this is to us as difficult to understand as the Japanese custom by which the creditor puts an obstinate debtor to confusion by committing *hari kari* on his doorstep, but it is probable that some similar motive accounts for many Papuan suicides. Suicide is not uncommon in Papua; it is generally connected with a love affair, and is perhaps often prompted by a desire to create some such feeling as *Meh* in a faithless lover or a successful rival.

Mr. Williams fortunately combines the scientific spirit with exceptional literary gifts. Probably no one could make the enumeration of the component parts of a canoe particularly exciting to a reader who is not a trained anthropologist—is not the Catalogue of Ships itself a rather tedious episode?—but Mr. Williams can give those very dry bones at least a semblance of life, and even the most unpromising passages are illumined by a variety of interesting and appropriate stories, as that of the giant woman *Bobokoia*, as big as an island, who rescued the children from the flooded lake, and the treacherous 'crocodile man' who volunteered to buoy up one side of the raft. These two stories are of course native legends, but Mr. Williams makes a skilful use of actual happenings in order to elucidate the points which he is discussing. For instance the reference to Mr. Flint's account of the man who could not fell a tree for fear of cutting his baby's throat, and of the interpreter who, by washing his clothes, caused the death of his child, illustrate an association of ideas hardly comprehensibe to us except by direct instances.

Other interesting stories are those of the *Aiga* natives who mistook the miners' boys for women, of the boastful Handaupa, and of the practice of assuming the name of the man whom you have killed. It is, I believe, the custom not only of the Orokaiva but also of the Western Papuan, as far as Dutch New Guinea, to collect the names of slaughtered foemen, and to distribute them among the children of himself and his friends. A very famous warrior on the Mambare, renowned throughout the Territory for various more or less mythical feats, was always known as *Busimai*, and I think there are very few who ever suspected that this was not his real name; but he told me some years ago that it was not— it was the name of a man whom he had killed on the *Opi* River.

Mr. Williams mentions some other curious resemblances

between the customs of the Orokaiva and those of the Gulf of Papua and the West. He is careful to avoid any definite expression of opinion upon a possible common origin, but on the principle that 'fools rush in', I may venture to suggest that some such connexion is quite possible, for, so far as I understand these matters, Dr. Haddon's theory that the culture of the *Purari* Delta came from the North, across the main Range, from the former German New Guinea, is now generally accepted. There is a further coincidence of custom, which I think is not mentioned by Mr. Williams, in the prohibition against eating the man that one has killed oneself. This custom exists both among the Orokaiva and in the Purari Delta, subject in the latter case to one strange exception which I have mentioned elsewhere.[1]

Incidentally Mr. Williams has done good work in refuting the idea that the native lives a life of idleness and makes his wife do all the work, and in exposing the fallacy that the native is a child and not a man—a false analogy which seems to be generally accepted almost as a matter of course. Mr. Williams points out that a native is a man with the same groundwork of passions as an European; and it is a neglect of this very obvious fact that is responsible for much of the trouble that has arisen between white women, in various parts of the world, and their native servants.

It will be seen, from what I have said, that this book offers a many-sided attraction, but to an administrator the most interesting part is the last chapter. For in that chapter Mr. Williams deals with a phenomenon which has always appeared to me to be very difficult to understand, though it is common enough in Papua, and that is the well-ordered regulation of a peaceful society with apparently no government and no administration of justice to support it. There are no chiefs with any authority worth talking about among the Orokaiva, and the same is true of nearly the whole of Papua, and there are no Courts and no recognized method of enforcing native law or custom, and yet within the community, within what Mr. Williams calls the 'sympathy group', life is probably as peaceful and as orderly as it is

[1] See *Papua or British New Guinea*, p. 180.

with us. How this result can be obtained in the absence of any objective sanction is one of the puzzles of native administration.

Various explanations have been given of this phenomenon, most of them very ingenious, but none of them, to my mind, at all convincing, though I think it may be fairly said of Mr. Williams's effort that it is the most promising and the most reasonable of them all. The practical administrator can perhaps afford to leave the problem unsolved, for it seems clear enough that, whatever the explanation of the mystery may be, it can offer nothing upon which one can work or build upon as a foundation. Sorcery is mentioned by Mr. Williams, and has been mentioned by others, as a deterrent to law-breakers, and doubtless the fear of sorcery is at least as effective as the fear of physical violence or anything else, but we are surely not justified in assuming that sorcery is used only against evil-doers, and that the dread of it is confined to them. In any case the most ardent advocate of indirect rule could not approve of an administration of justice founded upon sorcery, and sorcery, 'the most hated of crimes' as Mr. Williams calls it, is, in fact, the chief cause of disorder in the villages of Papua even to this day.

The practical administrator may therefore leave the problem unsolved, but every one interested in the government of native races should read this last chapter, for it contains many suggestions of interest and value. In what the Orokaiva call *Meh* the Papuan has developed a feeling which is foreign to the ordinary European; it will be strange if we discover that he has also developed a sense of civic duty which enables him to secure tranquillity and good government without all our administrative and judicial paraphernalia.

J. H. P. MURRAY

PORT MORESBY,
19 *Sept.* 1929.

I

THE OROKAIVA PEOPLE

Territory

THE Orokaiva occupy the major part of the Northern Division of Papua. From Oro Bay, some little distance below Buna on the north-eastern coast, a line might be drawn westward, skirting the foothills of the Hydrographers and the Lamington group and passing over the small divide of the Kumusi and Yodda rivers, to the neighbourhood of Kokoda; thence, curving round the Ajura Kijala, it would proceed northwards, keeping on its left the uninhabited mountains which are merely eastern appendages of the Main Range, and passing through Ioma would continue on to the border of the Mandated Territory. This line, together with the territorial boundary which coincides with the 8th meridian, would enclose the demesne of the people whom we call Orokaiva. One cannot do better than follow the distribution given by E. W. P. Chinnery and the late W. N. Beaver, both of whom travelled the Northern Division more widely than the present writer,[1] and the actual boundaries of the Orokaiva country which appear in the map are approximately theirs.

It must be understood, however, that while marking the limits of those people who are distinctly and exclusively called Orokaiva, these boundaries are nevertheless somewhat arbitrary. In a general treatment it would be permissible to include, for instance, the people of the lower Waria and beyond, although they go by a different name. Similarly in the south the specified boundary beginning at Oro Bay cannot be regarded as a rigid limit, for along the coast of Dyke Ackland Bay almost as far as Cape Nelson, there are settled several groups of people who are virtually identical with the Orokaiva although commonly named Okeina. The present report, however, will observe the limits already set down.

[1] *Papua Annual Report*, 1914–15, Appendix III, p. 161.

The Name 'Orokaiva'

There has always been some mystery as to the meaning of 'Orokaiva'. By now, however, the name has established itself in the Territory, and appears more suitable than any other. W. N. Beaver wrote:

'... we are at a loss to find a generic term to describe all that group of tribes who are considered to belong to one stock and who speak affiliated languages. It seems to me cumbersome to be continually referring to geographical boundaries or to places which are less than mere names to most people, and consequently I have been in the habit of using "Orokaiva" as a general term. ... I would welcome a more correct general term, could one be found.'[1]

It is doubtful whether any more correct general term could be found. It is common experience that a very large group of primitive people will have no distinctive name for itself. Among the people we are about to discuss both clan and tribal names are definite enough; but when we seek one generic name for all the tribes we must not expect to find it actually in use among them. Small differences of custom and the friendships and enmities of his own immediate group with its neighbours bulk large in the eyes of a native. It may be only the outsider who sees those comprehensive similarities which join all the tribes in one people. With regard to the Orokaiva, a more than usually quarrelsome and disunited people, it may be fair to assume that they never possessed that sense of unity which would necessitate or justify a common name. One thing at least is quite certain, that they did not themselves use the name Orokaiva. This, however, is by no means a disqualification, and we may conclude that the name has come to stay.

An alternative in common use is the rather clumsy phrase 'Binandele-speaking'. This is justified by the fact that all the tribal groups speak kindred dialects, the best known of which is that of the Binandele tribe in the north of the Division. The name 'Binandele' alone is sometimes applied to the whole people, and so again is the name 'Mambare'— because the Mambare river happens to be the home of the Binandele proper. But neither of these latter names should

[1] *Annual Report*, 1918–19, pp. 96, 97.

be retained. A southern Orokaiva would be indignant to hear himself described as Binandele or Mambare.

When Sir William MacGregor ascended the river Mambare in March 1894 he was greeted with cries of *Orokaiva!* from those who wished to be friendly. 'On the Mambare', he wrote, 'the password is "orokaiva", which seems to mean "man of peace". It, at all events, puts one on a friendly footing.'[1] Then apparently, as now, the native of the north was given to vociferous welcoming of his friends. Nowadays, when a party of travellers enters a village, men, women, and children will send up an irregular chorus of cries which may be almost deafening and disconcerting to a European, though it fails entirely to affect the *sangfroid* of a well-bred Papuan. Strangely enough the cry of *Orokaiva!* is heard now comparatively seldom. It has been supplanted by *Oro, oro!* which will be heard in almost every village.

It appears, however, that *Orokaiva!* was never the universal cry of the whole people. Different tribes had their distinctive cries of welcome. Among the Binandele it was commonly *Tepo Tepo!* which, as the word means 'empty' or in pidgin English 'for nothing', may be taken as a cry of reassurance from the villagers to their visitors. The conventional cry of the Aiga was *Javau javau!* with the second syllable of the word prolonged into a cacophonous shriek. Those who used it could give no interpretation of this startling mode of salutation. The 'Salt Water' People sometimes used the cries *Pesau!* and *Savesau!* I am told that at Bakumbari on the coast, for instance, visitors from the north would be hailed with *Pesau!* and those from the south with *Savesau!* and it was suggested that the former was the name of a certain fish, and that the latter meant 'swimmers', though in neither case was the appositeness of the words made at all clear. It is plain then that, prior to the coming of the whites, *Orokaiva!* was not universally used by the Binandele-speaking peoples.

The fact appears to be that the first explorers who penetrated the Mambare heard this cry, which they interpreted as one of peace or welcome, and accordingly took up as a

[1] *Annual Report*, 1893–4, p. 33.

ul password. It is evident that they used it in prosecuting their explorations in parts where the cry was not even known, for an old man of the Aiga tribe told how on the first coming of the whites to his village they had entered shouting *Orokaiva, orokaiva!* and he, then a youngster, not knowing what they meant, had joined with the others in answering *Evari peka!* 'Sleep in peace!' To be short, however, the characteristic cry used by some of the people has been adopted as a name for all of them. Even now, it is true, a native of the north may refuse to acknowledge the appellation, and I know a diminutive armed constable who threatened assault on a Kiwai corporal solely because the latter had referred to him as an Orokaiva. But none of this need deter us from using what is a useful and happily chosen name.

The actual meaning of the word remains in doubt, though it is interesting to note that in modern speech it stands for native tobacco. Here again, however, a similar difficulty arises: is the name anterior to the coming of the whites, as some informants have maintained it is; or is it a comparatively modern transference of a name from the people to one of their distinctive possessions, viz. the inferior kind of tobacco? It may be worth adding that *oro* means 'men's house', and *kaiva*, a mysterious word, is the name of one of the principal kinds of taro.

Ethnic Neighbours

The ethnic neighbours of the Orokaiva may be briefly enumerated. (1) On the sea coast immediately to the south are a branch of the Okeina[1] who are in every respect closely akin to them. Beyond these are the Baruga people of the Bariji river who speak a different language and are culturally distinct, though generally similar in appearance. (2) In the Hydrographer Range and on the southern slopes of Mount Lamington are found the group of peoples commonly named 'Managalasi'. Between these and the Orokaiva the distinction is immediately apparent, not only in culture but also in physique. The Managalasi are as a rule lighter in

[1] Another group of this people occurs near Cape Nelson, North-Eastern Division.

colour, shorter in stature, and somewhat sturdier in build. They have not the lean and well-marked features of the plainsmen, but broad faces on which their more vivacious temperament shows itself in broad smiles. (3) At its south-western corner the territory of the Orokaiva abuts upon that of the Biagi peoples. These are typical mountaineers of the Koiari type, with whom Capt. Barton strikingly com-pared the plainsmen, as 'dark-skinned, lanky, naked people, with their hair worn in long tags, in marked contrast to the stalwart, be-petticoated, light-skinned mountaineers'.[1] They have not been examined with any great thoroughness hitherto. (4) Along the western flank the Orokaiva plain is bounded by a wide belt of uninhabited mountains separating the Yodda valley from the plain. It would hardly be right to speak of the Chirima people (i.e. those who inhabit the valley of the Chirima, the second great affluent of the Mam-bare) as neighbours of the Orokaiva, because prior to the penetration of the Chirima valley by Europeans there was apparently no existing contact between the two peoples. (5) On the north-west, inhabiting the Upper Waria, are the group of peoples whom Chinnery and Beaver called Tahari. Except for a branch which has extended to the Upper Gira, it might be said that they also were virtually out of contact with the Orokaiva. (6) Along the lower reaches of the river Waria are a number of tribes, Mawai, Yarawi, and Jia, who bear some resemblance to the people with whom we are concerned in physique, culture, and language. Contact with these, friendly or warlike, has evidently been fairly close before as well as since the coming of the white man. With them we may class the Yema who are found on the middle Gira and the Eia. These latter, however, are becoming merged in the Binandele population.

Tribes and Cultural Differences

The Orokaiva are divided into a number of large tribes which may be named at this point. The classification rests mainly on a basis of language and follows, with a little am-plification, the list made by Chinnery and Beaver. It must

[1] *Annual Report*, 1904-5, p. 7.

be understood, however, that the present is a very rough-
and-ready statement of the case; for there is far more blending and complexity than appears in a bare list of nine tribes.
A fuller treatment of the classification of tribes will be given
in Chapter X; in the meantime the principal of them are:

1. Binandele and Jeva Buje.	6. Sangara.
2. Tain-Daware.	7. Dirou.
3. Aiga.	8. Wasida.
4. Yega.	9. Hunjara.
5. Sauaha.	

Their disposition may be seen on the map.

The native roughly classifies these tribes according to
their environment. The River People are called *Umo-ke*, lit.
'water-language'; they comprise the Binandele of the Mambare and Gira rivers and the large branch of the same tribe
called Jeva Buje, inhabiting the lower Kumusi. The coastal
Tain-Daware and Yega are called *Eva-Embo*, 'Salt-water
Men', and the inland tribes are collectively known as *Autembo*, 'Bushmen', or more often as *Pereho* (*Berepo*), a word
which has the same general meaning, or more specifically
stands for the 'little bush-pigs' that are captured wild in the
forest. There are naturally some environmental differences
between these large groups, but it appears that such differences are not essential. There seems to be no good ground
other than group-conceit for the opinion of an Aiga that the
Bush People were *momoseja*, attractive and 'pretty' (the same
word would be applied to a brilliant croton leaf), while the
River People were *kamoseja*, ugly and unattractive, with
black skins like Kiwais, ringworm, and elephantiasis.

Apart from certain cultural differences which are probably the direct result of environment, as e.g. in methods of
fishing and their appliances, there are others of greater
significance which are probably due to some contact influence. The most important of these consists in the religious
and social ceremonies involving the use of the bull-roarer
and the sacred flute. These objects are known in the
southern part of the Division, but their use is discontinued
with some abruptness when we reach the Aiga, the Binan-

(a) An Aiga Native

(b) A Wasida Native

(c) An Aiga Native

PLATE I

dclc, and the Tain-Daware. They then reappear on the river Waria, to the north of the last-mentioned tribes. Their distribution excludes in the main that of the small dramas for which the Orokaiva are famous, these latter belonging especially to the Aiga, Binandele, and Tain-Daware.[1] Thus bull-roarer and flute on the one hand, and drama on the other tend to be mutually exclusive. It is noteworthy that the miniature drum, *saunda*, is confined to those three tribes who practice the drama.

Another significant distribution may be mentioned, viz. that of the yam. This vegetable is grown over the whole of the plain, but far less commonly in the north than the south, though it is not, as far as I know, debarred by climatic causes from flourishing in any part. But the yam-house and the extensive cultivation of yams disappear north of Divina Kovari, so that their distribution seems to correspond in some degree with that of the bull-roarer and the sacred flute.

Save for these few distinctions between South and North, the exclusive presence of bull-roarer, flute, and yam in the one, and of the drama and the *saunda* in the other, I have not been able to see any really important distinctions between the various component tribes of the Orokaiva. It may be stated with some confidence that the groundwork of their customs and institutions is the same throughout.

It is on the assumption of general uniformity among the tribes that the present report claims to refer to the people as a whole. The tribe with which I am best acquainted is that of the Aiga, who seemed to offer the best opportunities for research because they are fairly central and as yet less contaminated by European influence than most of the others. Out of a total Orokaiva population of some 9,000, this tribe numbers approximately 1,300, who are scattered in nearly fifty villages on or between the Opi and Kumusi rivers. To avoid confusion it will be the rule of this report to use the Aiga dialectal form for native words.

[1] I am not ready to say that the drama never appears among the Southern tribes. At any rate I cannot speak with any certainty about the Hunjara.

Provenance

It is only by wide research among the near and distant neighbours of a people that we are likely to form a correct opinion of their provenance. The present writer cannot claim to have made any such research, and therefore no definite hypothesis will be attempted. The internal evidence (as we might call it) is not altogether straightforward. The legends for the most part (though not invariably) point to the Waria and the Gira as the original home of the people; and the general similarity between the Orokaiva and the present inhabitants of the country immediately north of the boundary is quite in keeping with such a theory. But the historical evidence—if so we may call the more recent memories of tribal feuds, dispersals, and migrations— would seem to indicate a movement from the opposite direction. While it is evident that tribal affairs have been involved in a veritable whirlpool of strife, migration, and counter-migration, there is nevertheless proof that certain large groups have pushed or have been pushed steadily northwards.[1]

It may be that both these movements southward and northward have taken place. As a purely tentative suggestion it may be that the original Orokaiva population occupied the plain from the direction of the Waria and have since been subjected to a pressure from the south which has driven them back over their tracks. The presence of the bull-roarer and the sacred flute in the south and their gradual progress northwards would seem to indicate that a new culture at least, and perhaps some new people, had entered at the southern end of the plain and caused an ethnic backwash towards the north.

Rather against such an hypothesis is the presence of the bull-roarer and the sacred flute on the Waria itself, which might make it appear that the Binandele, Aiga, and Tain-Daware constituted an intrusive element who had driven the bull-roarer people out of their way. The general uniformity of custom and language, however, gives some

---

[1] See Chinnery and Beaver, *Annual Report*, 1914–15, Appendix II, p. 158.

ground for assuming that the exceptions, viz. especially the bull-roarer and sacred flute, are later introductions.

The present report, which aims at describing the Orokaiva people alone, may proceed without pretending to solve this question.

Physical Characters

It remains to give some idea of the physical characteristics of the people with whom this report is to deal. To any one who has overcome the antipathy of mere strangeness the Orokaiva may well appear a handsome and prepossessing race. The best example will be a man of medium height, clean-limbed, muscular, and spare. The colour of the skin is predominantly darkish brown, though there is variation in both directions. The hair is of the woolly texture common to natives of Papua, and black in colour. The features are fairly clear-cut. The nose, usually straight, is not unduly broad in appearance and is often well defined. The brow ridge is somewhat marked and the jaws strong. The lips are sometimes full but not specially so. The mouth is commonly firm, and the face often shows deep lines.

In general appearance the Orokaiva may stand midway between the typical Papuan and the typical Melanesian. He has neither the prominent convex nose and the narrow forehead of the former, nor the broad and somewhat smooth countenance of the latter.

The results of measurements upon 81 individuals are given below. Of these 36 belonged to the Aiga tribe, 28 to Wasida, and 17 to Sangara.

Cephalic Indices.
General average: 74·2 .   .   . { Aiga 74·7 / Wasida 73·8 / Sangara 73·9
Extremes: 66·6–81·9.
Modes: 72–3 and 74–5.

Nasal Indices.
General average: 91·4 .   .   . { Aiga 89·1 / Wasida 92·7 / Sangara 94·2
Extremes: 70·4–110·6.
Modes: 88–9 and 100–1.

Height.
General average: 159·7 cm.   .   . $\begin{cases} \text{Aiga} & 159\cdot7 \\ \text{Wasida} & 159\cdot8 \\ \text{Sangara} & 159\cdot6 \end{cases}$

Extremes: 148·5–170·5
Mode: 160–1.

Chest.[1]
General average: 83·7 cm.   .   . $\begin{cases} \text{Aiga} & 83\cdot75 \\ \text{Wasida} & 84\cdot2 \\ \text{Sangara} & 82\cdot5 \end{cases}$

Extremes: 73–92.
Mode: 80–1

Weight.
General average: 112·5 lb.   .   . $\begin{cases} \text{Aiga} & 124\cdot7 \\ \text{Wasida} & 111\cdot6 \\ \text{Sangara} & 105\cdot7 \end{cases}$

Extremes: 90–150.

I am unable to refer the skin colour to any standard, and can only describe it as darkish brown. But an observer will note three fairly distinct categories, viz. (1) the usual darkish brown, (2) a distinctly darker shade on the one hand, and (3) a lighter shade on the other. The darker colour approaches that of the Gulf native and the lighter is commonly seen among the Eastern Melanesians of New Guinea. In measuring the natives I have noted whether they are Medium, Dark, or Light:

Skin Colour (75 cases):
Medium   .   .   .   54·7 per cent.
Dark .   .   .   .   29·3   ,,
Light .   .   .   .   16·0   ,,

The typical Orokaiva nose is straight in profile; but many cases show more or less marked degrees of convexity and concavity. The marked convexity of a true Papuan nose is seen, but not commonly.

Nose Profile (80 cases):
Straight   .   .   .   47·5 per cent.
Convex   .   .   .   36·25   ,,
Concave   .   .   .   16·25   ,,

[1] Taken at the level of the nipples with the arms raised above the head.

(*a*) A Woman of Wasida   (*b*) An Orokaiva Profile

(*c, d*) Two Orokaiva Profiles

PLATE II

II

ENVIRONMENT

The Country

THE homogeneity of the Orokaiva in language, culture, and physique may be due in some degree to the nature of their country and its boundaries. The plain of the Northern Division is bordered on the west by the Central Range with its spurs and foot-hills—considerable mountains in themselves; on the south by the Hydrographers and the cluster of which Mount Lamington is the centre; and on the east by the sea. Its northern boundary is roughly speaking the river Eia. But between the Eia and the northern neighbours of the Orokaiva there rises a succession of small but difficult ridges, the last of which descends almost precipitously to the narrow valley of the Waria. In fine it might be said that the country of the Orokaiva was more or less completely encompassed on the landward side by mountains, and was thus effectively fenced off from its neighbours.

Near the southern border of the plain there stretches out a process towards the west, a well-populated valley, watered by numerous tributaries of the Kumusi, and extending towards the Government station of Kokoda. Taking this into account the total extent of country whether plain or piedmont, in which the Orokaiva have established their homes, might be set down at about 1,800 square miles. A certain proportion of this is no more than trackless swamp; but by way of compensation there are wide border areas of mountain and hill which, though uninhabited, are visited by hunting parties and thus make their contribution to maintenance.

The great majority of the Orokaiva are plainsmen. Their country has been built up by sediments borne down from the mountains and now consists of a wide plain which slopes towards the sea coast at a barely perceptible gradient. A few lonely hills on the western side, like islands in a calm sea, break the almost absolute level of the plain; and from the old German boundary down to the mouth of the river Opi a low irregular range marks the line of the coast. But except for these features the plain is remarkable for its flatness. Seen from the summit of one of the bordering hills, basking in the haze and sunshine of the eighth meridian, it yields a peculiar impression of placidity which proves to be somewhat oddly at variance with the character of its inhabitants.

Along its western margin the hills stand up rather abruptly from the plain; but in the south they are approached by long sweeping slopes, scored by ravines and rivers, yet affording extensive areas of fertile land. This piedmont area, formed by the northern slopes of Lamington and the Hydrographers, is closely populated and, in comparison with others, closely cultivated; and here the innumerable garden clearings, relieving the close monotony of the bush, make it possible to take in the beauty of the surroundings. With its comparatively bracing climate and the charm and opulence of its scenery, this region may be counted among the most fortunate of Papua. A somewhat discouraging contrast is found in the forests of the plain proper, which are sometimes gloomy and water-logged. In many parts the land degenerates into sheer swamp; in others it is low-lying and of wholly inferior quality. In fact it is a matter for wonder that an environment so depressing to the European sojourner should produce so small a trace of depression on its native inhabitants.

The Rivers

Through this wide alluvial tract of the Northern Division there flow, pursuing a north-easterly course with a noticeable curve towards the sea, some half-dozen very considerable rivers. Among these the Mambare is the greatest and the Kumusi the next. Both of them have their sources far up in the mountains and bring down huge volumes of water, flowing steadily up to their very mouths. Swift and wholesome in their middle reaches, they become sluggish and meandering when once they have left the hills.

The Mambare and Kumusi are navigable by launch, the latter as far as Bogi, where in mining days the stores used to be put ashore some fifty-five miles from the mouth. But here already the flow of the stream is too strong for native transport, and canoes are rarely seen among the people of the neighbourhood.

While the Mambare and Kumusi are both powerful and impressive rivers they do not possess the same charm as the lesser Gira and Opi. Of the Gira Sir Wm. MacGregor, having admired the landscape of scattered hills and the elevated and fertile banks with their frequent villages, concluded that it was 'the most populous and certainly by far the most pleasant of our north-east coast rivers'.[1]

Sir George Le Hunte was sufficiently charmed by the lower Opi to write:

'I do not recollect ever being on a more beautiful stream. The banks lined now with the handsome dark-leaved nipa palms springing from the water, now with the spreading sago palm with its curious candela-bra-shaped flowers rising straight above it, here a village landing-place with a group of tall graceful areca palms, across which a leaning coco-nut would curve above a cluster of red and golden crotons. . . . The water a deep brown, on which the reflections were so vivid that it was sometimes difficult to distinguish the real from the image. . . .'[2]

Had it been possible for Sir George to ascend the river further than 'about six miles', he would have found a strong flowing stream whose rocky bed is visible through its swift transparency, and which is alternately overshadowed by tall forest or exposed to the sunshine in some broad expanse of rapids; and he might well have been tempted to write with equal vividness and still more enthusiasm.

The northern rivers, however, do not always bear this idyllic aspect. They are subject to sudden rise, and the clear stream of yesterday is transformed overnight into a brown swirling flood, sweeping down masses of forest wreckage and rising over its banks to cover the surrounding country. At such a time it is hardly possible to stir abroad except on canoes or rafts, and some time after the subsidence of the water one may not be surprised to find one of these stranded high and dry among the trees.

[1] *Annual Report*, 1896–7, p. 31.   [2] *Annual Report*, 1898–9, p. 21.

The experience of a Government official in the early days will show to what extent these floods may go:

'From the date of our arrival (Oct. 12) until the end of May we had one long series of floods in the Mambare River. Scarcely a week passed without a flood, and sometimes we had five or six consecutively at night. On six or eight occasions the floods were exceptionally heavy, and the water rose from two to three feet above the level of the banks. The highest ground is immediately adjacent to the river, for in the forests a short distance back the water was many times 6 and 8 feet deep.' [1]

The rapidity with which the flood-waters sink is somewhat surprising when we consider the very gradual fall of the ground. Sometimes, it appears, the damage to native gardens may be serious, but this is not often so; and the pile-built village, although often enough within reach of the flood, sustains no permanent injury.

The Seasons

The floods belong to the 'North-West' season, i.e. they occur roughly speaking between October and March, when the north-west monsoon is blowing. This is the period of greater rainfall throughout the territory.

Reports published in 1922 give the following results for the three Government stations in the Northern Division.[2]

Station.	Period.	Mean Rainfall (Annual).	Three Wettest Months.
Buna	12 years	113 in.	Nov., Dec., Jan.
Kokoda	12 ,,	131 ,,	Nov., Jan., Feb.
Ioma	11 ,,	161 ,,	Dec., Jan., Mar.

The difference between the 'North-West' and the 'South-East' seasons is fairly well marked, though it is one of rain, temperature, and humidity, rather than one of wind, as the names would imply. Whatever winds may fly overhead there is an almost dreary stillness in the forests of the plain,

---

[1] John Green, Government Agent, in *Annual Report*, 1895–6, p. 77. The writer adds: 'The natives during the heavy floods had to sleep in their canoes.' It may be remarked that such a situation would be entirely exceptional, for the flood-water very rarely reaches the floor-level of the house.

[2] *Annual Report*, 1921–2, p. 87.

varied, indeed, by occasional squalls that may do considerable damage among the luxuriant but flimsy vegetation.

The South-East season is perceptibly drier and much
more pleasant than the North-West. This becomes especially apparent to the traveller who in the former season can
make a good pace over excellent native tracks, but in the
latter must do more than a little wading. A former *Annual
Report* gives the following account of the Aiga country:
'The track between Bogi and Tamata has the reputation of
being in bad weather the worst in the Possession. The
greater part of it passes through flat country, intersected
by sluggish creeks and pandanus swamps. After heavy rain
it is flooded for miles waist deep.' [1]   One may reasonably
doubt whether the Aiga country is often deserving of this
description; but making allowance for a little pardonable
exaggeration on the part of one who had evidently met with
unpleasant conditions, we may take his word for it that in
bad weather the tracks are very wet.

The contrast afforded by the drier months of 'winter' may
be striking. Sometimes a long spell of sunny rainless
weather, with refreshing, almost chilly, nights may lead to
a serious dearth of food, and compel the natives to supple-
ment their diet with a variety of leaves, roots, and fern-
fronds from the bush. Although such scarcity never reaches
the point of famine it may nevertheless be serious enough.
The drought has in fact far more terrors for the Orokaiva
than the destructive flood.

Conditions of temperature remain fairly equable. The
following are figures for the official year, 1924–5:

Station.	Dry Therm.	Wet Therm.	Maximum.	Minimum.
Buna	82·2	77·5	87·3	68·4
Kokoda	74·5	72·3	88·5	67·5
Ioma	77·4	74·4	91·5	72·9

Vegetation

By far the greater part of the Northern Division is covered
by forest. Some of this has at one time or another been

[1] *Annual Report*, 1904–5, p. 5.

cleared for native gardens, some is still virgin, being distinguished by the presence of giant trees with spreading flanges or buttresses. The forest presents an infinite variety, with this important characteristic, that the variety is for ever repeating itself, so that a man who requires any particular product usually has not far to seek.

With few exceptions the trees are soft-woods, and these supply easy material for canoes and much of the house-building. One or two varieties of hard-woods are used for spears, but these weapons as well as the wooden 'sword' are usually made from the tough and springy *Koropa* palm. Other palms provide the slats used in flooring; and the pandanus, most useful of all, is valued for its fibre which is twisted into rope, and for its broad leaves which are sewn together to form the sleeping mat. One variety is prized for its fruit, a long red seed-cluster, which is boiled down to a porridge.

One of the greatest natural assets of the Orokaiva is his sago. In the interior the palm is comparatively rare and each tree is carefully husbanded, but along the lower reaches of the rivers, where they are bordered by swamps of very great extent, the sago grows in a quantity which, as far as native wants are concerned, is probably inexhaustible. As a diet it is secondary to the taro, but among the river-dwellers at least it provides an unfailing resource in times of scarcity. The sago leaf thatches the house, and the midrib nowadays commonly forms the walls of the house. In the dismal swamps of the coast the *Nipa* palm furnishes another material for thatching, and the mangrove one of the most adaptable of native timbers.

Comparatively few fruit-bearing trees are found in the bush. The only exceptions of much consequence are the several varieties of bread-fruit, the *Okari* nut, and the tree called *Puga*. Mangoes are uncommon and of inferior quality, and of the numerous varieties of wild fig only one or two may be called edible. But there are numerous herbs, ferns, and tree leaves which always lend variety to Orokaiva cookery, and when scarcity prevails at the height of the South-East season may even become a stand-by. Indeed, the various natural resources of the bush would probably enable the native to tide over a period in which the taro gardens failed completely.

Such clothing as he wears is made by beating out the bark of a *ficus* tree; his belt is plaited with thin strips of cane; his pipe is a tube of bamboo; his cheeks are streaked with a red paint obtained from a seed; his ready-made luggage-strap or the mooring cable for his canoe is a creeper withe or a length of rattan cane. These are only a few of the uses to which the Orokaiva, true forest-dweller that he is, may put the multifarious products of his environment. One cannot fail to be impressed by his wonderful familiarity with the forest—so perplexing to one who is not a woodsman—and with his extempore skill and resource in turning all its products to account.

Wide areas of the plain—though still but a small proportion of its total extent—are covered with *alang alang*, or long grass. The apparent spread of these grass patches, and the corresponding deforestation have caused the Government some anxiety. As yet, however, this aspect of the matter has made no appeal to the native. The grass patch, entirely unproductive as it is, and almost invincible to cultivation, yet provides an annual supply of game when it is burnt off by the hunting party. It seems, indeed, as if the grass were regarded in the light of a special asset to its owners.

Fauna

Of the wild animals which these burnings drive into the nets of the hunters most important is *sus papuensis*, that fierce long-legged animal which abounds throughout Papua. But there is an unclassified multitude of marsupials ranging downwards in size from the wallaby, all of which are welcome to the Orokaiva, who despises no meat that comes his way. Of the tree-climbing marsupials the most notable is the cuscus, with beautifully dappled fur of white, yellow, and brown, which is cut into strips and worn in long streamers from the armlet of the warrior; and in the hills a larger animal, the tree-kangaroo, whose rich brown fur is used for the same purpose. Most beautiful of all is the

delicate little *Hajojo* which resembles a flying squirrel, and
which makes the prettiest if not always the most docile of
pets. There are many more bush creatures perfectly known
to Papuan (if not so well to European) zoology, and all,
while they serve the more utilitarian purpose of diet, are
especially interesting because their names constantly recur
in the Aesopian legends with which Orokaiva folk-lore
abounds.

Reptiles are not less common than in other parts of the
Territory. Snakes, from the python to the smallest and
deadliest, are regarded with a queer mixture of feelings in
which sometimes veneration, sometimes horror, and sometimes hunger gains the upper hand. The lizard is killed,
its flesh dried in the smoke against some future feast, and its
skin stretched over the drum as a tympanum. Crocodiles,
the most terrible of the Papuan's natural enemies, abound
near the river-mouths, and their attacks have sometimes
been so frequent on village pigs and dogs and on women
filling their gourds at the water's edge, that favourable
settlements have had to be abandoned. Yet even the crocodile is often outwitted in the legends and occasionally caught
and eaten in reality.

Flying-foxes or fruit-bats are numerous and destructive.
From their camping-grounds, where they hang by day in
lazy myriads from the branches, they steadily wing their
way at evening to the gardens which they mean to plunder,
and after this nocturnal migration may be seen steadily
beating back at earliest daybreak. To the Orokaiva as to
ourselves there is a hint of the spectral about the flying-fox,
and it is not surprising that it should find a place in their
legends and theories of the life after death.

Birds are of interest to the northern native mainly as
providing the plumes which, fastened together in head-
dresses, make him, as they are meant to do, more attractive
in love and more terrifying in war. Thus parrots, kingfishers, and birds of paradise supply in their brilliant plumage
one of the principal kinds of convertible wealth. The
domestic cock is valued for the same reason, being merci-
lessly plucked and bereft of his sweeping tail feathers in

order to serve the vanity of his owner. The great corrugated beak of the hornbill is valued as an ornament, and apparently in earlier times was an emblem of the homicide. The bird is frequently seen as a pet, being accommodated like the parrot or the white cockatoo in a little house of its own. Sometimes the young cassowary is domesticated, until as he grows up his aggressive manners and sharp claws make him an unmanageable member of village society, when he usually takes to the bush and rejoins his own kind. The cassowary is common in the hills though comparatively rare on the plains.

Even in so sketchy a list of the creatures which as friends or enemies share the habitat of the Orokaiva one should not fail to make a passing mention of the insects. It is well enough known that the most terrible predatory creature of Papua is the mosquito, and parts of the Northern Division, particularly the lower Mambare, deserve the bad reputation which it has given them. A magistrate wrote, I think without exaggeration, of this district:

'It is infested by multitudes of the most voracious mosquitoes, so that for that reason alone, one falls to wondering what could induce any one to live there. The native is not by any means immune to the bites of these pests. On my visits to these villages, I have seen the people sitting full in the acrid smoke of large wood fires, or beating their bodies with palm fronds, and they have complained to me that life is unbearable on account of the mosquitoes.' [1]

The scourge of mosquitoes has been bad enough to drive out whole village communities. Manau is said to have migrated from the present site of Bebewa, some distance up the river simply to escape them. Leaving behind the mosquitoes, however, the emigrants have established themselves in a region of countless sand-flies, and it is questionable whether their second state is not worse than their first. These infinitesimal insects (whose irritating bite is out of all proportion to their size) infest the brown sea-beaches of the north-east coast. But while they make life unbearable for a European it would seem as if the natives enjoy a certain amount of immunity from their poison.

[1] S. A. Greenland in *Annual Report*, 1912–13, p. 127.

One might mention other insects that appeal to the imagination of the Orokaiva—the innocent-looking March-fly with its treacherous sting, the carpenter bee that riddles the light timbers of native houses, the warlike black ants with their sudden migrations, the fire-flies in which, floating and luminous, he sees the eyeballs of the dead. None of these have much practical importance, but it is interesting to note that the Orokaiva, making his farewell address to the dead, bids him go to a place where March-flies and mosquitoes will cease from troubling him.

III

DAILY LIFE

The Day's Work

THE villager wakes and rises with the sun. Being at liberty to take his repose at any time of the day, whenever indeed he feels a tiredness in his limbs, he is not likely to be a lie-abed in the morning. If the weather be hot he is early at work in the garden to have his day's task through before the sometimes grilling heat of noon; if the night has been a cold one (for many New Guinea nights are cold to those who live in New Guinea), he issues forth from his house bringing some of the night's fire with him, to meet the sun and to profit by the warmth of its first rays.

There is no bustle of preparation for breakfast. A lump or so of cold taro or a fragment of roast sago left overnight constitutes the morning meal, and often enough a man is content to go with none at all. If he have work before him in the garden he will soon set off accompanied by his wife and children, with his axe and knife in his hand and his rude digging-stick over his shoulder; usually, too, with a long spear against some chance of game. If there be no immediate call for his masculine strength in the garden he allows his wife and children to go to their work alone, to perform the drudgery of weeding and grubbing while he employs his mind and fingers upon some more interesting or creative task—such as the fashioning of a spear, the plaiting of a cane belt, or the chopping of a mess-bowl from a block of wood.

Such employments as these he follows with a deal of comfortable assiduity, for not only does he see the object take shape as he proceeds, but the nature of his work permits of a seat in the shade and, like knitting or hemstitching, does nothing to hinder conversation.

Some women will have remained at home to perform

sedentary tasks of their own—different always, for none of the crafts are shared by the two sexes. So we may see the clay pot growing coil by coil in the hands of the housewife, the bark-cloth spreading out into a sheet under the blows of her mallet, or the furnace of green leaves, rolling out clouds of smoke, from which she will obtain a small residuum of salt. These and many other such tasks are woman's province, upon which there is no male encroachment.

Some work therefore will be going forward in the forenoon, but there is not unusually a quietness in the village during this part of the day. The children may have remained, but they are as likely to be down by the river-side or playing at work in the garden with their elders. Of those men and women who chance to be unoccupied none will think it shame to sleep, and there will be no loud life about the village, perhaps no sound but the ceaseless regular whacking of a bark-cloth maker's stone mallet upon the log.

Meanwhile the bulk of the village population is probably employed in the garden. If it be the mere routine of weeding and of gathering a bagful of taro for the pot, gardening is women's work; but whenever the business of clearing, planting, or fencing is afoot, then the whole family will be engaged, or sometimes all the families of a clan, in a somewhat unorganized and happy-go-lucky working bee.

The heat of the garden clearing, fenced in by a high wall of forest, may be almost insufferable to a European, but the native, hatless and streaming with sweat, bears it well enough. The party may be cutting into the bush to increase the area for fresh planting. The women and children clear the undergrowth and trailers and the men deal with the tree trunks. Amid the sound of axe-blows and those loud expulsions of breath—'*ugh, ugh!*'—which accompany them and with which the Orokaiva seems to convince himself he is working very hard, may be heard occasionally the clear yodel-like call, something between a shout and a song, which shows the workmen to be in his highest spirits. And when from time to time he brings down a tree, he accompanies the prodigious crash of its fall with a not less prodigious Orokaiva hoot, and turns to the next, or throws

(*a*) On the Middle Opi

(*b*) The Village of Poho

PLATE III

down his axe and turns to his string bag hanging on a stump for refreshment of betel-nut and a breather.

After the felling of timber there is the burning of it, which is hot work with a vengeance, for the hottest day is regarded as the best opportunity for making a clean sweep of the litter which clearing has left behind it. In none of his gardening operations, however, does the Orokaiva display unnecessary haste. He moves hither and thither, gathering armfuls for the blaze, and gives it a desultory poke or raking with his long stick. Meanwhile, the atmosphere is visibly dancing with the heat, and broad leaves are caught and floated upwards by the ascending currents of air.

Maybe the work on hand is that of fencing. One or two men are driving the stakes and laying the rails that constitute the primitive fence. Theirs is the skilled work—if so it may be called—while it is for the women folk to maintain the supply of materials. Among these unskilled labourers the unmarried daughters, strapping young women who have discarded their bark-cloth skirts for greater freedom, move through the garden as naked as Eve through Paradise, supposing the mother of mankind to have worn at least an armlet or two or a flower in her hair for ornament. The children—particularly the little girls, who show an earlier disposition for work than do their brothers—bear their small and irresponsible share. The baby, meanwhile, hanging in a knitted string bag from some convenient tree-branch, sleeps undisturbed.

The housewife has probably pulled some taro and gathered some of the edible leaves with which it is to be seasoned; and now when the morning's work is over she will stow these into her string bag, which has incredible powers of distension, squat beside it to arrange upon the crown of her head the band which serves as handle, and so rise to her feet to plod contentedly homeward. The baby hangs, still sound asleep, in a second bag upon the woman's stooping back, and her husband, shouldering his spear and digging-stick again, leads the way.

So in their own time most of the families will have returned by noon to the village. There may be something to eat, made ready by some woman who has been at home during the forenoon, but, whether or no, the toilers will probably retire into their houses for the siesta.

If the day be warm there will be drowsiness in the village atmosphere and almost universal somnolence among its inhabitants for an hour or two after midday.

The Evening's Recreation

The real activity of the village commences at about three o'clock. The women will soon begin peeling the taro, each seated on the ground before her own house. The diurnal grand repast is in preparation, and what with the peeling of vegetables and the cooking of them a housewife has perhaps an hour and a half of final work to do. Not that this is hard or unpleasant, but rather of a sociable nature, for little groups gather round the pot in which the taro is slowly seething under a covering of leaves. The men have risen from their rest and may foregather to chew betel or will sit before their respective houses renewing some sedentary task of yesterday—for such tasks may drag on unconscionably. Often a man is content with the society of his immediate family, playing fondly with his younger children and carrying an infant in his arms.

Women and girls will go for water, and youths perhaps for firewood. Young bloods may appear, with a dash of paint on their cheeks and an ornament of boar's tusk or shell on their breasts. Their hair is glossy and greasy and their fine young figures set off with a sheen of coco-nut oil. In the most indirect manner and with a somewhat studied nonchalance they are, if the truth be known, bent on courtship, desiring principally to show off their masculine charms in those quarters where it suits them.

As the cool of the evening approaches the village grows more animated. If one game or another happens to be in vogue, youths of all ages will be boisterously engaged in it. The favourite games of the Orokaiva have something of war or chase about them. A number of players, with darts poised for throwing, stand in a kind of extended order while one boy bowls a disk-shaped section of banana stem along the ground before them. Then the waiting spearmen discharge their darts at the flying disk, seeing in imagination the wild pig flying past the hunter. This, like most native games, has no finality and no winner. Whoever lodges his mock spear in the rolling disk utters his shout of triumph—maybe his own name or that of his clan—while all rush forward to recover their weapons and form into line again for the next attempt.

A more uproarious pastime is the sham fight between two contending parties, when mock spears are thrown with great violence and evaded with great address. The spear is usually the six-feet-long stalk of a large herb weighted with its rhizome, a very solid knob, which gives power and directness to the missile and makes it worth one's while to dodge. The shield is a miniature of light palm spathe. Armed with these weapons the parties attack one another, launching their spears or parrying or dodging those of the enemy with all the cries and actions of true warfare. When the game is played by small boys, the contending parties draw closer and closer, snatching up and returning the spent weapons of their adversaries with gradually mounting spirit, until the combat thickens and may become a hand-to-hand scuffle in which the spear is turned into a club. An unlucky hit may compel one of the combatants to withdraw weeping from the fray, but one never sees bad blood engendered in these village games, however warlike, and a stand-up fight must be a very rare occurrence.

With the approach of dusk the various families of the village will forsake amusement and employment, or the lack of either, for the business of eating their evening meal. About this there is little or no formality. The housewife is responsible for the due preparation of the repast, which is the only regular one of the day. If she be a dutiful spouse she seldom fails in punctuality, for the hungry Orokaiva husband is short-tempered and any break-down in the catering of his household will cause domestic disagreement. (Indeed, it would appear that neglect of household duties may be as just and potent a cause of divorce as actual infidelity.) There will be a few friendly gifts of food. If a man has made a catch of fish his wife, having cooked it in the evening, will carry portions across to her neighbours; but for the most part the meal is prepared for the immediate family.

After dark there is conversation and the liveliness of the village will continue. Any happening of the humdrum day will have passed from ear to ear, and one may now hear occasional shouted comments, greeted with yells of laughter from a distant fireside. Some incident of slighted feelings during the day may lead to an angry outburst in the evening, when the victim pours forth his feelings in a molten stream of indignation, which may call forth fierce retorts, but is more likely to be heard in silence by the rest of the village. Sometimes an individual, either to air his own grievance or express his opinion in an inter-clan dispute, will parade back and forth among the houses, shaking his spear and denouncing his enemy. But happily, though swift to anger, the Orokaiva is content to allow it a verbal overflow, and very seldom comes to blows with his fellow villagers.

Often the menfolk of the village will be met in a cheerful company to enliven—or some would say make hideous—the night with song. The singers assemble in the *oro* or men's house, drawn into a close circle about a fire or preferably a kerosene lamp. Three or four drums and a conchshell are the instruments of music, the last in the hands of a smallish boy who, though thrust somewhat into the background, willingly supplies the wind for an instrument which is more exacting of endurance than of musical finesse. When everything is in readiness the drums begin to beat and some precentor strikes up on a high pitch, singing with spirit and not without a certain taste one or two bars of a melody to words that are for the most part meaningless. As he finishes, his song is caught up and repeated in a very full-throated manner by the chorus, accompanied by the drums and the well-timed but not always harmonious blasts of the shell trumpet. The leader sings again and the chorus follows, till, after many repetitions, they all pause from their exertions and refresh themselves with betel-nut. With frequent changes of tune and frequent pauses this singing may go one till late at night; indeed on occasions of festivity

(a) A man of the River Gira

(b) Woman and child of Wasida

PLATE IV

it is no uncommon thing to see the singers dispersing for their night's rest at break of day. But happily, when a European is in their village they have the politeness and the deference to the common European habit of sleeping by night, to discontinue their concert when he extinguishes his lamp. Then the older folk and the mere boys will retire to rest and the young men will follow their own devices, either turning in or going a courting. No one will see them creep into the houses of their sweethearts where by pre-arrangement they are assured of a welcome.

The village is now in complete silence. It may be warm and drizzling rain, or it may be clear and cold. In the latter case the fires will be burning underneath the pile-houses, and now and again one will hear the voice of the father gruffly rousing one of his children to go down and stir the embers or add fuel. Then follow the sounds of sleepy and complaining acquiescence, the fire flares and crackles, the youngster creeps back to his sleeping mat, and all is silence once more.

At times in the dead of night one may waken to hear a woman's voice raised in a solitary dirge for dead husband or child—long-sustained, clear notes whose effect is singularly sad. From the standpoint of music it must be confessed that such performances are variable, yet sometimes they are of the purest tone and uttered with an admirable restraint. Long-drawn, and with a suspicion of *tremolo*, the dirge ends characteristically with two or three high-pitched sobs or whimpers. There are now no sounds other than the tireless croaking of the frogs in the swamp, the hooting of owls, or the occasional flapping of a fruit-bat among the bananas, until the tailless rooster on the house-top thinks fit to salute the coming dawn.

Occasional Activities

Such is the uneventful routine of the Orokaiva day. Yet although there is undoubtedly a general absence of varied interest and incident in native life compared with our own, it must not be supposed that the typical day which I have endeavoured to describe is by any means invariable. There are in the first place the exigencies of nature: the flood with its opportunities for fishing and the pursuit of small game; the heat of the early North-West season when the grass-burning will go forward and great hunting parties assemble; the long dry spell when the villagers must turn to making sago, or go down to a fishing camp, the streams being then at their shallowest.

There are also the many new activities, not always welcome, which Government control has occasioned. The village must clear its allotted span of track with every moon; the passing of an officer means a turn out of carriers (and the Orokaiva are reputed to be as sturdy and cheerful as any in the Territory); and the approach of a patrol means a mild bustle of diligence in which the village must be made to look its best for fear of magisterial wrath. Again the Plantations scheme and the presence of a supervising officer mean labour of a somewhat new kind, which for those who live from hand to mouth seems irksome because unrepaid by immediate returns.

Now and again the recruiter of native labour passes, lays out his trade for those who will bargain to go with him, and leaves perhaps with a batch of young men to 'sign-on' for European employment. But the sadness of parting, however real, is not more moving than the demonstrative welcome at the labourer's home-coming, when his women folk, who threw themselves down and beat their foreheads on the ground for sorrow at his going, do the same again with equal violence for joy at his return.

Apart from these sources of interest, and from events of birth, marriage, and death, and again from the more startling incidents of thefts, quarrels, and occasional murders which are all but necessary to any human society, native life is varied by a number of festive and ceremonial occasions which constitute a very important part of it.

Not a few of these are associated with the rites of mourning and with the placation of the beings who survive death. When a death occurs mourners, summoned by long blasts of the trumpet, gather from far and wide to the scene and give themselves with what one suspects to be almost joyful abandon to the indulgence of grief. The house of the dead

is thronged with mud-smeared wailers and the corpse is
hardly to be seen for those who are mauling and caressing
it for the last time. The funeral, despite the undeniably
genuine sorrow of the mourners, even of those who are but
remotely connected with the deceased, is not without re-
deeming features. The mourners disperse with the satisfaction of having performed a necessary rite, of having
participated with a crowd of their fellows in an exercise of
emotion, and of having been well feasted.

It is not the purpose of this chapter to give any detailed
description of mortuary ceremonies, nor of the rites of
seclusion and initiation with their spectacular *finale*, when
the youths and girls emerge as 'new children' bedecked with
feather head-dresses and loaded with crude but magnificent
ornaments of shell and ivory. All ceremonies, however, are
accompanied by feasting, for the primitive virtue of liberality
is not less strong among the Orokaiva than others. Food
will have been gathered from the gardens and bountifully
displayed on platforms. The guests, arriving in their several
parties, come striding single file into the village, each party
headed by its man of first importance, befeathered club on
shoulder. No smile adorns his face, but rather an expression of fierceness, which, however unsuited it may seem to
the hospitable occasion, is nevertheless Orokaiva good
form. Tempestuous shouts of welcome greet the visitors,
which they accept without a flicker of weak-minded gratifi-
cation, unless it be on the part of some silly girl; and so they
file majestically through the village until they reach the
place allotted them, when they seat themselves somewhat
abruptly and relax into a more sociable attitude. Meanwhile,
the women have been busy at peeling and chopping the taro,
and the pots are cooking in rows. If it be an occasion of any
importance the pigs are slaughtered and, having been dismembered, lie in reeking heaps on the high platform where
the butchering is performed in rather studied publicity.
The stench may soon be almost nauseating to a European,
though to Orokaiva nostrils it has no doubt a pleasant and
promising savour. An onlooker who would appreciate the
gaiety and charm of the scene must not be too fastidious.

Towards the end of the day comes the formal distribution of food. The master of the feast, conferring anxiously with his friends, has been setting out the taro in heaps, making them correspond by laborious arithmetic with the number of his principal guests. Now that the tally appears satisfactory, he turns, with an enthusiasm bordering on violence, to the distribution. With loud shouts he and his assistants rush back and forth depositing, or often rather hurling down, bunches of taro before the guests, who accept them with a fitting appearance of indifference. In the same way the pig flesh—legs, quarters, chines, and entrails—are bestowed on top of the taro heaps, and the guests are ready to depart. They have been sufficiently regaled throughout the day; the food thus finally distributed is to be carried home. The women pack it into their string bags and prepare to move off. Men and children will bear their part. One remembers the spectacle of a diminutive child bearing away the blood-spattered head of a huge pig, balanced with difficulty and pride upon his own small crown. Thus laden with proofs of friendship the guests depart to await the time when, in a year or so, they will make a similar return of hospitality.

With certain of these festivals there will go the dance and pantomine. The Orokaiva ballet will be described in greater detail in another chapter, but in passing one may claim that its brilliant natural setting, the sudden theatrical entry of the performers into the sunlit village, their paint and feathers and voluminous costumes of dyed palm-leaf, the inspiriting beat of the drum, and above all the swift movements of the dance, full of grace and power, all combine to make a spectacle that one might even call magnificent. The mime comes as a dramatic interlude in the dance, and presents as a theme some legend or incident of village life, enacted with great spirit and humour, and sometimes with considerable taste, upon the most realistic of stages—the village itself, and in the midst of the audience who are on such intimate terms with the actors as occasionally to add an extempore touch of their own to the play.

Such social amusements as these still continue, one is happy to say, to add some zest and interest to native life.

The more engrossing pastime of war, one is still happier to say, is now a thing of the past. The Orokaiva are a high-spirited and warlike people, and at no very distant date were frequently engaged in raiding, killing, and eating one another; and life in those times must have involved an anxiety, but also an alertness which are now entirely absent.

Nevertheless, the Orokaiva still loves the appearance of battle—perhaps more, indeed, than he ever loved its deadly realities. No sight is more typical of the people than that of the constantly recurring *esu*, sham-fight or hostile demonstration, with its charge and counter-charge, the forming in line of the warriors, crouched behind their shields and with spears in readiness. Such a demonstration is likely to occur whenever one group of clans enters the village of another, whether to accept hospitality or upon some business such as that of obtaining the bride-price of one of its daughters. On such an occasion one may always hear fierce harangues and altercations, the speaker running back and forth between the two parties, pausing before his auditors and brandishing his spear-point at their very throats. When he retires one of the opposite faction will assume the role of abuse and threatened violence. As a rule this will all pass off in friendliness unless perhaps some man lose his temper in earnest at the resuscitation of some especially bitter grievance, or as sometimes happens, the inflammatory taunts of an old woman, armed aggressively with her long quarterstaff, set the whole in a blaze. Then the sham fight turns into a real *mêlée* in which blows of spear and club are dealt with great freedom and received for the most part safely on the shield. But still the restraint of modern times will prevail. The village constable (unless he has forgotten his office in the heat of the moment and is already wielding a spear) dashes forward with his jangling handcuffs prepared to make an arrest—most likely no doubt on the side opposed to his own, the uproar dies away with nothing worse than a few cuts and bruises, and the business and hospitality of the day will even go on as if nothing had happened. Such friendly bouts as these are all that remain of the fighting days of the Orokaiva.

IV

PERSONAL ENHANCEMENT

Clothes

ONE of the earliest observers of the Orokaiva, John Green, who was Government Agent in the year 1895, reported that 'The majority of the men who live on the Mambare are quite naked'.[1] Sir Wm. MacGregor noted a year earlier that in the neighbourhood of Gona Bay the men wore 'a strip of painted mulberry cloth', but that many wore nothing; and again in the same *Annual Report* he writes, 'On the Ope the men are naked'.[2]

In these times one seldom sees a man without the perineal band of bark-cloth, *bo*. Old men and sick men sometimes go quite naked for the sake of comfort; and boys until they assume the *bo* some time before puberty. The perineal band is a strip of bark-cloth passed round the waist, drawn between the legs, and knotted loosely in front. Because of this method of adjustment it is called *bo-abo*. It always covers the penis, but a native apparently feels no shame about exposing his testicles. When the strip is long enough it is so arranged that the end will hang as an apron or tail-piece which is painted with rude but effective patterns. This latter fashion belongs to the Bush and Salt-Water People rather than to the River People.

The woman's dress consists of a bark-cloth skirt, i.e. a wider strip passed round the hips and supported by being tucked under a belt in front. At the rear it is not tucked under but hangs somewhat below the belt, and young and attractive women allow it to show a glimpse of their buttocks. These younger women and *atamei*, or unmarried girls, wear the *bo* short, not reaching to their knees, but with older women it is sometimes of an ungainly size. Newly made, the cloth is coarse and stiff, but being painted with

---

[1] *Annual Report*, 1895–6, p. 76.   [2] *Annual Report*, 1893–4, pp. 4 and 33.

Typical Bark-cloth Designs

PLATE V

designs in red, brown, and black is not unbecoming. A good specimen may be regarded much as a party frock, and a woman is fully conscious of being well dressed when she wears it. It is amusing to see an old dame in expectation of a visit dart into her house and reappear in her best piece of bark-cloth. Growing older the garment grows softer and dirtier and loses all claim to beauty.

Among the Bush and Salt-Water People the woman's *bo* is worn from puberty onwards; among the River People only from marriage onwards. Nowadays a new sense of modesty in the presence of white men has altered this, but one may still occasionally see fully-developed young women among the Aiga or Binandele who go quite naked and without any trace of shame. The assumption of the *bo* by girls as well as boys will be referred to in a later chapter. A few examples of patterned bark-cloth are shown in the accompanying illustration. The method of beating the cloth and painting it are described under 'Arts of Life' (pp. 77–8).

The palm-leaf petticoat, commonly known by the Motuan name *rami*, is found as a sign of mourning among the Dirou tribe and on the lower Opi (see p. 222 n.). It is also reported at Lake Koena without any suggestion that it is restricted to mourning;[1] and further as worn by the Yema at Bovera on the Eia, where the older women use it as the proper dress of their people, while the younger have adopted the bark-cloth skirt of their Binandele neighbours.[2]

The Bark-cloth Hat, Pohu. The heads of old men are sometimes covered with a small sheet of bark-cloth called *pohu.* It encloses the mass of their hair, and falls over the back. Usually ragged and greasy, the *pohu* is no ornament but yet a mark of age and importance. No young man is seen wearing this unsightly rag. He would be at once too vain of his appearance and too modest to assume a headgear that is the prerogative of age.

The Widow's Cowl. Upon her emergence from seclusion the widow wears a cowl-shaped headgear, also called *pohu.* This, as she hangs her head, conceals her whole face and

[1] Beaver, *Annual Report*, 1914–15, p. 14.
[2] F. R. Cawley, *Annual Report*, 1922–3, p. 25.

covers the curious shame which she feels on this occasion. It is made of bark-cloth or of string netting, and is embroidered, sometimes completely covered, with the seeds known as Job's Tears. Being made and decorated with great care, however, it is later worn rather as an ornament under which the widow's charms suffer no concealment.

The Widow's Vest, Baja. This is usually a straight sleeveless shirt of knitted string completely covered with Job's Tears (*Coix lachrimae*). It reaches usually to the waist but sometimes as low as to the knees. *Coix lachrimae* seeds are of two kinds, the one a delicate grey, the other fawn, and with the introduction of black and sometimes red seeds the garment may be very effectively decorated.

The Bark-cloth Mantle. This is merely a broad sheet, three feet square or more, which is wrapped round the shoulders in cold weather. It is also used very prettily by girls in the dance. Holding it by two corners, the dancer swings it to and fro as she moves or allows it to float out behind her head. The bark-cloth is gaily painted and the girl's movements are light and graceful, so that in this guise she is not ineptly called *horiri*, 'the butterfly'.

Bi-kaio, the Apron. This is a small square of knitted string which hangs from the belt in front of the body. It is worn only by old men of distinction, and is seldom seen even on them. It may be only a partly assimilated introduction from the hill neighbours (Biagi, &c.), among whom it is certainly found more commonly. In the only example which I saw the string was knitted in patterns of red, brown, black, and white, and the fabric was decorated with black seeds and tufts of cuscus fur. W. N. Beaver mentions the *bi-kaio* in his list of *otohu*.[1]

Hair-dressing

The Orokaiva commonly allows his hair to grow long, and with the frequent application of coco-nut oil the close ringlets become clogged in a series of tags. The typical *coiffure* is therefore a mass of tails about the thickness of a

---

[1] 'Notes on Homicidal Emblems among the Orokaiva', &c., *Annual Report*, 1918-19, p. 97; under *Ve Hajo*.

lead pencil which fall about his shoulders something in the manner of the Chief Justice's wig. Notwithstanding grease and dirt, it is a distinctly becoming mode, particularly when to the profusion of his locks he adds the tassels of red-dyed *kapiya*, the transparent skin that lines the inner side of the areca spathe. To an Orokaiva his hair is assuredly felt to be a crowning glory, though it is often far from being the well-trimmed and flowing mass that I have pictured. His head is sometimes scraggy and sometimes even bald—a state which is regarded with curious aversion and attributed to some early indiscretion or ceremonial neglect.

The hair is cut short in mourning, and sometimes as a last desperate measure to free it from lice. In the former case it is an example of the self-sacrifice or self-castigation which is so common in sorrow, though a man may allow himself a little decorative effect as compensation for the loss (*vide* concentric circles on Plate XXVII). Nowadays many wear their hair short for mere convenience.

A woman's hair is dressed in the same way as a man's while she is young, i.e. with tags and red streamers. At marriage she is likely, though not bound, to cut it short; and when she has borne a child or two she will certainly do so. This I am assured is a case of modesty: a matron does not care to masquerade as a 'flapper' (and the same reason is given for the fact that married women wear comparatively few ornaments). Some informants have also suggested that a husband does not care to see his wife make herself too attractive to other men, and others that a mass of long hair interferes with the carrying of the *eti*, or string bag for taro.

Natives are clean-shaven except for some old men and some who have allowed their beards to grow in mourning. The beard is never of very strong growth. Nowadays moustaches are commonly copied from the white man and especially affected by those who have served in the Armed Constabulary. Shaving is done with a glass fragment (formerly one of quartz); with twisted fibres; and by plucking out the hairs with a bivalve for tweezers.

Deformations, &c.

Every child has the ear lobes and the nasal septum pierced; the methods employed are described on p. 98. Raised scars, *pupuho*, are commonly seen on the chests and shoulders of women, where they are self-inflicted, usually in the extremity of grief. Other scars, particularly those on the forehead, are the result of the practice of blood-letting to relieve pain. In some few instances we see keloids on the arms and across the sternum which, hideous as they seem to European eyes, are said to be made with the sole idea of personal enhancement.

There is no deformation of the genitalia. Informants have invariably been both astounded and amused at the notion of circumcision. And yet we have two early notes—both of them from competent observers—which state definitely that the practice existed. Mr. H. O. Forbes made a voyage up the north-east coast in 1885 and got into touch with the natives of Holincote [Holnicote?] Bay, who waded a long way out to his boat. He remarked on the poorness of their houses, the mean description of their ornaments, and the fact that they 'were all circumcised'.[1] Eight years later Sir Wm. MacGregor wrote of the natives about Gona (presumably the same district) that 'some are circumcised, others not'.[2] This was Sir William's first visit to the locality, and I cannot but believe that he was guilty of an unaccustomed malobservation. Nowadays, so far from practising circumcision, the native regards the exposure of the *glans penis* as shameful and ridiculous, and even employs the expression *bi panjari* (bald) as a term of abuse. Probably what the two observers saw was not due to a surgical cause but to nature, or else we must assume a very remarkable change in custom of which I have discovered no hint or recollection.

Tattoo (*Taroro*) is uncommon and, where it is found, wholly inferior. It is seen usually on girls, but is not a general habit of the people.[3] Tattoo is entirely voluntary

---

[1] Memo. in *Report on British New Guinea*, 1886, p. 45.
[2] *Annual Report*, 1893–4, p. 4.
[3] Nevertheless the habit is evidently of old standing. MacGregor on first visiting Oro Bay wrote: 'A few had some tattoo-marks on the face, but this was neither well done nor deeply marked.' *Annual Report*, 1890–91, p. 16.

Hambo or Ornaments

PLATE VI

and has no ceremonial significance. It is made by inflicting innumerable punctures with a thorn over a pattern made on the skin with charcoal.

Personal Hygiene

The Orokaiva is as dirty as and no dirtier than the next native. He hates the feel of cold water unless he is already hot and perspiring, and he would rather take a bath to get cool than to get clean. After his bathe he anoints his body and hair with the oily milk of the coco-nut, which he uses at all times with freedom. The somewhat rancid smell which one notices at times may be rather the effect of this oil than a genuine body odour.

The native uses a variety of perfumes which are not always alluring, and are sometimes even repulsive to the senses of a European. He wears sprigs of scented leaf in his armlet which he thinks will increase his sexual attraction. It is interesting to note that the delightful aroma of the lime tree (an introduction found in every village) has actually been declared unpleasant by some informants.

Face Painting

Faces are painted as a rule on gala occasions alone, but a young man who is intent on the self-display which constitutes the earlier stage of native love-making may on his own initiative wear a forehead ornament and decorate his cheeks. Nowadays he uses a trade mirror; formerly he poured water into a wooden bowl (*teva*) or one of those stone mortars which are still to be found in the Northern Division, and for which this use, viz. that of a mirror, is the only explanation a native can offer.

The paints used are a red seed (*ohonda sari*), red ochre (*ohonda opasi*), red clay (*niani*), grey or whitish clay (*onu*), charcoal (*oku*), and a leaf called *sopapa*. The last is crushed and mixed with lime and spittle, and forms a bright greenish yellow. I have discovered no trace of clan or tribal markings, the only approach toward distinctive patterns being found in the one or two devices employed by sects of the Taro cult.[1]

[1] 'The Taro Cult', in *Orokaiva Magic*, p. 67.

Feather Head-dresses

It cannot be denied that when the Orokaiva is in 'full dress' the *tout ensemble* is strikingly fine. We cannot claim that he has shown a great aptitude for the decorative arts in general, but he has shown no small amount of artistry in the decoration of his own person. The most imposing feature of his make-up is the head-dress of feathers. It is seldom worn complete save in the dance; in the warlike expedition (which I have never seen) it was no doubt considerably reduced.

The head-dress is built on piecemeal. The individual feathers are fixed in sets on arc-shaped frames, and one after another these sets are bound upon the mass of hair which is gathered behind the head. The following is a description of a dancer's head-dress which may be taken as fairly typical. (1) The lowest stratum was a mass of the black hair-like feathers of the cassowary which fell back over his shoulders like a great mane. (2) Above this came a number of sets of the large white tail-feathers of the hornbill; (3) a set of hawk's feathers, dapple grey; (4) three or four sweeping plumes of the red-brown bird of paradise; (5) and lastly, several tiers of close-set feathers obtained from the smaller and more brilliant birds such as parrots, &c.

As I have named the various parts of the head-dress from back to front, the first may be pictured as falling over the back and shoulders, the last, viz. the tiers of parrot feathers, as rising above the forehead. The whole is well set off by a band of shells and dogs' teeth encircling the brow.

Ornaments

The ornaments, or *hambo*, of the Orokaiva are by no means without a certain richness and beauty. They are made for the most part with boars' tusks, dogs' teeth, and various kinds of shell, which components are set together in some half-dozen bold patterns or styles. The mellow colours of old ivory, the white and rose of shell, and the vivid points of scarlet seed find an admirable foil in the native's brown skin. The *hambo*, it is true, are often dirty enough to blind the fastidious to their artistic worth; but

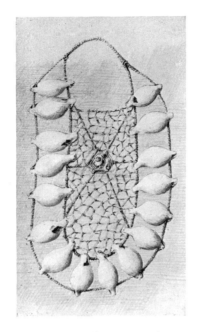

(*a*) *Erumo*, about 18 in. long

(*b*) *Gana*, about 8 in. by 7 in.

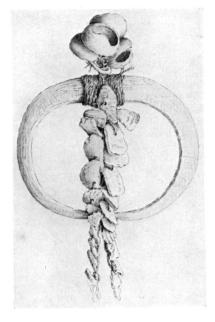

(*c*) *Hono*, about 6 in. wide

PLATE VII

as a little grime and age may add to the beauty of a building, so they probably add to the beauty of an Orokaiva ornament. It is certain that a newly-made ornament needs to be worn some time before it looks its best.

In the ensuing brief catalogue (which does not profess to be complete) the *hambo* are classified according to their use:

(1) *Teeth-held Ornaments.*

These are held in the teeth when dancing or fighting, and at other times are pendent on the breast. There is always some small appendage at the back of the ornament for the teeth to grip.

Hono (Plate VII). Two pig tusks forming a circle and supported by strings of irregular shell slabs. The latter (*ori*) show rich colours of red, salmon, and brown.

Huave. This ornament is similar to *hono* but instead of the pig tusks has two circles of white shell (giant clam), about three inches in diameter. It is supported by a string of *ori*.

Gana (Plate VII). A symmetrical arrangement of smaller pig tusks branching outwards from two main *rami*. It is thickly studded with red seeds, or nowadays often embroidered with trade beads. When held in the teeth at the lower junction of the two *rami*, the ornament forms a frame for the dancer's face.

Jauro or *Pako.* A circle, sometimes seven inches and more in diameter, cut out of the melon shell. It is white in colour and concave, somewhat resembling a china saucer. The couples in the ballet, each man holding one of these in his teeth, will clash them together as they dance. They are held by means of a string passed through two holes in the shell.

Erumo (Plate VII). *Ovulum* shells, called *Erumo*, are usually attached to a cane framework which, when not held in the teeth, is slung over the shoulder. The inner part of this frame may be netted. Another kind of *erumo* ornament is shown on Plate VI.

(2) *Forehead Ornaments.*

Peremo, the Hornbill Beak. The corrugated beaks of the hornbill are arranged on a frame so as to form a halo of spikes about the head. The use of this—as well as other *hambo*—for homicidal *insignia* will be referred to later (*vide* pp. 178 ff.).

Forehead Bands. These are composed in the main of the oblong shell slabs, red-brown in colour, known as *ori*, or of the small red shell disks called *pore* (commonly known in the Territory as *sapsap*). They are bordered with the minute white shells (*saima*), or with dogs' teeth (*bati*). Rosettes of the latter may be fixed at either end of the band.

Forehead bands are of great variety and beauty, and commonly figure as the ceremonial gift or *otohu* (*vide* p. 188). The example pictured in Plate VIII (*a*) (*Nanemo*) is only a dingy and disreputable specimen which happened to be at hand. It shows the shell slabs *ori* bordered with the small white shells *saima*. Plate VIII (*b*) shows a somewhat different style, viz. a tiara of white shell and cassowary feathers. I have not recorded its name.

(3) *Nose Ornaments.*

The usual nose-bone is a plain spike of white shell. Another style, which is found especially among the Binandele, is figured. It hangs from the septum over the lips. Known as *mekia*, this ornament has been aptly described as 'magnet-shaped'. It is not affected by younger men.

FIG. 1. *Mekia.*

(4) *Ear Ornaments.*

The common form is a small plain ring of tortoise-shell, or sometimes a series or bunch of them. The elaborate pendant shown in Plate IX (*a*) is, however, frequently seen. From a small pearl shell are suspended strings of shell fragments, dogs' teeth, a black banana seed known as *supi*, &c.

(5) *Necklets.*

These are of dogs' teeth or shell; frequently of the small white variety called *saima*. The large black seed *supi* forms a heavy but rather handsome necklet.

(6) *Armlets, &c.*

Two kinds of armlets are fairly distinctive of the Orokaiva. One is *samemi*, the narrow pearl-shell circle obtained from the trochus; the other is *siha*, the circle of coco-nut shell. Armlets of plaited cane or fern fibre are also common.

The skin of cuscus (*pauri*, *koviro*) may be attached to the armlets in the form of long streamers on which tufts of feathers may be tied at intervals. (The tanning of the skin is done, I am told, by powdering with red ochre or lime.)

(7) *Belts*.

These are mostly of plaited cane strips, sometimes with simple patterns made by introducing a darker material. The commonest of these patterns is shown on Plate IX (*b*).

Examples of finer texture are plaited with the strands of a creeper called *angoro*. A belt of another kind is made from the creeper named *sita*. Strands of this are plaited into a fine rope, black in colour, bearing a polish, which passes round the hips in multitudinous coils. The creeper is obtained only in the hills and is highly valued.

V

THE FOOD QUEST

Gardening

LIKE most inhabitants of Papua the Orokaiva are essentially gardeners. As their methods have already been described and criticized in another report,[1] they may be dismissed rather briefly in this; though it will not be forgotten that gardening is the first and foremost activity of the food quest and deserves more space than it will receive here.

The principal product is taro (*ba*); others of importance are sweet potatoes (*keroja*), yam (*kai*), banana and plantain (*pije*), sugar-cane (*jou*), and a variety of andropogon called *ina*. Coco-nuts (*bu*) and betel palms (*sa*) are cultivated everywhere, and the bread-fruit (*oga* and *eumba*), a food of some importance which grows wild, is also found in many villages and gardens.

Though effective enough the gardener's methods are primitive and wasteful. Fresh ground is continually cleared for new plantings, the crop matures and is harvested, and after that the plot is surrendered to the bush. Thus many areas are cleared and planted in succession, until in course of time the gardener finds himself at work on an area which he or his fathers cleared perhaps a score of years before. The gardens of a number of families, sometimes of a whole village, lie side by side in the same clearing, which will often enough be 100 acres and more in area.

When clearing is in progress an advance party of wife and children tear or cut away the undergrowth (*undaki*), and the husband follows with his trade axe. He cuts the trees at a level of some three or four feet above ground, and thus leaves an untidy forest of stumps which continue to sprout luxuriantly as the garden grows. An especially large tree may be left standing, but if the clearers have the requisite

---

[1] 'Orokaiva Garden Culture' (Report No. 7), in *Orokaiva Magic*.

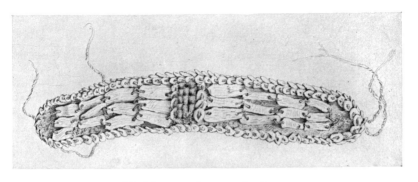

(*a*) *Nanemo*, about 18 in. long

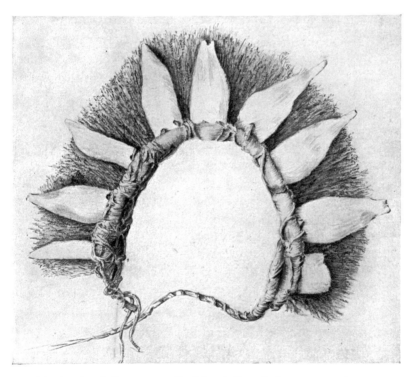

(*b*) Forehead Ornament of white shell and Cassowary plumes

PLATE VIII

energy they erect a scaffolding around it to enable them to attack the trunk above the wide buttress-like flanges which are characteristic of so many Papuan trees. Of the smaller tree-trunks some are laid out to mark off one plot from another—for the gardens of the whole clan are likely to be grouped in the same large clearing—others are stacked in pyramids to dry for firewood. The litter of branches and leaves is gathered into heaps and burnt. It would seem that the ideal is to have the ground as bare as possible before planting, and an exceptionally neat gardener will even go to the length of sweeping up the ashes from the burning. But the larger obstacles remain, and the garden will inevitably be obstructed with tree-trunks and those knotty roots which lie on the surface in the tropical bush.

There is no tilling of the soil and no manuring save indirectly through the burning of leaves and branches. There is no attempt at drainage or irrigation; indeed, both would be somewhat difficult on the plains, owing to their low gradient. In the sometimes protracted dry spells the taro offsets must be planted near swampy ground.

The only implement used in actual gardening is the digging stick—usually a hardwood stake which may be improvised on the spot. Sometimes it takes the form of a well-finished crow-bar of black palm-wood with a spatulate point. In planting, the digging stick is driven into the ground and levered back and forth so as to increase the size of the hole. Then the gardener, not deigning to stoop, shoots his taro-top cleverly into its place, adjusts it, if necessary, by means of his nimble great toe, and lightly treads in the earth. Yams are propagated from shoots, being kept in the darkness of the yam-house until the shoots appear. The gardener knows how to plant from cuttings (sugar-cane and *ina*), from suckers (banana), and from seeds (tobacco and some minor garden products), and he transplants rooted seedlings of trees (bread-fruit and the *ajimo* or bark-cloth tree).

The garden is weeded from time to time by women, but when once the taro is well established, it is often left to contend with the weeds. A rough fence surrounds the whole clearing and protects it more or less effectively against the bush-pigs. Until the whole circuit of this fence is completed it is necessary for some people to live temporarily in the garden, where a smoking fire and an occasional shout are sufficient to scare away the intruders. Sometimes a man will lie in wait by moonlight hoping to spear a pig among his taro, which is a dangerous game and results in many casualties. The various traps and snares which are meant for pigs and others spoliators of the garden will be described under Hunting.

There is little to say concerning the harvesting. A woman gathers from time to time enough for her family's immediate wants, and the taro tops will be replanted. There are thus a number of plots at different stages of advancement in every woman's garden. Sometimes, however, when all the gardens of a clan are well stocked, there will be a simultaneous harvesting to furnish forth a feast. The products of the garden are then loaded ostentatiously upon platforms in the village before their final distribution to the guests.

Coco-nuts are placed under a tabu when a large feast is pending and, as they fall, are accumulated in long lines on the ground, or else strung to poles set up as a tall pyramid in the centre of the village. In the southern part of the division yams are kept in a *harasi* or yam-house, the actual repository being a small dark attic under the gabled roof, while the lower story, merely a raised platform, is used as a sitting-place. Only two other methods of food-storage are worth mentioning. *Tauga* nuts are strung together on poles and suspended over the house fires, where they become black and dry; and *Puga* nuts are concealed in holes in creeks, where the moving water in the course of several months purges away their poisonous properties.

Hunting

Although hunting is only a secondary phase of the food quest, the hunter is distinguished by some skill and ingenuity, by a remarkable keenness for meat, and by a very sensible catholicity of taste. Bush-pigs, wallabies—of the bush and of the grass-lands—rats, birds, lizards, frogs, and

(a) *Dende* or ear-pendant   (b) Belt of plaited cane

PLATE IX

snakes are all pursued with eagerness. If any kind of food is debarred it is more often because of some magico-religious tabu than through a feeling of aversion.

Individual Hunting. When an individual travels in the bush he goes armed with his spear and followed by his dog so as to lose no opportunities. As the floods are subsiding the villagers will prowl about, a man and his wife together, with a fair certainty of bagging some small game which has been driven out of its shelter; and if they can do no better the woman will, at least, succeed in catching frogs.

If his dog puts up a bush-pig a man will not hesitate to attack it single-handed. He will even do so in the perilous uncertainty of the moonlight. The strength and fierceness of the bush-boar, with his tusks ground to continual sharpness, make him no mean enemy, and argue considerable pluck on the part of the individual hunter. Even concerted hunts are not without danger. An old man named Tumai relates how, during a pig-drive (while the river Opi was in flood and the pigs more or less cut off), he speared one of these animals as it rushed into the net. The spear broke and the pig, disengaging itself from the net, 'looked about as if to say, who speared me?' Concluding rightly that it was Tumai it turned upon him, ripped first one thigh, then the other, then his chest, then his knee. (The scars remain on the old man's body as proud evidence of his adventure.) It was at this stage that his son came to the rescue, only to be bowled over in his turn. But now Tumai, despite his four wounds, threw himself bodily upon the pig, and the son was enabled to get to his feet and kill it. Such incidents are common enough. There is no denying that the bush-pig is a formidable beast and the Orokaiva a fearless hunter.

Concerted Hunting. There are two principal methods of concerted hunting. One is the drive through the bush towards a pig-net; the other is that of the grass-burning.

The pig-net (*monga*) is strongly made of pandanus fibre. The mesh is about four inches wide; the net stands about four feet high; and each section may be twenty yards long. It is propped up by a series of stakes (*tetere*). Formerly these stakes were the only means of holding up the net, and it was frequently charged down by the pig. But once while the hunters were sheltering from the rain a small boy found himself cowering in a hollow tree. He was startled by a cry of *Duve hange, duve hange!* from above his head in the interior of the tree. He ran out terrified and told the men, who proceeded to cut out part of the hollow trunk. As they were doing so a *sovai* or monster came tumbling down and glared round on the hunters. Some were brave enough to threaten him, but he told them to restrain themselves as he was about to make them a present. With that he dragged down interminable lengths of rope from the interior of the tree, and passing them through the meshes of the pig-net above and below, made them fast at either end to strong stakes. The rope is called *duve* and the stakes *hange*, and since that time both have been used with satisfactory result. A similar but lighter net is used for wallabies. With either the method of procedure is the same. Beaters (*dogo*) advance with loud halloos, and the pig fleeing before them charges into the net, where he is speared by the *monga-embo*, or netsmen. A number of privately-owned nets are stretched end to end, and the quarry belongs to the owner of that particular net in which it is caught.

Annually towards the end of the South-East season the tracts of grass-land are burnt off. The weather is hot and dry and the grass burns furiously, only to spring up afterwards with renewed vigour. The grass tracts are owned by individual clans, but at this season there will assemble large hunting parties composed of many clans and villages.

At one hunt which I attended there were some sixty people, including a number of women. They assembled from various quarters at one village and left for the scene of the hunt, at about 9 a.m., so as to commence operations in the heat of noon. After a walk of about seven miles they rested in a small village and arranged their campaign. Four firing-parties split off and made their way as quietly as possible to four positions on the edge of the selected grass patch. The remainder distributed themselves around the patch. The men of the firing-parties work in pairs. One goes in front and, holding his spear horizontally, thus

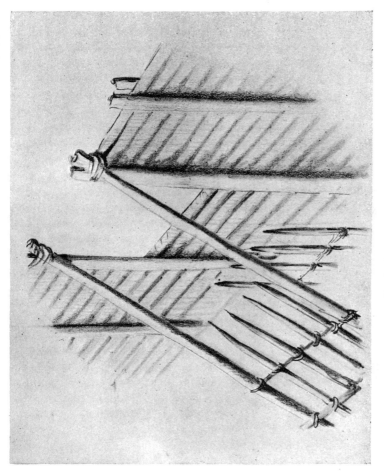

Kombu Bage or Pig Trap
PLATE X

presses down the grass and forms a path; meanwhile his companion behind him applies the torch to the inner edge of the path. They move as swiftly as they can and the four parties endeavour to set their fires going simultaneously. Thus the retreat of the pig, which is presumably somewhere in the centre of the patch, is largely cut off by the flames. The burning strips are extended, and the hunters move forward close behind them like troops under a barrage. The heat is almost intolerable. The tufts are left red-hot and crackling, and the sparks are still flying. It is almost incredible that bare feet should endure it, but the hunters press on with their spears poised for any quarry that may turn and break through the flames.

But mistakes occur. Too much noise in preparation may warn the pig to make good his escape; or the fires may be ill-timed. On the occasion here described the total bag (when I left late in the afternoon) consisted, as far as I know, of no more than three bush-rats. But the party remained, and subsequently caught many more, with the aid of their dogs, who ferret among the gradually cooling debris of leaves and fallen branches around the edge of the grass-patch, and bring out lizards, rats, and such small deer, alive or already scorched to death.

Traps and Snares. Several traps and snares are in common use throughout the whole of the Orokaiva country. The log-trap (*bage*; Binandele *wau*) consists of two parallel fences (*a*) some eighteen inches apart, made of upright stakes with a weight of heavy logs between them (*b*) held up by a lever (*c*). This lever rests on a fulcrum (*d*), formed by a strong forked stick leaning against one of the fences. The lever is held in position by a line. To this line is attached a short peg (*e*) which, being passed round the base of the fulcrum, is made to meet the trigger (*f*) (*bage-bi*) end to end at the point (*x*). The other extremity of this light trigger bears upon one of the stakes of the fence on the opposite side. If the adjustment at (*x*) is made carefully the trap is set, the string is kept taut and the lever holds the logs in position. But along the ground between the fences and underneath the *bage-bi* there lies a split palm-trunk, which constitutes the bait. The wild pig roots at the pith of the palm-trunk (*g*), enters between the two fences, and made heedless of its suspicious surroundings by its enjoyment of the palm-pith, pushes on until with a vigorous jerk of its

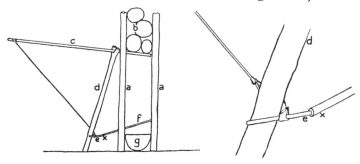

FIG. 2. *Bage* or Pig Trap.

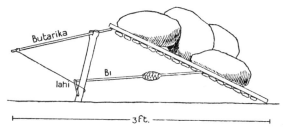

FIG. 3. Rat Trap.

snout it disturbs the *bage-bi*, and breaks the all-important contact at (*x*). Then in one instant the peg flies, the lever is released, and the weight of logs is home on the pig's back. The animal is either killed outright or effectually imprisoned.

The *bage* is sometimes made to lead off from a gap purposely left in the garden fence, and in this case the bait consists not of a palm-log, but merely of the temptation to enter the garden. The *bage-bi* will be then attached to a small sloping platform or ramp over which the pig must pass in order to enter the garden, so that its weight will serve to set the mechanism in motion. Rat traps are made on precisely the same lines but in miniature. A variant form is shown in Fig. 3. Here a small tilted platform of sticks is weighted with stones and left under the house as a rat-trap, or else

A Rat Trap

PLATE XI

in the bush, as a snare for small ground birds. The bait is attached firmly to the *bage-bi*. These miniatures are often in the nature of toys rather than serious contrivances.

The pit-trap (*hoto*) is common in all parts of the Division. It is placed where bush-pigs are known to pass, and a roughly camouflaged fence, some 30 or 40 yards long, will guide the pig to the fatal spot, viz. a gap in the centre where the pit is dug and concealed with leaves, twigs, and earth. It is about 6 feet deep and the bottom bristles with spikes of hardwood or old spear-points. The pig is not driven, and the only means other than the fence of inveigling it to the pit is the magical one of ginger-root or pig-medicine hidden close by. The *hoto* is not without danger to dogs and wandering children, and a number of recent casualties have compelled the magistrate to place restrictions on its use.

The pit is sometimes dug on the inner side of the garden fence opposite an intentional gap. Another kind of trap is similarly placed but consists simply of an array of sharpened stakes set in the ground. It is calculated that the pig, leaping over, will land among the points and be stuck through some vital organ, say the liver; so that in Wasida this device was given the expressive name of *kombu-bage*, or 'liver-trap'.

The miniature pit-trap called *oivo* may be mentioned in passing. It is a shallow hole set with small spikes and covered with leaves. Placed in the garden it was a protection against thieves, and, in the environs of the village, against night-walking sorcerers. I was told that *inja*, or sorcerer's medicine, might be placed on the points to make it something more than a mere burglar-alarm. Several instances of accidental stumbling into the *oivo* were recounted to me, but none in which a real culprit met with his deserts. It appears that one really guilty would lie low in the endeavour to conceal the injuries that proved his guilt. Nowadays, it is said, the *oivo* has gone out of fashion.

An interesting though trivial variety of trap is made by children in rat-infested gardens. A hole is dug with smooth shelving sides, and projecting half-way across it is set a light stick, half-fractured at a point not far from the end. The rat ventures out towards the bait and as it passes the point of weakness the stick breaks, and it is thrown into the hole from which there is no escape. (Plate XI).

The springe (*ihive*) is used for wallaby and other small game. It is set either on a track known to be frequented by wallaby or else by a hole in the garden fence, where a wallaby might enter. A strong pole (*butarika*) to which a running noose (*ivasi*) and a light rod (*bi*) are attached is bent down and held in place by a cross-piece (*iahi*) as shown in the diagram. The wallaby disturbs the *iahi*, over which the

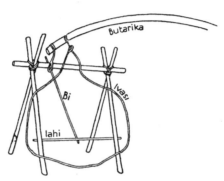

FIG. 4. *Ihive* or Wallaby Trap.

noose is spread, and so releases the spring and is caught. A rather odd transposition of names will be seen by comparing the sketches of the wallaby trap and the rat-trap.

Bird Catching. Bright feathers, such as those of the common bird of paradise (raggiana), parrots, kingfishers, and numerous small but brilliant varieties, are a definite form of wealth with the Orokaiva, and are preserved with great care. A fledgling may be kept and eventually treated with kindness as a pet, but if a man find a beautiful little bird defending her nest in the hollow of a tree it will not cross his mind to be compassionate. The feathers are too tempting.

The commonest method of catching birds is that of a running noose (*huri* or *ni-sai*) attached to a long line. The noose is spread along the branch of a flowering or fruiting tree which is frequented by bright-plumaged birds, while the snarer, usually a boy, remains in concealment holding his long line. A sudden jerk at the right moment and he has a fluttering captive. It does not occur to him that it would be merciful to kill the bird immediately; he rather enjoys its squeaking and struggling. The bird-snarer is ingenious enough to cover a pool with broad leaves, leaving only a small surface of the water exposed. Close by he sets up a little perch horizontally with his noose spread over it, and then waits till the bird after its bathe will hop on the perch to preen itself.

A large net of loose mesh called *hute* or *goga* is used for catching those birds, such as cockatoos or hornbills, which make their nests in hollow trees. The *hute* may be attached

FIG. 5. *Utuha.*

to a handle after the fashion of a butterfly net, and while one man holds it over the hole, another will beat the tree trunk until the bird is scared out and enmeshed. A more primitive method is that of simply knocking a sleeping bird off its perch. For this purpose, I am told, there is a roughly contrived instrument called *utuha*, which resembles a highly magnified 'fly-swat'.

Lastly, there is the sling *Taiha* (see p. 83) with which it is said birds may sometimes be brought down; though if one may judge from the amazing inaccuracy of trial shots, the *taiha* cannot nowadays be very effective.

Miscellaneous Traps, &c. In the Isivita district may be seen an ingenious trap for fruit-bats or flying-foxes. This consists of a small meshed bag, roughly made of bark-string, and of the right size to contain a bread-fruit. Attached to the bag are numerous running nooses, which form a general tangle about it. The fruit-bat noses and claws at the bread-fruit, and is probably awkward enough to get itself caught in one of the nooses.

A second method is that of the *asora*. A bunch of trailers

of the climbing palm is tied to a long pole. These trailers are armed with sharp recurved thorns, and the bat-snarer takes his stand beside a banana or pawpaw tree, the scene of the animal's nightly depredations. One sweep of the *asora* at the right moment, and the flapping wings are caught in the hooks.

In the caves near Ioma it is, I believe, only necessary to go in and lay about with a stick and the bats may be slaughtered wholesale. Unappetizing as they seem to ourselves, they are welcome enough as food to a native who is perforce mainly vegetarian.

FIG. 6. Lizard Snare.

The large monitor lizard, besides being eaten, serves another useful purpose in furnishing the skin for the drum. If a native catch sight of one, he will leave whatever he is at in order to give chase. The lizard takes to a tree for refuge and the native hastily improvises the special implement required for the occasion. This is a light pole with a running noose of some fairly stiff material, such as split cane, attached to the extremity, and a hook made by binding on a small stick obliquely. He now climbs the tree after the lizard, hanging his pole by means of the hook to any convenient projection as he ascends. When within range he stretches out to noose his victim, which constantly moves to the far side of the branch on which it has taken refuge, only to be driven round again by sticks, stones, and shouts from those who are standing below. Finally the lizard stands as if mesmerized and permits the noose to be gently slipped over its slowly waving head. It seems bent on going forward to escape and the noose tightens hopelessly round its neck or middle.

Having dealt with various methods of snaring animals and birds from *sus papuensis*, the wild boar, downwards, I may conclude by describing two methods of catching the domestic fly. Incidentally it was almost with surprise, considering the all-devouring taste of the Orokaiva, that one learnt the domestic fly was never eaten. The first of these fly-traps is called *orari* or *barara*. The light midrib of a coco-nut leaflet is bent back at one end and tied so as to form a loop with a handle. This is passed through a number of spiders' webs until the space enclosed within the loop is a thick mesh of cobweb. The little boy with a sore on his leg—and there are too many such—is continually plagued with flies. He dabs at them with his butterfly net of cobweb, and the fly is made a secure prisoner.

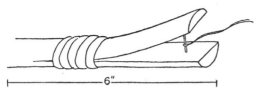

FIG. 7. *Teonda-tahi* or Fly Trap.

The second fly-trap is called *Teonda-tahi*. A piece of sugar-cane is split and bound near the extremity. The two halves, which tend to spring together, are forced apart and kept open by a tiny peg attached to a fine string. The behaviour of the fly and the fly-catcher are obvious, and the device, which is no more than a child's toy, is quite effective.

Fishing

Hand-nets. The commonest kind of fishing contrivance (one which has a wide distribution throughout Papua) is the small hand-net supported on a loop of cane. Among the Orokaiva it is called *eutu* (also *eundu, isimbo,* and *angoro*). The mesh is fine and the loop varies in size, but might average 20 inches long by 10 inches wide. It is used as a scoop in creeks and pools, the water having been first diverted by means of a dam and a race, or scooped out with sago branches (*kambo*). This net is used by women.

In Koropata and other villages along the middle course of the Kumusi is found a much larger hand-net called *hute*. The mesh is wider and supported on an elliptical hoop of

cane, with a handle passing through its shorter axis. The
net is used at night when the subsiding flood waters are
coursing down to the bed of the Kumusi. The fisherman
stands with his back to the current, which flows past

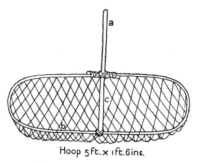

Hoop 5ft.x 1ft.6ins.

FIG. 8. Fish Net, *Hute.*

FIG. 9. Fish Net, *Siho.*

him through the net. He holds the handle at (*a*) and keeps
his foot on the loop (*b*) in order to keep the net steady. If
he feels a fish enter the net he stoops and grasps the handle
at (*c*) and raises the net horizontally in front of him.

Widely distributed among the Orokaiva is an interesting
little net called *siho*. It is often hardly more than a toy,
being used by children to capture the tiny, somewhat inert
fish of the creeks and pools. The net is very light and frail;
the mesh is often made of plain pandanus fibre, while the
framework is a loop (about 3 inches in diameter) of the
midrib of a coco-nut leaflet. The net takes the form of a
small bag, the mouth of which, sliding along the loop, will

open and close. It is held face down and then suddenly snatched away. The movement closes the mouth of the bag and the fish is held.

The coastal people have the triangular net (*yako* or *yavara*) (Fig. 10). The actual fabric is almost square, but it is fixed to two poles which form a triangle in the manner shown. The cross-piece is bound on at either end and acts as a handle. This net is used on the beaches.

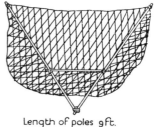

Length of poles 9 ft.

FIG. 10. Fish Net, *Yako*.

A number of fishermen, each with his *yako*, form two lines and slowly drawing together encircle a small school of fish. They keep their nets under water, and then holding the apex with the right hand and lifting the handle with the left they raise their nets together.

Drag-nets. The coastal Orokaiva use small drag-nets. These have a row of light wooden tabs for floats and a row of scollop shells for weights. At certain points along the coast we find a much larger drag-net called *Komboru* which is owned and used communally.

It is about 6 feet in depth and may be 100 yards long. Several villages will be joint owners of the net and must do their share towards keeping it in order. There is a 'chief' or *komboro-topo*, in some cases two—one for either end—and these never go with the canoe when the net is paid out: for some reason not made plain their presence would spoil the catch. There does not appear to be any definite allocation of tasks, and the spoils are distributed among all the villagers.

Stationary Traps. The most characteristic of the fishing methods of the Orokaiva is that of the *sirava* (also called *beturo*). This is common to all the River People and the Aiga, and is used by some of the coastal tribes for creek fishing. It is not found, unless exceptionally, among the Bush People. The trap consists of two cones, one within the other, made of strips of palm-midrib set fairly close together. Both are open at their apices, i.e. at the points (*x*) and (*y*). The net is set in small streams or in temporary courses of flood water. A barrier of sticks and leaves blocks the stream except where one or more of these traps allows the current to flow through. The *sirava* is set with its mouth facing upstream and the orifice at (*y*) is stoppered with leaves. The fish entering at (*x*) is unable to make its way out again, and in due course the net is taken up and emptied at (*y*). There is no kind of bait save perhaps a

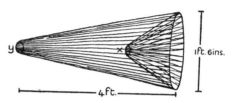

FIG. 11. Fish Net, *Sirava*.

magical one concealed in the bunch of leaves which acts as stopper. These traps are made by men and used by either men or women. They are constructed neatly and well, and their strength is attested by the tale of the over-confident man who chaffed his brother-in-law as he was engaged in making one. Declaring it was a poor job which a fish of any size would break in a moment he foolishly accepted a good-humoured challenge to break it himself. But having by some means insinuated himself through the hole at (*x*) when the trap was already set in the water he found it impossible to carry out his boast, and so the owner was afforded the triumph (particularly embarrassing to an Orokaiva) of catching and drowning his brother-in-law.

I have heard at Wasida of a stationary trap constructed on a different principle, viz. a conical frame lined with thorns; but never in the course of my stay in the Northern Division have I see one.[1]

A simple contrivance is employed for catching eels. In the South-East season many of the inland streams fall low, the water is clear and the large eels (*ohiti*) harbour in the

[1] Mr. Leo Austen, Assistant Resident Magistrate at Buna, has made special inquiries upon this subject and sends me the following verification: 'I have searched through the various tribes of the Northern Division and find there is no such thing as a fish-trap with thorns or spikes on which the fish become impaled.' If the thorn-lined trap is found at all in the division one ventures to think it was introduced by the Kiwai (lower Fly river) police who were employed there in the early days.

dark places under fallen tree trunks. The eel is a heavy-bodied creature with a blade-like tail and fierce jaws. When a number of them have been discovered the village may turn out in force. The younger men will dive and endeavour to dislodge the eels with sticks and spears, while the others, some upstream and some down, take their stand on convenient rocks and wait with poised fishing-spears to catch the eel as it makes a dart for freedom. If the efforts of the divers (who perform remarkable feats of endurance under water, and use their spears at no small risk to one another's legs) prove unavailing, they will have recourse to more insidious methods. The *poso*, a hollow log, some 6 feet long and 9 inches in diameter, open at either end, and furnished with a small window or peep-hole, 2 orches 3 in square, half-way down its length, is brought into use. Two divers will take this down and secure it under water near the hole where the eel is hiding.

The harrassed creature being now left alone and seeing a dark narrow hole—a retreat after its own heart—slips into the *poso* and rests secure until one of the young men diving again discovers its presence by means of the peep-hole. Then two men will go down, block each open end of the log with leaves and bring it to the surface, where the eel is ejected and killed.

Fishing-spears. Any spear will serve on emergency for a fishing-spear, but nowadays it is frequently furnished with a point of iron wire. The fishing-spear proper, however (*bosau* or *saita*), which I have seen among the Bush People, has two prongs of palm wood bound on to a long light shaft. In some of the coastal villages is found a long leister or spear (*sagi*) furnished with perhaps ten prongs of hard-wood bound on to a light shaft about seven feet long.

Line Fishing. Line fishing is of little practical consequence. The line itself is of pandanus or banana fibre, plain or twisted. Two kinds of hooks may be described. The first of them is hardly more than a toy. The leaf of the pandanus is edged with minute oblique thorns or prickles, and a small boy will attach to his line a little section of this leaf which acts as bait or lure and, by virtue of its little thorns, as hook also.

In the more usual method the hook is made of sago thorns or those of the plant called *sinegi* (apparently a kind of palm). The line is first threaded through an earthworm by means of a thin sharp sliver. Then three thorns (about 1 inch long) are bound together by means of the line itself and thrust into the worm so that the points project upwards, and thus

FIG. 12. Worm Bait and Hook.

constitute a hook. Line fishing is done by hand and the bait is allowed to dangle in the water.

Poisoning. The last, but not the least important, of fishing methods is that of poisoning, which is practised by all tribes in the inland creeks and pools. The poison is usually obtained from the vine *Anisi* (*Kanesi, Ainsi*), a variety of derris; though certain other poisonous plants with the native names *Ondoto, Pogera,* and *Imanya* are used, as well as the recently introduced chilli. Water is bailed out of the pool or sometimes run off by means of a race or gutter, and when it is sufficiently shallow the root of the *Anisi* is pounded on a log. It exudes a highly poisonous milky fluid which permeates the water and brings the fish stupefied to the surface.

Sago Making

Among the River People sago is a never-failing food supply, for on the lower reaches of the rivers large tracts of swamps are, I believe, not even explored by the natives, and their resources are but lightly tapped. Inland, where it is comparatively rare, trees are definitely owned and husbanded. Sago, however, is not a favourite food with the Orokaiva, and it is for the most part when his taro gives out that he resorts to it; and since this is likely to be in the midst of a partial drought, when the swamps themselves may have

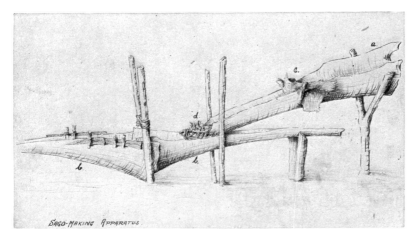

(*a*) *Beo* or Kneading Trough.　(*b*) *Ingi Gau* or Settling Troughs.
(*c*) *Usisi* or Strainer of Coco-nut Fibre.　(*d*) *Kuoro* or Strainer of
Coco-nut Leaves.

Above, *Evai* or Sago-scraper; *below*, *Gopiri* or Water-scoop

PLATE XII

dried up, the sago-maker's work, which requires a good supply of water, is not always easy.

The branches or fronds—often armed with the sharpest of thorns—being lopped from the selected tree, the leaves are spread on the swampy ground to make a temporary floor. The broad spathes are peeled off and the tree is felled. Next a section of bark is prised off and the sago-maker, taking his seat astride the trunk, proceeds to use his scraper (*evai*), which is hafted on to a forked branch so as to form a hammer-shaped implement. (The point of the hammer is slightly cupped and hardened in fire.) He accompanies his rhythmical strokes with strange ejaculations and musical cries, *eyeveyeyeyeye, o-dego-o-o-o-o o-deg-o-o-o-o*, and such-like, of which he cannot give any explanation. The pith is transferred from time to time to the trough at which another man is working. The apparatus is shown on Plate XII (*a*).

The kneading trough (*a*) (*beo*) is made of a sago branch, so also are the settling troughs (*b*) (*ingi-gau*) placed end to end and carefully adjusted. The narrow ends of these may be raised or lowered, and any leaks are stopped with leaves. The sago pith is kneaded in (*a*) and constantly watered. The real sago is carried down in suspension by the water, and passing through the two strainers at (*c*) and (*d*) settles in the trough. The first strainer, made of coco-nut fibre, is called *usisi*; the second, merely a bunch of sago leaves, is called *kuoro*. If the trough is too shallow its edges are raised by sago leaflets fastened on as if with clothes-pegs. An ingenious water-scoop (*gopiri*) is made from a sheet of sago spathe. The harder surface is chopped away until only a thin leathery sheet remains. This is doubled and bound into the cleft of a sago midrib, and any leaks are patched with leaves. The supports or props for the troughs are often made of sections of the sago midrib, so that it is interesting to note how the whole apparatus, with the exception of the scraper (*evai*) and the coco-nut-fibre strainer (*usisi*) may be fashioned from the sago palm itself.

The sago soon settles in the settling trough, forming a pulpy mass. When the kneading is finished the water is run off and the mass of sago is pressed and pounded into lumps of the requisite size. These are rapidly singed in a fire of dry leaves and so acquire a brown glazed surface, a sort of tough skin which preserves the interior against moisture. The work is now finished. The glazed lump of sago is neatly bound with sago leaves, packed into the hollow of a sago branch, and carried home. Under favourable conditions two or three men will easily make 100 lb. in a day.

Collecting

The Orokaiva is a collector only by necessity or opportunity. When a prolonged drought in the South-East season causes a scarcity of food, collecting assumes importance, and a reduced diet must be eked out with roots, leaves, and fern fronds. While it is only under such stress that he collects systematically, he nevertheless keeps his eye open at all times for chance blessings when he is working or travelling. For tearing down betel pepper (*hingi*) or the somewhat rare fruits of the bush he will tie a pair of poles together and bind on a small oblique peg at the end to make a hook. This crude improvisation called *kainpo* may have a reach of 30 feet. The native is, moreover, a nimble and daring climber. If, however, neither his *kainpo* nor his climbing are equal to the occasion, he will fell a large tree for the sake of a little honey or even a nest of edible insects.

Frogs, snails, and fresh-water bivalves are collected by the humbler hands of women, but not in any quantity; they amount to nothing more than savouries.

Domesticated Animals

The Pig. The village pig and the wild pig are of the same species, the latter being continually domesticated. When a wild sucking-pig is captured by hunters, it is brought to the village and gradually tamed. Its roving and lawless nature may be restrained by the constant companionship of a long stick tied to its hind leg; it is fed and petted, its ears are snipped, it is castrated, and finally becomes as nearly domesticated as any other native pig. It is accustomed to forage about the village and to roam the neighbouring bush, where females are served by wild boars. It is fed every evening, and probably sleeps under the house.

Always a restless and obtrusive creature, the village pig is sometimes aggressive towards strangers, so that more than one visitor, even of magisterial importance, has been compelled to seek safety in the altitude of a house verandah. But, however unattractive, the pig is treated with consideration and even fondness by the villagers. Its owners, man and wife, are referred to as its father and mother. While young it may be washed with a magical infusion to promote its growth. It is given a personal name, and as it grows becomes an identity of importance in the village. As the inevitable hour of parting draws near, its 'mother' will be genuinely grief-stricken; and when at last her pig is bound for the sacrifice and lies groaning and struggling under the house, she will sit beside it, stroking it and shedding copious tears.

The pig is carried in the usual manner, with its feet bound to a pole. For a long journey a pig-litter (*kakate*) may be used. It is a cage-like structure of cane which, as it were, is made to measure and fits closely about the animal's body (see p. 79). The conventional method of slaughtering is with the spear, and at a feast of importance this is done ceremonially, a number of pigs being set in a row and stuck simultaneously. On such an occasion I have seen one of the butchers, more elderly than the rest, fail to impart sufficient force to his thrust, and try again, amid a good deal of laughter, until he drove the point home. Then he levered the shaft of his weapon back and forth like a crow-bar to make his work the surer. On the whole, however, there is no special inhumanity in the treatment of pigs.

The actual butchering is performed on a platform. Two long incisions are made from shoulder to tail, and the skin cut off together with a thick coating of fat. Then the body is dismembered with axe, trade knife, and bamboo knife (the last-named, *ivi*, is still used because of its extraordinary sharpness). The carving is not a pleasing spectacle. The blood drips through between the rails of the platform and is eagerly lapped up by quarrelling dogs below. There may be some delay in the distribution of the meat, and then the scene of the feast becomes a veritable shambles. There is little squeamishness with the native, however, and even the entrails are not despised. As it was explained (whether naïvely or waggishly) on one occasion, fresh entrails are suitable for men; if they stink a little they are suitable for women; and if they stink a great deal they will do for the children.

The Dog. The native dog is small, though better grown than those in some other parts of the Territory. It is commonly not more than 12 or 13 inches at the withers, though some, notably those of the Gira and the Waria, are larger. It has pointed ears and snout, and the tail has a very slight suggestion of brush. In colour it is usually yellow-brown, though sometimes black. It is undeniably a game little animal, an excellent hunter of small game, and equal to bringing a bush-pig to bay.[1]

Dogs are treated affectionately enough by their owners. I have known an elderly man declare his intention of leaving his village and 'signing on' for a year because his dog had fallen into a pit-trap and killed itself. It is true he subsequently thought better of his decision, but he was no doubt sorry to lose his dog. However, the dog does not compare with the pig in Orokaiva estimation. It is always less of a pet than a servant, and is ultimately destined for the pot. In slaughtering it is seized by the hind legs and its body dashed against a tree, a method which seems brutal but is instantly effective. Many specimens are mangy and diseased. They are proverbially susceptible to the cold and are commonly seen crouching in the ashes of a hardly expired fire. Indeed, the dog is said to have a special prerogative over the fire by virtue of the legendary fact that he first brought it to the Orokaiva.

The Domestic Fowl. Nowadays there are some European fowls in the Northern Division, and many of a native breed. By common consent of many old informants these latter are pre-European. Both are called *hohora*. The native cock is

---

[1] The native dog of the Purari Delta (Report No. 5, p. 27) is no doubt a degenerate of the same species. From the canine point of view the Delta must be a very unfavourable environment.

smallish and in colouring resembles a brown leghorn with large sweeping tail-feathers; the hen is a neat little white or brown bird. The wings are well developed and the native fowl is often capable of flying to the top of a coco-nut palm. It is kept for eating or for its feathers; natives do not appear to fancy the eggs greatly. The cock is treasured principally on account of his long tail-feathers, which are shamelessly plucked; though natives realize that a European has queer notions regarding cruelty to dumb creatures, and more than once, inquiring about a tailless rooster, I have been assured that its feathers were torn out by a dog.

Preparation of Food

Fire-making. The indigenous method of fire-making is that of the stick and groove. From their mountain neighbours on the south the Orokaiva have learnt in recent times the saw method, with split stick and rattan. This is said to be more effective, but is not as yet very widely known.

The stick and groove method is called *kaja*, i.e. 'thrust', as, e.g., with a spear. The smaller stick is called *bi-kai* (*bi* = penis; *kai* is the root of *kaiari* or *kajari* = thrust). A shaving is peeled back on the piece of wood which acts as base. The *bi-kai* is grasped in both hands, knuckles up and thumbs down, and worked back and forth with increasing speed, till it is suddenly brought to a stop pressing into the end of the groove, where a little pile of smoking wood-dust has accumulated. If this is smouldering it is gently coaxed and blown and then transferred to a coco-nut husk. Although signed-on boys bring back matches to the villages, it is by no means to be imagined that the primitive method of fire-making has gone out of use.

Cooking. There is but one regular meal in the Orokaiva day, viz. in the evening. The housewife peels her taro and cuts it into lumps with a sharp oyster-shell or a keen-edged piece of coco-nut shell. She adds various leaves and herbs for flavouring, among the commonest being that of the taro itself, first carefully freed from its stalk and ribs. She may spray condiments out of her mouth into the pot, and finally covers it with leaves and allows it to seethe. From the earthenware pot (*obu*) the cooked taro is transferred to smaller pots, wooden bowls (*teva*), or coco-nut shells, in which it is served.

Food is placed in front of the principal people present, and the others soon group themselves round the various dishes. There is none but a tacit invitation, simply a jerk of the head. The meal goes on for the most part in silence—that is, in respect of conversation, though not always in respect of mastication and swallowing. The only table utensils are coco-nut spoons (*age*), in the form of little boat-shaped scoops, and three- or four-pronged forks (*sagi*) made of bone or wood. The latter, however, are said to be old men's implements. It was suggested that they were needed because of the clumsiness of an old man's fingers, but the fact is that there is something honorific about them. A young man would not feel at home with a *sagi*; he would be, in a manner, exceeding his rights.

Nearly all Orokaiva cooking is done in earthenware pots. They are even carried on expeditions. But on emergency there is the method of cooking with hot stones. The food is placed on a layer of leaves upon the hot stones; more leaves and more hot stones are laid on top, and the food slowly bakes. The method of cooking in a pit, with heated stones below and above is known, but I have never seen it put into practice. It is alluded to in some of the legends and is presumably an old fashion. The boiling of water by heated stones is used in fumigation. The medicines are placed together with water in a wooden dish (*teva*), and when the heated stones are thrown in, the steam rises and the sick man stoops over it to be fumigated.

Salt. The native shows the usual craving for salt, so that among the inlanders it is useful pay for carriers. Visiting the coast, these inlanders will even take calabashes and bring them home full of sea-water. The only means of obtaining it locally is by burning certain leaves and the husks of coco-nut or *Tauga* nuts. Over a layer of dry wood are set a number of large pottery fragments, and over these again are piled the leaves and husks. Ignited, the pile smokes abundantly, and when it has burnt away leaves a residue of ash in the pottery fragments. For actual use the ash, which has a salty taste, is placed in a half coco-nut shell and watered; and the salty water percolates through the eye-hole of the coco-nut into the cooking-pot.

Stimulants

The habit of betel-chewing is universal among men, women, and even young children. There can be no question that betel, a mild and comparatively harmless stimulant, does much to make the native's life pleasanter, especially by reason of the good-fellowship which is the best argument for all intoxicants. Areca or betel palms grow in every village. The betel pepper (*Piper betle*) called *Hingi* grows wild in the bush and is transplanted into villages and gardens. A superior cultivated kind is called *Hingi petani*. Legends of the origin or discovery of the areca palm and the betel pepper have been recounted elsewhere.[1]

Lime (*O-nasal*) is made by burning shell-fish from the sea or rivers. A small tower or pyre about 3 feet square and 3 feet 6 inches high is made of layers of dry sago branches laid criss-cross, and on each layer are set a number of shells. The pyre is lit from above in order to prevent premature collapse. It burns and cools rapidly, 'like paper'. The shells, which retain their shape, are transferred by improvised tongs to a sheet of banana leaf, which by being passed once or twice through the flames has become pliable. The shells are gently kneaded with mutterings of *ere ere!* 'Get up, hurry up!', which are meant to expedite the pulverizing process, and are cautiously sprinkled with water. Then the banana leaf is folded and left by a fire, presumably to hasten the slaking. If all this has been done carefully, the result will be a very fine soft powder.

The lime-pot (*O-kigi*) is a calabash with a stopper of closely woven strands of creeper. A somewhat more pretentious lime-pot, called *kananga*, is furnished with a shell mouthpiece set in black native beeswax, and encrusted with gems of scarlet seed and white shell fragments. The spatula (*O-ta*) is commonly of black wood. The point is thrust into

[1] *Orokaiva Magic*, p. 123.

the mouth of the lime-pot and then into the mouth of the chewer, who sucks off the thin coating of lime powder. Usually the spatula is very indifferently carved, for the Orokaiva is no wood-carver; the few examples illustrated are of somewhat exceptional merit (Plate XIII). With the large lime-pot (*kananga*) there usually goes a spatula of bone, and the two together may constitute an *otohu* or ceremonial gift made at initiation, though in use they are both appropriate to old age, and a youth or person of small consequence would not have the effrontery to use them. The old man makes a somewhat ostentatious rattling of the bone spatula against the opening of the *kananga*.

Tobacco is a late introduction in the Northern Division, having preceded the European by hardly more than a generation. The evidence clearly indicates that the mountaineers behind Kokoda first brought it to the Orokaiva, and that, travelling from the neighbourhood of Kokoda, it had not reached the Mambare or the lower Kumusi by the time MacGregor first visited these rivers.[1] Its original names are said to have been *orokaiva* (or *kaiva*) and *kuku*, the last being used before the whites brought their trade tobacco, which is now known throughout the Territory as *kuku*. The name *orokaiva* has already been discussed, but with regard to the others, *kaiva* and *kuku*, it may be worth while drawing attention to the singular coincidence that the two words are joined together in the Gulf Division and indicate a masked figure, *Kaivakuku*, and that in the Northern Division they are alternative names for the same substance, native tobacco.

Several other names, more or less local, are used, viz. *Hajojo* and *Tonaki* (derived from the resemblance of the tobacco leaf to those of the *Hajojo* and *Tonaki* trees); *Masati*, which is said to be the same word as *masa*, 'stink'; and *soka*, which bears a suspicious resemblance to the name *sokowa*, commonly used for tobacco west of the Fly river, and may have been introduced by the early Kiwai police. Several varieties are distinguished. The leaf is simply sun-dried, and is smoked either in the well-known bamboo tube (*poru*) or else rolled with some leaf or other into a cigarette.

[1] *Annual Report*, 1893, pp. 31, 34.

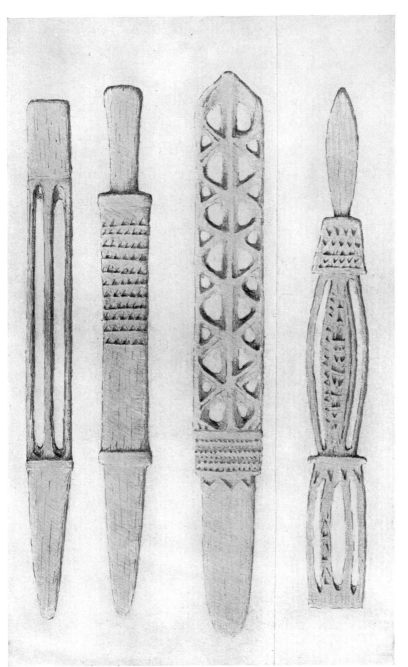

O-ta or Lime Spatulae

PLATE XIII

Certain barks are chewed as if they were stimulants, but it is questionable whether they have any effect other than in the imagination of the chewer. The most notable example is a hot and highly scented bark called *Pota*, used by *Baigona* men, i.e. the exponents of the almost extinct cult of snakes. But one might suppose that if the product had any genuinely stimulant properties it would have come into wider use.

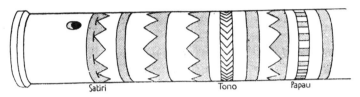

FIG. 13. *Poru* or Bamboo Pipe. Incised and partly scraped, the scraped surfaces being shaded.

Satiri or *Poki* (Fork)—The V-shaped cut in the top of a building post.
Tono—A kind of tree snake.
Papau—The hole made in a branch by a boring insect.

VI

ARTS OF LIFE

The Village

THE typical Orokaiva village would comprise hardly more than a dozen houses, and many settlements are much smaller. In former times, if native accounts are to be trusted, villages were more extensive through need of mutual protection against the raider; and a resident magistrate patrolling the river Gira in 1901 speaks of a village 200 yards long by two chains broad, which contained seventy-one houses and was 'barricaded in with a look-out and fighting platforms on the stockade'.[1] But nowadays pacification has brought about a tendency to scatter in small isolated groups.

The bush settlement is closely surrounded by walls of forest, so that the view is somewhat depressingly circumscribed; among the Salt-Water People the village stands virtually on the margin of the beach; among the River People it is invariably placed on the river bank. In most cases and in so far as the floods allow, it is well situated on dry ground. The modern village, by Government edict, is kept almost scrupulously clean, and when the visit of a patrol is imminent one may see old folk and children engaged in the meticulous removal of weeds. At all times, however, it is fairly well swept by the women. Refuse of coco-nut husks and the like is thrown away beyond the edge of the clearing, and for sanitary arrangements there is the privacy of the circumambient bush. Much of the credit for the cleanliness of the village is due to the tireless scavenging of pigs.

The House

In most instances the houses are set in two regular rows, facing one another. The space between, sporadically planted with coco-nut palms, is the scene of dances, plays, and inter-

---

[1] A. L. Walker, *Annual Report*, 1900–1, p. 53.

(*a*) Original type of Orokaiva house

(*b*) Yam-house, Dwelling, and combined Yam-house and Sitting-place

PLATE XIV

village scuffles. The old-fashioned house has been for the most part replaced by the 'European' model. This does not always mean any great change, save that the new house is loftier and airier and frequently possesses an annexe or 'kitchen' which seems as a rule to serve any purpose but a culinary one. But the general improvement is undeniable. The true native dwellings of the Orokaiva were so poor that W. E. Armit, an early resident magistrate, described them as 'miserable little things, small ramshackle erections', and referred to an Opi village as 'a collection of squalid hovels'.[1]

The original Orokaiva house (*mande*) is oblong and very low. The floor proper (*gaga*) is raised on piles, but the space beneath is roughly walled in so as to form a closed compartment called *su*. Above the floor proper there is often an interior platform or shelf (*hahari*) forming, as it were, a third story under the slope of the roof, but as a rule only along one side of the house, so that it resembles a sleeping-berth more than anything else. The ridged roof is so low that a man cannot stand upright on the *gaga*. The essential part of the whole structure is the *gaga*. This is built first on strong piles of its own, and then the roof supports and the walls are built around it independently save for bindings of split cane. In some cases, indeed, the walls are wholly separate from the *gaga*, which is enclosed as it were in a box. The piles and main posts are of various hard-woods, but the other timbers are soft and far from durable. The walls of the true native house consist of rails or logs laid horizontally, but in the more modern style their place has been taken by branch-midribs of the sago palm set vertically. The thatching is of sago leaf.

The interior of the house is dark, warm, and smoky. It contains a variety of pots, wood bowls, string bags, pig-nets, water calabashes, and other domestic paraphernalia; maybe several bags of *Puga* nuts, blocks of sago, and drying *Tauga* nuts attached to poles and suspended under the ridge-pole. Cooking is done out of doors in fine weather, and at other times underneath the house in the *su*. In cold weather

[1] *Annual Report*, 1899–1900, pp. 90; 87.

the fire burns all night through, and in the ascending heat and smoke the family sleeps warm and grimily, the householder on the *hahari*, his wife and family on the *gaga*, and his pigs and dogs in the *su*. Under the constant influence of the rising smoke the interior of the house acquires a curious metallic polish, and the poles of the roof become coated with a black lichen of soot. Conflagrations are rarer than one would expect under the circumstances.

Miscellaneous Buildings

The men's house is called *oro*. If built in connexion with a ceremony and intended as a male club-house or what might be termed a concert-hall, the men's house is called specifically *arijo*; it will occupy a central position and be of more pretentious size—say 40 feet long; and it may boast some decoration in the form of frayed sago leaf hanging in fringes from the eaves. These *arijo* houses are not seen very frequently. A peculiar feature of one or two of them is an outward-sloping wall, which gives the edifice the contours of an oblong haystack. The ordinary *oro*, which is simply the regular domicile of the young bachelors, may be small and without any distinctive feature.

A mere roofless platform is sometimes to be seen as a place of social intercourse. Among the southern tribes it is more usually combined with the picturesque little *harau* or yam-house, in which a small attic compartment above is the repository for the sprouting yams.

The Orokaiva, a true *improvisatore*, will find the materials for a house at a moment's notice. Overtaken by bad weather or benighted on the road, he will turn aside, fell a few saplings, make a selection of palm or wild banana leaves for thatch, and construct a lean-to or penthouse with a raised floor and a tolerably water-tight roof. A common trick of extempore construction is to use a slanting strut so tied to the upright that its upper end projects and thus forms a rest for a piece of cross-timber. See Plate XIV*b*.

Of tree houses (*savai*), which were formerly common enough, I have seen no evidence in the whole Division, except for certain large trees which are said to have supported them in less reposeful days. They were not fighting-tops so much as places of refuge in which a surprised village might keep its assailants at bay until the blasts of the wooden trumpets brought help from surrounding allies. They were built in the branches of large trees in or near the village (sometimes in several adjacent trees connected with cane gangways), and were furnished with cane-ladders or 'legs' (*savai-tei*). The stockade provided another means of defence, though this too has disappeared with the coming of the King's peace.

A method of dwelling which I believe to be unique in Papua is described by Beaver, and, though he had not the witness of his eyes, it appears that he was dealing with a reliable informant.

'I had many times heard', he writes, 'that the Dogi people used to live on rafts moored round the lake, and had been inclined to look upon the story as rather of the traveller's tale variety, but I found that it was actually the case. They used to live on the shore, but, owing to successive raids by the Iawabuie and Binandele, the Dogi built huge rafts —the water was too deep to sink piles—and constructed their houses on these refuges. Ninei, the present village constable, a man about 40, was born on one of these floating arks, and he tells me the people were living on them when first visited by Mr. M. M. Clark.' [1]

It was probably about 1895 that Mr. Clark was prospecting in this neighbourhood, and the lake referred to is presumably Lake Koena. I did not visit the locality myself and can only verify the legend of the eel and the flood which Beaver tells in connexion with the origin of the lake. I found this legend, however, coupled with the adventures of two surviving children rescued by a woman named Bobokoia, who was of great size, like an island, with sago palms growing on her back. The children lived on this floating island or woman until finally they settled on shore again. It seems hardly credible that the story of the raft-dwellings should have turned into that of Bobokoia within the time, though the likeness seems suspicious. It is not improbable that the raft dwellings were of no more than a temporary nature, and that the legend dates back much earlier.

[1] *Annual Report*, 1914–15, p. 14.

Transport

Tracks. Altogether we are unable to claim any high degree of engineering skill or architectural taste for the Orokaiva; but in magisterial estimation the excellence of the tracks makes ample amends. These are said to compare favourably with those of any other Division, though it is doubtful whether the Orokaiva of former days bestowed any exceptional care upon them; for if left to themselves they seem, with their naked legs and hardy feet, equally indifferent to the mud of swamps or the obstacles of the road.

But nowadays in some parts and at some times—particularly before the periodical visit of the magistrate—the track may be swept and garnished and guiltless of the minutest weed; for at the behest of the village constable the men turn out with trade knives and spade-like scrapers of tin, to nick, shave, and almost polish the surface of the road.

Bridges. Formerly, I am told, stretches of swamp were spanned by single logs supported on cross-trestles. The modern type of this bridge has an adzed surface to make walking safer, and is certainly preferable to the other style (viz. a raised gangway with clumsily laid cross-pieces) until, as is so often the case, the log is found to be slippery and aslant. Small creeks are crossed by single tree-trunks, over which the native, a fearless balancer, walks without misgiving, despite the queer and disconcerting vibrations set up by his footsteps on a long log.

One is told of the former existence of cane-bridges swung from the branches of tall trees overhanging the banks of a river. Nowadays these cobweb bridges are replaced by more workmanlike, though still somewhat precarious, fabrics, in which the cane is reinforced by steel wire. Such improvements are necessitated only by the presence of the white man, whose feet are delicately encased in boots, and who, apart from his fastidiousness regarding the mire, seems by comparison deficient in the nerve which altitude and balancing demand.

The rivers in their upper reaches are commonly forded. A party bound for a dance, fully armed and decorated, will remove their bark-cloth bands, take to the water and swim over, holding spear, shield, string bag, and bark-cloth band above their heads. A man may take a short length of light wood for a lifebuoy and, launching himself into the rapids of the Kumusi, will disappear and reappear many times, in a way which may actually alarm the spectator, until he emerges on the opposite bank some hundreds of yards down stream.

Rafts. Along the upper reaches of the rivers canoes are seldom seen. A primitive raft (*enga*) is constructed of half a dozen logs with two cross-pieces. Underneath are placed one or two much larger logs, which, though quite un-attached, remain in position and buoy the raft upwards. An even cruder makeshift is an *enga* of banana stalks.

This primitive device, the raft, continues to hold its place with the canoe. Although essentially temporary it is strongly made. There is a tale of a crocodile-man who in his human guise persuaded two youths to build a raft, instruct-ing them particularly to use grass in the building of it. He then volunteered to swim underneath in order to buoy up the raft like one of the detached logs. But he had betrayed himself by a smile which revealed the long pointed teeth of a crocodile, and the boys, unknown to him, used cane and strong creeper in binding the logs together. Then follows the sequel in which the swimmer, transmogrified into a crocodile, heaves and lashes his tail to no effect, thus point-ing to the necessity of making a strong job even of an *enga*. But, however well constructed, the raft remains an unstable craft, and in the main a temporary one. Being clumsy and unmanageable, it may be carried far down stream in transit, and it is easier to make another than to haul it back.

Canoes. The canoe (*ma*) is a hollowed log with a platform and an outrigger. The work of obtaining a suitable log and the rough hewing of it will call for the assistance of a man's fellow villagers, for which he makes them no reward except that of feeding them. After the initial stages he works leisurely at it himself; he gives a neat finish to the hewing with his adze (and sometimes still the old stone adze is pre-ferred for canoe work); he fits the platform and outrigger;

and finally paints the dugout a dull red with ochre or clay, possibly picking out a zigzag in black at prow and stern. The craft is launched with no ceremony save a 'trial spin', and may or may not be given a personal name.

The general appearance of the canoe may be judged from

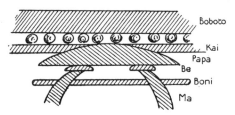

FIG. 14. Attachment of Platform to Hull of Canoe.

the accompanying sketch. The parts are named as follows:

Dugout . . . . . *ma.*
Platform . . . . *ma-bua.*
Outrigger float . . . . *taona* (from its resemblance to the banana *taona*).
Outrigger poles . . *ma-tu.*
Outrigger pegs . . . *ma-gi* (because made of spear-wood, *gi*).
Prow . . . . . *Kopuru* (head).
Stern . . . . . *Ao.*
Points at stern and prow . . *pepe* (the same word is used for sago thorns).
Incised zigzags at prow and stern *dengoro* (ear).

Between the platform and the hull the method of attachment is somewhat complicated. Along the two rims of the canoe are laid split rails or slats (*be*), their upper surface being rounded (which incidentally provides a moderately comfortable seat for the paddler who sits with one buttock on either rim and his feet in the dugout). The actual supports for the platform are two curiously shaped pieces of wood (*papa*), one at either end, which are laid transversely on the *be*, and thus intervene between the platform and the hull of the canoe. These two *papa* are slightly hollowed on the upper side so as to form troughs in which rest the two transverse rails (*kai*) that form the basis of the platform. The platform is made fast to the hull by lashing firmly to

(*a*) Attachment of Outrigger to Pole

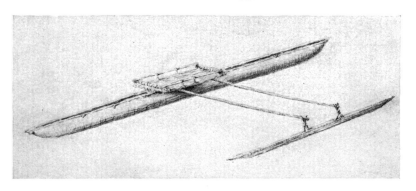

(*b*) Canoe. Up to 40 feet long

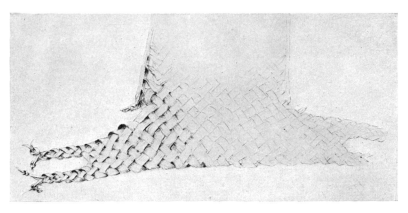

(*c*) *Tere* or Coco-nut Mat

PLATE XV

stout pieces of palm-wood (*boni*), one at either end, which pass through the wood of the hull. The purpose of the *papa* is no doubt to allow for a little give, i.e. to prevent undue rigidity between the hull and the platform. The actual floor of the latter is composed of light longitudinal

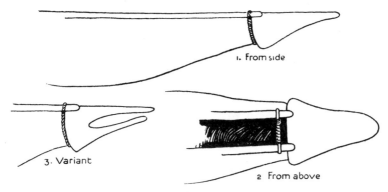

FIG. 15. Canoe Prows.

rails, and at either end of it is bound on a piece of wood constituting a low bulwark (*boboto*).

The outrigger poles are attached to the actual outrigger by pegs or 'spears' (*gi*) of black palm-wood, which are commonly six in number and arranged in the manner shown. They are simply driven into the wood of the outrigger.

The prow and stern are roughly the same. The usual forms are illustrated, together with an unusual variant seen on the Mambare.

The canoe varies considerably in size,[1] the largest being found on the coast and used for seafaring. While well adapted to rough water and open rivers, the outrigger canoe will not compare with the plain dugout of the Delta country for speed and for handiness among intricate watercourses.

[1] I am indebted to Mr. Leo Austen, Assistant Resident Magistrate, Buna, for the following measurements of a canoe from near Gona:

Length of hull	.	.	.	.	.	39 ft. 8 ins.
Depth of hull	.	.	.	.	.	1 ,, 10 ,,
Length of platform	.	.	.	.	8 ,, 6 ,,
Breadth of platform	.	.	.	.	6 ,, 9 ,,
Length of outrigger	.	.	.	.	18 ,, 1 ,,

The two outrigger poles were of slightly different length, 18 and 19 ft. respectively, measured from the inner edge of the platform.

Manufactures

Arts and crafts have reached no high development, nor, on the whole, do they make any pretensions to artistry. For the most part they are common knowledge and everyday accomplishments. To a very limited extent do particular crafts belong to particular districts; for instance, the people of Huhurundi (Sauaha) are said to excel in the painting of bark-cloth—which is probably a matter of tradition; and the people of the middle Kumusi to excel in the making of stone clubs—which is merely a matter of a supply of pebbles. Again, in a limited degree we see signs of individual pre-eminence. A man may specialize in the making of *teva* or wooden bowls by virtue of a steady hand and a good eye, or a woman may have a reputation as a bark-cloth painter. But such individual skill is, I am convinced, the result of natural gifts rather than of any special training. It appears that any and every man tries his hand at carving a bowl out of a block of wood, and only those who find they have a special aptitude care to persist and perfect themselves. Investigation proves that such crafts are not necessarily or even usually hereditary.

In the main, therefore, it appears that every man is an all-round craftsman. If he is a jack-of-all-trades he is likewise a fair exponent of all of them; and if he is a master of one of them he is likely to be a master of all, simply because he is born with a certain adaptable skill or handiness.

The only labour division of any great interest is the habitual one between the sexes. Pottery, bark-cloth, pandanus mats, string, and small fish-nets are made by women; weapons, ornaments, wooden bowls, coco-nut mats and baskets, plaited belts, and the larger fish-nets are made by men.

Pottery (Obu). The yellowish clay used for pottery is not found in all parts of the Division, and the collecting of it may mean a long journey. It is brought home in a wrapping of moist leaves, and beaten out on a large flat board (*obu-iri*), viz. the flange of a forest tree. The club is a piece of plain wood called *obu kungabu*.

(*a*) Orokaiva Canoes

(*b*) *Enga* or Raft

PLATE XVI

When the clay has been thoroughly pounded the woman commences to work with her hands. First she fashions a small saucer-like base (*obu-atu*). Then, taking a small lump of clay, she rolls it with the heel of her hand on a broad strip of bark which she holds in her lap for a rolling-board. Thus treated it becomes a long thin strip perhaps a quarter of an inch in diameter. This she coils round the rim of the *obu-atu*, and thereafter continues to roll strips and coil them one above the other so that the pot gradually grows and widens. Each coil is pressed home with the thumb and tapped lightly with a small baton (*tavi*). When three or four have been applied the potter moistens them with a few drops from a broken gourd of water by her side, and with the baton pats or smooths out the grooves on the outer side. She does the same more carefully on the inner side with the smooth surface and the sharp edge of a river shell-fish.

The completely fashioned pot is set aside till several are ready and may be burnt together. In shape it widens towards the mouth, which forms a good circle. Instead of being semi-globular the vessel shows a slight tendency to narrow down to a point at its base, so that its form has been compared to the more pointed half of an egg.

The modern pot is often devoid of ornament. Sometimes it has a few incised markings; sometimes raised pinched markings. Neither possess much artistic value. On the river Gira (and on certain earlier fragments from near the mouth of the Opi, where I understand pottery is not nowadays made) I have seen overlaid markings (formed by pressing on small strips of clay while the pot is in making) which have more artistic possibilities. They are called *bubuko* (the same word being used for the raised cicatrice sometimes seen on the arms and breasts of women).

Bark-cloth (Bo). Numerous wild trees (I have eight names which I imagine to be mostly ficus) yield *bo* or bark-cloth. The best is named *Ajimo*, which provides a very white cloth; it is sometimes transplanted and may be even cultivated in a small grove. The cloth from other trees varies in colour between white and brown. Beaten on a log, a strip of the proper bark spreads out to an extraordinary size, and when dried forms a coarse but tough material. The typical club is an elongated pebble (*kini*) with incised criss-cross lines (*jari*). The work is done by women, who make a common practice of withdrawing beyond the edge of the village, ostensibly to remove the annoyance of the loud continued tapping. The decoration—of which examples have been depicted elsewhere—is the artistic prerogative of women. It is executed in red and black. The red is a vegetable dye; the black is lamp-black obtained by burning a resinous gum called *ongo*. This, placed in a small receptacle, is lighted and covered with a large inverted fragment of pottery. The burning *ongo* gives off a heavy aromatic smoke and the soot is deposited on the under-surface of the pot. A little water is subsequently added and the black pigment is mopped up out of the pot with a sponge of grass and squeezed into a fragment of coco-nut or a cockle-shell, which is to serve as palette. Using for brush a tuft of frayed betel husk, the painter works quickly, confidently, and often carelessly. The workmanship is, as a rule, exceedingly crude, but the decorative effect is excellent, being somewhat enhanced when the garish colours are softened by a distant view and a shade of dirtiness.

Pandanus Mats (*Ohi*). The broad leaves of the pandanus are sewn by women into mats. The minute prickles on edge and midrib are shaved off and the whole leaf is rubbed with those detergent leaves that serve the native for sandpaper. This is said to hasten their drying and to ensure their flexibility. When dry they are sewn together in two complete layers with a partial transverse layer of narrower strips between them. The finished mat, together with a plain block of wood for pillow, constitutes the Orokaiva's bedding.

Coco-nut Mats (*Tere*). The mat for outdoor use is made of coco-nut leaf. A frond is split down the midrib and the leaves of either side are then woven neatly together to form a mat for which the halves of the split midrib form the side borders.

At the wider end of the mat two small appendages called *tengere* ('ears') stand out from either side. They are formed by plaiting the leaves which pass below the end of the mid-

(*a*) Beating Clay for Pottery

(*b*) Making Wooden Dishes, *Teva*

PLATE XVII

rib, and amount to a neat and ingenious way of disposing of the tag ends. Equally neat and ingenious is the suggestion made in an early *Annual Report*. 'Some of them [coconut mats] are even provided with appendages near the head of the mat, which is cut square across, resembling sleeves in outline. This is for the arms to rest on.'[1] The Orokaiva, however, does not lie on his back or his belly with a cruci-

FIG. 16. Orokaiva and Waria Patterns of *Kambije* up to 2 ft. long.

form outstretching of the arms; and until this posture has been actually recorded, the above suggestion, like many more weighty ones in anthropology, must remain unsubstantiated.

Leaf Basketry. There is no genuine basketry among the Orokaiva: the *kambije* hardly deserves the dignity of the name. It is made on the same principle as the mat *tere*, viz. by splitting part of a coco-nut frond down the midrib and by weaving the leaves together. The two halves of the midrib are now made to constitute the mouth of the bag or basket, which opens or closes like a Gladstone bag. Imported from the river Waria comes a larger and better-made example which has become fashionable on the Gira and the Mambare. In the smaller, which is the usual Orokaiva form, the plaited tag ends of leaflets become appendages to the top of the *kambije*, near its mouth, and are called *tengere* or 'ears' (Bin. *dengoro*). In the Waria style they appear at the bottom of the basket and are called *jimi* or 'tails'.

The Cane Pig Basket (Kakate). A kind of litter is devised for carrying pigs on long journeys. The pig is first bound and laid on the ground. Two hoops of cane are fitted over it, to ensure that they are of the right size, and then each hoop is made the frame of a strong rough network of split cane. The two fabrics are finally bound together with the

[1] *Annual Report*, 1893-4, p. 5.

pig inside, enclosed as if in a made-to-measure basket. It remains questionable whether the pig travels more comfortably thus than in the normal way with its feet tied to a pole.

Plaiting. Belts are made by men with very thin strips of cane. Several effective patterns are done in yellow and black of which I have recorded only the commonest one (*vide* Plate IX). Belts and armlets or leglets are made from a species of brown creeper fibre, plaited very closely into bands of varying width.

String and Rope. String such as is used in making small fish-nets is made by women. They tease out pandanus fibre and roll it on the thigh. Rope, e.g. for pig-nets, is made by men from pandanus.

Woodwork. Wooden bowls (*teva*) are cut out of blocks of soft wood. The work is done with a light adze and the surface is smoothed with sandpaper leaves. The finished article is a light boat-shaped vessel, with or without a handle at one end; though entirely without ornament, it sometimes possesses a graceful outline. These *teva* are often made by men who appear to be experts, and they make the nearest approach to the stock-in-trade of a specialist.

The carving of hard-wood into lime spatulae has been already mentioned (p. 66). With somewhat rare exceptions such carving is inferior or careless; and in many cases scratching would be a better word.

Weapons

Spears. The principal weapon is the spear, of which several varieties are distinguished.

(1) The ordinary pig-spear (*o-ki*) is made of black palm-wood (*koropa*). It is heavy and long—often about 12 feet. The section towards the point is half oval, and there are two sets of barbs.

(2) The fighting spear (*overo*) is much lighter and only about 9 feet in length. It is made either of *koropa* palm or of a reddish hard-wood (*kimana*) which takes a high polish. The section toward the point is approximately square; there are four sets of barbs, often well cut; and some distance below

the point are affixed one or more bunches of coloured feathers. The feathers apparently serve only a decorative purpose.

(3) A spear round in section and without barbs is known as *hou*.

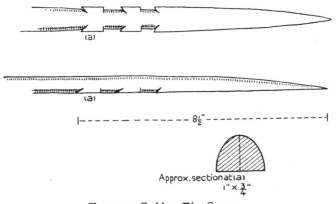

FIG. 17. *O-ki* or Pig Spear.

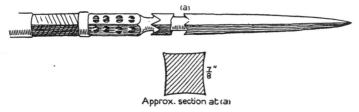

FIG. 18. *Overo* or Fighting Spear.

(4) A short thrusting spear or pike (*apau*) has a plain point at one end and a spatulate broadening at the other. This is meant less for throwing than for work at close quarters. In a recent inter-clan brawl, for instance, while one of the surprised villagers was clambering on to his house verandah in order to reach his spears there, he was rushed by his opponent and stabbed in the leg with an *apau*. It was no doubt this weapon—'a two-ended spear about 4 feet long'— with which a huge Orokaiva was about to kill one of Mr. Alec Elliot's police whom he had at his mercy, when a bullet from another policeman 'burst his heart'.[1]

[1] *Annual Report*, 1900–1, p. 12.

(5) There are other varieties of spears distinguished by minor differences; but one is used for a purpose which is perhaps unique. This is the *dega* or *kane*, which has a spiral of white feathers winding about it from top to bottom. The *dega* is not so much a weapon of offence as a standard meant for display and, as I was assured, the intimidation of the foe. When Sir William MacGregor saw a flotilla of war canoes ascending the river Musa one early morning in the year 1895, he remarked in particular 'two big men, each standing erect in the hull of a fine war canoe, one at each end of the square platform. They were in complete martial panoply, covered by paint and plumes, and each, as he remained in an attitude as stiff and silent as a pillar of stone, held his right hand on a great tall war spear, which he held erect, the lower end resting on the bottom of the canoe. These two spears were nearly covered with white feathers from end to end'. These spears, used by the kindred people of the Musa, were no doubt identical with the *dega* of the Orokaiva, which in these times of peace has been relegated from the hand of the warrior to that of the Taro man.[1]

Wooden 'Swords'. The wooden sword (*asivo*) is a blade-shaped length of black palm-wood usually some 3 feet 6 inches long. The point and edges are not so sharp as to pierce or cut, and the weapon is virtually a club. Being used with two hands, it is much less unwieldy than the stone-headed club, and probably gains in effectiveness by its lightness. The *asivo* is often painted and befeathered.

Woman's Quarterstaff. The woman's quarterstaff (*poreha*) is a long light staff of knotty hard-wood. Every able-bodied woman will keep one just underneath the raised floor of her house, where it is ready for a brawl. She carries it in a characteristic manner, resting on the crown of her head and held on either side in her hands. There is a certain technique in its use, and it is said to be 'correct, when warding off a blow, to hold the *poreha* simply between thumb and forefinger, with the fingers extended. Women bear their part in inter-village affrays and are not infrequently guilty of

---

[1] *Annual Report*, 1895–6, p. 27; and cf. *ibid.*, p. 14. The *Dega* is now frequently affected by Taro men, though I cannot say with what significance.

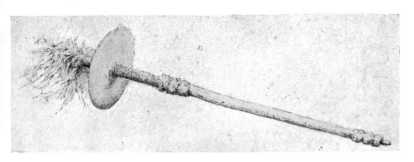

(*a*) *Emi* or Disk Club. Diameter of disk, 7½ in.

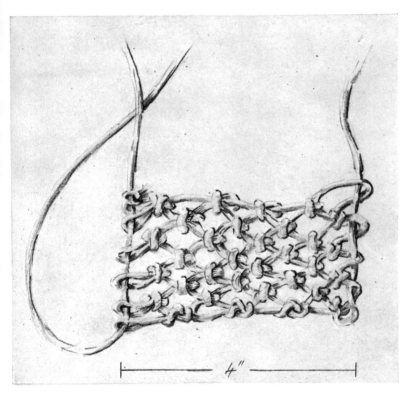

(*b*) *Taiha* or Sling

PLATE XVIII

inciting to violence. The other occasions on which the *pureha* may be put to use are, I am told, the quarrels of a polygamous household.

Stone Clubs. Stone clubs are of two principal kinds, the 'pineapple' (*gishi*) and the disk (*emi*). They are made from river pebbles. The former variety has a hole through the longer axis for the haft, and its striking surface is serrated by means of longitudinal and lateral grooves, which leave a number of processes or points. The latter is more or less disk-shaped, the outer edge being ground down to a fairly sharp cutting-edge. The 'star' club (*tingo*) is not common (the word *tingo* is used of a jutting broken branch), nor is the 'egg' club (*era*)—a plain knob with a hole through the longer axis. Club heads of quartz have been obtained in the Division, but are rarities and apparently antiquities.

The stone club was formerly made by striking and wearing down with another stone, the hole through the centre being made by a pestle-shaped pebble as striker, or what Sir Wm. MacGregor described as a small stone 'of the size and shape of a rifle bullet'. Nowadays the small pyramidal points of the pineapple club are made by means of a white man's file. The manufacture of these weapons has almost ceased, for their use has been brought down to one of mere display. However, the Orokaiva in full dress still rejoices to carry a befeathered club on his shoulder, like a sword at the slope.

The Sling. The sling (*taiha*) is said to have been once a genuine weapon, yet the early reports contain no mention of it as being used by the hostile natives. W. E. Armit speaks of the men of the Upper Kumusi and Yodda river as 'stone-throwers and rushing natives',[1] but other stories tell of the natives sometimes attacking with no weapons save large stones which they had picked up on the track, and there is no reason to suppose that the stone-throwers mentioned by Mr. Armit threw with anything but their hands. Now, at any rate, the sling is little more than a toy, though why elderly men should sometimes carry these playthings in their bags I have not been able to discover. In the typical example the pouch is of roughly netted string

---

[1] *Annual Report*, 1899–1900, p. 84.

(Plate XVIII*b*). Of the attached strings one is in the form of a loop, which is passed round a finger; the other is released in throwing.

The Shield. The shield (*beha* or *pere*) is made of light wood, about ½ inch thick, strongly bound with narrow strips of cane to prevent splitting. The handle is a loop of stout rattan which passes through the wood. The shape of the shield—square cut above and pointed below—caused early observers to refer to it very appropriately as 'Gothic'. It sometimes bears a device—in no manner heraldic but purely decorative—made by interlacing black strands among the yellow cane binding strips; and when this is well done the effect may be artistic and even dainty (Plate XIX).

The *beha* is held under-grip in the warrior's left hand, which also contrives to hold a club and even an extra spear. His right hand poises or brandishes the spear which he is about to throw, giving little jerks which cause it to vibrate like a twanged string. (At that moment it might well enough be called a 'shadowy spear'.)

Shields are used very adroitly in turning or intercepting missiles, and a broken spear-point buried in the wood is regarded as a trophy. Despite the fact that their serious use is over they are still very commonly kept in readiness —at least by the Aiga—and they always make a fracas possible. Like most other men the Orokaiva has no stomach for the plain spear, and he enjoys his inter-tribal brawl much more when he has a *beha* in his hand.

Miscellaneous Implements

The implements used in gardening, sago-making, fishing, &c., have already been described. It remains to mention a few used for general purposes.

The Adze or Axe. The adze or axe blade (*oto*) is a ground river pebble. This is bound with cane into a split tang, and the tang is driven into a groove in the forked branch which serves as a handle. Here it is held by a binding of plaited cane. The implement is either axe or adze according to the way the tang is turned.

The celt itself is made from a selected river pebble by

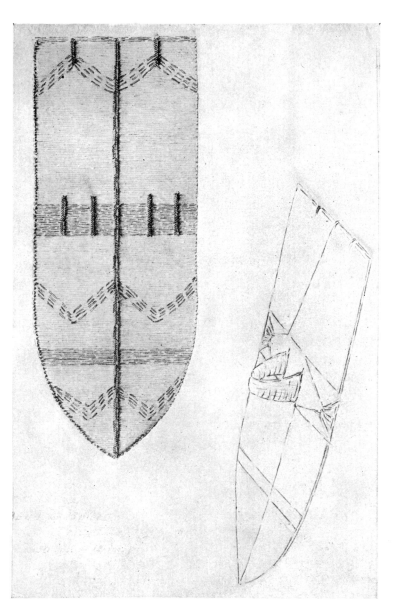

Beha or Shield, 30 in. by 12 in.

PLATE XIX

pounding and rubbing. Very few nowadays remain in the villages, but those that I have seen vary considerably in size and form. So much depends on the original shape of the pebble selected and there is such an infinite variety of pebbles which a native can see are easily convertible into adze blades, that I think it would be unprofitable to attempt a classification.

The stone adze is still used to some small extent in the hollowing of canoes, but for all other purposes the stone has yielded place to imported steel. The introduction of the steel axe and the trade knife has greatly simplified the work of gardening and building, though so far, I

FIG. 19. Hafting of Adze.

believe, it has not led to any great improvement in methods.

Cutting and Scraping Instruments. For small cutting instruments there are the bamboo knife (*ivi*) which is given a razor-like sharpness by simply peeling off the edge; the cockle shell which is the Orokaiva pocket knife; and the

FIG. 20. *Jino* or Bone Needle.

hari, a disk of coco-nut or oyster shell with one section of its edge kept sharp, which is used for peeling taro. For scrapers the edge of a cockle shell and the thicker edge of a boar's tusk are used. There are three kinds of files: (1) a kind of pumice called *nidiri*; (2) the skin of a certain fish (*Seh*) which is dried and stretched over a slab of wood; and (3) the rough leaves of various trees.

Needles, &c. Bodkins (*poma*), which a woman wears thrust in her hair, are made of flying-fox bones. So also are needles (*jino*), the eye being made through one side of the hollow bone (Fig. 20).

Drills. Two kinds of drill are in use. The commoner is

the well-known pump-drill (*arase*), known, I believe, in all parts of the Division. It possesses no unique feature unless it be that the fly-wheel is composed of several layers of pottery fragments bored through the centre.

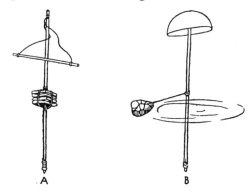

A   B

FIG. 21. Binandele Drills. A. *Arase*; B. *Jigogora*.

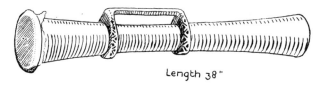

Length 38″

FIG. 22. *Ino* or Drum.

A more primitive and far less effective mechanism (called *jigogora* or *paihona*) is still in occasional use. This has no fixed fly-wheel but instead a stone attached by a string to the shaft and made to fly round and round it. The top of the shaft rotates in a cup-shaped receptacle (e.g. a coco-nut shell), while the bottom with its point of quartz bears on the object which is being drilled. A slight movement of the hand which grasps the coco-nut shell keeps the stone flying in a circle. The point is usually of quartz (*kase*) and some-times, when procurable, of flint (*biru*).

Musical Instruments

Drums. The Orokaiva are fond of music and naturally musical, though they possess no instruments of much poten-

Boy Playing the Pipe, *Hiviro*

PLATE XX

tiality. Drums are of three distinct kinds. The largest is called *ino* (which also means 'dog'). It is used in the dance called *Java-kuru*, which is the original dance of the Orokaiva, so that the *ino* may be the most primitive of the three drums. It is sometimes as much as 3 feet 9 inches in length and has a very deep tone. The second is called *ehu*. It is of medium size about 2 feet in length, and is used in the *Si* and *Paruka* dances. The third (12 or 13 inches long) is called *Saunda* or *Tatau* (both words being perhaps onomatopoeic), and is used in the *Saunda* and *Puga* dances. This drum is confined to the Aiga, Binandele, and Tain-Daware tribes, though in recent times its distribution is growing wider.

The drum is a hollow tube narrowing somewhat to a waist in the middle. The hollowing is effected by slowly burning out with the aid of a bamboo blow-pipe. The larger drums are usually fitted with a handle, *tei* ('foot'); the smaller ones are often without it. All have two raised rings at the waist called *pupunga*. *Pupunga* is the name of a kind of opossum or cuscus, from the skin of whose tail are made finger-rings. Hence by a somewhat fantastic explanation, which is not improbably correct, comes the name *pupunga* for the rings on the drum.

The closed end is called *hohoru*, 'head'; the other is *abo*, or literally the fundamental orifice. A tympanum of lizard skin (obtained usually from the monitor lizard, *ange*) is stretched over and stuck on with starchy cooked taro, and is then bound on tightly with bark-cloth. It is tautened by applications of beeswax, which is said to be essential to a good tone. A lump of this material is stuck to the side of the drum, and little pellets are detached and applied to the lizard skin.

A good deal of care is taken to ensure a proper resonance before a concert begins. The *pupunga* bear incised decorations (chevrons and zigzags) of mediocre quality.

Trumpets. The Orokaiva chorus is accompanied not only by drums but usually also by a conch shell, blown by one of the most juvenile of the performers. This instrument adds much to the volume but little to the harmony of the concert. It is commonly a large spiral shell with a hole, but an alterna-

tive, somewhat rarely seen, is made of wood. Both are
called *hui*. The principal use of the *hui* is for making sound-
signals, such as the alarm of war, the announcement of a
death, or the approach of a party bearing a pig. For such
purposes there are distinctive rhythms of long and short

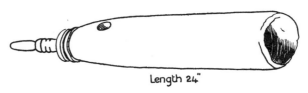

Length 24"

FIG. 23. *Hui* or Wooden Trumpet.

notes, though it cannot be said that they amount to any
elaborate system.

An interesting extempore trumpet (*tayana*) is made from
the stem of a large fern. The soft pith is hollowed out for
the greater part of its length, the narrower end remaining
closed. Near this closed end is placed the mouth-hole. The
instrument, which is made in a few moments, is about
18 inches long with slightly trumpet-shaped mouth. It
gives forth a surprisingly loud and resonant note.

Bamboo Pipes. A pipe called *hiviro* is made from a long
internode of light bamboo of say ¾ inch diameter. The
mouth end is open, the other closed at the node, except for
a small hole in the centre of the node itself, and two more,
distant about 3 inches and 6 inches respectively from it.
With his fingers on the stops and his mouth on the edge of
the open end a player produces very sweet though very
tootling music.

The 'sacred flutes' (*sepiri, inagu,* or *gauro*) used in the
initiation ceremonies by the Southern Orokaiva, are tubes
of bamboo some 4 or 5 feet in length and about 1½ inches
in diameter.[1] They are closed by a node at one end. Six

---

[1] It may be that on the river Waria the small pipe (such as *hiviro* above described)
is to some extent an esoteric instrument. Describing the *Guhu* (which is apparently
the seclusion-house) and its contents, Mr. C. H. Karius, A.R.M., notes a set of two
flutes or bamboo pipes. The full set comprises four pipes. Two are played inside
the *Guhu* and two are played outside. Never by any chance is the order reversed.
The two sets of flutes or pipes are of different size and the method of playing them
is different. The set used inside the *Guhu* is the larger of the two and the flutes are

inches or more from this closed end is a hole. The player holds the flute horizontally. He sets his lips to the edge of the hole and covers one ear with one of his hands. Sometimes he covers both ears and holds the flute in the crooks of his arms. Thus two men facing one another play with great intentness and evident enjoyment, each bowing and scraping a little to his partner in the duet (Plate XXIV*b*).

The very limited number of notes is doubled by the fact that the instruments are differently pitched, and being played antiphonally they are together capable of producing little cadences or phrases that are pretty enough, although trifling and endlessly repeated. Such tunes have different names which they sometimes derive from their resemblance to bird-calls and responses.

Miscellaneous Instruments. These sacred flutes are of course esoteric instruments and seem to be invariably associated with the bull-roarer, *umbubu.* This familiar instrument is a thin slat of palm-wood with a hole drilled through one end. It is attached by means of a string to a long stick. Being swung round and round the slat revolves rapidly, producing a wide range of noises which may be described as whirring, booming, or howling. The Orokaiva example of this widely dispersed object is usually without ornament.

A third instrument—if so it may be called—which belongs to the initiation ceremonies is the *koni pamoni.* This is merely a hollow shell of the tree *Puga,* by blowing on the edge of which a thin expressive whistle is produced. Like the notes of the flutes and the booming of the bull-roarer, this is meant to represent the voice of the *siango* or *embahi,* spirits of the dead, who are crying out for food.

A jew's harp (*pingoru*) is made of bamboo as shown in the sketch. It is held in the mouth, being gripped by finger and thumb of the left hand, while the string is lightly jerked by the right hand. The vibrator is called *pingoru-bi.*

A rudimentary stringed instrument, also called *pingoru,* is made from a young sago midrib. A strip of the green bark

played by blowing through a hole in the side. This set is known as *Saragarapa.* The set used outside the *Guhu* is known as *Neworarapa.* The pipes in this case are blown from the end (*Annual Report,* 1925-6, p. 90).

is prised up but left attached at the points marked *x* (with or without binding). Small pegs are inserted at either end to keep the strip taut. It is held in the open mouth at *y* and played by lightly tapping the string.

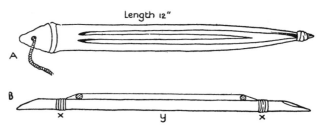

FIG. 24. A. *Pingoru* or Jew's Harp ; B. *Pingoru* String
Instrument.

VII

INDIVIDUAL, FAMILY, AND CLAN

The Members of the Family

THE Orokaiva family is a well-defined group under the immediate authority of the father (*mama*). When (as in the usual instance) it is monogamous, its members live under one roof, and the father and mother clear and cultivate one area of ground, with what help their children may be fit to give them. The family group is therefore in large measure self-supporting and in its internal affairs may also be called independent. The father is master of his wife and children, and if he thinks fit may chastise them without interference from fellow villagers. This is natural enough, as the wife, under normal patrilocal conditions, is a stranger. An instance such as the following is not uncommon. A man named Tiembo set off to the garden accompanied by his wife, his two young daughters, and his dog. The dog set upon a neighbour's pig, and Tiembo, a fond parent but a very excitable man, set upon his wife and elder daughter and thrashed them for not minding the dog. The girl, in a mixture of anger, grief, and indignation (a peculiarly native frame of mind called *sisira*) absented herself from home for two days, and the wife in a huff delayed the cooking of her husband's dinner that evening. But all were very soon reconciled, and the villagers were no more than tickled by the whole affair. Such an instance shows that it behoves the father to practise restraint (which indeed he usually does), but it also illustrates his unquestioned authority over his own family. In this he is backed up by his clan, among whom the wife is virtually a stranger. Indeed, one may doubt whether the severest punishment inflicted upon the stranger woman would arouse anything more than passing disapproval in the clan and village of the husband. On one recent occasion a man of Deunia who had killed his wife in a fit of temper, fled for his life instead of surrendering himself to the village constable. He gave himself up at the first opportunity to another constable, a good many miles distant. The reason for his flight was simply that his wife belonged to his own village and to the clan of its constable, so that he feared a too summary punishment. Had this murder occurred before the country was brought under control, one might venture to say that the murderer would have had the actual support of his own clan against that of his wife if a violent retaliation had been attempted. As a rule, however, the Orokaiva is fond of his wife and indulgent to his children. Squabbles do not often occur; too frequent wife-beating is deprecated; and bad temper is regarded as bad conduct.

The Position of Women. The wife and mother is largely occupied with matters of *ménage*, and takes little part in wider social activities. Completely overshadowed by the male she seems very well satisfied with her relative unimportance. A woman takes no initiative in matters which concern the clan as a whole, though, when a number of clans are together at a festival and feeling is perhaps strained, she is sometimes known to blow upon the coals. She has a weapon, the *poreha* or quarterstaff, and in former times would sometimes accompany cannibal raids, acting the part of armour-bearer or assisting in the commissariat.

In private life she is not aggressive, although I may quote a rather striking exception in order to prove the rule. A man named Siavije, having no children by his first wife, married a second, who was compelled, however, to reside in her own village nearby because of the jealousy of the senior wife. Under these circumstances Siavije hardly dared visit his second spouse, and was constantly involved in quarrels with his first. Being an inoffensive man and rather small, he was hardly a match for this large raw-boned woman who was known to worst him on more than one occasion and even to pursue him, crying for help, from end to end of the village.

Polygamy is relatively uncommon. In most of the instances which have come under my notice the wives manage to get on successfully enough with one another, though it is frequently said to be otherwise. I know of one man who 'threw away' his first wife because she could not live in amity with his second; of a second wife who, after a quarrel with the first, poisoned herself with *derris* or 'New Guinea Dynamite'; and of a husband, formerly a village constable, who was so upset by the wrangling of his two wives as to go away and hang himself. But these instances once more are exceptional, and the polygamous household may be said as a rule to be a peaceful one. Very commonly each wife occupies a separate house, and invariably she works a garden area of her own, so that mutual independence does much to prevent friction.

To sum up on the social position of woman we may say that she is nominally and often actually under the control of her husband, but that by virtue of his restraint on the one hand and her powers of personal expression on the other, the married couple usually get on very well together as a working unit. In public life, i.e. in the affairs of clan and village, the woman takes only a small part, but is well contented to have it so. She works longer hours than her husband, but her share of labour is not entirely disproportionate; indeed, the popular belief that women do all the work in a native village while their men-folk sprawl about in idleness is quite mistaken. A fairly systematic investigation in two Aiga villages[1] showed that of a total potential working time, men were idle 50 per cent. and women 33 per cent. On the whole it may be safely said that the position of Orokaiva women—indeed of native women in general—is not so slave-like and degraded as popular sentiment imagines.

The Control of Children. Children become members of the father's clan and naturally assume his clan emblem. They thus belong essentially to the father rather than to the mother. In cases of divorce, for example, it is normal for the child to remain in the custody of the father, unless it be an infant at the breast, when the matter may be waived, though compensation is due to the husband. The case of orphans is similar. Although there appears to be no formal adoption they are cared for in the normal case by the people of their father, being regarded indeed as their property.

[1] *Interim Report on Native Labour,* 1927.

The maternal uncle (*nobo*) has no real authority over the child, and his ceremonial obligations towards it are somewhat vague. However, there exists a cordial relationship between the two, and the *nobo* is treated with respect as a relative of importance. It is worth remarking that an Orokaiva child, while belonging to the people of its father, is very ready to identify itself also with those of its mother. When living with the latter and helping the maternal uncle in his work the child feels itself to belong for the time being to the maternal clan. At such a time it will use the maternal plant emblem, and indeed at all times it will name that emblem as subsidiary to the one it inherits from its father. In short, where the child, who belongs indisputably to its father's clan, is still on such friendly and intimate footing with its mother's, we might say that the system, although patrilineal in theory, was almost bilateral in effect.

Regarding the actual control of children we may note that they are seldom struck or smacked even in anger, and that they are never chastised by way of correction. A scolding seems always sufficient to check a naughty child. On the whole parents are very tolerant and children well-behaved.

From Childhood to Manhood

Childbirth and Infancy. In childbirth a woman is attended normally by women alone, though male 'doctors' may be called in to assist, not so much directly as by massaging, punching the back, and blowing into the ears of the woman in labour. The cord is tied, but I have no information as to its disposal. The afterbirth is treated by various alternative methods, some of which are thought to affect the mother subsequently. It may be placed in a small receptacle built in a tree where it is left to decompose; it may be buried (if at the butt of a coco-nut tree the roots would enclose or constrict it, and the result would be to render the mother barren in future); I have been told it may be given to a sow to eat, 'when it is supposed to effect a transfer of fecundity from the women to the pig'. In some cases a small enclosure is built underneath the house expressly to prevent the pig gaining access to the afterbirth, which is allowed to fall through the house floor; and it is probably the same notion at work: if the animal were to eat the afterbirth it might have an adverse effect on the woman's fecundity.

In the one instance of which I have definite information the confinement took place in the afternoon and the child was at the breast next morning. Suckling may continue till the child has long passed the stage of learning to walk, though it is treated to a variety of solid foods as well.

During the first few days of the child's life its father must avoid the dangers of gardening. If he were to strike at a young sapling with his axe it would be as if he struck at his baby's neck, with the possible result that 'the blood would come up' and the child choke and die. This association of ideas I have met with several times, and Mr. Flint records the same, as if it were a somewhat ghastly obsession. 'One man told me he could not fell a tree until his child was two days old. I asked him the reason. He informed me that if he did so it would be the same as cutting his baby's throat.' This couvade-like practice is very general. In rather extreme form it appears in another of Mr. Flint's instances. His interpreter at Kokoda had washed clothes the day his first child was born, with what proved to be fatal results. On the birth of his second he applied for two days' leave from the office, lest this child should die too, and needless to say received it from a sympathetic master, though his work consisted merely in interpreting.[1] It is for a somewhat different reason that the father refuses to plant taro too soon after his child is born: here he is considering his garden, for the plant would rot in the ground like the buried placenta.

It is said that abnormal children would be strangled at birth and buried, and this is probably true. But whether a mother would destroy a child who simply made one too many in her family and necessitated unwelcome work and trouble, is certainly a matter of doubt, although it has been declared to be the case by one or two witnesses. It is at least certain that a child who had lived long enough to find a place in its parents' affections would not be deliberately killed. But as life in itself is regarded very lightly, it is by

[1] *Annual Report*, 1924–5, p. 47.

no means impossible that infanticide is practised. Upon this vexed question, however, I have on the one hand no tangible evidence, and on the other a great number of denials.

Naming. It is necessary to make sure that the child is to survive and thrive before a name is given it, though the reason for this delay is not made clear. There seems to be no actual formality of name-giving, but some person is asked to stand godfather or godmother to the child, who will take his or her name. This person is called *tato* (a reciprocal term between godfather and godchild). There is no reluctance on the part of the *tato* to undertake the few obligations which belong to this relationship. A man wishes to have his name carried on by another after his death. If he have children he hopes that one of them will honour him by bestowing his name on a grandson. If he be childless he exclaims, 'Who will catch my name?' and hopes that some friend or relative will solve the difficulty by asking him to stand as *tato* to one of his children. An old woman said she expected one of her daughters to name a future child after her; adding, however, that if she did not—well, it would not matter; she would just die without leaving her name behind her. I know of no article of belief which would make this namesake system necessary. The principal motive appears to be the desire not to be forgotten. Not infrequently the relation is a posthumous one: the relatives of the deceased say they are 'very sorry for him' and must not allow him to be forgotten. The two *tato* do not stand in any special kin relationship to one another. In various instances noted, the elder has been to the younger either *ahije* (pat. grandfather), *ahije* (mat. grandfather), *mama* (pat. uncle), *nobo*, and *simbo*; and in the case of women, *ahije* (mat. grandmother) and *tata*. A woman may pay a second husband the compliment of naming his son after her first husband, so as to perpetuate the latter's memory.

A few mutual obligations belong to the *tato*. At the child's birth his *tato* brings firewood for the comfort of mother and child; and a female *tato* is supposed to wash the new-born baby. Continual presents of food are given, and the elder *tato* will take an interest in and make a pet of the younger. It appears that it is his special duty to make the perforations in the child's ears and nose. Return presents of food are made by the child's father; and it will stay from time to time in the elder *tato's* house and give him some assistance in his garden.

An Orokaiva child invariably has two alternative names, and frequently more. The 'name proper' (*javo be*) is that of its *tato*; the alternative, a nick-name, is called *javo isapo*, the 'small name'. A child may acquire his *javo isapo* by some accident of birth, e. g. one is called Ijita ('In the Sun') because she was brought to birth in a hot sunny place; another Bokoru ('Swamp') because he was born in a swamp; another is Pokoembo, because of a congenitally malformed foot. Such nicknames may be given for what must seem to us the most bizarre reasons. A man returning from a flood-time hunting expedition happened to fall into a hole full of water; on reaching home and finding that his wife had presented him with a child, he named it Hotera, 'In the hole'. Another returning home found that his son had died and was already wrapped or swathed (*egari*) in pandanus mats for burial. He cried, 'Open the mats for me to see my son', and gave to a child born shortly afterwards the somewhat ghastly name of Egari.

The *javo isapo* may be acquired at any age. A boy is named Sombi because as a youngster he captured a small lizard (*sombi*) and showed it to his parents. Another is Dumai, because on the occasion of a former cannibal raid he ran with the speed of a *dumai* or meteor—whether towards or away from the enemy was not specified. A third is called Jipari or 'shaker', because having survived a blow from a stone club, he startled or impressed his friends by the jerking or shaking (*jipari*) of his head. The commonest source of Orokaiva names, however, is simply the bush, and the frequency of botanic names, i.e. of trees, plants, and so forth, will be referred to in Chapter VIII, where it will be shown to bear on the question of the Plant Emblem.

Still another method of acquiring a name will call for notice in another place. This is the assumption by the slayer of the name of the slain. Whatever be the reason for this practice the new name (that of the slain) almost entirely supersedes the old; and, what is of importance here, the name of the slain warrior is sometimes taken not by the slayer himself but by his son. Instances of this are not uncommon.

Body Deformations. The perforations of the ear-lobes are made within the first few months of the infant's life. The piercing of the nasal septum is delayed until it is perhaps a year or so old. Among nearly all the Orokaiva both operations are performed simply by clamping on a tortoise-shell ring (*siatu*) which gradually works through the flesh. Strictly speaking it is the duty of the *tato* to provide the *siatu*, but the rule is not always observed.[1] Among the Hunjara tribe, I believe, it is the custom to defer the making of the nose-hole until the initiation ceremony, when youths and girls, sitting in a row, have to submit their noses to a painful and sometimes bloody thrust with a bone needle.

The Assumption of Clothing. Young children—boys or girls—go naked. With boys it is usual among all the tribes to assume the perineal band (*bo*) at various ages before they reach puberty. This is certainly the modern usage, and I believe it was the former usage also. Whether it was formerly permissible for the boy to adopt his *bo* without any ceremony (as he sometimes does nowadays) I cannot say; but it appears that any festivity might be made the occasion of bestowing it. For instance, at a dance which forms one of the earliest of the mortuary ceremonies, a youngster received his *bo* as a sort of extraneous incident in the day's procedure; and the same occurred in another ceremony in which the widow was finally discarding her mourning. The formal bestowal of a *bo* means a present to the man who bestows it, so that when a pig is killed for any major ceremony it is a good opportunity for providing a share as payment for a minor rite. The occasion for honouring the child is all the more fitting as a large number of spectators will be present.

---

[1] In *J. R. A. I.* lv, 1925, p. 407, I wrote: 'The maternal uncle has certain ceremonial duties to perform, e. g. that of piercing the child's nose. . . .' It appears, however, that this duty does not belong necessarily to the maternal uncle or *nobo*.

At the initiation or seclusion the candidates all receive new *bo*, which are stained red. As it is usual for the candidate to be fully developed he has nearly always assumed his *bo* previously through motives of modesty; but it is now bestowed again. On only one occasion have I seen a youth brave it out, and wait for a formal opportunity of assuming a perineal band even after he had obviously reached the age of puberty.

The *bo* is given by any of a variety of relatives. Among fifteen instances it was given six times by the true father, six times by the maternal uncle, and once each by the paternal grandfather, the maternal grandfather, and the elder brother. For the actual investiture a man of distinction may be asked to officiate, just as in the more important *Otohu* ceremony the *otohu* is bestowed by a noted warrior.

The girl's *bo*, a skirt of bark-cloth, is assumed at the termination of the seclusion which follows the first appearance of her menses. When she makes her début, it is with a spear or club in one hand, a bunch of betel-nuts in the other, and a bark-cloth skirt about her waist with a hole in it which is supposed to, but does not, show her genitalia. No satisfactory reason was given for this last detail, except that a girl would be subject to ridicule afterwards if it were not carried out. In the majority of the Orokaiva tribes the girl continues to wear an ordinary *bo* skirt after the ceremony; but among the Aiga and the River People this investiture is only an incident. The girl, although fully developed, goes naked until her marriage, only wearing a *bo* during her periods. This custom, viz. of unmarried girls going naked, is falling into disuse.

The Initiation Cycle. Usually about the age of puberty, but sometimes earlier, boys and girls undergo an initiation; though it is only among the Southern Orokaiva that the ceremony takes a definite and unmistakable form. Here the candidates (male and female) are subjected to a good deal of horse-play at the hands of men impersonating *embahi* or *siango*, i.e. spirits of the dead; and in the course of it they are introduced to the bull-roarer and the sacred flute, which are of course objects of mystery to the uninitiated children.

Among the Aiga and the River People, where the bull-roarer and the sacred flute are unknown, it seems that the place of this initiation ceremony is in some degree taken by the mime or drama. In this drama the initiate may play a minor part, and he is brought into contact with an impersonation of the dead.

After the initiation, or the dramatic performance which takes the place of an initiation, there follows a seclusion of some months. At the termination of the seclusion the initiates make a formal début, and are presented with certain gifts, consisting principally of feather head-dresses, to which is given the general name *kokumbari*. The word means literally 'decoration', and the ceremony amounts to a formal investiture which is necessary before a boy or a girl is entitled to wear a head-dress.

Another kind of gift is often made on the occasion of the *kokumbari*. This is known as *otohu*, and consists of a specially valuable and distinctive ornament or object which the candidate is thenceforward permitted to use. Its possession involves certain ethical obligations, and formerly in some cases it constituted a distinctive ornament of the homicide. The bestowal of the *otohu* may be reserved for a subsequent occasion, but in the majority of instances it appears that the moment of the début is regarded as favourable for the presentation. I shall therefore deal with the *otohu* as if it formed an integral part of what we might term the initiation cycle. Various precautionary or cleansing rites, principal among them being the eating of a ceremonial stew called *suna*, bring the cycle to a close.

To summarize on the matters of initiation and seclusion it will be seen that there is a series of distinct episodes, viz. (1) initiation to the bull-roarer and the sacred flutes (or among the northern Orokaiva the mime or drama which probably takes the place of initiation); (2) seclusion; (3) début with the *kokumbari* or decoration; and (4) presentation of the *otohu*. The whole cycle concludes (5) with the eating of a purificatory stew called *suna*.

The above summary disregards one or two minor differences between tribes as to the sequence of the episodes.

There is also in some tribes a brief seclusion preparatory to initiation. But the essential features may all be gathered under the above five headings. A full treatment of them is reserved to Chapter XII.

It is normally after initiation that the youth proceeds to marriage, and thereafter he follows the even tenor of his way to old age. There are no striking social changes after marriage. In the normal instance the father lives in his village and brings up a family and grows old working. If he be a man of character his influence will probably increase with his years; and whether this be so or not, he is reasonably assured—by a pleasing trait of primitive life—of the respect and consideration of his juniors.

The Constitution of the Clan

Having dealt with the immediate family and given an epitome of the social progress of the individual, I may proceed to the constitution of the clan.

Although the clan is a fairly well-defined group, it is difficult to find a satisfactory native name for it in the abstract. Among the Aiga the nearest approach seems to be the expression *embo-javo*, lit. 'man-name'; but this might stand in another context for the man's personal name. Among the Binandele there is a more definite term *oro-be*, 'the true *oro*' (the usual meaning of *oro* is men's house). In the Sangara dialect a word *araha* stands for either a village clearing or a clan. In the absence of a suitable native name I shall continue to use the word 'clan'.

The Formation of New Clans. The Orokaiva clan is patriarchal in constitution; it develops directly from the family in which the father is undisputed master. The clans vary greatly in size, but for the most part they are small; one of a dozen families might represent the average.

Consequently they are very numerous, and, as each and every one shows a tendency to split, they are not decreasing in number. Indeed, at the present time, when pacification has made it less essential to cling together for protection, it is possible there are more clans than ever before.

As the multiplying family merges into the clan it is not always easy to set a limit or a definition. But when the descendants of one man come to be known regularly by a distinctive name, it may be said that they constitute a new clan.

In some instances the clan is quite or nearly coincident with the village, i.e. the village is populated solely by one clan, and the clan is limited to that one village. Such a case is probably an elementary one, and the clan of comparatively recent origin. I will suggest a reason for this state of affairs and for the origin of the clans in general. There is an evident tendency for small family units to split off from the main body and form independent settlements. The reason is sometimes a quarrel and the fear of retaliatory magic, but more often, I believe, it is simply the lax method of horti-culture which necessitates the clearing of many areas in suc-cession and sometimes a temporary settlement on a distant site. This distant site is planted with coco-nut and betel, and, when subsequently the garden is again made on or about the same spot, it becomes the temporary home of a small settlement. But now one or two men may establish themselves here permanently with their families. So long as they retain their original clan name the settlement can only be regarded as an offshoot; but when they wax in numbers and begin to be known by a separate name, they become *ipso facto* a separate clan.

This process goes on continually. It means that originally the clan occupies a single village (a fact which is hinted at by the dual meaning of *araha*). In the hamlet of Borugata, for example, there are three houses and a combined yam-house and shelter. The head of the village is one Pipire, a man of middle age, who has three wives and thirteen chil-dren (an unusually large quiverful for an Orokaiva). The wife and son of his deceased brother are the only other occupants of the village. This small village of Borugata is an offshoot from another, Tandeti, inhabited by the clan Anjaha. As yet Pipire and his children retain the clan name of Anjaha; but it will be seen that we have the makings of a new clan, and it is only necessary for this small and essen-

tially patriarchal group to receive a distinctive name for it
to become a separate clan.

While in origin the clan and the village are co-extensive,
this state of affairs is by no means always maintained. War,
dispersal, and migration have scattered some clans and
drawn others together; so that now on the one hand we
may find representatives of one clan in a number of villages,
and on the other a single village comprising several clans.
In the latter place it is found that the several clans occupy
more or less distinct locations.

The Origin of Clan Names. It has been said that the essential feature which gives identity to a clan is a distinctive
name. Beyond this it has a further mark of identity in the
shape of a specific plant-emblem, called *heratu*. The *heratu*
will be the subject of another chapter. I may here continue
to discuss the first of these essential features, viz. the name,
and account for its origin.

It is by no means unusual for a man to identify himself
by the name of his parent or ancestor as well as by his own.
An interesting example of this is seen in the cries of triumph
uttered by the warrior or the hunter. As he drives his spear
into the victim or the pig he shouts, not his own name, but
some such expression as *Embogetahije!* (*Ahije*, or descendant
of Emboge); *Hositamei!* (lit. 'Son of Hosi', though in the case
in point Hosi is the paternal grandfather); or *Kaiepa-ta-bijari!*
(begotten of Kaiepa).[1] A woman making a big haul of fish
might be elated enough to cry *Handau-ta-du!* (sister of Handau, who is the 'big man' of her clan). In other cases the
successful hunter cries out his clan name, e.g. *Jagasitahije!*,
or *Sarahu-ta-bijari!*, in which Jagasi and Sarahu are the names
of the clans rather than of any definite or well-remembered
person.

Again all the underlings of any 'big man' will be known
to others under his name. In the Sangara dialect there is a
word *tekahoka*, of which I do not know the literal meaning,
but which appears to stand for a 'following'. When, at a
gathering of the clans for war, or for some peaceful cere-

---

[1] In some cases it appears that the man cries the name of his maternal relative,
either grandfather or uncle.

mony, the several parties make their appearance each following in single file behind its leader, a cry will go up, 'Here come the people, the *Tekahoka*, of Embuja, of Ehari, of Andari!'—whoever the big man may be. So in the Aiga language there is a word *ambotani*, which embraces all a man's junior relatives; and thus a number of more or less unimportant individuals may be known to others as the juniors of a certain big man and identified by his name.

There is no well-defined chieftainship among the Orokaiva, but merely a recognized ascendancy of the old men. The leader and ruler of any clan is the eldest of its men, provided he is not so old as to be incompetent, and provided always that his personality is equal to his position. It is consequently difficult to find a word which would correspond with our idea of 'chief', and unsatisfactory to use the English word 'chief', as too pretentious for even the most important of clan leaders. The Orokaiva expressions as far as I know them are *embo-be* (a proper man), and *embo-peni*, *embo-pajirari*, *embo-paitukiari*, and *embo-siakabada* (all of which mean no more than 'big or important man'); and these terms may be used of men of importance who cannot claim to be actually leaders. There are two other terms, however, which seem to possess a more specific application: they are *embo-javoari* and *embo-penjavo*. The first appears to mean 'the man who gives the name' (*javo*), and the second is no doubt a contraction of *embo-peni-javo* (man—big—name). The implication is that the real chief is the man who gives his name to his followers, i.e. the man by whose name they are collectively known.

It is readily understood how in this simple patriarchal organization the group may take its collective name from the leader or patriarch. Further, one may be surprised on asking who is the *embo-javoari* of a certain group, to be given the name of a man who is dead. Chieftainship among the Orokaiva is so rudimentary that a successor may not yet, so to speak, have taken shape. But that does not matter. The group is content to be known as the followers of the dead man.

All this leads to the conclusion (if it be not too obvious

to require proof) that the clan name is naturally derived from that of the clan's founder or ancestor.

There are many cases in which this is known to be the case because the eponymous ancestor of the clan is remembered in tradition. An instance is provided by the clans Serugahije and Samanahu: their founders were Seruga and Samana, concerning whom there exist more or less trustworthy accounts. (It was also said that Samana was originally a Serugahije man, so that the Samanahu is an offshoot of the Serugahije clan.)

I do not wish to suggest that this is the invariable rule. Indeed one could cite a number of contrary instances in which the clan has derived its name from a locality which it occupies or formerly occupied, e.g. Poitahu from the creek Poita; Sonami (a branch of the Eugahu clan, so called because it settled on the creek Sonami); Autembo, a branch of the Sekihu who fled and settled in the bush (*aute*).

But in the majority of cases it seems that the clan name is that of an ancestor. To illustrate the tendency for a group of people (in this case a village) to take its name from its leader I may quote the experience of a magistrate on the Gira.

'In the Government map of the Gira River . . .,' he says, 'when endeavouring to identify the villages marked thereon, I was struck by the fact that only two or three seemed to be known, the names of the others merely causing polite amusement. For some time I could not explain this, as the map was only made eleven years ago. Then it occurred to me that natives often give the name of the head man when asked for the name of their village. So I asked if there had ever been big fighting chiefs named Wore, Gubabai, &c. This instantly solved the enigma and I was able to identify nearly every village. . . .' [1]

Just as the village names itself after the leader, so also may the clan, which in the elementary stage coincides with the village. The name may be more or less temporary; for any offshoot will have no difficulty in finding a new and distinctive name, viz. that of its leader. But when this becomes well established and remains after the death of its actual owner, then we see in his followers and descendants the material of a new clan.

[1] H. L. Griffin, quoted in *Annual Report*, 1908–9, p. 22.

The Clan Spirit. It remains to say something of the clan spirit. The earlier part of this chapter dealt with the immediate family which was described as in large measure self-supporting and in its internal affairs independent. The family group is a definite social entity within a larger entity, the clan.

It does not often happen that the two interests, that of the clan and that of the family, come into conflict; but when they do it remains uncertain which takes precedence. It is largely a question of whether a man should place the interests of his wife before those of his kinsmen. Under normal conditions of peace the family of the husband remains on excellent terms with that of the wife, though in earlier days, when marriage by capture was common, the matter was not always so simple. The case in which the captive wife, with the connivance of her husband, warned her people of an impending raid illustrates how the conflict might arise. I may give a definite instance in which a man chose to cleave to his wife rather than his kinsmen. A very old man of Bologasusu named Bearivu was formerly married to a woman of the Aiga people on the right bank of the Kumusi. In an inter-clan fight these people killed some men of Bologasusu. This left Bearivu in a very uncomfortable predicament, for he feared that his clansmen would take an easy revenge by killing his wife, who was of a kin with the raiders. He accordingly migrated and settled with his wife's people on the other bank of the Kumusi. In due course the retaliatory raid was made, and Bearivu fought against his own clan in defence of his wife's. When the woman died Bearivu changed his coat, returned to his clan, and in subsequent encounters fought in turn against the people of his late wife.

But under ordinary circumstances we do not find the husband's people at variance with those of his wife, as if he should be pulled in different directions. When he takes a wife she is economically absorbed into his clan, and her life in all important respects belongs to that clan; and he by certain elaborate precautions, of which name-tabus are an instance, takes care to remain on good terms with his relatives by marriage. Save for any untoward happening, therefore, the life of the family will fit into that of the clan.

It is only necessary to stress the point that the immediate family is recognized as a social unit; and the mere fact that a man sometimes quarrels with the members of his clan and migrates with his family or settles somewhere apart, proves that the family interest may compete with that of the clan. Both units are co-operative, the family especially in respect of the food quest, the clan in respect of ceremonies and feasts, and more importantly of fighting. The clan owns the garden land, but the family cultivates its own patch and reaps its own harvest. On the whole, since the clan displays a constant tendency to split into smaller groups of which the family is the nucleus, it is difficult to draw a line between the two. Yet for the same reason we may be right in saying that the family, as the indivisible unit, exerts the stronger hold.

Whatever the difficulty of deciding between these two, however, there can be no doubt that both of them, family and clan, mean more to the individual than does the tribe or the somewhat loose confederacy of clans within the tribe. A man's strongest sympathies certainly lie within the limits of the clan. Quarrels between families, i.e. within the clan, are inevitable, but they are easily adjusted. Not so the quarrels between clans themselves—land disputes and the like—which are prosecuted with great bitterness. Indeed, as sorcery cases show, it is almost invariably the stranger beyond the pale of the clan who is suspected. Any one within the clan is presumably a friend; any one without it is a potential enemy.

There is another kind of group-spirit with which the clan may have to contend, viz. that of locality. Once more the two are not frequently opposed. Often the village is occupied wholly by one clan, and in such a case the conflict could not arise. But when representatives of one clan (A) live in the village of another clan (B) (although the *modus vivendi* is usually satisfactory), there may arise the situation in which the clan (A) as a whole falls out with the clan (B). Witnesses have commonly assured me that a man would stand by his clan rather than his village in such a crisis, and this is no doubt usually the case, though I have two definite instances in which the individuals fought on the side of their adopted villages against their own clans.

It is interesting to note that immigrants from other clans into a village (e.g. those who for any reason become domiciled among their wife's or their mother's people) are not always readily assimilated. In one case that came to my notice a man of about thirty years, who had lived in a certain village since going there as an orphan child with his mother, fell out with his neighbours over a question of fishing rights, and was so cold-shouldered that he had to change his place of residence again.

It has been shown that the Orokaiva clan is usually a small unit, that it is often of comparatively recent origin, and that it often bears definitely the name of a founder and ancestor. From these facts it will be seen that its limits may hardly surpass those of kindred. There are many cases, those of scattered clans, where the kindred connexion is virtually lost sight of, but typically the clansmen may be said to be united by feelings of actual kinship. Where this is so, such feelings may be expected to prevail over any opposition from the locality spirit. However, as I have said, such a conflict seldom arises. To sum up, it may be repeated that the Orokaiva's strongest sympathies are limited to his own small clan and to his family within the clan.

Relationship Terms

The following is a list of the principal relationship terms. The speaker is a married man. The word for husband is *ivu*. This together with *ai* (wife), *mei* (son), and *iai* (daughter), is used in periphrasis when there are no set relationship terms, e.g. *tata-ivu, betere-ta-ai, simbo-ta-mei*.

mama	father, father's brother, all males of the father's clan and generation; elders in general.
aja	mother, mother's sisters, all females of the mother's clan and generation; elder women in general.

bitepemi	elder brother, all males of the speaker's clan and generation who are senior to him.
biteambo	younger brother; all males of the speaker's clan and generation who are junior to him.
du	sister, elder or younger; females of the speaker's clan and generation.
tata	father's sister; females of father's clan and generation; maternal uncle's wife.
nobo	mother's brother; males of mother's clan and generation.
ahije	grandparents (paternal and maternal); ancestors in general; grandchildren; descendants; sister's children (sometimes called *mei-ahije*).
mei	son; males of the succeeding generation within the speaker's clan.
iai	daughter; females of the succeeding generation within the speaker's clan.
simbo	child of the father's sister; children of all *tata*; child of the mother's brother; children of all *nobo*, i.e. cross-cousins.
ai	wife (*pamoni* or 'woman' is also used).
atovo	wife's father; males of the preceding generation within the wife's clan.
imboti	wife's mother; females of the preceding generation within the wife's clan; wife's father's sister.
nabori	wife's brother; males of the wife's clan and generation; sister's husband and males of his clan and generation.
hovatu	wife's sister; females of wife's clan and generation; brother's wife and females of her clan and generation.
imi	daughter's husband.
meindai	son's wife.
betere	husband of cross-cousin (*simbo*); husband of sister's daughter (*ahije*); wife's mother's brother; children of wife's mother's brother.
jaivu	husband of wife's sister (*hovatu*).

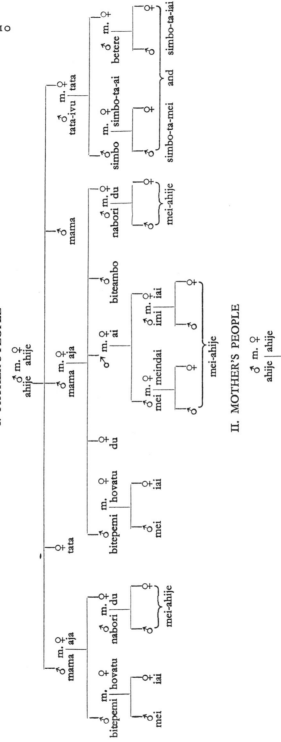

III. WIFE'S FATHER'S PEOPLE

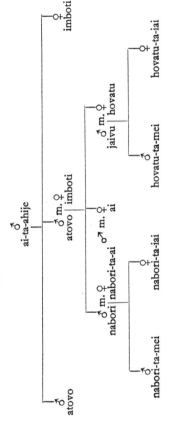

IV. WIFE'S MOTHER'S PEOPLE

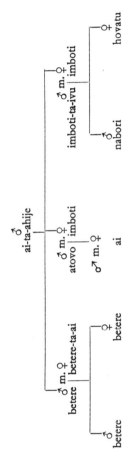

VIII

THE PLANT EMBLEM

The Nature of the Heratu

THE clan has a distinctive emblem or associate. Among the Aiga tribe (of whom my information is the fullest) this is called the *heratu*, and throughout the remainder of this chapter the word *heratu* will be used as the equivalent of plant-emblem. *Kenatu* is the form in the Binandele and Tain-Daware languages; in Wasida a different word, *hae*, is used; and, throughout the whole Orokaiva people, alternative names are *evobo* and *ahije*, or some nearly equivalent forms.

It may safely be said that every clan has a *heratu*, and almost invariably it is some plant or tree. The Orokaiva are mostly forest people. In the tropical bush there is infinite variety, and (what makes the bush so difficult for the timber-getter and so easy for the native) this variety is for ever repeating itself. Give a native a moment and he will look about him and pluck you his *heratu*. The botanical names are of no consequence—fortunately so, as I cannot give them. There are large forest trees such as *Boruga* and *Siruga*, the 'canoe tree'; creepers and bushes; grasses and weeds. Sometimes they have an economic value; commonly they have none whatever. It is certain that they are not selected as *heratu* because of any use they may have. They are seen most frequently in the form of a twig or an unpretentious handful of grass.

Since the *heratu* is in so great a majority of cases a vegetable species, the phrase 'plant emblem' seems to be justified. There are, however, some interesting variants, including a number of bird associates and certain simple emblematic devices. Though I describe these somewhat in detail it must not be forgotten that they are relatively speaking a very small category, and that the *heratu* is normally a plant or tree.

In the Wasida tribe I came across three bird associates,

Kombu, a certain black bird whose name '*Kombu*' is meant to reproduce its cry; *Hiviki*, the hawk; and *Hororo*, a small ground forager. These were all subsidiary emblems, and the clans to which they belonged had *heratu* of the ordinary botanic kind. Further, they were not, as far as I know, used for the regular purpose of the *heratu*, viz. as a badge or token of identity. However, among the Binandele there was the *Diriu*, or common blue pigeon, of the Diriu clan; and among the Tain-Daware the *Bangai*, or eagle hawk of the Bangai-unji; and it was claimed that the feathers of both these birds were used as identity marks. The blue pigeon (with a slight dialectal change of name) is again *heratu* of the Dirou about the Hydrographer foot-hills, but I have no very trustworthy note in this instance. Among several score of *heratu* I have lighted upon only these six instances of birds, so that they may be considered very rare.

A few examples may be given of the semi-mechanical devices which sometimes serve as *heratu*. Among the Aiga the Honia-Noduru clan use a split stick—not a particular stick, but simply any small branch torn from a tree by the track and split half-way down its length. The Samberota clan has for its *heratu* a *sambi*, i.e. a green stick flattened or squashed at the end as a wooden peg is splayed out by hammering. The Simborota, besides their plant emblem *Simboro*, have a habit of stamping their heel (*atu*) into the soft ground to leave the print of it as their mark. Among the Binandele we find *topo*, any broad leaf rolled into a spiral with the same quick turn of the hands which we see behind the grocer's counter; and *pono*, a foot or so of creeper fashioned into two tangent circles in imitation of the ornament *pono*, which consists of two circular pig tusks. The Umbengi clan of the Tain-Daware have for their *heratu* *umu-bengi*, literally 'water clod', i.e. the clod of earth continually dislodged by the stream from the river bank.

Further instances of this nature could be given. It will be seen that all these, like the usual plant *heratu*, have this much in common, that they may be extemporized in a moment. A native cannot lay hold of a bird or an animal whenever he wants it; consequently birds are rarely adopted as *heratu*, and animals or fish, so far as my investigations go, never.

It is common, almost regular, for the clan to have one or more alternative *heratu*. For this there are several explanations which may be regarded as concurrent. In the first place it is well to have an alternative or emergency *heratu*. If the tree *Tuvira* is not handy, then *Ehe jakara*, a grass stalk, will do; or failing that again *Komusu*, a leaf of any kind made into a scroll; and by one or the other of these you may know that a Serugahije man has passed.

Secondly, there is a sort of hierarchy of *heratu*. As was said before, the clan is continually subdividing. The subclan or incipient clan, even the individual, may adopt an independent *heratu*, but, still belonging to the parent body, continue for a time at least to use the parent *heratu*. Thus two branches of the clan Simborota, while retaining their original *heratu*, the river-grass *Simboro*, have each their distinctive mark, one the tree *Ominga*, and one *atu*, the imprint of a heel.

Thirdly, a man uses both the paternal and the maternal *heratu*. As I have previously mentioned, the *heratu* proper is the former, and the contrary instances which do occur are exceptional. The *heratu* of the father is passed on by inheritance, whereas that of the mother is not normally handed down beyond the generation of her offspring. However, so close is the intimacy between the two branches of the united family, that the son or daughter may be as familiar with the mother's *heratu* as with the father's. Within the clan, indeed, it is the distinctive mark of the household, and a man may often employ his father's and his mother's emblems simultaneously so as to make his identity the clearer. Further, as it is customary for a man to spend some of his time in his wife's village, it follows that the son must spend some of his time in his mother's village, and while there he may use his mother's *heratu* in preference to his father's, which would be less familiar among the surrounding villages and clans.

Uses of the Heratu

(a) *As an Identity Token*. So far I have not mentioned the uses of the plant emblem. If one asks a native what he actually does with his *heratu*, he will assuredly answer: 'I place it on the track so that others who may follow may know I have passed that way.' This, indeed, though not the only use for the *heratu*, is the commonest. At the juncture of two paths I have come upon eight different kinds of leaves or grass, placed there during the morning and as yet scarcely wilted. My boys, who were inhabitants of the district, were able to identify each clan by its *heratu*; the owners of them had passed this spot at intervals, all bound for one village as guests to a feast and dance. The stem of the leaf, the root of the grass, or the butt of the branch, should point in the direction which its owner has taken, but apparently this rule is not observed with strictness.

There is another use similar in principle. When a hungry man sees a ripe bunch of bananas in the garden of his friend he will not hesitate to help himself. It is to be feared that he would not hesitate over long if he met the same temptation in the garden of a stranger. In the first instance, however, he will eat his fill of the bananas, or whatever it may be, and leave his *heratu*. When the owner comes to his garden and sees this, he will be satisfied, for no native grudges food to his friend.

I have had occasion myself to use this simple expedient. Finding a village where we meant to lunch deserted for the time, we steal a bunch of bananas, cook them, and go on our way with invigorated and cheerful carriers. To account for this act of pillage we need only leave a stick or two of tobacco by the remains of the banana bunch, tied to a sprig of croton, which happens to be the *heratu* of a rather distinguished old native who is with me. We may then feel that we have not only made payment but given the fullest possible account of our behaviour.

In these two uses the *heratu* is an identity token, having a sort of evidential value in proving presence or agency, like a national flag left planted on the North Pole, or a visiting card slipped under the front door. It may be remarked that the *heratu* is never worn or carried by a man simply as a badge. It is an identity mark *in absentia*.

(*b*) *As a Mark of Individual Abstinence.* The next use for the *heratu* is a somewhat singular one. It is used by individuals as a sign of abstinence, a sort of self-inflicted tabu, whenever such abstinence has been the outcome of some quarrel or grievance. The Orokaiva is very prone when his feelings are hurt to punish himself rather than the man who has hurt them; or, perhaps better, to take revenge upon the other party by punishing himself.

Thus, if a man fall out with his wife, he will thrust a sprig of his *heratu* through his armlet, and while he continues to wear it will receive no food of her cooking. Not that he altogether starves himself into relenting; some friend will cook for him until his mood softens, and then there are interchanges of gifts between the wife's people and his own, and, as I am assured, invariable reconciliation. Similarly a wife who has been accused by her husband of sponging on him, not working for her keep, will advertise her grief and indignation by wearing her *heratu*, and will for the time being refuse to eat another taro out of his garden.

A bunch of drooping leaves may be seen tied to a coconut palm in the village. The owner has fallen out with his neighbour over the boundary of his garden. The row of tree-trunks which constitutes the usual garden border has been displaced and shows an encroaching and unwarrantable bulge. Therefore he has set up his *heratu* to indicate that he has been imposed upon, and has broken off friendly relations with his neighbour; he will accept no hospitality from him (and give none) until the matter has been adjusted. Another man nurses some resentment against a near-by village. If he were bidden to a feast there he would go, but with his *heratu* in his armlet; and when the wooden dish of savoury taro was placed before him, he would wave it aside, or lay his *heratu* upon the food to show that he could not accept the hospitality of those who had wronged him. Then the offender would be put to shame and punished, and be sorry for what he had done.

(a) The *Naterari* or Tabu Post

(b) Coco-nuts stored under Tabu

PLATE XXI

(c) As the Naterari or Village Tabu Post. The *heratu* appears again in its most interesting character as the village tabu post. In many parts of the Territory it is the custom long before a feast to set up some tangible sign of tabu upon the coco-nuts. Among the Orokaiva this sign commonly takes the form of a wooden post or pillar, roughly carved and painted, and this post should properly speaking be of that particular wood which the clan owns for its *heratu*. This, however, cannot be a universal rule, because the *heratu* is often a grass or some small plant; but it may be said that when the *heratu* is a tree the tabu post is a stump of that tree. (In the other cases it may be a post of some alternative wood, or—a frequent substitute—one or two wands of the very light timber called *pamba* tied horizontally to a palm.)

Among the Aiga such a post is called *naterari*, and this word will be used as an alternative for tabu post. The *naterari* will be described more fully in Chapter XIII, but I may here anticipate one or two points in that description because they throw some light on the nature of the *heratu*.

In the first place the feast for which the *naterari* is set up is a mortuary feast; it is in honour of, or placation of, certain departed spirits. Further, offerings are made to it as if to the departed spirits; it is hung about with mementos of the dead; the feast is laid out before it, and it is called upon to witness the food; it is treated and disposed of with something like reverence; lastly, it often bears a faint and sometimes a decided anthropomorphic character. These various points show that the *naterari* is closely associated with the dead man, and they do much to justify the suggestion that the wooden pillar actually represents the dead, or even that it stood originally as a crude model.

The Heratu as Ancestor

Having described the uses of the *heratu* I may now endeavour to explain them. The fact of first importance is that the *heratu* of the clan is constantly referred to as 'our ancestor'. The words used are *evobo* and *ahije*; the former (which in this connexion is the usual one) seems always to have the extra connotation of 'ancient'; the latter may mean either literally 'grandfather', or else an ancestor more remote. It is always difficult to determine the proper limits of native categories. *Heratu*, which I have used as synonymous with plant-emblem, would seem with some informants to have a rather more limited application, i.e. it refers to the plant emblem especially *qua* mark of identity; whereas *evobo* is rather a more comprehensive term, covering not only the special plant-emblem ancestor, but the whole march-past of forefathers. However, the plant-emblem is called an ancestor; and when a man is dead and lies awaiting burial, the women may be heard crying to him as the offspring of his *heratu*—'*Asava-jai, Hombiga-jai!*' i.e. 'Child of Asava, child of Hombiga!' the word *jai* being used in everyday speech as we might use the word 'piccaninny'.

Now I have on a number of occasions asked the native what he means by calling the plant emblem his ancestor. Sometimes he cannot give an answer, but very commonly he can, and then it is always the same: 'Our real ancestor', he says, 'was a human being, not a tree; *it was a man with a tree name.*' For once, I believe, our native has given the really true explanation. I will proceed with the evidence for this hypothesis, viz. that the normal *heratu* is a species of plant representing a human ancestor of the same name.

There are certain reasonably authentic incidents in which a human namesake, or rather original, of the *heratu* is well remembered. Thus there is a Binandele clan named Yega-boda whose *heratu* is *watora* the reed. During their latter migrations these people hid from their enemies among the reeds, and here a baby was born to whom was given, in a very characteristic fashion, the name Watora. In due time this child became the chief man of his clan, which adopted *watora*, or the reed, as its *heratu*. So again we find two widely separated branches of the clan Samanahu, one among the Aiga, the other, an emigrant section, among the Binandele. The Aiga section, still retaining their name of Samanahu, have now the alternative *heratu, asava* and *hombiga*, evidently acquired subsequently; while the Binandele branch has kept its original *heratu*, the tree *samana*. Both sections, however,

told the same tale of Samana. He was their common ancestor—not a tree of course, they affirmed, but a man, and
one who, as it chanced, acquired his name from the fact
that he was brought to birth under a *samana* tree.

(It happens that in each of these two cases the ancestor
has acquired his tree name in much the same way; and in fact
this habit of naming a child from some odd circumstances
attending its birth is very common; instance the names
Abiga, 'Ashes', and Ijita, 'The Sun', given for precisely
similar reasons. But whatever the origin of the tree names
for human beings, I shall presently have to stress the fact
of their extraordinary frequency among the Orokaiva.)

To give further instances, a man of the Aiga clan Johari,
whose *heratu* is *saga*, declares that Saga was a man of flesh
and bone, and gives with confidence a genealogy in which
he proves to be his great-grandfather. Another, an old man
with *heratu okomba*, says that he remembers seeing in his
boyhood the real Okomba. In a certain village on the
Kumusi the *heratu* is *juara*, a creeper. This will not make a
suitable tabu post, so the chief, one Euga, cut out a post
from the *euga* tree; and on another occasion used the tree
hananya, because a paternal ancestor had borne that name.

Of individual *heratu* I shall have more to say presently;
but an instance may be given here to show how the individual *heratu* also represents the human being with the tree
name. The Pure clan on the Mambare has for its *heratu* the
plant *pura*; but two individual clansmen possess *heratu* of
their own, one the tree *goru*, from his paternal grandfather
of the same name, and the other a pair of alternatives, *simbiri* (the croton), his mother's name, and *eua* (a kind of
bread-fruit?), his father's name. Instances could be multiplied. From constant questioning I have come to form the
opinion that in the very great majority of cases the *heratu* has
been adopted in this manner, viz. as a tangible emblem of
the synonymous ancestor.

I have four cases in which a contrary explanation was
offered. A fugitive section of the Serugahije clan, making
its way northward toward the river Mambare, settled for
some time in a place of abundant sago, and thereafter aban-

doned the original *heratu tuvira*, and adopted *ambe*, or sago. A clan of the Tain-Daware named Giriri had for its original ancestor one Bono. But they were constantly using a certain hardwood called *giriri* for building, and consequently took this for their *heratu* and clan name. The Gonini clan of the Tain-Daware have for their *heratu gonini*, and occupy four villages. In one of these, Sivariri, there is growing a large tree of the same name, and its inhabitants have taken this species (*sivariri*) for their *heratu*. The fourth instance is that of the Binandele clan Diriu. These people, who long ago lived on the Kumusi, were fishing in a small creek when the body of a blue pigeon (*diriu*) came floating down. They accordingly named the creek Diriu, and, it would appear, adopted the name for themselves and their *heratu*. Though the clan was long ago driven out by the Aiga, this same creek and the adjacent village are still known as Diriu, a circumstance which gives a colour of truth to the legend.

These four cases, however, are not typical. The usual explanation is the one I have given above. In many cases, of course, no explanation whatever was offered; yet it came as a rather pleasant surprise to the investigator that the natives should suggest as often as they did the same plausible origin for one of their customs. After some acquaintance with the Orokaiva, one may safely say that, although of a highly imaginative nature, he is not such a fool as really to believe himself descended from a tree.

Identity of Clan, Heratu, and Ancestor

We have now, therefore, reached this proposition: the *heratu* is both tree and ancestor, and it is so by virtue of the circumstance that the name of the tree and the name of the ancestor were identical.

Now I have already shown (Chapter VII, pp. 103 ff.) that groups of men tend to take their collective names from the individual names of their leaders, and that the clan name is frequently that of its original leader or founder. There is no need to elaborate that theme, but I may draw attention to the facts (1) that clan names are very commonly tree names, and (2) that very commonly the clan name and that of the *heratu* are identical, or the former incorporates the latter.

To illustrate these two points I give a list—fairly complete—of the clans of the Aiga tribe. The terminations of the clan names require a note. *Ahije* means 'descendant'; *uhu* means literally and somewhat picturesquely 'the trunk of a tree', much as we should say 'stock'; *embo* means 'man'; *aha* may mean 'mother', as it does in one Orokaiva dialect (Hunjara), though not in that of the Aiga; -*ta* is simply an associative or possessive suffix.

(1) There is first a class of local names which more or less explain themselves.

Clan Name.	Meaning.	Heratu.
Angerihani	(*angeri* means 'beyond, over yonder'; *hani* may mean 'friends, comrades', or possibly 'tree branch'.)	Isuga, Soriho.
Angeriuhu	. . . . .	Potana, Hamana.
Autembo	(*aute* means the 'bush, forest'.)	Saga.
Poita-uhu	(Poita, the name of a certain creek.)	Boruga.[1]
Seva-uhu	(*sevahi*, the 'bush'.)	Siruga, Seki, and Tanderi.
Tiri-Humusi	(*tiri*, 'hills'; Humusi, the river Kumusi.)	Hambora, Garava.

(2) There is one solitary bird name of which I can give no explanation.

Jega-Karenga (*Jega*? ; *Karenga*, parrot) . . ?

(3) There is thirdly a miscellaneous class of names of which I have no explanation, but will put down only for the sake of making the list complete. These may be nicknames, ancestral names, or tree names.

Clan Name.	Heratu.
Airahije	Horo.
Ata	?
Evija	Isuga.
Horipahije . . .	Ongo.
Jarutuhu	Embara, Kitikukumi, Ehe.
Johari	Saga.
Koariahije . . .	Tanderi.
Komahije . . .	Tutengi.
Ngiriahije . . .	Boruga.[1]

[1] The same *heratu* may belong to apparently unrelated clans.

(4) Lastly there is a long list in which the clan name is that of a tree or plant.

Clan Name.			Heratu.
Ango-uhu	.	.	?
Aseahije	.	.	Pogera, Ase.
Borugaha	.	.	Boruga.[1]
Bove	.	.	Simbiri.
Eugahu	.	.	Euga?
Honia-Noduru	.	.	? (a split stick).
Hojavahije	.	.	Hojava.
Isugahije	.	.	Isuga.
Jautiahije	.	.	Jauti.
Jega-Juaraha	.	.	Juara.
Koropahije	.	.	Tutengi, Tambara.
Ongoahije	.	.	Ongo.
Paingoahije	.	.	Paingo.
Samanahu	.	.	Asava, Hombiga.
Samberota	.	.	Sambi (a squashed stick).
Sauhu	.	.	Sahu.
Seheo-Buje	.	.	Buje.
Sekihu	.	.	Seki.
Serugahije	.	.	Twira, Ehe-jakara, Komusu.
Simborota	.	.	Simboro, Ominga, Atu, Boruga.[1]
Soriahije	.	.	Soriho.

If we exclude the third category, of which I have obtained no explanation, it will be seen that the last category contains the majority of the remaining names. And it will be seen also that in fifteen cases out of twenty-one, the clan's name, besides being that of a tree or plant, is that of the particular plant which is its emblem or *heratu*. In the typical instance, I believe, the names of clan and *heratu* correspond. And when we remember that the clan takes its name from its original leader or founder, it will appear that in the typical instance the names of the clan, the *heratu*, and the founder correspond.

On the whole I think the clan and its *heratu* come into being simultaneously and in this manner: an individual secedes from the parent clan and his family grows into an independent clan. This clan comes to be known by its founder's name and adopts for emblem a plant bearing the same name, or one similar to it.

---

[1] The same *heratu* may belong to apparently unrelated clans.

The exceptions (i.e. where the clan name and *heratu* do not correspond) may be explained in several ways. (1) A sub-clan may retain the old *heratu* but take a new name. So the Autembo are a fugitive section of the Johari who took to the bush (*aute*) in order to avoid reprisals for a murder. While they are known as Autembo they have kept the original *heratu* of the Johari, viz. *Saga*. (2) A local branch of a clan may keep its original clan name but adopt a distinc-tive *heratu*. A migrant section of the Simborota still call themselves Simborota, but have assumed *Boruga* as their *heratu*. (3) A clan may discard the old *heratu* and take the synonymous plant of a new leader. Thus a very old man tells me his *heratu* was formerly *Tumena* (a variety of taro), but nowadays it is *Bari*, because his son *Barigi*, an ex-sergeant of Native Police (made famous by C. A. W. Monckton), has taken his place as leader of the clan.

Plant Names for Human Beings

I have mentioned (p. 97) the frequency with which plant names are used for human beings among the Oro-kaiva. It is time that this statement should be substantiated. In the first place we are dealing with a people of the forest, who depend on its products for countless purposes, and who know its multifarious flora in a way that no European could know it—unless he were a botantist. It need not altogether surprise us, therefore, that they should draw upon this inexhaustible store for their own personal names.

Name-giving customs have been dealt with already (Chap-ter VII, pp. 96–98). Suffice it to say here that, besides the formal names passed on by god-fathers and god-mothers (*tato*), there are countless nicknames (as we should call them) originating from some chance circumstance of birth or early youth. The formal names appear to be as odd as the others, and have no doubt arisen in the same haphazard manner. Most personal names permit of interpretation, and pro-vided their owners or their owners' parents are present, the interpretation will often recall some homely anecdote of childhood.   But, however they may have arisen, plant names form a large proportion of them.   In a random list (two series of men who submitted themselves for physical measurement) we find such names as Half-cooked, Shell, Lizard, Pus, Cry-baby, to Stretch, to miss with the Spear, Wet, Roasted, and so on. But by far the largest category is that of plant names. In a list of 57 names (13 of which were not interpretable) they added up to 15, i.e. 26 per cent. of the whole, or 34 per cent. of the interpretable names.

The Heratu as Badge

(a) *The Use of 'Nearly' Synonymous Heratu.* As only a proportion of men have actual plant names, it is obvious that not every one can have a synonymous *heratu*. There is, however, an important consideration which does much to remove this difficulty. Although a man may not have a plant name, nevertheless some plant with a name *resembling* his will be made to stand for him. The instance of the altered *heratu Bari* (p. 123) is a case in point. *Barigi*, as far as I know, is not the name of a plant; but *bari* is a sufficient approximation, and will do for the *heratu* of Barigi's clan. So we have *pura* as *heratu* for the clan Pure, and *anderi* for the clan Andere. Again for the clan Samberota (named from the plant *Sambero*) we have *sambi*, the flattened stick (vide p. 113).

(We even find a closely related variety of plant made to do service for the proper *heratu*, though it has an entirely different name. Thus the tree *benoma* may be a substitute for *samana* of the Samanahu (Binandele branch); *omba* for *Piri* of Piri-bijari; *pogera* for *ase* (both varieties of Job's Tears) of the Aseahije.)

What with the frequent occurrence of plant names and this convenient possibility of using as *heratu* a plant that is only nearly synonymous, it is almost impossible that any and every Orokaiva should not have his plant emblem.

(b) *The Individual Heratu.* This brings us to the individual plant emblem, which has already been touched on here and there. The matter does not require a long consideration, for it will be obvious that the principle of the individual plant emblem will be precisely the same as that of the clan plant emblem; indeed, in all typical cases the latter has apparently come into being as an individual emblem. One sometimes finds a man living as a member of a clan and owning its *heratu*, but at the same time boasting a private sign for himself. We have seen a man, Euga of the Jega-Juaraha (*heratu juara*), setting up a *naterari* of *euga* wood (vide p. 119), and two members of the Pure clan distinguishing themselves by the synonymous plants of their grandparents or parents. Among the Binandele clan of Diriu is a man Taimi, who, besides the feather of the blue pigeon (*diriu*), has a *heratu* of his own, viz. *tai*, a root. No doubt the pigeon feather is not always at hand; but the root of any plant placed conspicuously on the track is enough to show his friends that Taimi has passed by.

(*c*) *Summary on the Heratu as a Badge.* It remains to say something more of the *heratu* as a badge or identity token, and lastly to discuss its bearing on the question of totemism.

Of the three main uses of the *heratu* previously described, viz. (1) as an identity token, (2) as a mark of individual abstinence, (3) as the *naterari*, or village tabu post, the last will seem tolerably clear. The *naterari* stands as a symbol of the dead man in whose behalf the tabu is imposed. Formerly it may have been something more than a formal symbol of the dead, in fact a crude image. This association between the wooden post and the dead man which it represents is strengthened by using his particular namesake tree: then, besides other associations, the two have this important bond between them—a common name.

The second use remains somewhat obscure, though it has this in common with the *naterari*, that in both the *heratu* is really a tabu sign.

The first use, however, is the fundamental one. The *heratu* is a badge; and it is a badge by virtue of the fact that it bears the same name (or nearly the same name) as the man or men it represents. We may therefore call it a synonymous badge. A man named Waiwa once explained the matter to me thus. 'You white men', he said, 'have your books. If you went to your friend's garden and took his taro, you would write your name in the book, and when he came and saw your name there he would be content, knowing that his taro had been taken by a friend. But the New

Guinea man cannot write his name on paper so he leaves his name behind him in another fashion. I should look about me', he said, 'and find some tree with a name like "Waiwa", break off a branch of it, and leave it by the broken taro tops. Then my friend, the owner of the garden, when he saw that sign, would say "Aha, Waiwa is welcome to my taro".'

In the article referred to elsewhere in this report, viz. 'The Movements of the Tribes of the Mambare Division of Northern Papua' (Chinnery and Beaver), there is an interesting anecdote,[1] still well remembered in the region of which it is told. The Binandele, led by a man Waia, had been raiding on the river Gira, and searching for their real enemies had in error attacked the Yema tribe, killed the chief, and captured a youth Jiani. For this unhappy mistake Waia expresses his sorrow, and desires that Kewatai, the absent son of the chief, be sent on a visit to the Binandele country in order to effect reconciliation and alliance.

'Then Waia said, "My name is Waia; can you remember this name?" Jiani replied, "Yes; we call this tree (pointing to a certain tree called Warawa in Binandele) Waia." The chief then cut off a piece of the bark, and gave it to Jiani for remembrance, and told him to put it in Kewatai's house, and to tell him that he (Waia) was sorry.'

When Kewatai does visit the Binandele country, it is only by remembering the name of Waia that he saves himself from being eaten.

In such uses as these the *heratu* is something more primitive than a pictograph; it is a very material symbol, a sort of vegetable signature.

The Heratu as Totem

Throughout this chapter I have avoided the word 'totem', using in preference the non-committal, if awkward, phrase 'plant emblem'. I may now review the evidence which might have justified the use of the former term.

(1) The *heratu* is normally connected with a definite social group, viz. the clan (though sometimes with the individual and his immediate family).

[1] *Annual Report*, 1914-15, p. 159.

(2) The clan is usually exogamous in practice, though by no means strictly so (vide p. 131).

(3) The clan commonly, in the typical case always, takes its name from the *heratu* or, more strictly, is synonymous with the *heratu* (vide p. 122).

(4) The clan uses its *heratu* first and foremost as a badge.

(5) The *heratu* is called an ancestor (though the Orokaiva does not really believe that his ancestor can be plant or tree).

Thus far it would seem the *heratu* has conformed very nearly to the tenets of totemism. It remains to be considered whether the clan possesses any magico-religious sentiment for its *heratu* such as typically unites the group and its totem.

The evidence is here somewhat conflicting. Generally speaking the plant emblem (except as *naterari*) is treated with no semblance of respect or reverence. In clearing the bush a man will fell his *heratu* tree without a thought; if it bear edible fruit like *topu*, the wild fig, he will eat it; if it be, as in one case it is, *ambe* or sago, he will not forswear one of his principal means of subsistence. There is a large clan, the *Umondaha*, one of whose *heratu* is nothing more nor less than 'Water'.

In one or two instances, however, informants have claimed that they will not cut down their own tree; though such are distinctly exceptional. No case has come to light of a useful *heratu* which its owner will not use. With the rare bird *heratu* the case is almost the same. A Diriu man, ex-constable, averred that he had shot many *diriu* (blue pigeon) for his master, and would be only too glad to shoot and eat another if I would lend him a gun. Perhaps at first he was like the other who 'sighed as a member of the cockatoo totem but obeyed as a policeman', but his scruples are long since gone if he ever had any. A man whose subsidiary *heratu* is the bird *Kombu* says that, while he would not hesitate to kill it (if he could get near it), he would still refrain from eating it. It is apparently for reasons of sentiment alone that he would not eat it, for he declares there would be no evil effects upon him if he did (as I believe he might) yield to the temptation.

On the other hand, however, a man of the Bangai-unji, or 'children of the eagle-hawk', who use one of its speckled feathers for their mark, avers that he would neither kill nor eat the bird; and, further, volunteers that if a *bangai* fledgling, being caught and kept in the village, were to die, it would not be eaten or thrown away, but buried. Lastly, there is one isolated note which may have some significance. The bird *Hororo* (mentioned on p. 113) belongs especially to a certain man Erupa. Should its cry be heard near the village, the people would say, 'Erupa will be successful in the hunt to-day'.

In passing I may mention a point of some interest. Among the Orokaiva there are certain strict rules of etiquette between relatives by marriage (particularly between the man and his parents-in-law), exemplified by a very strict name-avoidance. Now, although a man will cut down his own *heratu* tree without mercy, he will hesitate to do the same with a tree that happens to bear the name of his *atovo* or *imboti*, i.e. his father-in-law or his mother-in-law, and may request one of his companions in the clearing to fell this particular tree for him. Similarly he will not eat any food, animal or vegetable, which happens to be synonymous with either of his parents-in-law. Now this rule is based on sentiment; there are, as far as my knowledge goes, no magico-religious sanctions to it; and where a similar tabu is observed with regard to the *heratu* we may probably assume that this is likewise no more than a sentimental avoidance.

The foregoing evidence has been set down for what it is worth. On the whole there would appear to be no very special regard for the *heratu*, though here and there will crop up a strong manifestation of such regard. It may not be surprising that this is relatively more marked in the few cases of birds than in those of the usual botanic *heratu*, because the former, with their more definite personality, are in themselves likelier objects of regard than the latter.

In fine it is of little consequence whether the plant emblem be called a totem or not; it will be obvious that it is very much like one. There is in my own mind little doubt as to how the system came into being. The *heratu* is a synony-

mous badge for the leader of the clan, and through him for
the group to which he gives his name. It has been maintained that totemism was evolved in more ways than one.
More thorough-going totems may well enough have sprung,
like the plant emblems of the Orokaiva, not from communal
nicknames, but from names, and furthermore, from individual names. The conclusion of the present chapter may be
summarized very briefly. The clan's *heratu* originates from
the individual *heratu* of its leader or ancestor; and the individual *heratu* is some plant which serves as a token of identity
because it bears the name of its owner.

IX

MARRIAGE

THE customs relating to marriage will be better understood if it be made clear at the outset that there are four distinct methods by which an Orokaiva can obtain a wife. They are (1) Purchase, (2) Exchange, (3) Elopement, and (4) Capture. The first three of these methods are in continual use to-day; the fourth has fallen out of fashion, but only since the pacification of the country by the white man. Cases of marriage by capture have been very common, and the custom is not so long obsolete but that many women are still to be found in the Division who first met their husbands as members of a hostile raiding party. I shall return to a discussion of these several methods at the end of the chapter.

Polygamy and Exogamy

In the great majority of instances marriage is monogamous. Whether in the fighting days there existed that surplus of males over females which the modern census reveals, it is impossible to say; but apart from this we are told that every mature and normal man had a wife, so that one finds it difficult to conceive how polygamy could have been very prevalent. In present-day instances the polygamous husband rarely has more than two wives. A certain young man Orari of Isivita, who is of more than usually prepossessing appearance, has divorced one and at present owns three. Asked why he had so many he said it was the girls' fault; they all wanted him. It seems probable, however, that wealth and power rather than personal attraction are the means of winning extra wives. The record instance, as far as my knowledge goes, is that of a man Buninia whose wives are numbered by his surviving contemporaries at eleven. Buninia was a man of great influence among all the Aiga clans, and was notorious for bad temper and bullying. It is said that he was greatly feared. It will go without saying that he was wealthy. I do not know which of these attributes had the greatest influence in winning him eleven wives.

Normally marriage is patrilocal, though instances to the contrary are not infrequent. Nor is it unusual for a man to spend long periods in the village of his wife, for, as we have found, there is usually a close intimacy between the two sides of the united family. It is said that a kindly husband will make allowance for his wife's homesickness. But in cases of what seems more or less permanent matrilocal marriage, the offspring still belong emphatically to the father's clan.

The evidence regarding exogamy is not entirely consistent. Some witnesses have said it is not permissible for a man to marry a woman of his own clan. For this two arguments have been put forward, but neither throws much light on the matter. If a girl married a man of her own clan, where, it was asked, would the pay or bride-price come from? On another occasion a witness said that if a man and wife of the same clan happened to quarrel they would both find themselves calling the name of the same *heratu* or plant emblem; and the neighbours overhearing would shake their heads or turn up their noses at the idea of marriage between two of the same clan. Other informants have expressed repugnance at the suggestion of marriage with a *du* or 'sister', so that it would appear that in general theory at least the clan should be exogamous. As for the village group (in which there may be several clans), it cannot be called exogamous even in theory. It has been stated, on the contrary, that in a village where there happens to be a number of attractive girls it is a wise thing for the young men of that village to marry them and keep them at home. And this precept was made applicable to the clan itself by some informants; for the rule of clan exogamy was actually in some cases denied.

When we consult the facts we find that marriage is usually outside the clan, but that the exceptions are numerous enough to prove that clan exogamy is not a hard and fast rule. It also appears that marriage is usually outside the village, though the exceptions are just as numerous. The most notable example came from the Aiga village Ehenada (a large and rambling one, it is true), where of twelve men questioned, all of whom belonged to Ehenada and the clan Asiahije, no less than five had married women of the same village and the same clan. Again in two neighbouring villages of the Simborota clan I found five inter-marriages.

Marriage is common between first cousins, though in no recorded instance did these cousins belong to one and the same clan. We may probably assume that the marriage of first cousins within the clan is forbidden, although the general rule of clan exogamy is often disregarded. There is no rule against marrying out of one's generation, and I have several cases of marriage between a man and his *iai*, or daughter in the classificatory sense.

It will be seen that there is no great severity in the matter of marriage prohibitions; and as for positive regulations I cannot find that there are at present any prescribed classes into which a man is obliged to marry. The two following examples of marriage relations within the clan were not regarded with any disapproval:

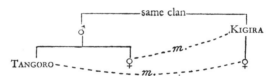

(Tangoro called Kigira *Mama* until the latter married Tangoro's sister, when he called him *Nabori*. Now Tangoro has married Kigira's daughter and therefore calls him *Atovo*. It will be noted that the wives are of the same clan as their husbands.)

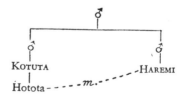

(In this case Kotuta and Haremi are respectively *bitepemi* and *biteambo* to one another, and Hotota is *iai* to her husband.)

We may be surprised at the laxity of marriage regulations,

but there is no reason to suppose that they are due to degeneracy or a modern neglect of old social laws. The above facts relate to the Aiga, and although this tribe has long been under Government control and has sent many boys to indentured labour, it has never had white residents among it and has not been under a missionary. I cannot see, therefore, what new influences as yet should have broken down the old marriage restrictions, such as they were, among the Aiga tribe.

It may be mentioned that there is in native life always a certain degree of local endogamy following as a necessary result from the tribal enmities which make it dangerous for a man to go too far afield. Among the Orokaiva, however, where the tribes are very large, this is less pronounced than in some other parts of the Territory, and it cannot have given rise to that degree of inbreeding which is found in those parts and which has been by some so seriously regarded.

Courtship. Young children are sometimes betrothed by their parents. This transaction is called *kerari*, and from the beginning the boy's father will make continual presents of food to the girl's people, by which he lays them under an obligation. The *kerari*, while perfectly regular, is relatively uncommon. Witnesses have said that it invariably implies an exchange, i.e. the adult parties to the transaction each have both a boy and a girl at their disposal. Consequently the gifts of food are in the ordinary instance reciprocal. The *kerari* betrothal will probably reach a happy ending in marriage, but it is always subject to a sudden alteration when a pubescent girl or boy begins to show wayward preferences. It is said that a parent will urge his daughter to marry the boy she is pledged to without undue delay, for fear she should take a fancy to some other and let her father down by decamping.

One is happy to say, however, that courtship usually takes a more romantic form than that of child betrothal. There is a word with a somewhat intriguing sound, viz. *kigi*, which implies clandestine meetings and love-making in the bush. A boy will go to where he knows a girl is at work in the garden, and hiding himself in the bush nearby, will break a dry twig in his fingers, so as to make just enough noise to attract her private attention. The word *kigi* would seem to apply specifically to this trick. Another way is to make the noise between lips and teeth which by ourselves is commonly associated with kissing, but which bears no such implication to the Orokaiva girl at work in the garden, as she is ignorant of this kind of blandishment. Again, in a man's *hetava* I have seen an article called *bohiva* which resembles a seed-pod but which is really a receptacle made by an insect for holding and hatching its eggs. It is dry and empty, and when pressed makes a clicking noise like a ping-pong ball. It is used expressly for *kigi*, and a little girl of eight or nine was covered with the prettiest confusion when the *bohiva* was pressed before her.

Sometimes, as we shall see, a youth and girl elope, and in that event we may assume that their previous meetings and love-makings are mostly in secret. But when there is no likely objection to the marriage, he will visit her from time to time by night in her father's house. He knows exactly where to find her, and as the matter has been pre-arranged he is not likely to meet with a rebuff. There is no actual prohibition against sexual intercourse before marriage, but it is nevertheless regarded as the proper thing for the young couple to abstain. It may seem unlikely that they do abstain, but nevertheless it has been so frequently and consistently asserted that the boy and his sweetheart sleep 'for nothing' that one must believe that the statement is at least partly true. It is quite unlikely that young men, when they realize that their questioner has nothing censorious in his attitude, should endeavour to conceal from him what they know is a matter of indifference. I am therefore convinced that there is some truth in the constant assertion of my informants that a great deal of the love-making, even the 'sleeping together', is, as we should call it, innocent.

It has been rather shrewdly suggested to me that when a youth has been courting a girl for some time, he will seduce her in order to nail her affections the more securely, and will subsequently marry her. Illegitimate children are rare. It is said to be the custom to do away with them, though this is certainly not invariable.

Except of course in the case of *kerari* there is no necessity for a 'long engagement'. In one instance a girl had asked her sweetheart to take her away and marry her quickly, as she feared that if the matter were delayed some other boy might come along and disjoin her affections from him.

An Orokaiva youth is not put to the necessity of waiting till his income is adequate to matrimony. There are no expenses of upkeep in an Orokaiva household, and it is solely a question of furnishing a bride-price, for which he will be able to draw upon his father and his sympathetic clansmen.

✦ *Marriage Ceremonies.* The actual ceremonies of marriage—such as they are—depend in some degree upon the nature of the transaction. In most cases of capture and elopement there are naturally enough no rites celebrating the first cohabitation of husband and wife: the former simply appropriates the latter or entices her to his home. In the instances—frequent as they are—where the bride's people withhold their consent or are taken by surprise, they will come in force next morning to the village to abuse husband and wife, and they may even endeavour to drag the latter away. On one occasion I saw a runaway bride very roughly handled by the women of her own village and finally led away, stripped and weeping, to her home. But in the usual instance it appears that this visit from the outraged people of the bride is nothing more than a form. They make a pretence of dragging away the woman, but they really acquiesce with a bad grace in her remaining. Thus an elderly woman of Korisata tells how she clung to a corner of her husband's house when her own people came to remove her by force. Her people returned without her and, as in all such cases, received payment in due course.

Where the bride's people do not actually lay hands on her, they may content themselves with vituperating her husband. Sometimes he is subjected to indignities of a more tangible nature. Endeavouring on one occasion to elicit something about marriage ceremonies, I began by telling my informants of the pretty customs of throwing rice and confetti; and then asked if they ever did anything of the sort themselves. This did not meet with a very encouraging response until one of the group answered with perfect seriousness that they sometimes threw human excrement at the husband. This somewhat stunning reply became more intelligible when my informants explained that this was an example of the humiliation of the bridegroom by the indignant relatives of the bride. An old man whose daughter had recently eloped, being asked if he had dealt out this treatment to the young husband, gave another surprising answer when he said, 'No, he had used the man's name to his face.' The really strict mutual tabu on the names of *atovo* and *imi* (or father-in-law and son-in-law) makes this perhaps an even graver insult than the other.

This humiliation of the bridegroom amounts to a custom (though it is not resorted to in cases of regular exchange or when the match is arranged). The wife's relatives invade the husband's village and strew it with leaves and rubbish; they damage his house and play havoc in his garden. To this vandalism the husband's village submits with the best grace possible under the circumstances, and the bridegroom sits with his head hung in shame, even while, as in one case, a potful of ashes soaked with water is capsized over it.

When, in cases of exchange or purchase, both families, i.e. bride's and bridegroom's, are consenting, there may be a definite form of welcoming the wife to her husband's village. This form, however, to which is given the name *asanga*,[1] does not always accompany even the more regular kinds of marriage, and many cases of exchange seem to be absolutely without formality. On the other hand the *asanga* may be given subsequently to a girl who has eloped, as if, from the bridegroom's side at least, to regularize the match.

For the *asanga* a platform is constructed in the village. It has no roof but flimsy walls of frayed palm-leaf. Around it are suspended numerous gaily painted sheets of barkcloth, which are presents from the husband's village to the bride, and through her to the bride's people. For three or four days (some witnesses have said as long as a month) the

---

[1] Binandele *nya-tagari*='the cooking of food', or *anumba*='the sitting down'.

bride sits here daily, and dishes of food are presented to her
by members of the husband's village. Of course she cannot
eat such a quantity of food herself but distributes it in turn
among the donors.

She does no work, nor is she bound to sit in state the
whole time. She occasionally mounts the platform during
the day, and by night sleeps indoors with her husband. At
the end of the *asanga* she is loaded with ornaments and taken
to see her husband's garden, and from then on lives the toilsome life of ordinary wifehood.

Except for these two forms, the *asanga* or welcome on the
one hand, and the dragging away of the bride and the
humiliation of the husband on the other, there are, as far
as I know, no actual ceremonies of marriage. There is
nothing in the nature of a sacrament, and nothing to cele-
brate the first married union of the couple.

Marriage Payments. The actual marriage payment takes
place after the husband and wife have been living together
for some time. The price is called *dorobu,* which, as natives
have explained, is a compound of *dora* (wealth in the shape
of ornaments) and *obu* (pots). It varies considerably in
quantity, but always comprises ornaments (*hambo*), feather-
sets (*di*), a quantity of garden food, and one or more pigs.
In one typical instance the bride-price consisted of 10 ornaments (including *peremo, hono, huave, saima*), of 38 sets of
feathers (14 of cassowary feathers, 16 of hornbill, 5 of
parrot, 1 of the Bird of Paradise, 1 of the hawk *Guvera,*
and 1 of a red and black bird *Ungaiavo*), of a great tower of
taro, bananas, and coco-nuts, and of a pig. The feather-sets
are affixed to a spear driven into the ground. The taro is
usually tied in bundles about a betel palm, or two palms
growing close together between which cross-pieces are tied
in the manner of a ladder. In many cases the whole payment is not made on one occasion. A man of Wasida, for
instance, has given six pigs for his wife in instalments of
2, 1, 1, and 2.

The payment for the bride is never an entirely private
transaction between the husband's family and the wife's.
The whole clan as well as the maternal relations will com-

monly contribute; and on the other hand the *dorobu* will be distributed among the bride's clan. At the taking over, which will be described presently, a number of more or less closely related villages will come to support both parties, donors, and recipients, and the price itself will be very liberally shared among the latter. I have seen a father of the bride on such an occasion give away to his friends all the costly ornaments which the *dorobu* comprised except for one set of hornbill beaks which he set on his own head.

In a large percentage of instances a return present of equivalent value is made by the bride's people to the bridegroom's. The bride-price is called specifically *a-dorobu*, and the 'bridegroom-price' *bi-dorobu*. *A* means vulva and *bi* penis. It would seem that where a *bi-dorobu* is given the bride herself virtually goes for nothing, because informants generally insist that the two prices are of equal value. Several explanations have been offered. It has been said that the bride's people do not like to be outdone in liberality and regard it as a creditable thing to return pound for pound; indeed they would be ashamed to make no return payment. It has also been said that the *bi-dorobu* will make the husband a better friend of his wife's people: he will be more likely to help them in their work and make them presents of food. But the usual explanation is somewhat different: if no return payment were made, the husband would be apt to ill-treat his wife, or he would feel at least that he could ill-treat her with impunity. If, however, the *bi-dorobu* had been paid, an ill-used wife might return to her parents and the husband would have no claim. In a certain case where no *bi-dorobu* was given or expected, the father of the bridegroom said that if his son beat his wife there would be no protest from the latter's family: they would say, 'Well, we have our price for her, and her husband may do as he pleases.' In one district I was told that the custom of giving a *bi-dorobu* was dying out, for nowadays the people placed reliance on the Government and thought it less necessary to insure against ill-treatment of their kinswoman in this way, viz. by making a payment to her husband.

By virtue of the *bi-dorobu*, therefore, it would seem the

wife's people retain an interest in her welfare. While we may not entirely disregard this explanation there is another and a simpler one. In many cases there is a *bi-dorobu*; in many cases there is not. It is difficult to understand why, if any of the above explanations be the real one, there should not be a *bi-dorobu* in every case. The fundamental explanation is, I prefer to believe, that the *bi-dorobu* accompanies an *exchange* (*mine*) of brides between two groups. This does not mean, of course, that the exchange is simultaneous: the second marriage which is to square the first may be deferred, but the exchange is nevertheless contemplated. In such a case the returning of *bi-dorobu* for *a-dorobu* is at least a logical transaction; whereas if there were no girl in the husband's group who could eventually be given to a boy in the wife's group, then the giving of a *bi-dorobu* equivalent to the *a-dorobu* would be a poor business proposition, for the woman would go for nothing.

Instances in which the *bi-dorobu* is refused have been explained in precisely this manner. For example, an old man of the clan Asiahije has a son and daughter. The daughter elopes with a man of the clan Koropahije, who eventually pays *a-dorobu*, because, as he explains it, there is no suitable girl in the Koropahije clan for his son to marry. So in effect he sells his daughter and keeps the price. He made it clear too that she was worth the price as she no doubt had many children inside her—an argument which was offered more than once in similar circumstances.

From an economic standpoint, therefore, the *bi-dorobu* is not compatible with actual marriage by purchase, but only with present or future exchange. This does not mean that exchange is always accompanied by *bi-dorobu*. Sometimes the exchange is made without payment on either side, i.e. without either *a-dorobu* or *bi-dorobu*. Sometimes, again, a woman may be married by purchase proper, i.e. without *bi-dorobu*, and eventually a man of her clan may marry a girl of her husband's clan. In this second marriage, which virtually completes an exchange, the circumstances of the first marriage are not forgotten and the *bi-dorobu* is withheld. Apparently characteristic of most Papuan, if not of most primitive, peoples is their love of making gifts; but not less characteristic is their habit of expecting a return. Even the friendliest and most hospitable of transactions are in the nature of a 'square deal', and marriage, whenever it is carried out regularly, is no exception to this rule.

Regular marriage is not only a contract between individual man and wife, but, economically, is a transaction between two clans. The woman passes into the ownership of her husband's clan. The communal nature of the transaction is evidenced by the fact that the clans as a whole give and receive the bride-price, and further by the fact that, as we shall see, they appear in united force at the ceremony of payment. The position of the widow is in keeping with the same idea. Having entered her former husband's clan she belongs to it after his death and may automatically become the wife of one of his 'brothers'. I have an instance of a son marrying one of his father's widows, and a fairly old one at that. The woman, however, is not in any sense bound, and in the majority of cases that I have noted her second marriage is with an outsider. In such event the payment for the widow (which is much smaller than that for a maid) goes normally to the former husband's people; though very commonly some additional payment is made to the woman's own people, who are thus paid twice for the one woman. I cannot say whether this additional payment is complimentary, or whether it may have some relation to a *bi-dorobu* paid in the first place.

Transfer of the Bride-price

The actual taking over of the bride-price, which occurs some time after the union of husband and wife, is, from the clan point of view, the legalizing of that union. There may be some considerable delay. In one case the bride's people were constantly blowing the *hui* to advertise the fact that they were still awaiting payment and to expedite a settlement by putting the bridegroom's village to shame.

When the *dorobu*—which includes a great quantity of food—has been got together, the supporting clans of the husband's people are invited to the village. Here they will

(*a*) A Bride with part of the Bride-price

(*b*) Preparations for handing over the Bride-price

PLATE XXII

meet the supporting clans of the bride's people, who come in a body to take receipt of the payment. The proceedings are very warlike. The bridegroom's clans are the first to gather, and each body as it arrives will enter the village fully armed and at the charge. This warlike manœuvre (called *esu*) is highly characteristic, and I will proceed to describe an actual instance of paying the bride-price in which the *esu* was performed with great spirit. The bridegroom belonged to the village of Totemburari, and his clansmen were awaiting the arrival of their supporters from Poho and Koninida. These latter had already joined forces on the track. Now they enter the village at a steady run uttering loud shouts, or rather a continuous roar, while the Totemburari people, who have rushed to arms at the first signs of their approach, range themselves in a close-set line facing the entrance to the village and brace themselves as if in readiness to receive an assault. The Poho and Koninida people as they draw near suddenly split into two bodies diverging to either side, and then sharply turn about and come to a halt forming one line, with the Totemburari people in the centre. Now without a pause the latter advance at the same steady run to the entrance of the village where they face about and stand glowering at the newcomers. After a few moments they charge back and occupy their previous position in the centre of the line. The whole body of warriors stands thus for a matter of five minutes while a few individuals perform excited excursions. Then their attitude suddenly relaxes and the visitors sit down and are made welcome.

These preliminary manœuvres did not compare with the actual reception of the bride's people. These, who had first collected themselves in Korisata some miles distant, entered the village in a solid phalanx. The husband's people having ranged themselves in a wide half-moon advanced to meet the charge, and considerably outnumbering the newcomers swept round either flank and took them in the rear. The Korisata faction, assailed from every direction, sometimes stood their ground and sometimes made determined sallies. The proceedings appeared to grow more and more confused, though real clashes were carefully avoided, until at length the two companies found themselves facing one another at either end of the village. While both maintained their threatening posture the leader of the Korisata party (i.e. the bride's), named Tembari, advanced across the open space and harangued the supporters of the bridegroom, pausing repeatedly to shake one or other of them by the hand. Having said his say he retired backwards, leaping and dodging from side to side, and striking the front of his shield with the handle of his stone club, evidently pretending to fence off an attack from the Totemburari party. He was followed by the latter's leader who delivered a harangue in his turn; and he again by others from either side.

These individual harangues consist for the most part of half-serious threats. The two factions have been at enmity before (probably the same could be said of any two factions among the Orokaiva clans), and it is not impossible that they may be at enmity again. One man, dancing and brandishing his spear, shouts that he once killed a man of Korisata and he may yet kill another; so let them look out. Another says the people of Totemburari and those of Korisata have fought before, and it is only the fear of the Government (touching the village constable's handcuffs with the point of his spear) that prevents them from fighting now. A vociferous old woman who holds the arena for some time informs the Korisata party that they need not imagine, because they are receiving all these gifts and this great quantity of food from the Totemburaris, that the latter were afraid of them.

Very commonly again, one may hear indignant comparisons of the present *dorobu* with some previous gift made by the one party to the other. On such an occasion old grievances may be revived and in the excitement of the moment may lead to a real clash of arms. Yet this is not often the case. As a rule the fiercest denunciations end in a smile and a hand-shake and good humour prevails over the whole scene.

When these harangues have come to an end and the overheated warriors have slaked their thirst with coco-nuts and

refreshed themselves with betel, the *a-dorobu* is set out.
Some one brings forward a spear to which are attached the
feather-sets and drives it in the ground before the high
column of taro; the *hambo* are placed on a mat, and the pig
is brought out by two of the bridegroom's people. (In the
instance I have been describing the bridegroom was one of
them.) At a word from the leader of the opposite party two
or three young men will rush forward, scale the column of
taro, and beginning from the top hand down the bunches
from one to the other. Tembari, the leader of the Korisata
party, plucks the spear out of the ground and carries it to
his own people, followed by another man of importance
with the *hambo*. The actual father of the bride, an old man,
bears no very active part, but shares out the ornaments
among various of his own party and assists in allotting the
heaps of taro. Great excitement prevails even in seemingly
unimportant details. When, for instance, the leader tells his
people to begin cooking, he shouts 'Cook your food!' four
times in rapid succession, and when they run for firewood
they hop and dance and shout themselves hoarse.

While the sharing of the *dorobu* is in progress, Tembari
faces a number of the bridegroom's people and addresses
them. He shakes hands with the bridegroom again and
again and adjures him to treat his wife kindly, not to quarrel
with her, and never to speak ill of her father and mother.
He turns to the bride and soundly scolds her for having run
away with her husband at such an early age; he reminds her
that her mother did no such thing (and harps on this subject
for a long time, while the shamefaced young bride looks at
the ground). He addresses himself with repeated hand-
shakes to several others in turn, and particularly to one
elderly man who, it appears, had the reputation of an ill-
tempered husband. Still holding him by the hand Tembari
turns to the bridegroom and cries, 'Do not be like this old
man who used to beat his wife.' At this there is a flutter of
amusement among the bystanders in which the old man in
question joins somewhat grudgingly. Tembari concludes
his address by turning suddenly, catching up a spear that is
stuck in the ground behind him, and racing back and forth

in the open space of the village with shrill cries and shouts. The old man who has gone back to sit with his people, viz. those of the bridegroom, now springs to his feet and rushes upon Tembari with rage and indignation fairly flashing out of his eyes. The two performers in this very characteristic scene swerve and avoid one another with amazing skill. The old man is shouting that his wife did not cook for him nor look after his comfort and therefore deserved to be beaten. After one or two almost hair-raising dodges the two retire from the arena in the best of good humour, the old wife-beater's face covered with smiles.

The proceedings come to an end towards evening, when after a feast the several parties disperse. Neither bride nor bridegroom has borne a part of any importance. The former has for the most part been a spectator from a house verandah.

The martial demonstrations which have been described in the foregoing pages, especially the charge and counter-charge known as *esu*, are very commonly associated with the marriage payment, but they are by no means restricted to this occasion. Nor, on the other hand, is the marriage payment always accompanied by an *esu*. It is said that where villages are entirely friendly there will be no such seemingly hostile demonstration, and that the bridegroom's people may even take payment to the village of the bride. I do not know that the *esu* is ever performed at the acceptance of a *bi-dorobu*. The occasion above described is of course that of accepting an *a-dorobu*, or bride-price.

The Four Forms of Marriage

It remains to consider and compare the four forms of marriage, or the four methods of obtaining a mate, which were named in the beginning of the chapter. It will be understood that the following remarks refer to marriage as it obtains among the Orokaiva, and are not meant neces-sarily to apply to the usages of other primitive peoples.

Marriage by capture has been of very frequent occurrence. It was the practice in cannibal raids to kill and eat the men and the older women, but to make captives of any women who were sufficiently young and attractive. It is not to be supposed that women and girls were always spared, for they sometimes met death in the heat of the moment. A very old man named Barepa enumerates ten victims of whom three were women. On the occasion of his first raid he was a mere boy, but in the scatter and pursuit he had captured a girl somewhat older than himself. When his people were mustering again he stood on the track holding her by the wrist. Up to that time he had been cherishing a youthful intention of keeping her till he should be of an age to marry, and when some of his elders laughingly said that she was too big for him and would escape he replied, 'Not she!' Next moment she had wrenched herself free and made off into the bush. Barepa gave chase, caught her, and dragging her back to the track deliberately killed her with a blow from a stone club, thereby showing his clansmen 'that he was not such a boy after all'. On another occasion he was holding a woman captive when she unexpectedly kicked him in the stomach and knocked him on to his back. Under this treatment Barepa's intentions suddenly changed and he sprang to his feet and clubbed the woman to death.

But instances in which the woman has been taken back to the raider's village and has settled down there as a wife are very common. For instance an Aiga man tells how his father and a friend had observed a Jeva Buje man in a canoe with his wife and daughter on the Kumusi. While the man remained in the canoe the two women had gone ashore to gather pandanus leaves. The two Aiga men stole upon them, clubbed the older woman and made off with the younger, while the father, hearing an uproar which he no doubt construed as a large attack, paddled for his life downstream in the direction of his village. The captive woman, who I believe still survives, became the mother of my informant.

An old woman of Sangara married originally a man of Wasida. She was subsequently captured by some of the Sauaha tribe and became the wife of a Sauaha man. In the course of a raid by Sangara upon Sauaha she was captured once more. In the confusion of flight she had leapt on a fallen log and screamed the name of her paternal uncle, who was of course a Sangara man. One of the attackers, hearing the familiar name of his fellow tribesman, bore her back to her original village and married her. This old woman, captured, recaptured, and thrice married, was found living in contented old age with her third husband. But she said she had been well enough satisfied with each in turn and refused to express any retrospective preference.

Instances could be multiplied without making the matter clearer. A captive wife is called *jigari*, which simply means 'captive'. When, as in the usual instance, she is of another tribe, she is called *baira*, a 'stranger', though this word does not necessarily connote captivity as well.

Sometimes the captive wife was allowed to bring an infant with her, and it appears that both mother and child were well treated and settled down in their new surroundings. Buninia (who was mentioned as the husband of eleven wives) captured a woman and her young daughter. He kept the latter until she grew up and then found her attractive enough to marry also.

Marriage by capture evidently did not always result in good feeling between the wife's people and the husband's. An elderly man who married his paternal uncle's widow (a captive) has never to this day visited her village, and avers that he is still afraid to do so. In another case an elderly woman never saw her people after being captured until the spread of Government control recently made it possible. Though, on the other hand, I have an instance in which the husband of a captive woman agreed to her warning her people of an impending attack; and in the making of peace between tribes such women were the recognized emissaries. This points to the possibility of compensation for the capture which would follow on or be a condition to reconciliation between the tribes; though I am unable to give an instance of such tribal compensation.

In nearly all the cases of which I know, the captive woman has come from another tribe, rather than from another clan within the tribe. That is to say she has been taken as a true prisoner of war. But I have a few instances in which a woman has been captured or abducted from one clan by another within the tribe; and in such cases it appears that the clan, in the absence of due compensation, would attempt a reprisal. A Bologosusu man killed the dog of a Sapute man. The latter enlisted the support of his friends, and together they raided the Bologosusu gardens, carried off a girl whom they found at work, and married her to one of their number. Now the Bologosusu people—with what exact intention is not clear—got together their supporters and attacked the Sapute faction, but were defeated with the loss of four killed against their opponent's two. Unfortunately I have no information as to how the matter ended, but it is hard to believe that the Bologosusu party, which is a strong one, should have allowed the matter to rest without some compensation from their near neighbours of Sapute. In another case the people of Koninida surrounded a girl of Suporasusu who was working in a garden with her brother. They decoyed the latter away and seized the girl. According to the Koninida informants the Suporasusu people were too weak to attempt a reprisal.

To sum up on the question of marriage by capture it is fair to suppose, in consideration of many examples, that capture has been since the beginning a common method of obtaining a wife among the Orokaiva. It is of course regarded as highly unsatisfactory by the wife's people unless they receive some compensation. In the event of ordinary capture in a cannibal raid on another tribe, the only likely form of compensation would be the capture of another woman in a retaliatory raid; though it is also conceivable that compensation of some sort, e.g. payment, should be made at the truces or peace-makings (*peka*) which occasionally took place between enemy tribes; of this, however, I can cite no examples.

In the event of a capture or abduction within the tribe it is, I believe, necessary to assume that some kind of adjustment, i.e. compensation by exchange or payment, would be made before the clans and villages concerned could settle down to live in their normal amity. Failing some such compensation the transaction remains economically unsatisfactory to one of the parties, and would inevitably lead to reprisal.

The same disadvantage, that of a one-sided bargain, belongs to marriage by elopement. Of this again there are many examples. It appears that a nubile girl is regarded as a valuable asset to her people and in the ideal circumstances she marries into a clan which can return another nubile girl by way of exchange. But not infrequently a girl forms a love match in an undesirable quarter, and will go to her lover's village without the consent or knowledge of her parents. It is quite common for the girl to take the initiative (for proposals may come from either side) by asking her lover to take her. Then will follow the quarrelsome scene in which the bride's people demand restitution, and in which they may succeed in reclaiming the girl. But, as we have seen, the matter is usually compromised; due compensation is made and the girl remains with her husband.

There are two ways in which the due compensation may be made, viz. either by exchange (*mine*), or by paying a bride-price (*dorobu*). I am inclined to think that marriage by exchange is the Orokaiva ideal, and the great objection to elopement is that it may frustrate the intention of exchange. I give two instances to illustrate this feeling.

A young man of Korisata eloped with a girl of Koninida. The latter's people were infuriated and at first refused to consider the proposition of payment. They abused the young husband, cried out his name to his face, called him *pureambo*, a 'loafer', and *sovai-ta-mei*, the son of a supernatural monster. Eventually, however, they came out and accepted payment. But the leader of the Koninida people went so far as to lay hands on the young daughter of the leader of the Korisata party. The latter, however, said he had no intention of letting her go as he had a son of his own whom he wished to marry off, and he meant to keep this girl so as to make a suitable exchange.

In another case a young man, backed up by his father, complained bitterly of the conduct of his sister who had run away with a lover. He wished eventually to marry himself, and had set his heart on a certain girl. He had proposed therefore to effect an exchange by giving his sister to this girl's brother. His plea is now that his own chance of marriage is seriously damaged by his sister's elopement.

From such instances as these it appears that marriage by exchange is preferable to marriage by purchase—at least in the eyes of the marriageable man, and probably also in the eyes of their elders who sympathize with their desires. We may perhaps go so far as to say that the actual buying of a wife only takes place when circumstances make present or future exchange impossible.

Exchange may take place without payment of any kind from either side; or it may be accompanied by equal payments from either side, viz. *a-dorobu* and *bi-dorobu*, which do not affect the balance. Further, there seems to be a likelihood that the *bi-dorobu* or 'bridegroom-price' is always associated at least with the expectation of an exchange; or in other words we can speak of definite purchase only when the *a-dorobu* is given and the *bi-dorobu* withheld.

We thus find that of the four kinds of marriage, Capture, Elopement, Exchange, and Purchase, the first two, while taking place very commonly, are economically unsatisfactory. With regard to capture we may assume, and with regard to elopement we may actually see, a tendency to make the affair regular by giving or extracting compensation in the form of exchange or payment, and thus striking the economic balance which is so dear to the native's heart. Capture would still be common if it were not for the *pax britannica*; elopement is still common as it is. These are both in keeping with the nature of the Orokaiva (and one presumes of any other equally warlike and primitive savage). But except in the case of two enemy tribes between whom negotiation is impossible, they tend to resolve themselves subsequently into exchange or purchase. The remarkable gestures of hostility against the husband's people which sometimes characterize Orokaiva marriage, i.e. the attempted dragging away of the bride by her people, the humiliation of the bridegroom, the damaging of his village, and the bellicose demonstrations at the taking over of the *dorobu*, all properly belong to the irregular methods of capture and elopement; they are the aftermath, the retaliation. In so far as they constitute ceremonies of regular marriage they may be survivals, symbolizing not capture itself, but the adjustment of an irregular match, as if payment were not so much given as exacted.

This is not to say that exchange or purchase necessarily and always develop from capture and elopement; or in other words that capture or elopement are the original forms of Orokaiva marriage. Friendly exchanges and convenient purchases were no doubt made at any time and quite independently. All four methods existed simultaneously, and each operated from time to time. But capture and elopement tended to be regularized as exchange or purchase; and as there is little doubt that exchange, with or without mutual payments, is preferred to a one-sided purchase, it seems therefore that whenever it was possible, exchange was the ideal form of Orokaiva marriage.

X

THE TRIBES

Partial Blending of Tribes

THE principal tribes have been already named in Chapter I. It will be understood that the list is not entirely rigid. It could be considerably amplified by mentioning minor groups such as Hunjovarehu in the Wasida tribe, Haniahaja and Ahojega in the Sauaha tribe, and Sebaga-andere in the Yega tribe; and by dividing the Sangara into fairly distinct halves, viz. Kombu-Sangara on the east, and Ato-Pekuma on the west. The large Hunjara tribe also, of which I possess only scanty information, would no doubt admit of further subdivision.

On the other hand we may not regard the nine tribes as so many water-tight compartments. Dispersal and migration have brought about some blending, and it is not always easy to draw the line between any two of the nine. There are undoubted affinities, for instance, between the Aiga and their neighbours the Hunjovarehu (of the Wasida tribe) on the south, and also between the Aiga and the Binandele of the river Mambare on the north. So again the Binandele are closely related to the Sebaga-andere of the Yega tribe: indeed, Binandele (or Bina-andere) and Sebaga-andere sometimes lay claim to a common origin.

Chinnery and Beaver have given a very full account of the wanderings of the Binandele tribe, and of others with whom it came in contact.[1] Among the Orokaiva at large, however, the subject of tribal migration is involved in truly vertiginous confusion, and a complete account of the movements of every tribe is something more than I would attempt in this life. The work of Chinnery and Beaver gives a vivid picture of the turbulent and restless life of these people, with whom migration was, in the main, a matter of attacking, fleeing, and pursuing. As the authors say, 'The whole is a typical Papuan record of battle, murder, and sudden

[1] *Annual Report*, 1914–15, pp. 158–61.

death.' All I shall attempt here is to give some further details concerning the movements of the Aiga, which, since 'the whole series of (Binandele) migrations is a pressing of the Binandele north by the powerful Aiga', may be regarded as supplementing the work of Chinnery and Beaver.

Migrations of the Aiga

The Aiga are to be partly identified with the Evije-Tombaha or Timbariundi people, names of which there are now only scattered evidences. Timbariundi would appear to be a highly contumelious nickname, for *timbari* indicates that common phenomenon among Orokaiva children, a sore between the buttocks. The Timbariundi are said to have been more than usually restless and prone to wander. They deserved the name of *sisiki popoki*, or 'vagrants', which was also applied to the miners who moved from camp to camp in this region twenty-five years ago. Their first home, as far as tradition goes back, was at Barau, in the Sauni district. Driven from here by their western neighbours, they settled in the vicinity of Aususu, and soon came into conflict with the people of Koropata. It is said that they next moved eastward to the Ahojega people, by whom they were not very cordially received, and that they then dispersed, some remaining among the Ahojega, some going to Hamara, some to the Hunjovarehu, and some back to Aususu. In the last-mentioned neighbourhood they drove out the Koropata people, and once more established themselves. There are to be seen caves in the hill-sides, difficult of access and well concealed, in which refugees of either party, Timbariundi or Koropata, would take shelter when driven from their villages.

It appears, however, that the bulk of the Timbariundi moved northward to the neighbourhood of Bogi. It was here, at a village called Anjivu, that the menfolk, seated one day in a large *oro*, were amusing themselves by beating and rubbing the floor with coco-nut shells by way of a substitute for drums. A high wind blowing without increased the noise, and the men sang lustily a meaningless song, '*Ávara bóvora, ávara bóvora*'. During a lull, while they waited for a fresh gust of wind, they were shelling betel-nuts and throwing the husks at one another. Something happened to affect the hitherto pleasant temper of the party, and they took to exchanging heavier missiles, and finally, their feelings thoroughly roused, rushed outside and commenced to fight with spears. As a result of this unnecessary quarrel the remaining Timbariundi found themselves divided into two factions, and when in due course they moved northwards again, some settled on the Kumusi and others on the Opi; and, whether there be any truth in this legend or no, there is still some trace of antagonism between the Aiga on the Kumusi side and those on the Opi side.

We need not suppose that these simple traditions about the Timbariundi will adequately account for the origin of the Aiga tribe. That tribe is more likely to be of a composite origin, and the Timbariundi to form merely one of the component elements. Such evidence as there is, however, all points to the south for the former home of the Aiga.

When they reached what is their present territory they found it occupied by Binandele people, especially by a branch of them called Kiriri Gaimoda. It appears that at first the Aiga and the Kiriri Gaimoda settled together, but that when quarrels subsequently disturbed their friendship the former drove the latter 'like pigs' out of the district. Several explanations, some of them trivial (but not too trivial to be true when we remember how quick-tempered a man is the Orokaiva), account for the quarrel between Aiga and Binandele. We are told that an Aiga was overheard playing a reed pipe in solitude, and that some people called Ponadu saw in this a splendid opportunity and killed him. Subsequently a party of Aiga were guests at a Kiriri Gaimoda feast, and seeing a Ponadu man there killed him by way of revenge. This led to bad blood between hosts and guests, and after many quarrels the former were driven out. Another explanation has it that an Aiga pig trespassed upon a Kiriri Gaimoda garden and was speared (and this oft-repeated circumstance has been a fruitful cause of serious quarrels). But several times repeated I have heard the same odd explanation, viz. that the trouble arose over a pet parrot, some having it that the parrot was owned by an Aiga man and killed by a Binandele boy, others that the parrot was owned by a Binandele man and bitten by an Aiga dog.

It is certain, however, that a previous Binandele population were driven out by the Aiga, some of the fugitives settling on the lower Kumusi, others on the Mambare.

Subsequent quarrels among the Aiga, with constant repetition of the inter-clan fighting called *embogi*, finally led some of the Aiga to migrate northwards and rejoin the Binandele. It is said that these refugees in their anxiety to escape killed the old folk who impeded their progress and left them behind decorated with feathers but unburied. But a milder version of the same incident relates that one of the refugees taking his wife with him was so embarrassed by the clamorous grief of his *imboti*, or mother-in-law, that he silenced it by striking her dead with his club. There are now some Aiga clans represented among the Binandele, as there are also Aiga clans represented among the Hunjovarehu. And if any value can be attached to names, it would appear from cases in which they correspond that some of the clans are widely scattered among other tribes.

Legends of Origin and Dispersal of Tribes

I must confess to having no settled theory as to the movements of the tribes at large. There has evidently been a northward drift in comparatively recent times affecting the Aiga, the Binandele, and other peoples referred to by Chinnery and Beaver; but without reliable information (which I cannot supply) as to the movements of the other tribes, it is impossible to say whether this northward trend has been general.

Several legends (with many variations) are current as to the origin of the Orokaiva. In the south it is said that all the peoples issued from a hole in the ground or a cave situated somewhere in the Hydrographers, and that the first to emerge were the Orokaiva, who brought the taro with them, and left the yam and sweet potato for the mountaineers.

But the other stories point rather to a northern provenance. One of the best known of Orokaiva legends concerns a man-monster named Totoima who was in the habit of slaying all whom he met. His sister (or wife), however, while at work in her garden cut her finger on a leaf of sugar-cane and caught the blood in a leaf of taro. Wrapping this up she hid it away in a pot where it was transformed into two children, or, as other versions say, a great number of boys and girls. These children grew up, and with the assistance of their 'mother' managed to dispatch the tyrannical Totoima; after which they waxed in numbers and became the present Orokaiva people. It is only in some versions of the story, however, that these miraculous children born in the pot are made the nucleus of the Orokaiva. The legend necessarily presupposes a previous population on which Totoima could practise his persecutions, and in the more usual version the remnant of these people come flocking in from their hiding-places to devour various parts of the monster's body, and in consequence acquire the several dialects of the Orokaiva tongue. As for any light which this legend might throw on the provenance of the people, it may be said that, although the knowledge of the tale is as widespread as the actual depredations of Totoima are supposed to have been, it is associated especially with the river Gira, where the scenes of the monster's dramatic downfall are pointed out.

Another legend, associated with the Gira or the Waria (though more commonly with the latter), tells of a thickly populated inland water. Two youths, usually called Garia[1] and Simono, build a canoe on this lake in a miraculously easy manner, and then make an outlet by which the water flows to the sea in the form of a river—either the Waria or the Gira according to the rendering of the tale. Garia and Simono proceed down the river on their canoe, followed by a number of people who subsequently spread over the plain as Orokaiva. In another version, which differs rather widely from the above, the canoe is made by one Korevaja who, while travelling on it, pleads with his friends to hit him on

---

[1] Probably the same word as Waria.

the head with a stone club and throw him overboard. At last one of them consents reluctantly to do this, and Korevaja topples overboard and sinks. As he does so innumerable bubbles rise and turn into human beings who disperse themselves as the Orokaiva tribes.

In the fourth of these legends, a woman Buda lives alone with her husband Menina on the Waria river. Over their house grows a tall *Bendoro* tree, and every morning the woman must take her broom and sweep up a litter of fallen leaves. But she complains of the loneliness of their life, and one day at her work she wishes that men and women were as numerous as the *Bendoro* leaves. Next morning when she and her husband come out of their house they find no leaves but myriads of people. The woman Buda forthwith classifies these into the various tribes, presents them with weapons and implements of Orokaiva material culture, and sending them off to their respective regions, from Kokoda down to the salt water, bids them fight and wage war on one another, and make truces when they tire of fighting—instructions which they have carried out with much fidelity.

Individuality of the Tribe

These legends are as much concerned with the division of the Orokaiva into tribes as with their origin. The actual division into tribes is probably due in the first instance to kinship and clan grouping; but this is reinforced by local grouping, and eventually the local group, owing to the vagaries of settlement and migration, is found to comprise a variety of clan groups. Relative isolation serves to consolidate the tribe, to create a few idiosyncrasies of custom, and to give it a distinct dialect. But what more than anything else gives individuality to the tribe is the almost perpetual state of war with its neighbours. The tribe, therefore, is defined by (1) a common territory, (2) certain idiosyncrasies of custom, (3) a distinct dialect, and (4) its common enmities.

(1) It will not be necessary to deal at any length with the subject of tribal territory. The boundaries on the map are rough and ready. It will be seen that the distribution differs

slightly from that of Chinnery and Beaver,[1] but principally by a slight amplification. I have divided their Dobodura tribe into three, Sauaha, Sangara, and Dirou; and I have given the name Jeva-Buje to that branch of the Binandele inhabiting the lower Kumusi. By the addition of minor tribal names, such as are mentioned on p. 151, the matter would be complicated and not helped.

In one instance, that of Sauaha (and perhaps we might say in another, that of the Binandele and the Jeva-Buje), the tribal territory is not continuous, but in the others there is a fairly well-defined local spirit which belongs to a solid block of territory. This local spirit, which was in evidence among the clans (*vide* p. 107), is certainly of some moment. It is probably the principal motive behind the minor tribal groups and the temporary clan confederacies within the tribe. When, for instance, a number of clans band together to support one of their number in a semi-warlike dispute, it is, I have been told, because they are *pusu tahavo*, 'one ground', and, therefore, natural allies.

Although the boundaries on the map make it appear that the tribal territories are coterminous, there is commonly a no-man's-land of greater or less extent. This is particularly marked in the case of the Aiga, who (while in close touch with the Jeva-Buje) are separated from their other neighbours on north, east, and west by a good half-day's journey through virtually uninhabited country. In the more densely populated southern end of the division this territorial isolation is not so complete.

(2) Certain tribal peculiarities have been spoken of already in Chapter I. On the whole we may wonder at their absence rather than their presence. It is sometimes possible to distinguish men of different tribes merely by differences in their dress and ornaments. The Binandele commonly wear the bark-cloth perineal band with the end tied in a knot at the belt; the bush people in general have it suspended as an apron. The Aiga are said to be fond of the streamers of thin betel-palm spathe attached to the tags of their hair. The Tain-Daware and other coastal people especially affect

[1] *Annual Report*, 1914–15, p. 161.

the *huave*, a breast ornament of two circles of white shell. When Totoima's sister split up the people into tribes she allotted them various distinctive ornaments. To the Sauaha she gave the black feathers of the hornbill; to the Sangara the red feathers of *Ungaiavo*, *Orero*, and *Samba*; to the Aiga red-dyed betel spathe, *saima* (or small white cowrie) shells, and dog's teeth; and to the Yega the *tava* or palm-wood digging stick. The legend, of course, merely indicates that the men of these tribes show a modern preference for the articles named.

But these fashions are by no means exclusive, and perhaps the distinctions are little more real than those peculiarities of temper which are said to have come into being when the various peoples feasted on Totoima's body. In a version of the story given by an old Yema man the participants in the feast were mostly Waria people: the Bia and Mawai had eaten his legs, and were consequently speedy runners; the Yema themselves had eaten his entrails, and were therefore subject to stomachic disturbances which were the direct cause of a fierce temper; the Ono (?) had eaten his genitalia, and were highly erotic; the Jia had eaten froth or saliva, and therefore their language was unintelligible; the Gilita (who formerly occupied the present Binandele territory) had eaten his spleen, and were sullen men who used their spears more readily than their tongues; and the Berepo (i.e. the Aiga and other bush people of the Orokaiva) had eaten his head and mouth, and were therefore 'strong talkers', quarrelsome and abusive.[1]

(3) The eating of Totoima's body is generally made to account for nothing more than differences of dialect. There is a remarkable insistence in many renderings of the story upon the bubbles (*horo*), i.e. of froth, saliva, or grease, which in a manner not easily understood arose from the monster's body before or during cooking. In one version the refugees came flocking in when they heard of Totoima's death, and when they found him roasting or basting on the hot stones they fell to and lapped up the bubbles of scalding grease.

[1] In Wasida the story of Totoima is told of one Kokowaiko. *Vide* Chinnery and Beaver, *loc. cit.*, p. 161.

After that, as one might almost expect, they began to speak in different tongues.

The tribal vocabularies have been compared by Chinnery and Beaver.[1] They have been commonly called varieties of Binandele, not because Binandele is known to be the original or nearer to an original than any of the others, but because it has been more closely studied. The Rev. Copland King put together a vocabulary of this dialect which was published in 1901,[2] and it has since been mastered by members of the Anglican Mission. The dialects are mutually intelligible to the natives, though not always without difficulty. To a European they sound very different, and a knowledge of one does not imply a speaking knowledge of another.

Natives have their own way of classifying the tribes (or some of them) according to dialect. There is a word *midia*, which means 'There you are!' or *voilà!*; and natives will refer to the Wasida tribe as *Mitia* people, the Sangara and Sauaha tribes as *Mihia* people, the Hunjara tribe as *Mihja* people, and the Aiga as *Midia* people. (Binandele and Yega people apparently do not use the word.)

The Hunjara tribe is very commonly called *Aha-maha*, from their distinctive manner of pronouncing the words for 'mother' and 'father', which the other tribes find somewhat amusing. An informant will go on to explain that the Binandele are *Aiaha-mamaha*, the Aiga *Aja-mama*, the Yega *Aia-mama*, and the Sauaha and Sangara *ajaha-mamaha*. (The Wasida use the word *enau* for 'mother'.)

Somewhat remarkable is the fact that at least four different words are used to name the ghost (or the spirit of the dead, or, again, the supernatural monster, which comes under the same category). Among the Aiga the word is *sovai*; among the Binandele and Yega *binei*; and among the Hunjara *siango*. The other tribes appear to use either *siango* or *embahi*. I do not know that there are any distinctive differences between the ideas of the several tribes on this point,

---

[1] *Loc. cit.*, pp. 162 ff.
[2] *Vocabulary of the Binandele Dialect, spoken by the Natives of the Mamba River, British New Guinea* (D. S. Ford, Sydney, 1901). New Edit., 1927.

and believe that each of the four words is applicable to the same loose concept.

(4) The fourth of these features, which lend individuality to the tribe, is the fact that it is constantly at enmity with various of its neighbours, and that in the fighting which so frequently ensues it is a unit and not divided against itself. It is not to be imagined, of course, that the component clans of any tribe remained at permanent peace with one another, for that is hardly in Orokaiva nature. But inter-clan fights were not characterized by the deliberate blood-thirstiness of the tribal raid, and they resulted in comparatively few casualties. Furthermore—what is an important distinction —there was never, except in the most abnormal instances, any cannibalism within the tribe. The inter-clan fight is called *embogi*, and the raid or tribal expedition *isoro*. Most of the fighting described in the following chapter will be of the latter kind, in which men of one tribe attack those of another. Friends or allies are called *toho* and enemies *ki-toho*, and although the friendship or affinity between certain tribes allowed the use of the former word, it would be fair to say that in most cases the tribes were mutually *ki-toho*.

We are justified in adding a fifth essential in the delimitation of the tribe, viz. the recognition of a common name. I have already spoken (p. 2) of the difficulty of naming ethnic units. In the largest groups, as we see them, there is no recognition within the group itself of a common name; but as we descend the scale we reach a point where such a name comes into use, where the members of the group are able to say 'We are so and so'. Among the Orokaiva we reach this stage when we come to the tribes. They are in fact the largest units which are able consistently to name themselves. I would suggest therefore that the use of a common name, implying as it does a recognition of unity, is a very essential factor in the individuality of the tribe.

XI

WARFARE

THE Orokaiva have had something of a reputation as a fighting people, though others no doubt could dispute their claim to the doubtful distinction of being the most savage in the Territory. The fame of the Orokaiva in this respect is probably due to the resistance, more than usually determined, which they made against the miners some thirty years ago; and it is certain that they have held a more independent and fearless attitude toward the whites than is seen among many other Papuans. Among themselves they were bellicose in the extreme. Every village was on the *qui vive* against attack, and, except during the periods of rather ticklish peace and uncertain friendship, was probably joining in some plan of concerted aggression.

Although the title of this chapter is Warfare, the following pages will deal with indiscriminate fighting and killing as well as with the regular raid. There was no idea of sporting equality of chance when the Orokaiva was bent on killing. I have already given one or two random instances in which the solitary stranger was put to death as a matter of course. It may be fairly doubted whether a party of primitive Orokaiva meeting a lone stranger would hesitate to kill him any more than they would hesitate to kill a bush-pig. Nor does the warrior think it beneath his dignity to kill a woman. One is surprised at the pride which a man evidently takes in the slaughter of defenceless victims. A certain Pahua of Soroputa (one of the early village constables who still wears his uniform) accounted for three victims before he became a guardian of the law. The first was made on a raid on the Hunjovarehu people. The attackers having surrounded the village by night rushed it at morning; Pahua found a man sitting down engaged in eating his breakfast, and speared him before he had time to rise. His second victim was one of a fishing party caught at a disadvantage; Pahua speared his man in the side and he fell into the water. His third victim was a woman. Long previously Pahua had lost a brother killed by the Hunjovarehu people and was naturally nursing his revenge. It now happened that a Hunjovarehu woman, sister-in-law to one of Pahua's countrymen, was visiting his village of Soroputa. Pahua was informed that she was asleep in a house, so he stole in, speared the sleeping woman in the breast and struck her on the head with a club. He was not ashamed but proud of this exploit, which satisfied his long-delayed vengeance.

Inter-Clan Fighting

The raid, or concerted fight, may involve different tribes or merely different clans of the same tribe. I have already explained the general difference between the former engagement (*isoro*) and the latter (*embogi*), which is a comparatively trivial affair. It appears that the *esu*, an example of which has been described in connexion with the marriage payment, may upon small provocation develop into an *embogi*. Many such affrays took place during my stay among the Aiga, though I was only fortunate enough to witness one of them. This occurred at the taking over of a marriage payment. The charging and counter-charging had given place to the individual harangues in which old grievances were discussed with some bitterness. The excitement seemed to have died away, and the pig had already been killed when an inopportune taunt set the whole village in an uproar. Both parties rushed to arms and were immediately involved in a confused conflict with three or four lively vortices. In a scuffle of this kind there is a great deal of sham. The participants rejoice in the loud impact of their spears and clubs upon one another's shields, but they are not out to kill. Minor wounds are common, though they are concealed if possible from the Government. In the above-mentioned case I must report, almost with regret, that we succeeded in quelling the uproar before it had reached a more interesting stage. The most difficult to pacify were the women, who,

Esu performed at a Funeral

PLATE XXIII

while doing little actual violence with their *poreha* or quarter-staffs, were very successfully inciting to violence with their tongues.

The *esu*, as I have said, is not associated invariably with a marriage payment. On the recent occasion of a death, when some clans gathered as mourners, they soon found themselves engaged in a hand-to-hand fight which resulted in one serious casualty. There is a semi-traditional account of a quarrel between two branches of the Koie-Bumana people who formerly inhabited a portion of the present Tain-Daware district. One party visiting the village of the other at a feast caused some amusement by their efforts at dancing. 'You are like cassowaries', said their hosts. 'And anyway, why have you come? There are no girls for you here.' The guests retorted that their hosts danced with the elegance of flying-foxes, and challenged them to a tug-of-war with a long rattan cane. This contest proving indecisive, the two parties seized their weapons and took to fighting in earnest, with the ultimate result that, weakened by their own quarrels, they were exterminated or driven out by the Tain-Daware.

There are many causes of inter-clan strife—the depredations of village pigs, the killing of a dog, the defilement of a water-supply, and frequently the suspicion of sorcery. But such quarrels lead to the *embogi*, which is usually more of a lusty sham fight than a struggle to the death; and only in the most exceptional cases do we hear of cannibalism. In the feud between the Aiga clans on the right and left banks of the Kumusi there was eating of corpses on both sides. But this was spoken of as a horrible thing, that speakers of one and the same language should eat each other.

The Tribal Raid

The tribal fight (*isoro*) probably involves an expedition in which a number of clans combine. The war signal—either for the alarm or the assembly, for both mean the same thing—is a fast-throbbing rhythm on the *hui*, called onomatopoeically '*kikiki*. . . .' (In these days of peace the same signal announces the arrival of a Government patrol, though the alarm is happily less acute.) The attacking force having assembled by day usually travels by night, with the intention of surrounding the devoted village and surprising it at dawn. These tactics, however, are not invariable: the raiders are better satisfied with random victims, such as an isolated fishing party.

It was customary for women to accompany the expedition carrying pots of food; and they might even stand by their husbands as armour-bearers. Sir William MacGregor, ascending the Kumusi in 1894, noted that 'The men carried generally a spear and a shield each, with a woman behind him bearing two or three spears. The women were ablebodied, and unaccompanied by children or small boys. Apparently they were simply armour-bearers.'[1] Again, on the same river in 1895 he met many armed natives, 'the warrior being frequently followed by a woman carrying part of his panoply, or ready to relieve him of his arms when he was induced to dispense with them'.[2] The women were always ready to urge on the fighting men and even to mingle in the fray, as W. E. Armit found when in conflict with the natives of Papangi. For then, when the warriors rushed to the attack among the long grass, cheered on by the shrill cries, 'Cheep! Cheep! Cheep!', of their women-folk, it was found when they were finally beaten off that two of the women lay dead with spears in their hands.[3]

Villages were often built on hill-tops (where there were any hills) by way of defence, and many such sites are marked by clusters of coco-nut palms in the Tain-Daware district. In these easy-going times they have been abandoned for more accessible positions. Tree-houses (savai) were built as refuges in emergency, and, as they contained an armoury of spears and (it is said) a supply of food, water, and firewood, they enabled the refugees to hold out until help came from their neighbours. In their tree-houses the natives were for the time being secure enough, for an enemy armed with nothing more than the spear could not safely venture within striking distance. An interesting incident of the early days

---

[1] *Annual Report*, 1893–4, p. 34.   [2] *Ibid.*, 1895–6, p. xvii.
[3] *Ibid.*, 1899–1900, p. 91.

shows how much confidence the native felt in his retreat. In the Sisarita district Mr. Armit with his police and carriers entered what was apparently a recently evacuated village. Finding a tree-house in a garden, one of his carriers swarmed up the ladder intent on the search for loot, only to come howling down minus the index finger of one hand. Putting his hand on the airy threshold of the *savai*, which he took to be unoccupied, the unlucky carrier had received a blow from a stone which crushed off two joints of his finger. The still more unlucky refugee, who had no doubt hoped to escape detection, now began 'a lively bombardment with stones and spears' of a constable and several carriers, and, after frustrating all other attempts at capture by the constable, was finally shot—an end to the fray which perhaps astonished him in the rather pathetic security of his tree-house.[1]

Among the coastal people, when the villagers were at work in their inland gardens, sentries were posted on the beaches to guard against attacks from the sea. Sir William MacGregor, approaching several large villages below Oro Bay, found that his arrival was anticipated. 'Before we got within a couple of miles of the first one it was evident that the inhabitants had discovered our presence, and were preparing for our first visit to them. The glass showed the men to be assembling together, all dressed in paint and feathers, each man armed with shield and spear, as well as with a stone club. One man came toward us along the beach at full speed, and at about a mile from the village took two armed warriors from a post in the bush, where they had clearly been stationed as sentries. The three men then ran towards the village as hard as they could, and all the warriors of the tribe concentrated on one spot on the sandy beach.'[2] Among inland tribes the sentry was posted in the branches of a tall tree. One such overlooked the Kumusi near Bogi, and here for months on end two men were perched, one 75 feet, the other about 120 feet, from the ground, watching for carriers and police as they passed on the opposite bank.[3] False alarms were not unknown, as

[1] *Ibid.*, 1899–1900, p. 92.   [2] *Ibid.*, 1893–4, pp. 2, 3.   [3] *Ibid.*, 1900–1, p. 54.

these sentries, like others, had a way of 'seeing things'. A Tain-Daware man had on several occasions called in his fellow-villagers to beat off an attack of what proved to be merely *binei*.

It seems that in certain cases at least the village was provided with some kind of stockade, though no trace of these defences remains to-day. As a last point may be mentioned the miniature spear-pits (see p. 49) with which the paths were sometimes beset. They are mentioned as occurring in the Kokoda district, often beside a tree-trunk that has fallen across the path, so that the unwary might step over the log and into the trap. Several of the police had their feet spiked in this manner.[1] Near Bogi, again, Mr. Alec Elliot, attacking a force of natives established in a strong position on the opposite side of a garden, found this garden to be 'one mass of small spears and spear-pits'.[2]

Peace-Making

The lively monotony of warfare was broken by intervals of peace. A truce-making was called *peka*, and the first emissaries were women who, born members of one tribe, had married into or been captured by the other. In some cases it would seem that hostages (*otavo*, lit. 'friend' or 'mate') were exchanged. Two or three from either side would spend a few days and nights with the opposite party, and after this the two tribes would meet in armed force on some common ground between their territories to exchange gifts of pigs and ornaments. The proceedings even of a peace-making bore a characteristically warlike appearance, and sometimes the parties who had met to conclude a truce ended by joining in battle again.

It would seem that the position of the hostages was by no means secure, and the idea of exchanging them was to make sure of revenge if one party were done to death. There are tales of the meanest treachery. When after the conclusion of a *peka* a number of Hunjovarehu men had brought gifts to Wasida to make good the damage done in a previous raid, they were hospitably entertained and accom-

---

[1] *Annual Report*, 1899–1900, p. 93.   [2] *Ibid.*, 1900–1, p. 12.

modated over night, but in the early morning while sitting at their breakfast they were set upon and killed to a man. In comparatively recent times a party of five Waria men, having made peace with the Government, thought it safe to visit their Yema neighbours on the Gira. They were sitting about a dish of stew when five Yema men, having been methodically told off to their respective tasks, fell upon the five unsuspecting visitors and clubbed them to death.[1] It would seem indeed that these peace embassies miscarried somewhat frequently. W. N. Beaver noted that the particular homicidal ornament called *Horu* was 'a croton worn in the hair by a man who had killed a peace herald'.[2]

Resistance against the Whites

It is sometimes suggested that Papuan natives in general are cowardly, or at least that they do not care to stand up to one another in pitched battle. It is true that when bent on securing victims they are content with the easiest they can find; and that in most of the engagements of which we hear, one side is surprised, hopelessly outnumbered, put to flight, and massacred. It is certain, however, that when armed with their shields the Orokaiva will fight man to man with the greatest skill and address, and, I am prepared to believe, with the greatest daring. Even the way in which they deal with the perils of their environment should be sufficient to refute any suspicion of cowardice; and any fear they may have had of the white intruder is surely excused by the facts that the white man was to them nothing short of a supernatural marvel and that he possessed irresistible means of killing.

But the truth is that they resisted the Government and the miners with a determination that we can now only admire, and that they sometimes fought against armed police with astonishing fury and recklessness. Many instances in the *Annual Reports* from 1895 to 1901 show the native as a brave fighter, but none perhaps surpass that in which Mr. de

---

[1] For this one man Poivo was given six months in Port Moresby. To his first child born after his return he gave the name Garuma (stone) because he had been engaged in cracking stones in goal.

[2] *Annual Report*, 1918-19, p. 98.

Moleyns and his police were attacked in 1901 near Bogi on the Kumusi.[1] He, with a party of seventeen police, and a native corporal, with a party of five, sallied out against the hostile tribesmen, but 'Both simply couldn't make any distance; the natives were so numerous and harassed them every yard they went'. Returning, 'the natives followed them right back to the village and threw spears again from every track notwithstanding there were many dead on each track. This fighting, which was not of a desultory character but continuous and determined, lasted from 3.30 till dark'. Mr. de Moleyns estimated the attacking force at between 400 and 500; and it was thought that not one of the 200 rounds fired by the police was at a greater distance than 50 yards. One of these rounds, at any rate, fired from a Martini Enfield, is claimed to have gone through three men rushing in from a by-track, and another is claimed to have gone through two. Altogether, making allowance for a *soupçon* of exaggeration in the account, it seems obvious that the natives behaved in a very brave, even desperate, manner.

The Aiga people about Korisata tell a rather amusing story of their first acquaintance with Europeans. A party of miners, with an escort of a few armed police, had pitched their tents on the Upper Opi, and a number of inquisitive savages went to investigate this strange encampment. Among them was a man Kaiora who tells the tale of his adventure with considerable gusto. Watching the camp with his friends he observed several of the miners' signed-on boys who wore *rami*, or short calico skirts. Seeing these *rami*, which in the distance he mistook for the bark-cloth skirt worn by Orokaiva women, Kaiora leapt to the conclusion that the miners' boys *were* women. With a number of others he set off in pursuit, and for greater speed discarded his spear and club, so that he out-distanced his companions. For a moment he had lost sight of the 'women' and was peering about in the bush to see which way they had gone when he suddenly felt himself grasped from behind, and beheld the totally new spectacle of a uniformed policeman. Others came to the policeman's assistance, and

[1] *Annual Report,* 1900–1, pp. 55, 56.

Kaiora was hastily bound hand and foot to a pole like a pig. Now a white man—the first Kaiora had ever seen—made his appearance, and putting a gun to his shoulder fired a shot in the air. This was presumably to scare away the other Aiga who were not far off, but the prisoner, whether in the moment's distraction caused by the firing of the shot or in a sudden paroxysm of fear at the loud noise, wriggled or burst out of his bonds and made good his escape. The whole party of Aiga had for some reason fled, and were halted in an open space discussing the alarming situation and the loss of one of their number. Suddenly the flying figure of Kaiora appeared in the clearing, and on sight of him the whole body of Aiga set up a shout of terror and fled again, leaving the unhappy fugitive still far behind. Kaiora, a man of early middle age, is marked by premature greyness and an extraordinary wildness of eye which might well date from the time of this terrifying experience. According to himself he gave his friends, when he finally overtook them, an account of this new kind of human being and advised them to put aside their weapons and make peace. Disregarding this good counsel, however, they subsequently stole a cache of food left in a tent by the miners. For the rice and flour they had no use, but the tins of meat were punctured with stone tomahawks and their contents shaken out. This act of depredation brought an expedition from Ioma, and three Aiga men were shot dead. From then on they had a still better reason for fearing the white men, and they accordingly made no desperate resistance but a very sensible peace. I do not know whether we can accept this conclusion to my informant's story, though the rest of it is circumstantial enough to be true. The Aiga were as troublesome as any other tribe to the early whites, indeed it has been said that '. . . the people on the Opi river, between the Mambare and the Kumusi . . . were the worst offenders'; and they are described as 'truculent and aggressive'.[1] On the whole we may conclude that the Aiga as well as the other Orokaiva tribes made a very brave resistance against the white intruders.

[1] J. H. P. Murray in *Papua or British New Guinea*, p. 330.

Reasons for Raiding

The reasons for the inter-clan fighting are easy to understand: they are in the main nothing more than quarrels between hot-blooded neighbours. The reasons for the deliberate raid or *isoro*, which involves cannibalism, are not so obvious. Very commonly the raid was meant to avenge some previous victim, for vengeance was absolutely imperative to the relatives of a slain man; and the expression for revenge itself is an interesting one, viz. *diroga-mine*, or an 'exchange of *diroga*', the latter meaning the spirit of a man slain in fight in contradistinction to the spirit of one who has died in any other way. Instances of compounding are apparently rare, and it may be (though I cannot speak with certainty) that the practice of compounding for death obtains between clans only, and not between tribes. The compensation or blood-price, consisting of pigs and ornaments, is called *dorobu*, which word stands also for marriage payment. Between tribes, however, who normally stand in the mutual relation of *kitohu* it would seem that such amicable settlement is rare if not impossible. To show how imperative is the need for revenge I may mention the former rule that the widow of a man slain by an enemy tribe must continue her seclusion until the capture and killing of a man from that tribe made it possible for her to emerge from it.

I cannot find any binding ceremonial necessity for a raid other than the one just mentioned (and that is really a reason for returning a raid, not for making one in the first place). It appears that the corpses of victims were used in payment for marriage, either *a-dorobu* or *bi-dorobu*, or for gifts between relatives. But this was probably a matter of convenience: I have no evidence that a corpse was *necessarily* part of the marriage payment. Then again there is the matter of homicidal insignia. Although these are sometimes called *otohu* in common with the *otohu* given at initiation (*vide* pp. 201 ff.), it is not to be supposed that the latter were necessarily homicidal, i.e. that the killing of an enemy was demanded before a youth or girl could pass through the ceremony of receiving an *otohu*. In short, I do not know of any ceremonial necessity, other than that implied by revenge, which demanded a cannibal raid.

Cannibalism

The reason for cannibalism itself has been given by natives as the simple desire for good food. Indeed, we might profitably seek to explain why some people are *not* cannibals rather than why some people are. Anthropologically speaking the fact that we ourselves should persist in a superstitious, or at least sentimental, prejudice against human flesh is more puzzling than the fact that the Orokaiva, a born hunter, should see fit to enjoy perfectly good meat when he gets it. The aversion from cannibalism within the tribe is presumably to be ascribed to the same sentimental reason which, with a wider scope, turns us against human flesh in general. It was the custom to eat all victims made in an *isoro*, and they were only abandoned when the fear of counter-attack made the raiders leave in too great a hurry to be encumbered, or, as some informants have said, when the victims were so old, scraggy, and wrinkled as to be not worth the carrying.

When the victorious raiders returned they announced their success from afar off by a distinctive rhythm on the *hui* which (according to Aiga informants) may be represented thus:

— — – —, — — – — —.

There were conventional songs proper to the occasion, such as (an Aiga example),

Eruga tune	*kambaja-one*
Eruga leaf	seasoning
Isuga tune	*kambaja-one*
Isuga leaf	seasoning

by which the women were given to understand that they should prepare 'cabbage' for the cooking; or (a Sangara example)

Umo tihue kiari-ta koiko-ta,

which indicated that the enemy had fled (*koiko*), anxious to see (*kiari*) the familiar place where they drew water (*umo tihu*). The men who had not themselves secured victims would sing (another Sangara example),

U *sina nane arako, u sina nane,*

'Mine was like a water-fight', by which they meant that they had fought as ineffectually as children bathing and splashing one another with water.

The corpses of grown men were tied by hands and feet to a pole and carried face downward. In the case of a child one hand was tied to one foot, and a warrior would sling the body over his shoulder as a hunter might a wallaby's. Usually, perhaps always, the victim was dead before he was bound in this manner.

An ingenious, if gruesome, method of carrying human flesh was actually observed by a former Resident Magistrate in the Division.

'The limbs had been peculiarly treated. The ankle-joints had been severed, leaving the tendon Achilles intact. The bones of the leg had then been excised, and the pelvical bone removed. The ham had been neatly cut off. The boneless leg was wrapped carefully round a three-foot stick, and the foot secured to the stick by a piece of vine. In this manner the flesh could be carried comfortably on one's back.' [1]

Informants have said that no captives except desirable women, and sometimes little children, were allowed to live: it was a safer thing to kill them outright to prevent all chance of escape. There was, as far as I am aware, no such thing as torture, and the suggestion that one of the infant captives might be kept and fattened like a pig against some future occasion was regarded as horrible: how would it be thinkable to kill a child that was already calling its captives *aja* and *mama*?[2] True torture, as far as I am aware, was never practised, though C. A. W. Monckton, as Resident Magistrate of the North-Eastern Division, writes: '. . . the Dobodura attacked and defeated the Notu, driving them from

---

[1] W. E. Armit, in *Annual Report*, 1899–1900, quoted by J. H. P. Murray in *Papua or British New Guinea*, pp. 331, 332.

[2] Chinnery and Beaver, however, recount an incident in which the Yema 'killed a Gilita boy named Omba, who had been captured when very young, tied him up', and sent the body to the Binandele (*Annual Report*, 1914–15, p. 159). But here the case is somewhat different. Yema and Binandele were in alliance against the Gilita, and the Yema had just received a present of a pig from the Binandele.

their villages and subjecting such prisoners and wounded men that fell into their hands to such fearful tortures that the Notus were panic-stricken, deserted their villages, and appealed to me for help.'[1] It seems probable, however, that this passage refers rather to mutilations than to an intentional infliction of pain, which, indeed, the oldest informants affirmed was never a feature of the raid.

Brought home by the raiders the corpse of the victim was set upright in the village, still attached to its pole. During the night there was dancing to the accompaniment of *hui* and drum—properly the largest and most old-fashioned of the drums, viz. the *ino*. In the morning the body was taken down to the stream and cut up in the running water, in order, as I was told, to wash away the blood. Various portions were distributed as they are in the case of a pig, and little odds and ends were given to the children, who played at roasting them in the fires.

It was formerly the custom, I understand, to set up skulls of victims on a *gaga* or small platform in the village, just as pig-jaws are to be seen nowadays ranged along a branch of an old croton scrub. The pig-jaws are mainly in the nature of trophies, though it is said that to throw them away and lose sight of them would have an ill effect on hunting thereafter. I cannot say what were the motives for keeping human skulls, but presumably the same reasons would hold good.

Tabus and Purification of the Slayer

The actual slayer abstained from eating any of the victim's body. This rule was rigidly observed, though no satisfactory reason could be given. It may be remarked that the owner of a pig never eats any part of it when it is presented to another at a feast and distributed. But this seems to be no more than a point of etiquette, and perhaps offers no parallel. Beaver, who lays stress on the fact that the slayer must not eat of the slain, adds: 'Small portions of the liver, ceremonially treated with symbolic herbs, may be *bitten* into by the actual killer;'[2] though of this he does not record any explanation. It is tempting to suggest that by this rite the

[1] *Annual Report*, 1902–3, p. 33.   [2] *Ibid.*, 1918–19, p. 98.

slayer is assimilating some of the courage and fierceness of his victim, though it must be remembered that the liver is regarded as the seat of fear as well as of these more warlike emotions, and, indeed, it is presumably by his very deficiency in these latter that the victim was unable to look after his liver.

The tabu on the flesh of the slain applies not only to the slayer but to his father, mother, and nearest relatives. If they were rash enough to partake, their genitalia would swell, their joints grow crooked, and their heads turn bald. (Though in the case of an old man, it was said that these results need not be feared.) In view of such alarming risks it seems likely that there was in the person of the slain something like infection to that of the slayer. Other details confirm this view. The Orokaiva has a lively dread of *baupeni* (or elephantiasis of the scrotum) and swelling of the joints— both of which afflictions are seen in the Division. The slayer immediately removed his *bo*, or perineal band, and wore a leaf or nothing until he reached home and could effect a change of clothing: this was a precaution against *baupeni*. If he had dispatched the victim with a club he would straightway change this for another man's: on no account would he *shoulder* the club that struck the fatal blow, for he would run a risk of a swollen or distorted shoulder-joint.

Again the slayer must perform certain rites and observe certain tabus. He must not drink pure water out of the river, but only that which has been stirred up and made muddy by the feet of a non-slayer. He must not eat taro cooked in the pot, but only that which has been roasted in the open fire. He must abstain from sexual intercourse. These restrictions lasted for a few days and then the slayer ate the same purificatory stew (*suna*) which is given to initiates at the end of their seclusion (see p. 193). Among the Binandele I witnessed a mock demonstration of a peculiar rite which immediately preceded the eating of the *suna*. The slayer climbs into a small tree which contains a nest of those large and aggressive insects commonly called 'green' ants. The tree should properly be of the kind called *Bobo*, which is always swarming with them. While he crouches in a fork of the tree, branches are broken and laid over him so that he is almost completely covered and thoroughly bitten. Having endured this for some time, he climbs down and eats the *suna*, steaming himself over the dish and sponging his joints with handfuls of the stewed leaves. Another rite (also performed at the end of the initiate's seclusion) was to break a coco-nut above the slayer and souse his head with the milk.

It seems likely that all these observances and tabus are in a sense not only purificatory but defensive. As a rule, informants have no explanation to offer, but I have been informed directly that they are meant to drive away the *asisi*, or spirit, of the slain man. In support of this view I may quote what W. N. Beaver has written: 'I am not disposed to the sole view that the killer is "unclean". It seems to me rather that rites are necessary to throw off the power of the ghost or ghosts of the slain. . . .'[1]

Adoption of the Victim's Name

There is a very common practice, already referred to in Chapter VII, which we may be tempted to associate with the same idea. This is the practice of adopting the name of the slain. A man, originally named Koga, for instance, has killed another named Amburi: henceforward he, the slayer, is known by the name of Amburi, the slain. This custom is very common, and has been noted by others, so that it is unnecessary to give a succession of examples. It does not follow that the slayer entirely abandons his original name, which, I am told, may still be used occasionally by his more immediate friends; but his ordinary name is certainly that which he has taken from his victim. When a warrior of distinction has accounted for a number of slain he does not take the name of each in turn, but continues, as a rule, to be known by that of the first. This, however, cannot be an invariable rule, for a certain Ehari of Wasida, who can name no less than seven victims of his own hand, is known by the

[1] 'The Use of Emblems or Insignia of Man-killing among the "Orokaiva" tribes of the Kumusi Division', *Annual Report*, 1918–19, p. 97.

name of the second. His original name was Ata; his first
victim was Asi and his second Ehari. He is now called
Ehari though he has since killed five others.

Although the stoutest warrior does not disdain to take
the life of a woman, he does not assume her name. I have
one case, however, in which the slayer gave the name of his
woman victim to his infant daughter. The habit of bestowing the victim's name upon the child of the slayer (sometimes born subsequently) is again a common one. I quote
an example by H. L. Griffin:

'It is a common thing amongst the Binandele for a man who kills
a big chief to take the dead man's name, which he becomes very proud
of; but my orderly, Constable Gisi-Gada, received his name rather
curiously. His father, a Dauntutu man, went to fight on the Waria, and
killed a big Waria chief named Gisi-Gada. On his return his wife informed him that she was pregnant. He was so pleased at this that he
said that, if the child was a boy, he should have the name Gisi-Gada
instead of his father. Everything turned out as desired, and so my
orderly bears the distinguished name. But it was an instance of self-
abnegation on the part of the father that is very rare in Papua.'[1]

This is a typical example, though I cannot believe that self-
abnegation in general is very rare among Papuans; and the
particular habit of giving the name of the slain to the son
of the slayer is not rare but common.

It is interesting to note that in the case of an inter-clan
fight (somewhat unusually fierce) in which two were killed
on one side and five on the other, the slayers did not take
the names of the slain. For this I received the somewhat
bald explanation that the two factions lived at too close
quarters and feared magic.

The usual native explanation of the practice under discussion is that the name of the slain is adopted as a distinction. It draws attention to the fact that a man is *embo-dari* or
mai-dari, i.e. a man-slayer, and marks him, therefore, as one
of valour, *koropahuso*, 'strong or expert with the spear'. It
serves to commemorate his exploit.

Another explanation has already been suggested, viz. that
adopting the name of the slain is in some manner a protec-

[1] Quoted by J. H. P. Murray, Lieutenant-Governor, in *Annual Report*, 1908–9,
p. 23.

tion against the latter's avenging spirit or *diroga*. As we shall see, the Orokaiva dreads the spirits of the dead, whether slain in fight or dying in peace, and it may be that the tabus and observances which are customary with the man-slayer are in the nature of precautions against the spirit (*asisi* or *diroga*) of his victim. It may also be that by adopting the latter's name the slayer hopes to make himself invulnerable, because the dead would not assail the man who now bore his own name. This explanation, however, is merely a suggestion, and even if it be true, it is certainly not explicit in the native mind. Somewhat against it are the facts that a slayer of many men is known by the name of only one of them; that a man does not take a female victim's name; and that in an inter-clan fight the names of the slain were not taken at all. On the whole it seems that we must discard the tempting explanation (viz. that the adoption of the name is a precautionary measure against the spirit of the slain), and fall back on the simpler statement of the native, that it is in the nature of a distinction.

Homicidal Insignia

There is another kind of distinction, viz. the wearing of certain ornaments, &c., which may be described as homicidal insignia. To these is given the general name *otohu*, or the specific name of *esa*. The latter will be found more satisfactory here. The subject of these insignia among the Orokaiva is not so straightforward as we might expect, owing to the fact—a happy one from all points of view save the present—that homicide has long gone out of fashion, or at least no longer bears an honorific implication, so that the customs connected with it cannot be studied directly. The best written on the subject is found in the admirable article by the late W. N. Beaver in the *Annual Report*, 1918–19, pp. 96–9.

The source of confusion is in the fact that *otohu* ornaments are also given in connexion with initiation, where they certainly do not imply that the recipient has been a man-slayer. The concrete fact that they are given to girls as well as to boys or men is enough to prove this. Beaver made a distinction between homicidal *otohu* and 'pig-*otohu*', the former being conditioned by the killing of a man, the latter virtually bought with a pig. My own inquiries confirm this distinction, though I would attach more importance to the latter class than he does, and would prefer to state the matter thus, that the *esa*, or homicidal insignia, are a special class of *otohu*. The general subject of *otohu* will be discussed in the next chapter.

In the meantime it appears that the man-slayer, having undergone the forms of purification or exorcism, might at some convenient date receive his *otohu*, or, as I shall call it, *qua* homicidal insigne, his *esa*. I say 'might' because some of the older informants have assured me that an *esa* was not given invariably. Moreover, it seems that certain ornaments, which are rightly enough *otohu*, have been too freely regarded as *esa*, i.e. as implying that their possessor must be a homicide. My own inquiries have led me to believe that the variety of homicidal insignia was very limited. Beaver has given two lists, one for the coastal and central tribes and one for the Wasida and the trans-Kumusi. The first is of eight, and the second of twelve alternative ornaments or objects.[1] (It will be understood that the River People in the north observe similar customs and use similar *esa*.) I do not repeat these in full, but draw attention to several of the more striking. It seems likely that Nos. 1 and 2 (the hornbill beaks and the cuscus fur) were exclusive homicidal insignia or *esa* proper, i.e. they could be worn only by man-slayers. But save for these two, and possibly though doubtfully for the other three mentioned with them, I am led to believe that the long list of ornaments given by Beaver, as well as many others mentioned by native informants, were presented just as readily to the peaceful initiate as to the successful warrior.

1. *Peremo*: hornbill beaks arranged in a semicircle with points outward and worn on the forehead.
2. *Siropu, Koviro, Bauri*: different varieties of cuscus. Strips of the furry skin with small bunches of feathers tied at intervals are worn as streamers from the armlets or the club.

[1] *Annual Report*, 1918–19, pp. 97, 98.

3. *Gana*: an ornament formed of pig-tusks, suspended over the breast, or held in the teeth.
4. *Bati-ananya*: a forehead band of shell slabs and dogs' teeth, terminating on either side in a rosette of dogs' teeth.
5. *Ki-overo*: a spear decorated with tufts of coloured feathers.

Beaver has given some interesting hints as to the symbolism of various *esa*. For example, the *Bati-ananya* symbolizes 'the clawing hands and grinning teeth of the dead'. Again, 'simba—a head-dress of dogs' teeth, "sapi sapi" shells and beads, symbolical of the head smashed in by the stone club (?)'. The interrogation mark in the latter case makes it appear as if the writer did not entirely trust his informant, and while such symbolic interpretations are worth recording, we may well doubt whether they are the generally accepted interpretations, or, indeed, whether any general interpretation exists. It is not impossible that the above meanings are the extempore creations of imaginative informants reading their own meaning into the object on the spur of the moment; and I dare say that if we sought them we could discover a variety of symbolic interpretations for any one *esa*.

In the normal instance the *esa* will be provided by the father of the slayer, but the actual bestowal or investiture will be performed by some old warrior of renown who has made many victims of his own. After this ceremony the same old warrior will paint the face of the young slayer.

The main purpose of the *esa* is apparently honorific. To the Orokaiva it is, or was, an ambition to kill a man, and the man-slayer was in a manner lionized. When a warrior who already had a victim to his credit held an enemy at his mercy, he might forbear out of generosity and call on another to administer the finishing blow, and so earn the right of wearing what to an Orokaiva was perhaps the proudest possible distinction.

XII

INITIATION CEREMONIES

THE course of initiation ceremonies has been already summarized in Chapter VII. Except in reference to the southern tribes, where there are esoteric objects such as the bull-roarer and the sacred flute, it must be allowed that the word 'initiation' is used somewhat loosely. All the tribes, however, possess certain ceremonies, usually performed about the age of puberty, which are virtually *rites de passage*, and which convert the candidate (boy or girl) into an *ehamei* or 'new child'. These may be conveniently called ceremonies of initiation. They are usually the occasions of large festivals, and a number of candidates of varying age are passed through them together. I shall proceed to describe the initiation ceremonies in their successive stages.

Initiation

The first stage is that of the initiation proper, viz. the entering into the secret of the bull-roarer and the flute, and this, as we have seen, belongs only to the southern tribes. A vivid description of the ceremony is found in the article by Chinnery and Beaver in the *Journal of the Royal Anthropological Institute*, vol. xlv, 1915. It does not occur frequently, and it was not my good fortune to witness a full performance. I shall, therefore, take the liberty later on of quoting at some length from the above-mentioned source, for Mr. Chinnery not only saw the ceremony enacted among the Koko people of the Upper Yodda valley (Hunjara tribe), but 'was to a certain degree initiated himself into the Kokos'.

The candidates are of both sexes. On a recent occasion (at Wasida) there were, for example, seven boys and two girls; in another instance, nine boys and four girls. Those who pass through initiation and seclusion together constitute something like an age-group; and one member will refer to the rest as *nanamei*, 'my children', i.e. 'the children of whom I am one'. The age of the candidates is variable. Normally it would appear they are pubescent youths and maidens, but sometimes they are much younger, and sometimes, on the other hand, they may be married. Mr. Chinnery remarked that among the candidates which he saw near Kokoda there were women in a fairly advanced condition of pregnancy.

Before actual initiation the candidates are interned for some time in a house built at a little distance from the village. During this initial seclusion, which is only of short duration and not to be confused with the seclusion proper, preparations are being made for the festival. A great harvest of food is accumulated, and a stage or platform called *ohu* is built at one end of the village. The initiates meanwhile await their ordeal, which purports to be nothing less than a meeting with the *embahi* or *siango* (who are primarily spirits of the dead, but who are also conceived of, somewhat indefinitely, as malignant supernatural creatures, or—to give them a convenient or familiar name—devil-devils).

The *embahi* will be impersonated by men already initiated, and it appears that the candidates fully realize this before the event. A boy, for instance, was taken up to the *oro* for initial internment by his *epe* or maternal uncle, and told that the latter would 'wear his feathers'. This meant that the *epe* would impersonate an *embahi* and subsequently give the feathers as *kokumbari* or decoration to the boy. But the native enters with so much zest into the spirit of his ceremonies that one finds the border between make-believe and true belief to be very hazy. Writing of the candidates in the house of seclusion before the actual ceremony, Chinnery and Beaver say, 'The candidates being usually in a state of terror, they are warned that if they make a noise the spirit will take up the house and carry it away to some mountain and capsize it—their guide now tells them they are only going to see their fathers, but it does not appear that they are greatly reassured.' [1]

When the preparations are complete the younger children, who have not yet reached the initiation age, are taken away into the bush; the candidates wait in the *oro*; and guests pour in from the surrounding villages. All the men

[1] *Loc. cit.*, p. 72.

present will join in representing the *embahi* in the ceremony which is to take place at night. Their only disguise will be face-paint, ornaments held in the characteristic way between the teeth, and flowing or bristling masses of feathers; but in the imagination of the candidates, and for the time being in their own, they will approach very nearly to true *embahi*.

I cannot do better than quote the words of Chinnery and Beaver to describe the exciting scene in the village at night.

'As the moon rises, all present become deadly silent. The men depart for the bush, at the same time putting out all fires and lights. When the moon shines, a long procession emerges from the bush into the village, moving very silently and stealthily, figures wearing huge headdresses, masked with frames of pigs' teeth, and armed with stone-headed clubs. Women are present, but do not join the line.

'Having entered the village, they form two advancing lines until a large scaffolding is reached, erected at one end of the village. Turning, the men kneel down facing the entrance from which they have come and remain in this position, still keeping silence. It is at this stage that the candidates are presented. Faint cries arise from the bush, becoming louder and louder, and the words "Shi! Shi!" mingled with yells and shrieks are distinguished, and at the same time the candidates are marshalled in, led by their guides. They advance between the lines of men who, hitherto silent, now break up into groups, each catching a lad and running madly up and down the village, followed by the women, waving spears and all uttering cries and yells and rubbing the youngsters' arms, legs, and bodies. They now make a wild rush towards the scaffolding, throwing the lads on it, who endeavour to climb up out of reach, but are torn back by the mob and undergo further agony, until, utterly exhausted with fright and fatigue, they are allowed to climb away, not knowing what they may still have to put up with.

'Still retaining their group formation, the men rush forward to the scaffold uttering horrible yells, waving their heads sideways with faces upturned to the lads, and swinging their clubs, only to retreat again. Now and again a man will yell from the group, "*Namo shiango*" (I am the spirit), swinging his club to strike, but the other men will rush in upon him, throw him to the ground, and take his weapon away.'

This violence and pandemonium continue through the night. At daybreak the girl candidates are led in and subjected to the same treatment in somewhat milder form. Then the candidates, male and female, are mustered on the *ohu* platform, where they sit completely covered with hoods of bark-cloth. Trees are pulled down in the village

(*a*) Initiates secluded in the *Oro*

(*b*) Initiates playing the *Sepiri* or Sacred Flute

PLATE XXIV

by means of long lianas, and the bull-roarers are sounded, giving forth their peculiarly expressive and rather terrifying notes, which range from the deepest bass to a piercing siren-like shriek. To the boys and girls, who cannot see for their hoods of bark-cloth, these noises are evidences of the *embahi* or *siango*. Fathers and mothers cry out to the spirits to spare and not devour their children, while the spirits themselves utter a terrible chant or concerted cry, and gabble, '*Kambo, kambo, kambo!*' which means 'Bite, bite, bite!' It is not hard to picture the mood of the initiates who hear everything and see nothing from under their bark-cloth hoods.

And yet the candidate is aware that the proceedings are, in a sense, all sham. A young girl, who had been seized by a number of men and thrown into the air again and again, as if she were tossed in a blanket, said that these men were not bush-*embahi*, but village-*embahi*, meaning, as she explained, that they were not the terrible beings who in Orokaiva theory haunt the bush, but only villagers masquerading.

In the morning the candidates are shown the bull-roarers and flutes which they have heard sounded by the *embahi* overnight; the *embahi* retire to the river, bathe, and return as mere human beings, and the inevitable feast ensues. The candidates are now interned in the *oro* (the sexes being segregated), and there they remain for a long period of seclusion.

Seclusion of Initiates

The ceremony of initiation, which has just been described, is followed by a period of seclusion, and this again by a formal début with the bestowal of *kokumbari* and *otohu*. It appears, however, that this sequence is not entirely uniform. In Wasida I was informed that the *kokumbari* and *otohu* were given immediately after the *embahi* ceremony and before the subsequent seclusion; in Divina Kovari, where I witnessed a formal début, they were certainly given after this seclusion. Among the Aiga and Binandele it is customary for the seclusion to follow the giving of *kokumbari* and *otohu*. Without regard to this variety, however, I will describe separately the seclusion, the début, and bestowal of *kokumbari*, the bestowal of *otohu*, and the precautionary or purificatory rites (*ate-ate* and *suna*) which bring the cycle of ceremonies to an end.

Before proceeding with the description of seclusion, it is necessary to make one important matter clear, viz. that I am here dealing only with the seclusion that forms a part of the initiation cycle. There is another seclusion, viz. that through which girls must pass at the age of puberty. It appears that the manner of internment is in both cases much the same, but in order to avoid confusion I shall mention the distinction between them, calling one the initiatory seclusion and the other the puberty seclusion; and I shall reserve a description of the latter until the end of the chapter. A girl enters her puberty seclusion immediately upon her first menstruation, and may pass through it alone. Subsequently she may be one of a batch of youths and girls who are to undergo initiation together, and in that case she will pass through a second seclusion, viz. the initiatory seclusion. It is this which I shall proceed to deal with.

Seclusion is practised by all the tribes, north and south; and it appears that the same general rules are observed in all cases. The house of seclusion, removed a little distance from the village, stands in a small enclosure (*sama*) fenced about with palm-leaf barriers some thirteen or fourteen feet in height. The house is called *oro* (Aiga) [1] and may in some instances, I am told, accommodate both boy and girl candidates; for it is said that they are all 'brothers and sisters' and may, therefore, be trusted to behave. Usually, however, those who arrange the matter are less trusting, and the two sexes are confined separately. One house of seclusion which I saw was about 9 feet by 15 feet in area and consisted of a single large room in which nine boys were confined. The house was closed in on all sides and the eyes of the inmates seemed very wide in the perpetual semi-darkness. The secluded children are called *i-tekari-mei*, 'The children who are shut up above', or simply *i-mei*, 'the on-top children'. They occupy the upper part of a pile house, the actual ground floor of which is used by the old men who

---

[1] Binandele *wawa*; Hunjara *thrar* (Chinnery and Beaver).

look after them. They discard all ornaments, but it seems, nowadays at least, to be a matter of indifference whether or no they wear a *bo*. They must not wash, and it is said to be the proper thing to keep the house warm by a fire underneath; though this, I believe, is not meant as a trial to the initiates, but rather to make them comfortable. Whenever they please they may exercise themselves in the *sama* enclosure, and occasionally they go farther afield in the bush.

Chinnery and Beaver give a number of rules and precepts which the children are supposed to learn in their seclusion; [1] and I have been told that during this period they are instructed to be honest, obliging, and diligent. But we must not picture the *sama* enclosure as a severe school of tribal morals. It is certain that the initiates live a thoroughly indolent and easy life, doing no work save the plaiting of armlets and such tasks, in which there is more of amusement than labour. Their hardest task is that of learning to play the flutes (*sepiri*, *inagu*, or *gauro*), and it is said that the duration of their seclusion will be regulated by the skill which the school attains: the sooner they learn, the sooner they come out. But there is no doubt that the regulating factor is really the supply of food for the feast.

The method of playing these flutes has already been described (p. 89). It may be added that of the pair, which are invariably played in duet, one is called the male (*sianja*) and the other the female (*huega*). In Divina Kovari the former was called *sepiri* and the latter *inagu*; in Wasida, where *inagu* was a general term for 'flute', the male was called *otohu*, and the female *eh*. There seems to be no essential difference between the two save one of pitch.

While engaged in these very easy occupations the initiates are eating heartily, one might almost say deliberately battening. There is no restriction in the variety of their food, though it is served to them, not by their womenfolk who cook it, but by some old men who frequent the *sama* enclosure. It is the duty especially of the candidate's *nobo* and his wife (the candidate's *tata*) to ration him during seclusion.

[1] *Loc. cit.*, p. 76.

The internees must avoid being seen by people of the village—in particular, it would seem, by their own fathers and mothers. Sexual intercourse is prohibited. Chinnery and Beaver speak of other tabus: 'Should a boy happen to talk over loudly, one of the guardians would say, "Be silent, I will thrust a spear through the floor". Should a boy happen to drop taro through the floor, he would be killed.' This latter penalty is, of course, no longer inflicted in these slip-shod days, and personally I am very doubtful whether such severity could ever have amounted to a rule.

Début and Decoration

The initiate is not called an *ehamei* (or *meiha*), i.e. a 'new child', until he or she has terminated the seclusion and made a formal début. This is a spectacular occasion, the main purpose of which is perhaps to do honour to the initiate. It is signalized by the youth's first appearance in the feather head-dress, which thenceforward he is entitled to wear. Hitherto it has been strictly forbidden him, so much so that I have known a serious quarrel between two men resulting from the fact that one of them had given feathers to the other's younger brother before the right to wear them had been formally granted. The following description is drawn mainly from a ceremony which I witnessed near Divina Kovari in the Hunjovarehu country.

On the day of their formal reappearance the initiates, who have remained unwashed during their long internment, are taken down to bathe at early morning. They then gather in the bush beyond sight and earshot of the village, and in this sylvan tiring-room undergo the lengthy and laborious process of being decorated. Each sits on a mat and places himself entirely in the hands of the man who is dressing him. There are many others watching or helping: with a party of twelve youths and four girls at Divina Kovari, there must have been seventy or eighty onlookers. The tails of hair which have grown long during seclusion have red streamers tied to their extremities. In the middle they are gathered tightly together and bound with bark-cloth, so as to form a base for the mass of feathers which is to be tied on to the initiate's head. This decoration consists not only of feather-sets but of shell and ivory ornaments, particularly strings of dogs' teeth wound round and round the bunch of hair. One boy, when I saw him submitting patiently to the ministrations of his attendant, already had nine strings of dogs' teeth round his hair at the back, each consisting of perhaps 150 teeth, and he was then waiting for more. It will be easily imagined that the weight of this portentous mass of feathers and ornaments is very considerable, and as the process of decorating lasted some hours the eyes of their wearers were already blinking with fatigue at this early stage of the day. Oppressed either with the weight or the magnificence of their headdresses, they held their heads as still as possible or moved them stiffly, like a man unaccustomed to an evening shirt.

I have been assured that it is the function of the *nobo*, or maternal uncle, to present the *kokumbari*, for which he receives payment from the initiate's father in the form of a pig, and from his mother in the form of a pot (*obu*), a wooden bowl (*teva*), a water calabash, a *bo*, a netted bag (*eti*), a fish-net (*eutu*), and a spear. But, as so often in the case of such rules, we find on looking into the matter that other relatives may equally well perform the function. Thus in the present instance I recorded more cases where the *kokumbari* was given by the paternal uncle than where it was given by the maternal uncle. In other cases, again, it was given by the elder brother. On the whole, however, it may be regarded as proper for the *nobo* to give the *kokumbari*, as I have also heard that it is proper for him to attend to the initiate during his seclusion. But neither of these rules is observed with strictness.

While the decoration of the initiates is going forward, guests are arriving in the village. On such occasions it is the custom, not for the hosts, but for the guests, to perform a dance. (On a future occasion the invitation will be returned, and the hosts in the present instance will then be the performers.) In the ceremony at Divina Kovari two such parties of dancers arrived, one before and one after the formal entry of the decorated initiates. It is not necessary to describe their dances, which are entirely conventional and have no bearing on the ceremony in hand. They are, as far as I know, merely a form of entertainment.

The initiates make an ostentatious entry. The dancing is in full swing when a loud roar of voices is heard, and the *ehamei* appear assembled at the entrance to the village. They advance swiftly, flanked and covered in the rear by a mass of supporters so that the whole body forms a dense phalanx. Met with various gestures of resistance from the people in the village they come to a sudden halt in the centre, bracing themselves for a moment, and then advance again in the same irresistible manner. At the end of the village they turn about and charge down its length once more, and having done so, the compact body breaks up and resolves itself into the old-fashioned dance called *Kuru*. The boy initiates join in this, while the girls in the usual way dance apart, either in front or rear.

All the *ehamei*, both male and female, carry mock spears of light white wood, each with a piece of red-dyed barkcloth tied near the point. Many of them also carry stone clubs. Both boys and girls wear their *bo* which have been newly put on for the ceremony (though they have probably been in the habit of wearing garments of this kind long before). They almost stagger under their gigantic headdresses, and their persons are festooned with frilled yellow grass, tassels of which hang over the face so as to form a partial disguise.

The *ehamei* soon withdraw from the *kuru* dance, and while this and the other dances proceed with undiminished vigour, stand in line watching them, evidently uncomfortable and apparently almost stupefied.

Presentation of 'Otohu'

Late in the afternoon a number of the *ehamei* were presented with their *otohu*. Whereas every initiate receives his *kokumbari* feathers, not every one of them receives an *otohu*. However, as it is very usual to make this an occasion for presenting an *otohu*, I may pass on to describe the method of presentation as if it formed the next step in the series of

(*a*) Formal appearance of the Initiates

(*b*) Initiates wearing *Kokumbari* feathers

PLATE XXV

ceremonies. I shall return to the difficult question of the significance of *otohu* at the end of the chapter. For the present it may be said that it is a ceremonial ornament of great value and often of great beauty which is commonly bestowed on the occasion of the début and *kokumbari*.

It is the invariable custom to call upon some old warrior of distinction to bestow these ornaments: such a man is called *aguma* or *atemba*. On this occasion at Divina Kovari there were three of them, and I shall describe their part in the ceremony at some length.

The first was an old man of Togahu. Firm and self-possessed, he advanced to where the *otohu* had been laid on a mat, grasped them in two handfuls, and marched back and forth along a path which the spectators had formed between them, nearly a chain long and two or three yards broad. His business was to cry out the names of his own early victims, and having done this, he turned aside and handed over the *otohu* to the second *aguma*.

This was an old man named Handaupa of Hamara. Sitting somewhat apart he seemed loth to perform the office, and something like a murmur of applause was heard when he finally accepted the two bunches of ornaments and began. He was doddering with age and showed a tendency to corpulence or pursiness which is unusual in an Orokaiva. He commenced by shouting that as he was now a very old man he might not be able to summon all his conquests back to memory. Accordingly two younger men who remembered his exploits better than he did himself took their places one at either end of the path between the spectators. Handaupa now began to cry out the names of his victims, the tribes to which they belonged, and the circumstances in which they had been killed. He would run the length of the path while he dealt with each victim, and as the list continued the old man grew more and more energetic. He would bend his ear to the prompter at either end. Then, when a few words had roused his recollections, he would turn, hardly waiting for the prompter to finish, and career down the path again, shouting at the top of his voice. He gradually showed signs of fatigue, discarded first one bundle of *otohu*, then the other, and finally retained only two light switches of cassowary feathers. The catalogue of victims seemed inexhaustible. The sweat was pouring down Handaupa's lined old face, his voice was hoarse, and he was shaking with exhaustion and excitement. He paused to drink from a coco-nut and went on again, but just as his emotions seemed to be getting the better of him entirely, he suddenly said he must stop as he was tired, and with that he sank abruptly into a sitting position, and drained another coco-nut which one of the spectators held ready for him.

The third *aguma* was a very aged man from the neighbourhood of Divina Kovari. Feebler than Handaupa, he had a better memory, and was not so ambitious as to begin with the two weighty bundles of *otohu*. He was supported on either side by a younger man, and further assisted himself with a stick, but even his footsteps quickened as he warmed to his work and recounted the exploits of his youth and named his five victims.

The *aguma* exhorts the *ehamei* to bravery, and the reason for telling of his own prowess is to give them something to emulate. Such a demonstration, I understand, always marks the ceremony of investiture with the *otohu*. It is typical of a savage people to whom valour or mere bloodthirstiness is one of the first virtues. The Orokaiva is not only brave enough but exceedingly vainglorious: he loves to make a great show of martial prowess. It is interesting to note that this, like other ceremonies, has a sort of ambivalence, wavering between belief and make-believe, or between seriousness and banter. While the distinguished warrior is shouting his exploits, a chorus of young men stand by beating their drums and making fun of the old man in their songs. I have recorded one of the songs appropriate to the occasion:

Poponi opi be kajari keko

which means that the old *aguma* is a boaster and a liar, that he never thrust his spear through the body of a man, but merely poked him with a shoot (*opi*) of the *Poponi* tree.

When these lengthy declamations are over, several logs

are laid end to end and the *ehamei* sit down on them in a
row, all facing in the same direction. They must not sit
on the ground lest through contact with it they run the
risk of some physical deformity. A man stands behind
each boy (or girl), and the man who is to invest him with
the *otohu* stands in front. (In the normal instance this would
be the old warrior or *aguma*, but in the present case other
men officiated as well. The *otohu* is thrown above the boy's
head and caught and returned by the man behind him.
This happens again and again until the man in front leans
forward and binds the ornament in its place on the boy's
forehead. This throwing back and forth, called *ketumbari*,
or *iketumbo* ('giving and taking'), is said to be a precaution
against subsequent baldness in the initiate.

In other tribes the *aguma* will offer the *otohu* to the initiate
and, as the latter stretches out his hand to receive it, will
snatch it away again. This (called *itaraho?*) is likewise done
again and again till the *aguma* fixes it on the initiate as a
general might pin a medal on the breast of a private.
Another method of tantalizing the recipient is to throw the
otohu from one to another of the spectators before finally
giving it to him.

It is properly at this stage, while the initiate is waiting
to receive his ornament, that the *aguma* lays upon him certain injunctions of an ethical character. These are always
associated with the *otohu* and, as we shall see, they throw
some light on the obscure meaning of the word. As he
proffers and withdraws the ornament, the officiating *aguma*
exhorts the candidate to refrain from thieving, from adultery, from quarrelling, and from such lawless acts as killing
a neighbour's dog. It seems likely that the tantalizing delay
in bestowing the ornament is itself a means of showing the
youth that he must practice restraint, that he must wait his
turn, in fact that he must not snatch.

Subsequent Rites: Prophylaxis and Purification

The greater number of the initiates at Divina Kovari
received these *otohu* as well as the *kokumbari*, which is an in-
separable feature of the ceremony of début. When the in-

vestiture was over, the *ehamei* crowded on to the *ohu* platform at the end of the village on which were already strewn
heaps of high-smelling pig flesh. It was by now growing
dusk, but there was still enough daylight for them to make
a brilliant patch of colour against the dark background of
forest trees. The reason for this move on the part of the
ehamei was said variously to be (1) that all the people should
see them, (2) that they should see all the people, and (3) that
they should see all the pig meat.

During the whole of this time the *ehamei* have had to
support the weight of their *kokumbari* feathers and ornaments, to which has now in most cases been added that of
their *otohu*; and they have neither drunk water, nor, except
for banana and sugar-cane, broken their fast since morning.
These ordeals, however, must continue throughout the
night, which is occupied with singing and dancing and with
the *ai sumbasiona*, or abusing of the women. This latter
consists of highly obscene choruses and action songs, to
which the women respond in kind and with no lack of
spirit. It may be that under the circumstances morality is
loosened. I quote a sentence of Chinnery and Beaver's:
'In ordinary circumstances an initiation is a time of somewhat general licence, promiscuous intercourse being permitted between any initiated man and woman.'[1] Witnesses
have assured me that such promiscuity is confined to the
initiation ceremonies. The initiates bear no part in it, but
between their elders it is unrestricted. No husband might
object if another man made free with his wife, for, it was
said, he would fear retaliation by sorcery if he interfered.
Needless to say I have no more than verbal evidence for this
licence, but there is little doubt that at these times it does
occur.

Next morning the *ehamei* are subjected to a rite called
ate-ate, which appears to mean literally 'demonstration'.
Once more they sit in a row on the logs, each with a man
behind him armed with a stout stick. In front of the
initiates stand their respective mothers holding a taro in the
left hand, and the sharp peeler of oyster or coco-nut shell

[1] *Loc. cit.*, p. 77.

called *kari* in the right. When all is in readiness the women deftly slice off a piece of the taro, and with one motion send the fragment and the peeler across the head of the initiate to fall at the feet of the man waiting behind. The latter immediately smashes the peeler with his stick. This, I am informed, is a formal way of ending the tabu on the mother's cooking. Formerly, it appears, the cooking for the *ehamei* has not been done by his mother but by his *tata*; [1] henceforward after this rite his mother may cook for him without risk of any kind. It is said that this rite is once more a safeguard against baldness, the idea of which an Orokaiva so heartily hates. In other parts there is the custom of breaking a coco-nut above the initiate's head and allowing the fluid to fall over him; and for this the same reason (somewhat often called into service) is given, viz. that of preventing baldness.

But the partial fast of the initiates does not come to an end with the performance of this *ate-ate* ceremony. They are merely allowed to remove the heavier of their ornaments, a relief for which they must be heartily grateful. They continue to eat nothing more than banana and sugar-cane, and are still denied water until on the following day they eat the *suna*.

By this time all the guests have dispersed, carrying with them their presents of food, and the village is left very untidy indeed after the feasting, but in comparative quiet. The eating of the *suna* is a rite which pertains only to the initiates and their fellow villagers. The *suna* itself is a stew, a highly composite dish of which the ingredients seem to vary in different tribes. At Divina Kovari they were taro, pig flesh, *Tauga* nuts (*Terminalia Okari*), the fruit of the tree *Puga, Ina* (a kind of *andropogon*), and the leaves of the trees *Ega, Houra,* and *Sigoga,* and of the croton *simbiri*. The whole is stewed with the addition of coco-nut oil and pig's blood. I have been unable to discover any magical significance in any of these ingredients: except for the leaves, they are all

---

[1] Though other informants have said that the mother does cook for her own son while secluded. The matter is evidently of no great consequence, and the prohibition of the mother's cooking is not universal.

common articles of diet. Comparing five lists made in different parts of the Division, I find that they all contain taro, pig, and coco-nut in common; three contain *Puga* and *Tauga*; two bread-fruit and a kind of banana; while the other ingredients are various, with the exception of *simbiri*, or croton, which occurs in four of the five lists.

The initiates gather round the dish of *suna* and bend over it so as to be fumigated by the rising steam. They hold their hands in the steam, and then withdrawing them massage their joints. They take handfuls of the hot leaves and apply them to their private parts, their hip-joints, their elbows, their arm-pits, &c. They end by eating the stew. The other villagers stand by, themselves partaking and sponging their bodies with the leaves. The *suna* is sometimes set out in a wooden dish (*teva*) and a hot stone placed in it to increase the volume of steam, while the initiates stooping over the dish may be covered with pandanus mats to give them something like a Turkish bath.

After partaking of the *suna* the initiate is at liberty to resume his full diet. (During the last two or three days he has eaten nothing but banana and sugar-cane.) But even so he must be cautious. Before passing him a piece of taro one of the elders will pass it under his legs—a queer precaution which appears again and again in Orokaiva ceremonies, either as a purification or as a prophylaxis. Having thus received the taro, the hungry initiate must nibble it only and put it aside for a while. Furthermore, he must not handle it, but convey it to his mouth on a piece of stick as a fork. If he should handle it and afterwards scratch his head the penalty would be the severe one of baldness.

Meaning and Purpose of the Ceremonies

Initiation. The actual occurrences of the initiation cycle having been described we are now in a position to discuss their meaning and purpose. We may begin by considering the initiation ceremony described on pp. 180–3. Laying special stress upon the fact that the terrifying threats of the spirits against the candidates are apparently averted by the

(a) Eating the *Suna*

(b) Girls newly emerged from Puberty Seclusion

PLATE XXVI

prayers or efforts of the latters' elders, Chinnery and Beaver interpret the ceremonies as follows:

'As far as can be ascertained at present, the underlying idea of the ceremony seems to be to instil absolute and lasting terror into the candidates, and to make them think that their elders have beaten off the spirits; while in this receptive and chastened frame of mind, the lads, imbued with the idea of the power of the men, will pay attention to the instruction given. There appears to be an idea that the spirits of the dead are present, and that the initiated, i. e. the living, are keeping them away from the candidates.'

There is no doubt that the Orokaiva, whatever his age, has a very real dread of the real *embahi*. According to the above interpretation the initiated elders play upon this dread in the uninitiated juniors, and pose as the latters' saviours in order to reduce them to a receptive and obedient mood.

It seems to me that this interpretation may emphasize too strongly the pedagogical aspect of the initiation. We may reasonably doubt, I believe, whether the elders have any serious intention of reducing the initiates to a fit state of mind for subsequent instruction (though one does not deny that the painful experience of the youth may have considerable educative value in itself).

Furthermore, the interpretation does not, in my opinion, lay sufficient stress on the actual paraphernalia, viz. the bull-roarers and flutes, which play a more important part in the ceremony than would appear. The bull-roarer and the flute are esoteric objects in that they are never seen but only heard by the uninitiated, and it is always pretended that the notes and noises of these instruments, together with that of the hollow shell whistle called *koni pamoni*, are the voices of the *embahi*. Indeed, it might be said that the bull-roarer, the sacred flute, and the *koni pamoni*, together with the pretence that their notes represented the voices of the spirits, constituted the secrets of a secret society. The society is so comprehensive as to include the whole of the adult tribe, i. e. all those who have duly passed through the initiation cycle, and, like some generous societies who bestow a fellowship on receipt of a subscription, it is always ready to take any one into membership who can provide a pig.

S

To the uninitiated juniors who, at a discreet distance, have heard the mysterious sounds of flute and bull-roarer coming from the quarters where their elders are known to be, it has always appeared as if the latter are hobnobbing with the *embahi*; and this pretence, viz. that the initiated are in league with or familiar with the spirits, is the essence of the adult secret society. Chinnery and Beaver have written: 'The underlying idea about the bull-roarer is that it is a spirit that makes the noise, and this belief is strongly impressed by every device upon uninitiated women, children, and those who have not passed through the ceremony. This belief will usually be found wherever the bull-roarer is used in Papua.'[1] But it seems to me that in their interpretation of the ceremony they have not allowed as much importance to the bull-roarer (and the flute and whistle) as these paraphernalia deserve.

At an initiation ceremony, of which I saw some of the stages at Doboduru, the supposititious *embahi* were stamping, crouching, and leaping in the conventional manner as well as uttering their alarming cries, but they were also continually blowing the flutes, and one of their number was from time to time sounding the bull-roarer. Indeed, the flute and the bull-roarer formed very essential features of their demonstration; and it would, I think, be a mistake not to allow these instruments some importance in an interpretation of the ceremony.

The initiation ceremony, therefore, as practised by the southern Orokaiva would seem to be the acceptance of the junior into the adult society, and the process of acquainting him with the secrets of that society.

But why should the initiation involve such painful experiences for the initiate? One may hesitate to credit the elders with any serious motive. If they behave so as to reduce the initiates to a condition of fear and obedience it is not expressly in order to make them apt pupils for subsequent instruction. Rather would I compare the initiated to the members of a secret society who, on admitting new candidates, take the opportunity of enacting their pretence to

[1] Chinnery and Beaver, *loc. cit.*, p. 71.

the full, and incidentally of giving the candidates a thorough ragging. This is always the privilege of those who are already 'in the know'. In this case their pretence is that they are on terms of familiarity with certain dangerous and terrifying creatures—the *embahi*—who utter weird cries. They accordingly imitate the *embahi* in their gestures and conduct, and their cries on the bull-roarer, flute, and *koni pamoni*. Before giving away their secret, therefore, the elders make the most of it, and rejoice to see the learners thoroughly frightened.

At the same time—whether this be the deliberate intention or no—it cannot be doubted that this ragging must have the indirect effect of enhancing the power of the raggers. It, so to speak, knocks the stuffing out of a possibly uppish youth, and makes him an amenable member of the adult society to which he is now introduced. By feeling to his sorrow the full affect of this adult society's power he will enter it in a humbler and more appreciative spirit; and we may be sure that when his turn comes to act the ragger he will bear his part with all the greater vim for having been roughly handled himself.

I have previously spoken of the curious intensity of native make-believe, and it is quite possible that not only the candidates but also the adult impersonators may give themselves up to the belief that *embahi* are actually present. But I cannot imagine that such serious belief long retains the upper hand, and I feel that the ceremony admits of two constructions, that it may be viewed (not only by ourselves, but by those who actually practise it) as alternatively solemn and frivolous, at one moment as if the initiates were being brought into the sacred danger of contact with the *embahi*, the next as if the initiated were having a great deal of fun at the expense of the frightened and bewildered candidates. It may be remembered that, although I have from time to time used the expression 'sacred flute' (a New Guinea term perpetuated by Haddon), yet as far as the Orokaiva are concerned no sacred character appears to belong intrinsically to the flute or the bull-roarer.

Seclusion and the Purificatory Rites. We may next consider the purpose of seclusion and of the purificatory rites which follow it. It is often supposed that the seclusion through which natives commonly pass about the age of puberty is a period of intensive education in tribal lore and manners. I cannot find that this is so among the Orokaiva. It is true, I was told, that the youths and girls are instructed to observe certain laws, as e.g. against theft and adultery; but there is no evidence that they are consistently schooled, and indeed the suggestion that the house of seclusion was like a 'school' caused a great deal of laughter. As we have found, the internees spend a very idle time, and except for mastering the long flutes among the southern tribes, they have no set tasks to perform. I cannot think, therefore, that the purpose of seclusion is mainly educative.

If one asks either the elders or the initiates themselves for the reasons of seclusion, one will almost invariably receive the same answer: boys and girls are secluded to make them grow big. They do no hard work; they are advised to keep warm, still, and silent; they are forbidden sexual intercourse; they are overfed. It is said that to walk abroad and be seen by those who should not see them would impede their growth. The initiate's father and mother will not see him during his seclusion, but from time to time, I am informed, his *tata* will take the circumference of his arm or leg with a piece of string and show it as a register of progress to his parents. When they first set eyes on him on his emergence from seclusion it is appropriate that they should *titimirari*— 'be astonished', or 'hardly believe their eyes' at the progress he has made. If they were to see him during his seclusion it would, for some reason never made plain, check his growth. The real explanation for this queer prohibition is perhaps simply this, that for the boy's near relatives to see his progress at an intermediate stage would spoil the effect at his début, when, to their surprise and delight, they behold a son who has developed almost beyond recognition. He does not grow imperceptibly under his mother's eyes, but rather like the lad who, returning from a boarding school, seems to have leapt into long trousers.

The ideal Orokaiva is not a fat man, but well-conditioned.

Either by nature or by manner of life he is prevented from 'running to fat', so that the ideal never borders on adiposity. But he admires plumpness as he abhors skinniness. I was never able to discover a word in his language for fat, stout, or obese (indeed, there are, generally speaking, no such figures to be seen); but for a comparatively well-fleshed body he simply uses the word 'good'. Altogether I think we may attach a good deal of value to the native's own explanation of seclusion, and may conclude that the principal purpose of that seclusion is to make the initiate put on flesh, to bring him as near to an admired condition of plumpness as the physical make-up and the *milieu* of an Orokaiva will permit.

Just as the native admires a well-conditioned body, so he has a peculiar sensitiveness regarding physical deformity, and a horror of projecting bones and skinniness. An interesting evidence of this is found in the swear-words or terms of abuse which he uses. Besides such expressions as *Sovai-ta-mei* (son of a *sovai*) and *Pureambo* (waster or lazy-bones), there are *Temburite* (skinny-ribs), *Teperete* (spindle-shanks), *Kumuperete* (which means that the backbone is visible), *Abo-pokumo* (too much of the sacral vertebrae), *Utu-jahuti* (elephantiasis legs), *Tunga-dipori* (long neck), *Tengeu-pepeki* (big ears). Not a few of his ritual precautions are aimed at preventing these deformities, and it appears that he is specially liable to contract them at the end of his seclusion. Hence the precautionary and purificatory observances which we see at the end of the cycle. For instance, the initiate is not allowed to sit on the ground for fear of *baupeni* (elephantiasis of the scrotum). It is necessary to provide a mat for him to sit on while he is being decorated, and a log while he is going through the *ate-ate* ceremony. Similarly there are various precautions against baldness, which I have mentioned; and before he is quite free to come and go as he pleases he must pass through a general purificatory rite, viz. that of the *suna*. The object of the *suna* is expressly to prevent bodily deformities or afflictions such as the prevalent glandular swelling in the groin or the swelling or distortion of joints.

In fine it may be argued that the seclusion, together with the purificatory rites at the end of it, aim (the one in a positive manner, the other in a negative or precautionary manner) at the physical perfection of the initiate.

I have never met with any native rationale for the *suna qua* ceremonial observance; but a very similar process is sometimes used in the treatment of sickness; and as the argument is in this case fairly clear it may throw some light upon the rite in general. A man who has for some time been suffering from headache and general pains submits himself to treatment called *jura*.[1] Various leaves (*Teho, Hamanya, Bakimo, Haiva, Hamburi, Kore, Urga,* are the names of some of them—but there are many recipes for *jura*) are scraped and pounded in a wooden dish with coco-nut oil. The patient squats over it covering himself with a pandanus mat, a hot stone is slipped into the dish, and he sits in a cloud of steam. The only remarkable feature about the leaves used is that they all possess a more or less strong smell (*mune*), that of the *teho* being in European nostrils nothing short of abominable.

Now it is a very common Orokaiva theory that sickness may be due to the immanence of the spirits of the dead in the patient, and I have been assured on more than one occasion that they may be driven out by noisome medicines, simply, it is said, because they cannot endure the smell. The object of the *jura* fumigation, therefore, seems to be to drive out the malignant spirits; and (although I have not noted whether it possessed any strong smell) the ceremonial *suna* may possibly be used with the same idea. The novices during their true initiation in the *embahi* ceremony, and during their subsequent seclusion and association with the flutes and bull-roarer, have been in intimate association with the spirits of the dead—*sovai, embahi,* or *siango*. The fact that there is a vast deal of sham in the whole cycle of ceremonies does not altogether preclude a belief that the *embahi* are really present. As we have observed, make-believe and true

[1] See p. 297. The word is sometimes given to the ceremonial rite which I have called *suna* throughout, but I have not heard the word *suna* given to the 'medical' process.

belief seem with the native to merge into one another: they are too near extremes between which he may be said to shilly-shally. Therefore, when the time comes to be done with the ceremony for good and all, he takes the precaution of removing by a final purificatory rite all possible influences for evil which the *embahi* may have left in the initiates. The same explanation, it may be noted, is offered for the various rites, including the *suna*, observed by the man-slayer, who must rid himself of the peculiarly malignant spirit of the man he has slain.

The Otohu. It remains now to say something further of the *otohu*. I have already referred to the homicidal *otohu*, or *esa*, in Chapter XI, and described the rites observed in the bestowal of the ordinary *otohu* in the present chapter. It is now our task to consider the meaning—or the various meanings—of the word. The *otohu* may for the present be defined as one of a number of distinctive ornaments or objects which, at a price, are ceremonially bestowed, and which the recipient is thenceforward entitled to wear or use. It will be understood that any one who was, so to speak, masquerading with an *otohu* would be exposed to obloquy or ridicule. In earlier days it is doubtful whether any man would have had the hardihood or folly to attempt it. Where, therefore, one sees a man holding a highly ornamented lime gourd with a shell mouth-piece, or a string bag decorated with dogs' teeth, or wearing cuscus streamers tied at intervals with bunches of feathers, it may be concluded that he has paid the price for them (or probably that the price has been paid in his behalf) and that he is fully entitled to their use.

There is a considerable variety of these ceremonial objects, e.g. a specially ornamented *bo* or string bag (*eti* or *hetava*), decorated spears or stone clubs, bone forks for eating, lime-pots, belts embroidered with *saima* shells or made of black creeper cord, cuscus streamers, &c. More commonly they take the form of ornaments (*hambo*) for the breast or forehead—hornbill beaks set in a half-circle, *gana*, *huave*, *hono*, and the like (*vide* p. 39). They are always fine examples of their kind, and in some cases are extremely ornate, with pendants and rosettes of dogs' teeth and scarlet seeds. They do not take the form of feather head-dresses, which constitute what I have throughout called the *kokumbari*. It will be understood, though, that the word *kokumbari* means literally 'decorate', and might correctly be applied to the *otohu*. A distinction is sometimes drawn between *di-kokumbari* (bird or feather decoration) and *hambo-kokumbari* (ornament decoration), the latter, of course, meaning the *otohu*. However, I shall continue to restrict the word '*kokumbari*' to the feather decorations which every initiate receives, and which are, as it were, cheaper than the *otohu*.

I have been assured that, whereas the *kokumbari* is given properly by the *nobo*, the *otohu* is given by the *mama* (not the actual father, but one of the paternal uncles); but we find that the latter rule, like the former, will not come well out of the wash. It is customary, of course, for the candidate's parents to supply the pig which is the price of the *otohu*. (In some cases he does so himself.) The father will bespeak the services of some other—a craftsman—to make the actual ornament, and this man (the *otohu-embo*) is called upon as much for his skill and artistry as for any special relationship he bears to the boy. Among twenty-one cases it appeared that the *otohu-embo* was *mama* to the candidate in nine (in one of them he was the real father), *nobo* in six, *bitepemi* in three, *nabori* in one, *ahije* (grandfather) in one, and in the last he was of no recognized relationship but merely *otavo*, or friend, to the candidate's father.

There is no actual social necessity for every man to receive an *otohu*, though it seems probable that at some time or other nearly every one does. And these further points are significant, that one person may receive a number of them at different times, and that he may receive them at any age.

The usual occasion for presenting them is at the *kokumbari* ceremony in which the recipients are sometimes quite young children who are still a long way from puberty. Again, as we have seen, the *otohu* may be given to the man-slayer (though this is not absolutely invariable). But it appears further that an opportunity for bestowing an *otohu* might be made at any and every ceremony. Thus, for instance, at a dance in Petakiari, when a widow ceremonially discarded her mourning jacket of *baja*, or Job's Tears, she was presented with an *otohu* in the form of a specially decorated *bo*, and this with all the usual formalities.

In view of these facts we may regard the *otohu* as embodying a social distinction. It implies that its owner has paid a pig, or that it has been paid in his behalf, and thus the ornament has been formally and regularly acquired. Further, to the native who loves ostentation the *otohu* is worth having for its own sake, apart from any social distinction it may connote: it is a fine thing, for instance, to wear a 'magnet-shaped' shell ornament (*mendo*) passed through one's nose-hole and dangling somewhat awkwardly in front of one's lips, or to sit and rattle one's spatula noisily in the shell mouth-piece of an *otohu* lime-pot. In short the *otohu* has both honorific and decorative value.

It would seem that in Orokaiva custom as we find it there is no very essential difference between the 'pig *otohu*' and the 'man *otohu*',[1] or *esa*. They are of the same nature, but one is bought with the body of a pig and the other with that of a human victim. As we have seen, a victim's body may be used alternatively with that of a pig to satisfy social obligations, as, e.g., in the matter of a bride-price. It is therefore likely that a man who had a corpse at his disposal might equally acquire an *otohu* with it, and in this view it would appear that the homicidal *otohu*, or *esa*, was less an *insigne* conferred, *causa honoris*, upon the man-killer as such, than an ordinary *otohu* purchased with the body of his victim.

Against this view, however, are the facts that certain of the *otohu* ornaments assuredly do stand more or less distinctively as homicidal insignia, and that in conferring an *otohu* a warrior of renown always recites his past conquests and sometimes calls upon the candidates to follow his martial example. These facts may hint that all *otohu* were originally dependant upon the slaying of a man, the pig *otohu* being nothing more than a poor and unromantic sub-

[1] See p. 178; also Beaver, 'Homicidal Emblems among the Orokaiva', *Annual Report*, 1918–19, p. 98.

stitute. If such be the case, however, the change must have taken place or the substitution have been allowed in the very distant past, for we find that the well-established custom of the Orokaiva was to grant *otohu* both for human corpses and for pigs, and not only to man-slayers, but to boys, women, and young girls. So that an *otohu* together with the social *éclat* and dignity which its possession implies, is not only for the man-slayer but is within the reach of every one.

But the *otohu* with its social distinction may involve some social obligation. And this brings us to a discussion on the meaning of the word, which proves indeed a rather baffling subject. Beaver (who uses the Binandele form of the word, viz. *kotopu* or *Kortopo*) has said: 'I am not altogether clear whether the word "Kortopo" is strictly applicable to the act, the ceremony, the thing, the donor, the recipient, or to all of them, and, in describing the ceremony, therefore, the word may be used rather loosely. The Anglican Mission uses the word in the Binandele language to translate our "set apart", and therefore "holy". The sense, I gathered from my informants, was that of "superman", and indeed it is no great tax on the mind to connect the two.' [1]

While I would not deny that both these meanings may attach to the word, I still have not met them in my own inquiries. The only time I heard anything approaching the meaning 'superman' was when an Orokaiva, who had settled in another part of the Territory, gave *kotopu* as the equivalent in his language for 'chief'. The meaning of 'set apart' or 'holy' perhaps comes nearer to the results of my own questioning.

Adjectivally, the word seems to indicate 'well-behaved' in the widest sense of the term. It was applied to a law-abiding and amenable member of society, and perhaps the nearest equivalent in our language would be 'decent' or 'respectable'. The emphasis is certainly laid on the milder virtues rather than the more heroic. Thus a man was *otohu* or *otohu-embo* who did not quarrel, who did not beat his wife or children, who did not ill-treat his dogs and pigs, and who did not steal. According to one informant, an *otohu* man was he who went about his work quietly, who returned from his garden with wood on his shoulder and set it down, and then chewed his betel without 'rowing'. Diligence bears some part in this rather complex ideal, and so certainly does generosity: an *otohu-embo*, I was assured, would never refuse a request for tobacco. But it is on the negative virtues of respectability that the greater stress is laid.

Now I am bound to think that this concept of *otohu* as a good character bears directly on the instructions which the *aguma* gives the initiate at the bestowal of the *otohu* ornament. I have heard a number of versions of these instructions: the youth is adjured not to quarrel or brawl, not to steal, not to commit adultery. He is told to be diligent in the garden, in hunting, and in fishing; and to be generous and helpful, never refusing to fetch wood and water, or to give betel-nut to his friend. So a woman is told to lend an ear to what her husband says, and never give him 'strong talk' in return; to accompany him wherever he goes; to be faithful to him; and to keep her hands off other women's property.

It is at the actual presentation of the *otohu* ornament that these injunctions are laid upon the youth or the girl, and thenceforward, it appears, the initiate must live up to the *otohu* character. I have been told that a man might refuse to enter into a quarrel, saying, No, I am an *otohu-embo*; whereas one who had never received the *otohu* would grow up bad-tempered and a ne'er-do-well.

We may conclude, therefore, that the possession of an *otohu* does involve a social obligation. It is an honour and a privilege bestowed by society, but it means that the recipient should settle down as a thoroughly amenable member of that society.

I would not claim that this meaning, viz. decent or amenable to society, was necessarily the basic meaning of *otohu*. I should think rather that the name belonged in the first place to the concrete object or ornament, and that it came to be used for the negative virtues of respectability because those virtues were impressed upon the youth when the ornament was given him.

I am quite unable to offer any useful conjecture as to the

derivation of the word. It was observed that *otohu* was the name given to the 'male' flute at Wasida, though this seems to throws no light on its meaning. More interesting perhaps is the fact that among the Baruga, southern neighbours to the Orokaiva, *kotopo* means a clan badge; and that this badge commonly takes the form of some arrangement of white ovulum shells which are presented to the initiates (fixed to their arms or legs) when they emerge from seclusion. It is not impossible that the Orokaiva *otohu* (or *kotopo*) —although it has no clan significance—should have been originally identical with the clan badge of the Baruga.

Girls' Puberty Seclusion

The puberty seclusion of girlhood together with the formal ceremony of emergence may be treated separately, although they are in principle similar to the initiatory seclusion and the début which have been described in the foregoing pages. This last section should be regarded as an appendix to the present chapter.

As explained on p. 184, the girl enters seclusion directly her first menses appear. After a term of varying length she makes a début similar to that of the initiates and receives her *kokumbari* or feather decorations. She may be content with this, marry, and never pass through her initiation. But very commonly she will qualify for initiation and an *otohu*, and this will necessitate a second seclusion among the initiates. It is the first, or puberty initiation, which I shall now briefly describe.

The girl is confined in a specially constructed compartment of the house. I have cases in which this was variously the house of her father, her maternal uncle, and her husband's father (for a girl may go to the house of her husband's father before she has reached the age of puberty). She is commonly confined alone, though, if by a happy coincidence several girls in the neighbourhood reach this point of development at about the same time, it will be arranged that they come down out of their seclusion on one and the same occasion. It thus happens that the duration of their confinement varies considerably, one girl having to wait for another.

The seclusion will probably last several months; but in this, as in most other cases of seclusion, the time is not fixed, but depends upon the pig [1] and the garden produce. When these are ready the seclusion may be brought to an end.

The girl's confinement is not always of the strictest. She may retire to the bush either by means of a passage between palm-leaf walls at the rear of the house, or else she may walk out wrapped in an *ohi* mat. These precautions are meant, of course, to screen her from the view of the village. The compartment in which she lives is small and dark, perhaps a walled-off corner, though she is not confined there perpetually. In some cases I noted that she was allowed the freedom of the whole house. She is well fed, and lives in complete and probably contented idleness; nor can I hear of any special instructions which her elders may impart to her during this period. Her body is covered with a mess of coco-nut oil and charcoal, the effect of which is supposedly to make her complexion fairer (*panjari* or *hohoma*). In the broad daylight the skin of a secluded girl wears a somewhat yellow or sallow tint which is deemed attractive. She must avoid being seen by men, though this rule evidently does not apply to her father and immediate male relatives.

When preparations for the girl's début are complete she is carried down to the river at earliest dawn on the shoulders of a woman, and there the oil and charcoal are washed off. This operation should be over in time for the girl to be back in her house before full daylight, but one may be up in time to witness the curious spectacle of a woman staggering through the village with a full-grown girl, completely naked, sitting astride her shoulders. In the very touchy or susceptible condition in which a girl finds herself at the end of seclusion, it appears that there is a source of danger in contact with the ground. But this risk, if it is always felt, is sometimes ignored, for on one occasion I saw several

---

[1] One pig, indeed, may serve for several quite independent ceremonies. A man Tembari, for example, has his pubescent daughter and his widowed sister both interned in his house. He has a pig fattening, and when it has reached a satisfactory size it will serve for a feast at which his daughter and sister will terminate their seclusion and his son receive a perineal band.

girls who ended their seclusion together go down on foot to the river. Here they were washed by a number of older women, who engaged in a boisterous water-fight, and then all returned in a body dancing and singing extremely indecent songs.

After this bath at day-break the remainder of the morning is given to decorating the girl. Her skin is oiled again, the hair is shaved back a little from her forehead (merely for effect, I believe), and she is bedecked with feathers and ornaments.

The actual début of the girl, or in many cases of the girls, is made with some little dramatic effect. They have been brought together in one house, before which is set up a screen of palm-leaves with an opening or gateway concealed behind curtains of bark-cloth. When all is in readiness, the curtains are drawn apart and reveal the girls standing abreast, with a young man on either flank, apparently as escort. The girls are armed with spears or pineapple clubs; and in one hand they may carry a bunch of ripe betel-nuts, or a new-painted *bo*, rolled up, which will presently serve as a dancer's shawl. The striking feature of their make-up is the *bo* or bark-cloth skirt which they are actually wearing. This is of plain bark-cloth, unornamented save for splashes or smears of red; and in front and rear it has a hole which purports to expose their genitalia to the view of the onlookers. Thus attired the young women move slowly and in silence across the village and sit in a row on a log which their escorts have procured for them. After remaining some ten minutes on the log they rise and seat themselves on a coco-nut mat (*tere*) spread on the ground; and then after another ten minutes or so they rise once more and mingle with their friends. They will subsequently join in the dance which has been organized for the occasion, and they will not discard their ornaments till sunset. The ceremony has not ended until they eat the purificatory stew called *suna*, and steam their bodies over it.

I have never succeeded in obtaining any satisfactory explanation for the details of this procedure, i.e. the weapons, the betel-nuts, &c. The perforation of the *bo* is to the native an old custom: in after-life a girl would be put to shame if she were reminded that she had made her début without observing that inexplicable but important detail. Some said that the holes in the *bo* were safeguards against the bodily deformities and swellings which the Orokaiva so much dreads; though why they should have this effect remained a problem. It may be that the red smears on the bark-cloth were symbolical of menstrual blood, though no native witness gave that interpretation or any other to them. The sitting first on a log and then on a *tere* mat are both precautions against physical deformity: they exemplify the same ceremonial avoidance of contact with the ground which we have seen with initiates in the *kokumbari* ceremony. Lastly, the fumigation or steaming over the pot of *suna*, and the application of it to parts of the body, are all directed against the same possibility, that of physical deformity.

Among the southern tribes the girl continues to wear an ordinary *bo* (i.e. without perforation) after the ceremony. Among the northern she goes naked until her marriage.

XIII

CEREMONIES OF MOURNING

BEFORE commencing a full account of mortuary cere-monies it will be as well to anticipate by a summary to which the reader may turn back for reference in the course of a long and perhaps bewildering description.

(1) First comes the ceremonies of actual burial, which are followed by the widow's seclusion (pp. 210 ff.; 215 ff.).

(2) The widow emerges from her seclusion and assumes the jacket which is the special sign of mourning (pp. 218 ff.).

(3) The widow discards her mourning jacket, and the other mourners give up the voluntary tabus they have undergone (pp. 224 ff.). After a protracted general tabu on the food supplies, there follows,

(4) An important ceremonial feast and dance, accompanied among the northern tribes by a dramatic performance.

(5) The last of the mortuary ceremonies is the ritual dis-posal of the paraphernalia of this dance and drama (p. 253).

These five stages or landmarks may be separated from one another by intervals of many months. In the course of the present chapter and the next, continual reference will be made to them in order to keep the sequence of events clearly before the reader. The fourth and fifth stages will be dealt with under Dance and Drama, Chapter XIV.

Death and Burial

When death occurs in an Orokaiva village the women burst into loud lamentations, and rush to the nearest swamp to bedaub themselves with mud. Sometimes they mistake coma for death, and the dead man awakes in the midst of the lamentations. Sometimes—one might say usually—they begin wailing as soon as they are convinced that the patient is sinking and death is not far off.

I well remember such a scene about a dying infant. The poor child—if it retained consciousness enough to care—might well have been annoyed by a deafening clamour of grief, and its last moments were no doubt rendered fewer and more uncomfortable by the attentions of its relatives.

When the victim of this solicitude is finally dead, he is stretched out on his back. His face is painted and his head decorated with ornaments and a feather head-dress. Some of these will be buried with him; but his children will remove and keep the more valuable. The corpse of a man is entirely naked; that of a woman wears a *bo*.

If the deceased be a man of any importance, his body is laid out on a sloping platform (*bahari*) in the village. It is made of logs set at an angle of about 20 degrees, and the corpse is laid upon it feet downwards and with arms outstretched. This *bahari* is said to be meant for the convenience of the mourners who wish to embrace the corpse.

The posthumous honour of a *bahari* is denied to a woman for a curious reason which I have heard several times repeated. Women are too fond of *bivije* or adulterous intercourse, and are therefore undeserving of the dignity of an elevated position. They are laid on a mat on the ground, and the only real regret for them is said to be on the part of those who have enjoyed their favours. And since these latter are ashamed to weep for fear of betraying themselves, the woman goes unwept and unhonoured to her grave. This explanation, needless to say, was derived from male informants, and, in point of fact, the demonstrations of grief at a woman's death are hardly less extravagant than at a man's.

The mourners flock in from all villages in the neighbourhood, pausing on the way to smear themselves with mud, *pusu* (from which they get the name of *pusu-embo* or 'muddy men'). They desert their gardens or whatever work they have in hand at the sound of the *hui*, which repeatedly gives a very long-drawn note as a signal of death. Their attendance is not entirely obligatory, but it is regarded as a matter of decency to attend the funeral of a neighbour: and the relatives of the deceased will be offended if there is not a large muster. It is to be suspected, moreover, that the mourners derive some satisfaction from the very exuberant way they have of showing their grief, and, in the case of the many who are but remotely connected with the deceased, it is possible that they find some actual pleasure in surrendering themselves to a violent emotion. Nevertheless, one may definitely discount the belief of some Europeans that the grief of natives in bereavement is not genuine. My own observations have led me to form the contrary opinion, viz. that their grief is distressingly real. The fallacy may have its origin in the fact that a great number of the mourners do wilfully abandon themselves to the excitement of an emotion which is conjured up for the occasion. But one need only look at a bereaved parent or a widow to see that her sorrow, at any rate, is no counterfeit.

At the death of an old man, Handau of Korisata, when his body had been removed from the *bahari* because of rain and laid under his house, there was a continual striving among the mourners to get near him. Squatting or kneeling around they would hold him by the hands, the feet, or the neck, or fling themselves down and embrace him. One man, standing with legs astride the corpse, would jog continually up and down and howl in a manner which gave one an actual sensation of hoarseness by listening to him. Another was shaking, apparently uncontrollably, in every limb, while a friend tried to quieten him. A woman was dancing outside, or perhaps rather flinging herself about, while a second woman held her from behind with arms under her arms and around her breasts in the endeavour to restrain her.

It is, in fact, customary at such times for those who are less deeply affected to restrain or protect those who are really besides themselves with grief, or who, in other cases, are shamming too realistically; and sometimes these guardians may even tie ropes about the waists of their charges and thus follow them in order to keep them the better out of mischief. Women make a practice of cutting their foreheads, cheeks, and shoulders with quartz, glass, or knives. They beat themselves on the back with heavy stones. They will lick 'sand-paper' leaves till their tongues bleed, saying, 'He used to give me pig and taro to eat in my mouth: now I will make my mouth bleed'. It would seem that men are somewhat less severe on themselves, though they may cut

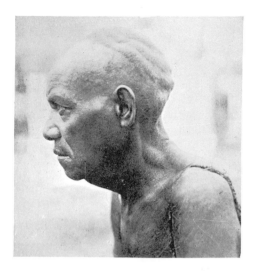

(*a*) Hair shaved in Mourning.
Not an usual mode

(*b*) The *Bahari* or Exposure Platform for the Corpse

PLATE XXVII

their shoulders or beat themselves on the forehead with their clubs. Mourners will chew a poisonous root until their mouths and throats are severely corroded; and I know one man whose scarred buttocks afford irremovable evidence of the fact that he deliberately sat down in the fire at a funeral. Even cases of suicide are not altogether uncommon. A village constable not long ago poisoned himself with 'New Guinea Dynamite' after his wife's death; a woman who saw both her brother and her son die within a short space of time went and hanged herself with a strip of bark-cloth; and a distracted widower of Wasida took a flying leap (though strangely not a fatal one) over a cliff of some thirty feet into a rocky river-bed. I dislike capping my own story with another man's, but cannot forbear to quote one of Mr. Flint's:

'An old man informs me that some time ago a woman held a tomahawk above her head and brought it down with such force that her skull was fractured. She died three days later from the effects of the injury. This woman had evidently been in the habit of hitting herself with a stone club and, to use my informant's words, "Did not savvy the white man's axe".' [1]

A woman once gave me an odd reason, but perhaps an understanding one, for these violent manifestations of grief. Grief itself is called *jo,* and this woman said that drastic measures such as the hacking of cheeks were meant to put a speedy end to the *jo.* Otherwise it would remain with the mourners for a long time.

After lying in state, so to speak, for perhaps a day and night, the body is wrapped in pandanus-leaf mats and bark-cloth for burial. The grave (*use*) is 3 or 4 feet deep. It contains an oblong 'coffin' (*detemba*), the floor of which is made of palm-wood strips like that of a house. The *detemba* is really no more than a strong framework of size sufficient to accommodate the body in a supine position. It is eventually covered with a roofing of poles and a large sheet of bark (*gapa*) to protect the corpse from the earth when it is thrown in.[2]

[1] *Annual Report,* 1924-5, p. 47.
[2] In the Sangara tribe (and possibly in others as well) the grave is undercut on one side at the bottom, the reason being once more to protect the body in its *detemba*

The grave is dug with knives, sticks, and finger-nails, and the earth scooped out with a wooden dish (*teva*). In one instance a number of young men acted as grave-diggers; the deceased (a woman) stood in the various relationships of *aja, tata, imboti, du,* and *hovatu* to them, and they came from six different villages. It seems clear, therefore, that the function of grave-digger does not belong to any particular relatives.

The body, whether of man or woman, is usually carried from the house to the grave by women. Many crowd around, and when the body is laid down in line with the grave there is a veritable scrum of mourners about it. Each is wailing or dirging independently, and to a listener at close quarters the atmosphere seems to be fairly dancing with the discord, though at a distance their combined voices resolve themselves into a rich monotone. The lamentation of the adult takes a lyrical turn in which extempore words are chanted loudly and with some semblance of rhythm, but I do not forget hearing the young son of a dead woman repeatedly scream, '*Aja, aja!*' as if perhaps his grief were too great even for the restraint of a dirge.

When for a few moments comparative quietness has been secured, an elderly man, holding in one hand a spear and in the other a bunch or ornaments, stands by the corpse and, pressing upon its feet with one of his own, as if to rouse (*ujari*) or attract its attention, he declaims what we might call a valediction. Of this I have several renderings which agree in essence but differ sufficiently to show that this farewell address is not a set form. The gist of it is as follows: 'Go now to a good place, not an evil one; go to the road of the sunshine, not to the road of the rains; go where there are neither mosquitoes nor march-flies, but where there are pigs in plenty and taro in plenty. Send us pigs and send us taro, and we shall make a feast in your honour, and pay-

from the superincumbent earth. In the hilly country of the Dirou tribe there is a system of cave burial which is foreign to the Orokaiva at large. The body is here wrapped in bark cloth and encased in a roughly meshed structure of cane. This, supported on a pole between two trestles or props, is set up in some inaccessible cave or fissure in the rocks, and allowed to decompose and fall. I am told that when the package has fallen to pieces and only the skeleton is left, the valuable *hambo* or ornaments which were attached to the body are retrieved.

(*a*) Crowding about the Grave

(*b*) Widow lying in the Grave

PLATE XXVIII

ment to those who have mourned for you.' The 'road of
the sunshine' (*iji-deita*) was said (when I asked where it was)
to be in the east, and the 'road of the rains' in the west,
where there are great downpours on the slopes of the
Central Range; but it may be said very emphatically that
there is no idea of a general Paradise or Elysium in the east,
but only of various scattered *sovai-ta-na* or 'villages of the
spirits', which are usually in fairly close proximity to the
villages of the living. The contrast between sunshine and
rain really points to the desired contrast between cheerful-
ness and gloom, not to that between east and west.

The spear and the handful of ornaments are presented—
only in form—to the dead, and he is adjured to present
them in turn to the other *sovai* whom he is to meet. He is
told to announce his name to them, and the name of his
father, to call upon them 'to make way for him, to blow the
trumpet, beat the drums, and prepare a feast', and he will
hand them these as, it would appear, conciliatory gifts.

When this address is concluded the body is lowered into
the grave. The women who are still clinging about it must
first be dragged or thrown aside, and this is done by one or
two young men with a roughness which is not inexcusable.
The grave is only partly filled, and the earth stamped down.
In the shallow depression which remains the mourners
throw themselves down—as many as can find a place—and
veritably wallow in their grief. They almost jostle for position, so much so that I have seen a bereaved husband compelled to push and shoulder his way through a throng of
mourners to secure a place at the grave of his wife.

Mourning Seclusion

It is customary among all the tribes for a widow to go
into seclusion for some time after her husband's death. In
certain tribes the widower is also secluded under similar
circumstances, but as this latter custom is not universal I
shall in the following section deal solely with the seclusion
of the widow.

When the excitement—for such it is—of the funeral has
died away, the widow (*doru*) of the deceased is left, perhaps

with one or two other women, at his grave. Formerly the grave was under the house of the deceased; now by Government regulation it is in the bush at some distance from the village. It is natural that the natives should do their best to evade this regulation, because the custom of burial under the house is no doubt based on sentiment. Informants repeatedly state that they dislike burying their dead at a distance because they are sad or 'belly-sore'. I have also heard that they dislike the thought of a grave neglected and overgrown; but the principal idea is, as informants have stated it to be, that the living cannot bear the parting with the dead. They cling as long as they can even to his inanimate presence. Sometimes in these days the dead are actually buried in the village, though if the fact is discovered or betrayed, the mourners are likely to work out their sorrow in gaol. More commonly the difficulty is overcome by a rather pathetic subterfuge. The grave is placed in the bush not far from the village, and a small house is built over it in which the widow secludes herself, just as in former times she would have been secluded over her husband's grave in her own house. When a Government patrol draws near, the grave shelter is of course empty.

The widow's seclusion is a long one, and the greater part of it she spends in her own house, i. e. that of her deceased husband. It is not clear when she is transferred from the grave shelter to the house, though it appears that this may be made the occasion of a feast. (Regarding this feast I have very little information, but it is of minor consequence at any rate, and cannot, I think, be regarded as a regular feature of the cycle of mortuary ceremonies.) While in the shelter the widow sleeps actually in the grave, above the corpse of her husband, which is covered only with a shallow layer of earth. I am told that she will from time to time burrow with her fingers in the earth, and whenever she discovers some maggots (*kanyeni*) she will carry them off and deposit them in one place in the bush nearby. Here they accumulate and disappear, being supposedly transformed into the *sovai* of the deceased. I do not know whether this belief and practice (which I found among the Aiga) are of general distribution. At any rate they illustrate only one of the theories as to the transformation of human beings into *sovai*. It is after this disagreeable rite has been performed that the widow moves from the grave shelter to the house, or in former times, we may assume, from the ground under the house to the living room above.

It is the general rule for the widow to be secluded in the house of her husband, though in some instances it appears that the house in which the deceased lived is tabu, being avoided on account of fear. But such cases are evidently exceptional. In the event of evacuation it was not the custom to destroy the house but to leave it, probably surrounded by a tabu string. A house is left when it is thought to be 'haunted' by a *sovai*, and it is not only in a house of recent death that this supposed situation can arise. I have known a young married pair abandon a house because their baby was continually ailing, a fact which they attributed to the presence of a *sovai*. Similarly a whole village may be deserted if its inhabitants get the idea into their heads that it is haunted by malignant spirits.

It is only upon the widow, not upon the other women-folk of the deceased, that rigid seclusion is enforced; though a mother will voluntarily remain for a long time at the grave of her child. In some tribes the widower undergoes seclusion. This is so, I understand, in the Wasida, Sangara, Sauaha, Yega, and Tain-Daware tribes. Among the Aiga and the Binandele he is not secluded. Of the other tribes I have no reliable information.

During seclusion the widow (or the widower) is engaged in making the mourning jacket *baja*—so called because it is made of *baja* (*coix lachrimae* seeds, or Job's Tears). She has no other work to do. She receives frequent friendly visits from the women of the village, who make her presents of food and assist her to make the *baja*, for which the seeds are gathered by her son or some relative of the deceased. She is not seen by the villagers, and her voice is supposed to remain unheard. Indeed, while living for some months in a village rest-house I was completely unaware that a widow was secluded in the house opposite, and that not more than thirty yards away. The reason given for the long seclusion of widowhood was the curious one of 'shame' (*meh*). The woman, it would appear from this explanation, cannot bear to face the people of the village; though I cannot believe that it is merely her grief which she is afraid of showing, for natives are not in the habit of hiding this emotion.

'Gorukari': Ending the Seclusion

The widow's seclusion comes to an end with a feast and a ceremony called *gorukari*. This, it will be remembered, marks the second stage in the cycle of mortuary ceremonies (*vide* p. 210).

When, in former times, the widow's husband had been slain by an enemy tribe, her seclusion must continue till a victim had been secured from that tribe; and it was the corpse of this victim which constituted the *pièce de résistance* of the feast. She was compelled to remain in seclusion till revenge was satisfied. In the fable where a crocodile devours a man, his wife goes into seclusion immediately; but when on the following day her son captures the crocodile and drags it to the house, she comes down, stands on the creature's body, and cries, 'Why did you take my man?'; and then the people dance the *kuru* dance, and her seclusion is over.

In peaceful modern times the victims would be unprocurable, and by the same token the necessity for them does not arise. The seclusion, therefore, is brought to an end when there is a suitable accumulation of food, and its duration is correspondingly variable. The feast on this occasion is called *pusu-ijuka*, lit. 'the counting of the mud', i.e. the reckoning by which the *pusu-embo* (p. 211) are paid for their efforts at the funeral. The people of the deceased husband provide the bulk of the provisions for this feast, but they are assisted by the people of the widow. All the mourners who paid the deceased the final compliment of bedaubing themselves with mud, of wailing, or of digging his grave, are invited to receive their 'payment'; but relatives on both husband's and wife's side will contribute. Apart, however,

(a) First stage of the *Gorukari* or Emergence of the Widow from Seclusion

(b) Second stage of the *Gorukari*

PLATE XXIX

from this paying of the nondescript body of mourners to which both groups contribute, it is evident that on the occasion of the *gorukari* the people of the deceased husband make some payment of food to those of the widow. In fact, amid some confusion of evidence it appears that it is virtually the people of the deceased husband who provide the feast which makes it possible for the widow to emerge from seclusion.

A few days prior to the actual *gorukari*, or emergence of the widow, the principal man of the village performs an interesting rite called *jage* or 'hailing'. Soon after dusk the people of the village are assembled, the younger men holding drums and standing in readiness for a dance. Now, while all maintain a tense silence, the chief man raises his voice and in long-drawn notes cries out the name of the deceased. There is heard an inarticulate reply from somewhere in the bush, and the old man then continues in the same sounding tones to bid the deceased to be present and witness the descent of his widow from the house of seclusion, and to witness the feast and dance. Then the drums strike up and the youths begin the *kuru* dance. The old man and the listening villagers appear to be fully satisfied that they hear the voice of the deceased, and, indeed, it is regarded as essential, for failing the encouragement of a reply the *gorukari* could not go on. I witnessed the performance of this rite on two occasions. On one of them I confess I heard nothing that resembled an answer from the bush, though the villagers declared they did, and seemed fully satisfied. On the other occasion there was a very distinct reply, an inarticulate halloo, which seemed louder than any echo I had heard in the neighbourhood. I could only conclude that a man had posted himself some distance away in the bush; but it is worth adding that this mundane explanation was laughed to ridicule by the natives present, and no one confessed to having played the part of the deceased.

A number of people will have assembled to witness this formal reappearance of the widow, or *doru*. As so often on such occasions one and the same ceremony may suffice for a number of candidates, so that several *doru* who have been

secluded in the neighbourhood may come out simultaneously. They are brought together in one house which is
surrounded by a barricade of palm leaves. Here they are
attended by a number of women and girls who spend the
morning in decorating themselves behind the concealment
of the barrier. Four men, who are to assist in the ceremony, also array themselves in full dancing-dress. Soon
after midday, when the waiting spectators have already been
entertained with a small feast, a few palm leaves are suddenly wrenched away, and in the gap there appear two of
the men squatting on their heels and tapping their drums.
Behind them is a long single file of kneeling women with
two more men bringing up the rear. They all advance
slowly, the women on their knees, the men shuffling on the
soles of their feet. The *doru*, who wear their jackets of
baja, are placed in the centre of the line. They cling to one
another, or to the women in front of them, and are in turn
supported by the women behind them. They wear a voluminous hood or cowl (*pohu*) of bark-cloth embroidered with
Job's Tears, and they hang their heads so that their faces are
invisible. Having crawled forward in this manner for some
twelve or fifteen yards they all rise to their feet, and, without
increasing their pace, proceed to follow a semicircular course
through the village. Then the four men withdraw, and the
women sit down in a group on some palm leaves which have
been laid ready. In their midst are the *doru*, their heads hung
low, and their faces completely veiled with the *pohu* cowls.
    The whole ceremony is somewhat melancholy. The line
moves very slowly, the *doru* dragging their feet and leaning
heavily for support on the women in front of them. The
spectators are seated in a wide half-moon, tapping drums
very softly, and now and then intoning a solemn low-
pitched 'O——, O——!' But this solemn performance may
be succeeded by a dance, which of course gives a new complexion to the scene. On one such occasion which I witnessed, the dancers made their appearance somewhat pre-
maturely, breaking cover at the edge of the village with an
inspiring thunder of drums. One of the principals rushed
forward dramatically waving them back, but, disregarding

him, the dance swept into the village, while the solemn *gorukari* procession went steadily on. In this case the *doru* were helped on to a house verandah, and the younger girls in the procession turned hastily to join in the more animated and attractive entertainment of the dance. Throughout the rest of the day, which witnessed a dance, a dramatic performance, and a feast, the *doru* (of whom there were three) sat on the house verandah without as much as raising their heads to see what was going on.

After this ceremonial emergence the seclusion of the *doru* is over. She continues to wear the *baja*, but may come and go at her ordinary work. She is free to marry again, and marriage may take place before the later ceremony in which the *baja* is discarded. It is said that the halting gait of the widow and her clinging for support upon her neighbour are due to the weakness of her legs after long seclusion; though if we feel inclined to accept such an explanation it must be merely symbolic. The gradual assumption of an upright gait, however, marks in some manner the caution which the native regards as essential in all transition stages. The hiding of the *doru*'s face is again attributed to the *meh*, or shame, which was said to be the reason of seclusion in general.

I was assured that among the southern tribes, who practise seclusion of the widower, there was no ceremonial emergence: the widower's legs were supposed to stand the strain of inactivity and he walked out of his seclusion unassisted. But this cannot be altogether correct, for Mr. Wurth has described, in reference to the Eroro district, a solemn procession in single file, each individual resting his hands on the shoulders of the person in front of him, and the widower wearing the mourning jacket of Job's Tears—in fact a ceremonial that corresponds in all essentials to the emergence of the widow.

Signs and Observances of Mourning

The widow continues to wear her jacket of *baja* (*vide* p. 217), and among the coastal people she smears her face and limbs with mud, which dries white and gives her a sufficiently ghastly appearance. (I have not noted in detail the distribution of this latter custom, but it is not practised among the Aiga or the Binandele.) The *baja* jacket is worn also by the widower, and various relatives of the deceased bear Job's Tears about their persons as a sign of mourning, sometimes in the form of jackets, sometimes merely as armlets or neck ornaments. The seeds appear to be of two varieties, pale grey or fawn, and with the addition of red and black seeds the *baja* jacket may be very effectively decorated. Except in the case of the widow, it appears that the *baja* may be put off at will: a man will wear it when he 'walks about', and doff it when he works. It is, in fact, rather in the nature of an ornament than of sack-cloth and ashes. However, I have been informed—quite gratuitously —that the *asisi* of the dead is in some manner immanent in the *baja*.

The hood (*pohu*) is either of bark-cloth or of netted string, in either case thickly embroidered with the seeds. A fish-net may be used for the purpose, or the *hetava*, i.e. string bag, which belonged to the dead man, and which now figures as a memento.[1]

There are many minor indications of mourning. A woman will wear mementoes of her husband such as a thick necklet made from his *bo* rolled as if into a rope and covered with *baja*, or a series of pendants—a fragment of the pot in which his food was cooked, a chip of the tree he chopped, his coco-nut spoon, his leglet, a tuft of his hair; and a widower may wear his late wife's taro peeler or her bodkin of flying-fox bone. A recognized symbol of mourning is a necklet of large white beads formed of cooked taro which has hardened. A man will wear a beard and cut his hair short in mourning. Both these practices are in the nature of self-castigation, for the Orokaiva fancy a glabrous beauty, and if a man have long head-hair it is felt to be a glory. In one case (to which I have previously drawn attention)

---

[1] An interesting mark of mourning is the *rami* or skirt of palm leaf. This is by no means universal, but is found in the Dirou tribe (where it is of coco-nut), and among the people of the lower Opi (where it is of pandanus). In regard to the latter people, it is said that the women of an earlier population, associated with a semi-mythical character, Bubugarere, all wore palm-leaf skirts; but that they dispersed, some to the north and some to the south, so that nowadays these skirts are to be seen on the one hand on the river Waria and on the other about Cape Nelson.

(*a*) The Widow sitting among her attendants

(*b*) The Widow, showing *Baja* jacket and *Pohu*

PLATE XXX

a man had shaved his hair in mourning for his brother, but
left a series of concentric rings; but this, which had a distinctly decorative, and, as the circles were slightly askew,
an almost jaunty effect, was, I imagine, quite unusual.
Women, who in the excess of their grief hack at themselves
with jagged quartz, often bear permanent raised scars on
their breasts or shoulders.

Formerly it was the custom to cut down one or more of
the coco-nut palms belonging to the deceased. This is now
prohibited by the Government, but it appears that the rule
was always adjustable to circumstances: if a man had many
dependents and few coco-nuts it was not carried out. The
felling of palms is only an example of the destruction of
some part of the property of the deceased, which is attributed to the *jo*, or sorrow, of his survivors. Pots, for instance, or wooden dishes are dashed to the ground and
broken. 'He ate from this dish,' they say, 'therefore we
break it'; or 'he ate the fruit of this palm, therefore we cut
it down'. I have never heard it suggested that the utensils
or the palms were in any way unclean or dangerous. The
reason for the destruction is always said to be *jo*. It may be
another instance of the native's habit of punishing himself
in sorrow, or simply a method of letting off steam: the pots
may be smashed in a fury of grief, just as wine-glasses are
sometimes smashed in ebullitions of a more joyous emotion.

However that may be, I think there is enough in the
severity of the native's mourning observances—so much
severer than our own—to argue the sincerity of his grief.
I may refer lastly to the self-denying tabu of mourning.
Such a self-inflicted abstinence is called *hajai*. The mourner
may abstain from pig-flesh, taro, tobacco, or betel, &c., or
dispense with such articles as a painted *bo* or a string bag.
These are very serious deprivations to an Orokaiva. Once
more the native is punishing himself in his sorrow. One
finds a man, for instance, who voluntarily does without his
hetava, or string bag, that veritable *vade mecum* which is the
receptacle for the lime gourd and many other indispens-
ables. His *nabori*, he may tell you, used to help himself in a
friendly way to the betel-nuts and lime pot in the *hetava*;

now that his *nabori* is dead he will make do without a *hetava*, and carry his lime pot in his hand. Another, who used to dance in a pair with his brother, has forsworn dancing after his brother's death. Another, who used to act as a clown in the plays with his brother (while the latter lived), has given up this also.

Discarding the Signs of Mourning

We may now turn to the third stage in the mortuary cycle (*vide* p. 210). Such tabus or *hajai*, as have been described above, are not for ever, but come to an end with a formal ceremony called *tepurukari*, which means literally 'forsake', or 'abandon'. (Another word applied to it is *ate-ate*, which we saw in connexion with the somewhat similar rite described on pp. 192–3.) The mourner makes a payment to an immediate relative of the deceased, and is in return formally relieved of his tabu. He is, for instance, presented with a new *hetava*, and may thenceforward use it; or he is presented with the conventional costume of a clown, and may thenceforward act his part. When the tabu is upon some particular food a peculiar rite (to which perhaps the term *ate-ate* applies more specifically) brings it to a formal conclusion. The subject holds his hands, palms downward and fingers interlocked, before his breast, while a little of the tabued food is placed upon them. This he throws backwards over his head, and the tabu is at an end.

The discarding of these *hajai* or tabus is properly made to coincide with the more notable ceremony of discarding the *baja*, which marks the third stage in the series of mortuary ceremonies. As, at the assumption of the *baja*, the feast was provided mainly by the husband's people, so on the occasion of discarding it the feast is provided mainly by the widow's people, who pay a pig to those of the husband, and make over to them the *baja* which the widow has been wearing.

Before the actual ceremony the widow, I am told, goes again to the grave of her husband, taps the ground with her foot, and cries out that she is soon to discard her mourning jacket. Later, when the pig has been slain at the feast, the woman takes off the *baja* and places it on the animal's body.

It is finally wrapped up with some of the fat and entrails and buried. In other cases it is hung up in the garden of the deceased and there left to rot in the sun and rain. This garden has been allowed to fall to rack and ruin since his death: none of its products have been eaten, though the young taro shoots may be transplanted to a new plot. In the Wasida dialect the word *kisa* was applied to such a garden. It appears that in this case the neglect of the garden was less a self-denying tabu than due to an actual fear of evil consequences—such as sore eyes, tooth decay, skinniness—if its products were eaten. And it is noteworthy that such effects would be felt only by the immediate relatives of the dead. It was possible, in fact, to make an exchange of gardens, so that the bereaved relatives would not be left without resources, the *kisa* garden being passed over to one who would take no harm from it, and another being given in exchange to the relatives of the dead. The evil potency of the *kisa* garden is apparently attributed to the malignant spirits of the dead—an explanation for which I have the direct testimony of one informant, although in many other cases it remained inexplicit. It is in keeping with the belief (which is a basis for a system of divination, cf. p. 281) that the dead revisit or haunt their gardens, and in general with the fear which the Orokaiva feels for his deceased relatives *qua sovai*. Among the various mourning tabus which have come to my notice, however, this, viz. the forbidding of the garden to the relatives of the deceased, was the only instance in which the motive was apparently one of fear. All the others were rather manifestations of sorrow.

The Naterari, or Tabu Post

The fourth major mortuary ceremony is a dance, which among the Aiga and Binandele is accompanied by a dramatic performance. The fifth is the ritual disposal of certain materials used in the fourth ceremony. Now I do not believe that the dance and drama are purely and wholly a mortuary ceremony, but that they are at least partly so appears from the facts that the dead are called upon to witness the proceedings, and that, when the proceedings are over, certain paraphernalia connected with the dead are ceremonially and finally disposed of. On the other hand, the dance and drama have their own intrinsic value as forms of art and amusement, and, furthermore, they commonly occur in connexion with the initiation and seclusion of a number of youths and girls.

The whole subject of dance and drama, however, will be discussed in the next chapter. In the meantime I shall deal with the tabu upon the food-supply which precedes the fourth stage, and which makes possible the large feast which is perhaps the most important feature of the proceedings in so far as they are of a mourning nature. The mark of this tabu is the *naterari* or tabu post, which has already been referred to in Chapter VIII, p. 117. As we saw there, it usually takes the form of a rough-hewn pillar or post, standing a few feet high in the open space of the village. Properly speaking it is made of the *heratu* wood of the clan; but when the *heratu* is not of a suitably solid nature the *naterari* may consist merely of a piece of light timber called *pamba* tied to the butt of a palm, or perhaps to a croton bush. *Na* means 'village', and *terari* 'to close up', as a creek is dammed up with stones, or as the hollow drum is closed at one end with the lizard skin. The Binandele word is *ao*, apparently a contraction of *ago* (another dialectal form): I cannot make any suggestion as to its real meaning. In Wasida the same object is called *itembari*, probably a compound of *i*, 'tree', and *tembari*, 'to place on top'. In Doboduru the word was *natembahije*: *na*, 'village', *temba*, 'to place on top', *ahije*, 'ancestor'.

Some months after the man's death the *naterari* is set up in the centre of the village, and from this moment the coconuts are not eaten green but allowed to ripen and fall, until at last there is a tremendous accumulation, perhaps laid out in lines on the ground or else piled on a mountainous tripod. Meanwhile the *naterari* has been standing in the village clearing as if silently watching the slow preparations, somewhat weatherbeaten by now, and with its originally garish make-up a little faded. It is, however, treated with a certain amount of care and respect. It is not uncommon to see a miniature four-legged shelter to protect it from the rain, with a gabled roof of sago thatch, and perhaps underneath the roof a little platform. On this platform may be found an old bamboo cylinder pipe, a lime gourd, perhaps a handful of withered betel-nuts; and besides these a few fragments—fresh or mouldy—of cooked taro. These are so placed for the spirit of the departed, or, to use the Aiga word, the *sovai*. It will come by night and refresh itself to that extent which is proper for a spirit, or as a native will say, with a twinkle in his eye, taking no more than an ant might eat. In addition to these offerings, there may be found certain mementoes of the deceased—an old banana-seed necklace, a shell bracelet, in one case a broken gourd that had been a urinary for an invalid and bed-ridden old man.

When the preparations for the entertainment are complete the *naterari* is removed, and with its removal the coconut tabu comes to an end. Normally, it would appear, the *naterari* stands through the time of feasting and is removed afterwards. Sometimes, I am told, the provisions for the feast are displayed before the post—row upon row of wooden dishes piled with cooked food—and it is called upon to witness the feast in its honour.

There is still something of reverence in the final disposal of the *naterari*. When I suggested chopping it up for firewood I was made to feel that this was rather a bad joke. In the inland village it was put aside in the outskirts of the bush, sometimes with a small platform close by for a continuation of the food offerings, and there allowed to decay. On the river Opi it is placed, with other paraphernalia of the dance, upon a raft; with some little ceremony this raft is guided into midstream and released to follow its unattended course toward the sea. Sometimes the *naterari* is stowed away in a house. At any rate it is not simply thrown away and disregarded. For this two reasons are given: first, that the *sovai* or spirit would be angry; second, that the people feel too sorrowful to treat the *naterari* thus.

It is worth referring to the forms or patterns of the tabu post. The variety is very great, for each example seems to take shape from the individual carver's imagination. There is no such thing as a distinctive clan device; and there are no names for particular patterns. In one village a newly erected *naterari* of an unusually pretentious character had been recently substituted for another of inferior workmanship. The latter, though discarded, had not been destroyed. Both belonged to the same clan and village and were set up for the same occasion, but they were wholly different in pattern and appearance.

The treatments range from the very simplest of formal designs to somewhat elaborate representations of the human figure. The latter probably throw some light upon the former. For instance, the prevalent device of cutting through the post so as to leave two separate supports may be reminiscent of the obviously human-like legs of more elaborate figures. There are many *naterari* which apparently do not conform to the implied explanation, but nevertheless it may be said that many do show a slight, and others an unmistakable, anthropomorphic character. The sketches (Fig. 25) were made at various times and entirely at random.

Enough has been said to show that the *naterari* is very closely associated with the dead man for whom the feast is to be made. I do not remember hearing in so many words that the *naterari* actually represented such and such a dead man; but, if I may repeat what was written in Chapter VIII, the fact that the feast is definitely made for the dead man, the care with which the *naterari* is treated, the offerings made to it, the mementoes of the deceased which are attached to it, and the ceremonious way in which it is finally disposed of, would all lend colour to the suggestion that it is regarded as a representative of the dead and is in imagination identified with him. One could not go so far as to say that it was actually an image of him; but in view of its occasionally striking anthropomorphism, it is not impossible that originally the *naterari* was in reality set up as a crude model of the dead. I may give one illustration to show that this idea, or a similar one, has not been entirely forgotten. In one sketch primitively painted on one facet of a post, may be seen the figure of a man. The *naterari* was cut out, set up, and painted by one Bararipa, pending a feast in honour of his deceased father Komona; and the figure, by Bararipa's word, was a picture of Komona himself.

A further bond between the *naterari* and the dead resides in the fact that the tabu post is normally formed of the particular wood which is his plant emblem, and hence is likely to be his clan namesake.

The most interesting point in regard to the *naterari* is the fact that food offerings are made to it. Of this subject I shall speak at greater length when we discuss the belief in survival after death. In the meantime I may give an account of the dance and drama which have at least some significance as ceremonies of mourning.

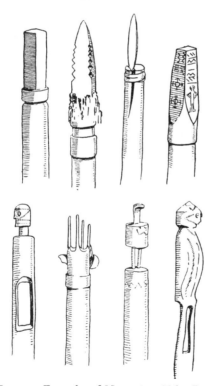

FIG. 25. Examples of *Naterari*, or Tabu Posts

XIV

DANCE AND DRAMA

BEFORE describing the dance and drama in detail it may be as well to set down a brief programme of events, i. e. the sequent stages of the festival. We may assume that the tabu is on the village and that it will remain until the occasion of the feast. If this feast is to be a considerable one, the first step will be the construction of an *arijo*, i. e. a men's house, which will be frequented by the men alone, and used for singing. This may be built a month or so before the festival, and from time to time the old-fashioned dancing (*kuru*) will take place in the open space before the *arijo*.

As the time for the festival approaches, the dancers practise the dance specially arranged for the occasion. There may be an enclosure, *java hamboru*, in or on the outskirts of the village, where they may rehearse in private. (Note that this *java hamboru* may be in the village where the feast and dance are to take place, or in another village. The latter is frequently the case because the dance is commonly performed by *visitors* who have previously undertaken to present it. They therefore rehearse in their own village, and stage the finished performance in the village where the festival is taking place.)

The preparations for the feast are now finalized, food being brought in from the gardens, and platforms or booths erected to stack the provisions or provide shelter for the guests. When everything is in readiness there is a formal semi-public rehearsal of the dance called *pamoni kiari*, or 'Demonstration before the Women'. This takes place on the afternoon before the festival, and is not witnessed by any save the villagers who are making the dance.

The remaining stages may be summarized as follows:

(i) During the night the stage fixtures are set up in the village, and any movable stage paraphernalia placed ready in the bush.

(ii) The morning of the festival sees all the guests assembled. The performers are decorating themselves in the bush.

(iii) The ballet makes its appearance at some moment during the afternoon.

(iv) After dancing some ten minutes or more the ballet goes off and brings back the movable stage properties.

(v) While they resume the dance the actors, *huvivi* and *binei*, make their entry and proceed with the play. This being concluded, they dance off and disappear in the bush.

(vi) The ballet proceeds for a while with the main dance, and then breaks off into a series of minor 'nature' dances.

The performance of the dance and drama may be said to end here. The paraphernalia of the play, however, are brought together, and finally disposed of in a ceremonial manner, but this may be a matter of months afterwards. I shall now proceed to deal with the Orokaiva dance in detail, giving an account—confessedly slight—of its technique.

The Dance

The general name for 'dance' is *java* (Binandele *ya*). As far as I have ascertained there are five main kinds practised by the Orokaiva, viz. (1) *Kuru*, (2) *Paruka*, (3) *Arijo* or *Saunda*, (4) *Puga*, and (5) *Si*. Only the first two are accompanied by song, and only the last three are accompanied by the drama.[1] The first, *kuru*, is without any definite formation save that of a group of men and boys clustered about several drummers. They dance slowly in one direction and then back over the same ground, singing meanwhile. Their movements are quite unpretentious, and might be described as rhythmical shuffling. In all the other dances the performers are in pairs one behind the other, forming double file. Each kind has its appropriate drums and rhythm, the drums being carried by the dancers themselves.

---

[1] The drama is not an invariable accompaniment of *Arijo*, for I have seen a performance of this dance without it. I cannot speak with certainty of *Puga* or *Si*, though I am given to understand that they are always associated with a dramatic performance.

(1) *Kuru*; also called *Gatari, Puruto, Jiwari.*
> *Form*: Dancers clustered about drummers.
> *Drum*: *Ino* (large) and *Ehu* (medium); accompanied by singing.
> *Rhythm*: Regular continuous beat. (Spondaic.)

Andante.

No Drama.

(2) *Paruka, Baruga* (the name of the southern neighbours of the Orokaiva).
> *Form*: Dancers in double file; the movements are lighter and more rapid than in 3, 4, or 5.
> *Drum*: *Ehu*; accompanied by singing.
> *Rhythm*: Time of three, with the stress on the second beat, the third being missed or made with an almost inaudible tap of the finger-tips. (Iambic.)

Moderato.

Natives call this rhythm '*Gurru Gúrru—Gurru Gúrru—.*' In pronouncing, the two syllables of *Gurru* must be run as nearly as possible into one.

No Drama.

(3) *Saunda* or *Arijo* (*Saunda*—the small drum; *Arijo*—men's dancing or singing house).
> *Form*: Dancers in double file.
> *Drum*: *Saunda* (small); no singing.
> *Rhythm*: Time of four, stress on third beat, fourth beat usually missed. (Anapaestic.)

Moderato.

Drama.

(4) *Puga* (*Puga,* or, in the Binandele form, *Bua*—the empty shell of the *Puga* fruit, used as a rattle. *Torepa,* which means the same, is another name for this dance).

Form: Dancers in double life.

Drum: *Saunda*; no singing.

Rhythm: Same as *Saunda,* but quicker, and the fourth beat heard more often. (Anapaestic.)

Allegro.

Drama.

(5) *Si, Shi, Ji,* &c. (the word means 'weeping').

Form: Dancers in double file.

Drum: *Ehu*; no singing.

Rhythm: Time of two, stress on first beat; occasionally varied by three short beats instead of two. (Trochaic and occasionally dactylic.)

Allegro.

Natives call this rhythm '*Kíngi Kíngi Kígigi*', &c.

Drama.

I can give very little information as to the origin of these several kinds of dance. It is generally admitted that *kuru* is the most primitive of them. It is of universal distribution, and seems to have attained to no kind of specialization. It is merely the old style of singing together and moving in unison, and is ready for any occasion. *Baruga* is a popular dance, and appears to be universally distributed. It is said to have come, as its name implies, from the south, but whether it is earlier or later than *Saunda, Puga,* or *Si* I am unable to say definitely.

Arijo (or *Saunda*) is now widely distributed, though informants have declared that it comes from the northern Orokaiva. As to *Puga* and *Si,* it seems likely that they at

least were confined to the Aiga and Binandele until comparatively recent times. It is said that *Puga* originated among
the Jeva Buje of the lower Kumusi, and that *Si* originated
among the Aiga. One need not attach much value to these
accounts, but I repeat for what it is worth a tale of the discovery of *Si*. An old man, Ororo, was seated on a platform
in the village of Petakiari, lost in contemplation of the river
which swirled by in a flood. Something catches the old
man's attention and he cranes his neck. Is it a crocodile?
No, a *sasa*, that is to say, a branch or tree trunk all but sub-
merged in the river. The water pours over the *sasa* and
presses it under for a moment until its resilience brings it to
the surface again, and this process goes on so that the branch
sways rhythmically up and down. Ororo, reaching for his
drum, lightly taps out the measure that the *sasa* shows him,
and thinks out the movements for a new dance. Meanwhile
his wife, watching the old man tapping his drum, is for some
reason so moved by the spectacle as to burst into lamentation. Thus the swaying of the *sasa* gave Ororo the inspiration for a new dance, and the weeping (*si*) of his wife supplied it with a name.

It will be seen that, with the exception of *Kuru*, all the
dances have double-file formation. When they begin the
dance the performers are two by two facing in the same
direction; and throughout all the movements this formation is retained, or at least regained from time to time. It
is very usual for the couples to be composed of boyhood
friends or *otavo* (see p. 166), who have been accustomed to
dance together, just as they shared many other tasks or
exploits. These couples have various parts to perform according to their positions in the column; and these positions
have definite names, from 'head' to 'tail', as if the column of
dancers represented an animal or reptile, though there is no
such picturesque fancy in the native mind. The most active
part is taken by the leading couple, who are called *hohoru*, the
'head'; and a characteristic detail of the dance is seen when
they, or the third couple, *saseri*, beat their drums over the
faces of the second couple, *tunga*, who bend their bodies
backwards as they dance.

(*a*) Dancers in the *Si* Dance

(*b*) Scene in a village during a Dance

(*c*) Performers of Dance *Arijo*

PLATE XXXI

The couples from front to rear are named as follows:

o	o	*Hohoru* .	.	Head.
o	o	*Tunga* .	.	Neck.
o	o	*Saseri* .	.	The branch set up as a shelter from the sun.
o	o	*Orohu* .	.	The first finger.
o	o			
o	o	,,		
o	o	*Saseri.*		
o	o	*Abo-tunga*	.	Tail-neck.
o	o	*Abo*	.	. Tail.

It will be understood that the column varies in length according to the number of dancers available. I imagine that any extra couples take their places in the middle, and are called *orohu*. As to the meanings of the words, that of *saseri* seems unsatisfactory, and no plausible explanation

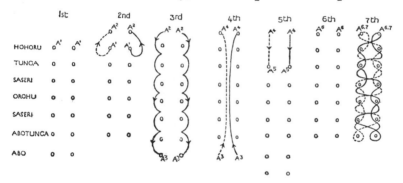

was offered. *Orohu* means 'the first finger', though it may be that this is not the only meaning of the word. *Abo* incidentally is used for the little finger, but the word stands for the rear, the tail, the anus, the last in general. It may be repeated that the various parts of the dancing column, despite their suggestive names, do not seem to be welded into any complete image in the native mind.

It has been impossible to record the figures of the dances in any detail. The above examples, however, which were noted at a performance of *Si*, may be regarded as typical. The leading pair, *hohoru*, are marked A, A, and the numbers show the positions they occupy at the beginning and end of each figure.

The column moves forwards and backwards more than

it is possible to indicate in the diagram, and it must be understood that every dancer is continually in action. In the fourth figure, for instance, while A³, A³ are dancing down the centre to their new position A⁴ A⁴, the rest of the dancers move in the opposite direction. In the fifth figure all the performers dance backwards for some distance, beating their drums heavily, and then in the sixth they advance on tiptoe over the same ground, stooping and tapping their drums almost inaudibly, all of which forms a very quiet and pretty contrast to the previous movement. The seventh figure, called *Tehokari* or ' crossing ', is a favourite, and very effective. It will be remembered that the above are merely typical examples and do not pretend to be a complete list of dance figures.

While dealing with the subject of dances in general we must notice the minor class of what might be called mimetic or nature dances. These, as reference to the programme on p. 231 will show, are usually performed after the drama. They are not to be regarded as essential parts of the major dances, but are in the nature of extras, cheerful little items which are added at the end of the entertainment. They are very numerous, and it appears that they are severally associated with one or other of the major dances, i.e. some are performed after *Si*, others after *Paruka*, &c. They are brief and animated. The dancers perform them with obvious zest, and pass rapidly from one to another as if they had any number at the tips of their toes. A brief description of a selection will show their general character.

1. *Gosevo Ijukari*—'*Threading the Fish on a Line*'. The fisher-woman, whenever she catches a small *gosevo* fish, threads it (*ijukari*) through the gills with a withe, until presently she has a whole succession of *gosevo* trailing behind her. The dancers form single file and move rapidly in a circle.

2. *The Purere Bird*. The *purere* is a small bird which seeks its food on the ground. The men dance on their heels and each revolves in a half-circle, regaining the usual two and two formation. The *purere* is hopping about in search of its food.

3. *Umo Ganigari*—'*The Rushing through of the Waters*'. When

fishing in the creek the native will dam up the stream and bale out the water below his dam. Sometimes the dam breaks, and a continuous stream of water rushes through. The two ranks of the dance column begin by moving in one direction, then turn outwards, back, and in again, so as to form a continuous swift movement:

4. *Huruga*—'*The Frog*'. The two ranks of dancers face inwards. They advance towards one another by short hops; the ranks pass through one another and about turn. The drums beat a slow deliberate rhythm which is reminiscent of the 'knocking' croak of the frog.

5. *Hohora*—'*The Cock*'. The dance divides into two bodies each in the usual double-file formation. A spear being set up between the two parties they dance towards it from either side, raising their drums as they do so; then they retreat, stooping, and with drums lowered. Meanwhile one man in the centre dances round the spear keeping his eye fixed on it. The whole dance is a pretty one, though it is not easy to explain its symbolism. The advance and retreat of the two parties, however, is oddly suggestive of the cock flapping his wings as he crows.

6. *Tongiju*—'*The Spirit of the Slain*'. The dancers form two bodies, each in a single file and each facing toward a spear set up between them. They all take several steps to the right, then several steps to the left, first shaking or jerking their heads to the right, then doing the same to the left. The *tongiju* is the spirit of a man who has been clubbed on the head and is trying to jerk the blood out of his ears.

7. *Ba Utera*—'*Pulling the Taro*'. The dancers sink almost on to their heels, striking the drums. Then they leap upright, raising the right hand as if pulling a taro from the ground.

8. *Pengoro*—'*The Tadpole*'. The dancers are in the usual two-and-two formation. Almost squatting on their haunches

they run forward a few paces and halt, and as they halt the
two leaders rise, turn, and beat their drums over the heads
of the pair behind them. The action, which is repeated again
and again, is suggestive enough of the large-headed tadpole
making short darts through the water.

The costume of the dancer requires some description.
The first of the major dances, *kuru*, does not call for any
special decoration, but in all the others the performers
appear in what may be called full costume, viz. feather head-
dress, face-paint, ornaments held in the teeth, and *ando*, i.e.
voluminous skirts or mantles of grass or palm leaf, frayed
and dyed. It is unnecessary to dwell on the effectiveness of
the *ensemble*. Bunches of croton add to the already brilliant
colouring, and the dancer, with his massive head-dress and
sweeping draperies, seems to be magnified far beyond
human size.

It is worthy of note, however, that the costume constitutes a virtual disguise, which is in some cases made more
complete by a veil of shredded palm leaf which hangs from
the forehead. This disguise derives extra significance from
the fact that there is at least an affectation of secrecy as to
the identity of the dancers. At the formal rehearsal before
the women, called *Pamoni kiari*, the parts are deliberately
'faked': the various positions are not taken by the men who
are to take them in the final appearance on the following
day. Again, prior to a dance which I witnessed, the names
and positions of the personnel were told over to me, but in
a whisper, and only within the confines of the *java hamboru*.
The native reason for this secrecy was that the effect upon
the women and the guests would be spoilt by divulging
the names of the performers.

There is one particular in the costumes to which I would
draw attention. In some of the dances—I have not carefully
noted which—certain of the performers wear a conical head-
dress of croton leaves. It is usually the leading pair (*hohoru*),
and perhaps also the last pair (*abo*), who appear in this uncommon headgear. Now at Bovera on the river Eia, which
is practically the northern boundary of the Orokaiva, I have
seen in a man's house several conical head-dresses strongly

made of cane and bark-cloth, which were virtually masks; and Mr. C. H. Karius informs me that he has seen on the river Waria what we should definitely call masked dancers, whose mask was once more of the same conical shape.

These particulars—the secrecy, the virtual disguise, also perhaps the use of palm-leaf skirts and mantles, and certainly the conical head-gear—all remind one of the masked dances of the Western Papuan, and in particular of the typical conical mask of the '*kaiva kuku*'. I would, therefore, put forward the very tentative suggestion that in the ceremonial dances of the Orokaiva we have a faint replica of the masked dance of the west. If this were so we should have a fair case for viewing the dance as a mortuary ceremony in which the dancers originally represented the spirits of the dead. For the present, however, this may be laid aside as no more than a conjecture.

The Drama: Stage Accessories

We may now turn our attention to the drama which always appears as a well-defined episode, and thus admits of separate treatment. I have used the word 'drama', despite its pretentious sound, because it is really the most non-committal; though 'mime' or 'farce' might have been more descriptive. As dialogue is almost completely absent, the expression 'dumb-show' would have been perhaps the most accurate of all. It is very difficult to discover a native word for the drama as abstracted from the remainder of the performance, i.e. the dance. The most satisfactory is *sesena* (Binandele *tetenya*) which means simply 'play', or 'play about'. Sometimes it is called *sovai-sesena*, 'the game played by the *sovai*'. Another word, of which I do not know the literal meaning, is *tehua*; and yet another—*yavetu*. It will be remembered that the play is proceeded or ushered in by the ballet. When the dance has been in progress for some ten minutes or more, the dancers suddenly leave in a body, retire into the bush near by, and reappear bearing the movable stage properties. These naturally vary according to the subject of the drama: they may, e.g., consist of a garden platform on which one of the actors is to sit, or a sago-log (represented by a stalk of a banana plant), or the ladder from the ground to the elevated hiding-place in which some of the actors are already placed. This stage-moving is done with rather remarkable expedition, and the dancers contrive to keep the stage furniture hidden from the spectators' view. This attempt at secrecy is rather noteworthy. Women spectators, for instance, may seize their mats and rush forward to help in concealing the stage properties as they are brought on, already well enough concealed as they are by the throng of stage-movers.

Very often some kind of fixture has already been erected in the village. This usually takes the form of an elevated place of concealment, and may consist of a hollow tree-trunk set on end. Sometimes the branches of a growing tree are lopped off short, and the tree is felled and set up in the village during the night. Upon the base formed by the spreading branches is built a closed superstructure, and in this retreat one or more of the actors must take their places before dawn and remain cramped and uncomfortable until they receive their cue in the afternoon.

When the dancers have set up the stage furniture to their satisfaction, they fall into their places before it and resume their dance. Now everything is in readiness for the appearance of the actors.

A Typical Drama Described

As a composite description is hardly possible I propose to give a fairly full account of one Orokaiva drama as I saw it, together with a brief abstract of several others. This method should suffice to give a fair idea of the drama as a whole.

The example chosen for description has this to recommend it, that having been performed at a 'Christmas' on a Government station it is devoid of obscenity. This does not mean that the performance is other than typical, because obscenity, although very common, is certainly not invariable or essential in the native drama. This has been selected from among the five examples which I have personally witnessed merely because it is, for the reason suggested, more easy to describe. It was performed at Christmas, 1923, on the Buna Bay station, by a party of Jeva Buje natives from the Kumusi.

The play is based upon the following legend or legendary incident, which was recounted to me shortly after by some of the players themselves:

A large *Boru* tree had fallen into the river (informants suggested the river Waria), and in the dark pool beneath this tree there sheltered a *dera*, or sword-fish. Now two girls came down the river fishing with a line, the younger taking charge of the fish as the elder caught them. When they came to the *Boru* tree and cast their line into the dark pool beneath it, the bait was seized by the *dera*. The united efforts of the girls failed to land so large a creature, and the line ran hot through their hands.[1] So they made it fast to a tree-trunk, and ran back to the village for help. On the way they were met by two youths who had followed them with the express intention of *kigi*, i.e. clandestine courtship. But the girls are too excited to dally with these young men. They tell them to wait till they call their father from the village, when all will go down to the river together and kill the *dera*. This all happens as they desire. The *dera* is dragged from the water, tied to a pole, and carried to the village where (to give a good ending to the story) it is cut up and eaten.

This simple and somewhat pointless story forms the plot of the drama which I now proceed to describe.

The scene of the performance was the parade ground, towards one end of which there had been set up during the night a small, roughly constructed shelter of palm leaves, about four feet high and six feet square, and with one side (that facing down the parade ground) left open; this shelter represented the *Boru* tree hanging over the water.

On the sea beach, perhaps a hundred yards away, and thus quite out of sight of the spectators, there was another piece of stage furniture. Under the shelter of a canoe, and completely covered with mats, lay a representation of a

---

[1] The only Orokaiva methods of line fishing of which I know (see p. 57) seem hardly in keeping with the details of this story. It has probably derived something from modern methods.

sword-fish (*dera*). This, which was made of wood, measured eleven feet. The body of the structure consisted of a hollow tree-trunk split down the middle, but various boards had been affixed for fins, and at front and rear there were features to represent the monster's 'sword' and his long tail. The model had been used on a previous performance,[1] and had evidently been well finished and decorated, though it was now somewhat out of repair. (During the performance it sustained further damage, but was kept nevertheless, possibly to be used on a future occasion.) Underneath, or rather within, this wooden model, which may be referred to as *dera*, the sword-fish, there lay a man whose business it would presently be to supply the fish with motive power and intelligence. I do not know low long he had lain in this hot and cramped position, but he was evidently bearing the discomfort quite cheerfully. It is worth noting that informants showed some reluctance in allowing me to see the *dera* and what it contained before the proper moment for its appearance.

The dancers and actors had meanwhile been attiring themselves in some place apart. In the present case I believe it was the police barracks, though in the usual village performance the 'green room' is merely a convenient spot in the surrounding bush. When their preparations, which occupy several hours, are complete, it is time for the performance to begin.

It is part of Orokaiva stage art, and quite in keeping with the affectation of secrecy which surrounds the dance, that the ballet should make its appearance upon the 'stage' from some unexpected quarter. Thus they do not enter a village by the usual pathway, but after a toilsome detour they make a spectacular incursion from the bush or the concealment of the long grass. They announce their arrival by a thunderous tattoo (*kuku*) on the drums, and one turns to see the column of befeathered dancers stooping or crouching at the edge of the clearing. The drums suddenly break into the

---

[1] It may be noted that the most valuable stage properties, i.e. those which have been very carefully made, are sometimes spared in the formal destruction. I have seen two well-made puppets kept apparently as mementoes of dramatic performances, or perhaps to serve in a re-enactment.

(*a*) The Ballet

(*b*) Bringing on the *Dera*

THE DRAMA *DERA*

PLATE XXXII

rhythm of the dance, and the leading couple (*hohoru*, the 'head') spring upright and come dancing into the open. Only a dozen or so paces and they dance back again, to be accompanied next time by the second pair (*tunga*, the 'neck'). Now the two couples dance back once more, and on the third advance are followed by the whole body of dancers, who, performing the ordinary evolutions meanwhile, move across the open and take up their position (which, in this instance, is opposite the shelter of palm leaves at one end of the parade ground). Here they continue the dance for some ten minutes or longer. I can give no more detailed account of this dance (which was of the kind called *Puga*) than has been given already in the general description, pp. 233 ff.

It is usual for the ballet to leave the 'stage' at the conclusion of this initial dance in order to bring on the paraphernalia, but on this occasion they were still performing when six men appeared carrying the *dera*. The ballet now dances forward to meet them, breaks up and surrounds the party so that the *dera* (which is covered with blankets) can hardly be seen. As this drama is being specially performed for the magisterial 'Christmas', it is not surprising that several rather officious village constables, carrying their books, should accompany the bearers and issue a multitude of instructions. These, however, though well-intentioned are quite unnecessary. The *dera*, which still contains the man whom we may call its manipulator, is carried to the shelter and placed underneath it, the blankets are removed, and the bearers and dancers withdraw, the latter to renew their dance. They are now, as previously, formed up before the open side of the shelter, and at a distance of perhaps fifteen paces from it.

The performance goes on for a moment or two when the attention of the spectators suddenly turns to two 'girls' who come dancing and leaping very gracefully through the coconut palms toward the parade ground, one following the other. These are, of course, the two sisters, who are impersonated by male actors called *huvivi*. Each carries the women's quarterstaff completely bound with red material, and the elder of the two has under her arm a fish-line with shell rattles attached to the end. When they have made an almost complete circuit of the ground the elder girl unwinds her fish-line and continually casts and draws it in as she dances. By now they are approaching the shelter where the *dera* is concealed, and the girl casts her line into it. This time she draws it in with a small wooden fish attached. The man underneath the *dera* has seized it and affixed one of a bundle which he carries. Three or four times the girl tries her luck under the shelter, and as often succeeds in catching a fish, which she unhooks and throws to her younger sister. But now she tries again, and this time it appears that she has hooked the *dera* or sword-fish himself. The girl attempts to draw in, but the *dera*, who still remains concealed, holds the line fast. The younger girl comes to the assistance of her sister, and together they pull without avail, until suddenly the *dera* comes scrambling a little distance out of his concealment. The girls are alarmed, but they drive a stake into the ground, secure their line to it, and dance off the stage as gracefully as they came on to it.

In a moment they reappear accompanied by two gaily bedecked youths. These are two more *huvivi*, the girls' lovers, who had followed them down the track. At some distance behind them comes a grotesque and hideous figure who represents the girls' father. He is an actor of another kind, called *samuna*, 'the bad one', or *sovai* (Binandele *binei*), 'the spirit of the dead, the devil-devil'. Staggering and lurching as he approaches he continually brandishes his mock spear of light *pamba* wood. He wears a ragged singlet and torn trousers, and his face is almost covered by two halved coco-nut shells, worn goggle-fashion.[1] Drawing near the spectators he makes darts and sallies, scattering them right and left. He hurls his light spear at any one within his

---

[1] It appears that the *samuna* (*binei*, *sovai*, or 'clown') sometimes wears European trousers nowadays; merely, I think, because they are in themselves ugly garments, and as foreign as one could conceive to the usual garb of the native. A missionary who saw a *samuna* attired in this fashion, and wearing the coco-nut shell goggles, told me he thought the man was 'taking off' the European, and adding a contumelious touch by imitating his spectacles. I think, however, he was mistaken. The coco-nut goggles (called *kiti monjo*) are quite usual: they are one of the conventional means of making the *samuna* look hideous or absurd, and probably the trousers were meant to serve the same purpose. For the usual costume of the *samuna* see p. 251.

(*a*) The Girls fishing

(*b*) The *Samuna*

THE DRAMA *DERA*

PLATE XXXIII

reach—not sparing the small party of white spectators—
and follows with prodigious bounds to recover it. For a
while the fun is running high, and the *samuna* is frankly
concerned with his own antics rather than the action of the
play.

At last he turns to where the four *huvivi* have surrounded
the *dera* in their efforts to capture it. The monster rushes
forth again and again while the youths and maidens dance
lightly around. But now at last the *samuna* has directed his
attention to the work in hand. He lunges at the *dera* with
his spear and after a few more capers succeeds in striking it
dead. The wooden model has suffered more or less serious
damage during the play, and it is necessary for the actors
to mend it or bind it about with withes. This they do very
expeditiously, and, the manipulator of the *dera* having
scrambled out of it, the two *huvivi* youths shoulder the
wooden shell and go prancing off through the coco-nuts.
Behind them follow the two girls, and the *samuna* still hurling his spear about brings up the rear.

The Plot of the Drama

The drama which I have just described is evidently
founded upon one of the innumerable Orokaiva legends, if,
indeed, one is justified in applying the word legend to such
an artless tale. These legends, or *hihi*, no doubt furnish the
plots of many dramas (see, e.g., No. 1, p. 247), but more
frequently, it would appear, the theme of the play is even
simpler, consisting of some trivial incident of village life.
Almost invariably this incident is one of comedy, so that the
drama may be little more than the re-enactment of a standing
joke. The following is an example. A woman of Poho,
named Anyanya, was fishing in a creek, and had left her
baby son, Barari, sitting on the bank. Seeing some reflection
that pleased him in the water, the child bent over, tumbled
in, and was nearly drowned. The mother, however, re-
covered him in time and, terrified and weeping, held him
up by the legs, while the water ran out of his mouth.
Another woman, Kombera, heard the uproar and ran to the
village to call the child's father, Saunda, and the latter's

brother, Evai. They all rush to the creek and rejoice to find
that the mother has brought the baby round.

This incident, which must have happened some eighteen
years ago (for Barari the baby is now a plantation boy),
obviously held some farcical possibilities, and within the
last few years was made the subject of a play by Evai, who is
now the principal man of Poho. The mother and father of
the child are dead, but the others survive. In the drama the
parts of the above-named men and women were taken by
four actors, and that of the baby by a wooden puppet.

I give another example which may be regarded as more
typical. It was enacted at Deunia on the Kumusi, where I
had the good fortune to see it. Many years ago when Kove,
the present village constable of Deunia, was a little boy, he
was sent one day to the gardens to gather wood. Approaching a sago-place he heard the sound of a man at work and
paused a moment at the edge of the clearing, where he witnessed an occurrence which eventually became the theme
of a play. Bigaba, a man of Deunia, was at work scraping
the sago log, while his wife, Warari, seemed to be pestering
him with amorous advances. At first Bigaba roughly re-
jected them, but gradually his manner changed, and finally
Kove observed the couple in the act of sexual intercourse.
All this he told of in the village, and it became a standing
joke of which Bigaba and his wife were probably not
unaware.

It was probably fifteen or twenty years after that the
drama which I witnessed was played. The part of Bigaba
was taken by Kove himself, who was a particularly clever
buffoon, and hugely amusing to the spectators; that of the
woman Warari by a young man; and that of Kove by a
little boy, who played the part of Peeping Tom, with a
bundle of sticks balanced on his head, as Kove carried a
bundle of firewood fifteen years before. The oddest feature
of all is that both Bigaba and his wife, now old people, witnessed the performance. It was by chance rather than intent,
I fancy, that as Kove (in the character of Bigaba) went dancing off at the close of the drama, he encountered the real
Bigaba face to face, almost indeed colliding with him.

Bigaba, who, whatever his feelings, wore an imperturbable countenance, stepped aside, but Kove met the situation by swinging a terrific blow at him with the long digging-stick he was carrying. The pole missed the old man's head by inches and met the ground with such force as to be shattered to pieces. After this improvisation, which earned him a parting roar of laughter, the clown went off, alternately shambling and bounding, to change his costume in the bush.

The following brief abstracts will help to give a general idea of the drama. I have actually seen only Nos. 7 and 8; the others were described to me.[1] It may be noted that there are two kinds of actors, the *huvivi*, whose parts are attractive, and the *samuna*, whose parts are at once comical and ugly.

No. 1. 'Totoima.'

Totoima was a man-monster who, in the early days, used to slaughter the Orokaiva. He was armed with tusks which, at the end of his day's work of killing, he would take out and sharpen. He was invincible until one day two youths secured these tusks which he had left aside while he bathed in the river. The youths had previously prepared a pig-trap, *bage* (see p. 48), and now pursued by Totoima, who is anxious to regain his teeth, they lead him on to the *bage* and throw them into it. Totoima blunders in after them and is caught. In the drama a pig-trap is erected in the village. Totoima (*samuna*) appears holding in his mouth the common two-tusk ornament (see p. 39). The boys obtain this from him and after a long pursuit throw it into the pig-trap, which collapses upon Totoima as soon as he enters it.

No. 2. 'Orehaha and the Drum.'

The Orokaiva did not know of the drum and *hui* (see pp. 86, 88) until they obtained them from Orehaha, the carpet snake. Orehaha used to beat the drum and blow the *hui* and, when the people came to discover the cause of the noise, would retire out of sight. This went on until they set a small boy to spy. He revealed the whereabouts of Orohaha,

---

[1] Another thoroughly typical example will be found in *Annual Report*, 1914–15, p. 14.

whom the villagers came and killed, thus obtaining the drum and *hui*. I have not the particulars of stage appointments, &c.

No. 3. 'The Snake in the Ants' Nest.'

A snake-man lived in an ants' nest (*siriho*) on a tree which leaned over a creek. A man and two girls come to bale out the water in order to fish, and as they work the snake puts out his head (made of cane and bark-cloth), and sways back and forth above them. Suddenly the man looks up and takes to his heels in a fright, shouting to the girls to follow. But the snake puts aside his skin and becomes a fine man. He overtakes the girls, and leads them into his *siriho* house.

No. 4. 'Cuscus Hunting.'

A woman goes to the garden accompanied by her dog. They come to a tree with a hole in it, at which the dog whines and scratches. Introducing a stick into the hole the woman prods, and from the noises which ensue concludes that she has found a cuscus. Now she goes to bring her husband, who appears as a *samuna*. The woman recommends obtaining further help, but the husband declares he is strong enough, and prods again and again. Finally a second *samuna* appears, who quarrels and fights with the first. Young men and maidens (*huvivi*) come from the village, but the cuscus is not caught until the dog finally drags him out by the tail. Then there is a pursuit, and it is finally killed by the *samuna*.

The parts of the dog and the cuscus are taken by small boys blackened with charcoal.

No. 5. 'The Girl in the Tree.'

A girl (*huvivi*) is found in a tree by a youth (*huvivi*). He brings his friends (*huvivi*) and one of them climbs the tree and brings the girl down. Now all desire to possess her, and there is a scuffle in which a *samuna*, who has appeared in the meantime, joins heartily, finding ample scope for his favourite methods. It appears that the drama ends when one of the *huvivi* secures the girl and the *samuna* is left lamenting.

No. 6.

A youth had visited the Mission at —— in order to pay addresses to one of the Mission girls. He was waiting in a tree by the track at a point some distance from the Mission where he hoped she would keep her assignation. It appears that in this he was disappointed, but while he waited he saw a man (of a village near his own) returning with his wife from the Mission, where they had been to make some purchases. Directly under his tree they stopped and had sexual intercourse. The youth did not reveal his presence but afterwards, of course, made the tale public in his village, where it subsequently became the theme of a thoroughly typical drama. This is a good example of the dramatization of a local incident.

No. 7. 'Roasting the Corn.'

A man and his wife (both *samuna*) go to the garden to plant taro. He works very energetically and scolds her for her laziness. She works with him for a time, and then, building a fire near the garden platform, proceeds to roast corn for a midday meal. Having finished his work the husband returns to the platform, and climbs on to it groaning with fatigue. From here he watches his wife, and his frame of mind changes. When she brings him the roasted corn he makes amorous advances to her, which, however, she rejects. He then turns his back on her in a huff, and refuses to eat her corn. At last she yields to him, and they have sexual intercourse on the platform. At this point a youth and a girl (*huvivi*) come into the garden, and dance round and round the platform. Suddenly the man, finding himself observed, leaves his wife on the platform, and scrambles underneath it to hide. After a few moments she also becomes aware of the spectators, and follows his example. The *huvivi* now dance away, followed by the disgraced husband and wife.

No. 8.

An old couple (both *samuna*) have been at work in the gardens. The wife returns first, feeling indisposed, and lies groaning on a mat by her house. A lover (*huvivi*) appears, arouses the old woman, and endeavours to have sexual intercourse with her. He is disturbed by a whistle, and dances about the village trying to discover whence it has come. In the meantime the husband returns from the garden carrying wood and vegetables as a woman does, for he is doing his wife's work. He throws these down and, in the usual fashion of the Orokaiva drama, begins to make advances to her. But he now finds evidence that she has been visited by another in his absence, and there is an angry scene. Meanwhile the lover has discovered that the whistle was made by a boy and girl in the woman's house. These two (*huvivi*) thereupon come dancing down, and all the actors leave the stage.

There was some confusion as to the interpretation of this plot. The most sensible version I heard was that the two children were son and daughter of the old woman, and that they had whistled in order to prevent the lover from interfering with their mother.

The foregoing examples will show that the theme of the play may be furnished by some domestic incident as well as by one of the accredited *hihi* or legends; and, indeed, the former is more usually the case.[1] Any episode that provides sufficient scope for farce and indecency may be turned into a play.

Actors, Stage, and Audience

It will be readily imagined that there is no playwright, unless one can give that name to the man who suggests the theme for the play. It would appear that the selection of a plot devolves upon the individual who institutes the feast and the accompanying dance and drama. But his ear is open to suggestions. Thus we find a man of Papaki who goes first to Totemburari, then to Ohoraburari, and finally to Poho for a plot, and in the last village accepts the *hihi* of Orehaha (No. 2, p. 247). Another (No. 8, p. 249), per-

---

[1] I find that Beaver made the same twofold division of the subjects of the drama: 'The Yavetu may be broadly divided into two classes—(*a*) myths or legends, (*b*) märchen, in which may be included imitations of local or village incidents and farce.' Quoted by Sir J. H. P. Murray, *Annual Report*, 1914–15, p. 14.

formed at Petakiari on the Opi, actually came from a plantation near Samarai in the Eastern Division, where the story was told one night in the labourers' sleeping quarters.

If there are no playwrights there are, nevertheless, those whom we might call actors. Certain men become celebrated for a gift of buffoonery. They are called *ate-huso*, i.e. expert in *ate*, or the art of demonstration, or *sovai-huso*, i.e. expert in representing the *sovai*. Such men are much in request, and I have been surprised to note—though this may not be invariable—that the man who takes the *samuna's* part, viz. that of the *binei* or *sovai*, is usually one of years, character, and some importance. It is not a part for the village idiot. The *huvivi*, who play prettier but less important parts, are usually young men of good appearance. There are no actresses on the Orokaiva stage: all female parts, whether of *samuna* or *huvivi*, are played by men.

The acting consists almost invariably of dumb show; and dialogue, where it does occur, is no more than elementary. In only one of the dramas I saw myself did any of the actors open his mouth to utter more than an inarticulate cry; though it is true that in this instance (No. 7, p. 249) the two *samuna*, husband and wife, kept the audience amused by shouted interchanges. As a rule, however, the *samuna* relies on exaggerated gestures and silent caricature.

The conventional costume of the *samuna* is made of *pipiga*, an extremely rough and ragged kind of bark-cloth, and it covers him like a hooded cloak. By immersion in swamp mud it is dyed to an evil grey-black, and where it leaves his limbs exposed the actor may apply charcoal. Over his eyes he wears a pair of half coco-nut shells, like huge goggles, which are pierced so that he may see through them. These great eyes are called *kiti monjo*. His make-up is rendered more terrible or absurd by such things as boars' tusks for teeth and fringes of cassowary feathers for whiskers. A red *hega* fruit represents a sore between his buttocks, and if he is a male he wears very ostentatiously an imitation penis. Altogether his aim is to make himself hideous enough for a real *binei* of the bush, and to behave obscenely and comically enough to make his audience laugh.

The paraphernalia of the stage have already been described, but I may draw attention in passing to the disguises
or devices for representing animals, &c. Babies were evidently represented by puppets. I have been told that the
parts of dogs and cuscus were taken by small boys blackened
with charcoal. A snake, or the head of a snake, was made
of cane and bark-cloth. We have already seen that players
could go to considerable trouble to make a wooden model
of a sword-fish, but there is in the Papuan Collection a
representation of a crocodile which is a far more finished
piece of work. It is almost nine feet in length with gaping
jaws. Its back is studded with small pyramidal prominences
which give a very fair idea of the creature's rough skin, and
the whole is skilfully hewn from one piece of wood. This
model was acquired by Mr. C. F. Jackson at a dance on the
Mambare. Mr. L. P. Armit informs me that in the same
district he saw a representation of a flying-fox which stood
three or four feet high and had reticulated wings which
were made to flap during the dance.

The action of the play goes forward in the open space of
the village. There is nothing in the nature of a stage or
a closed arena, and if I have used the former of these two
words in the course of the present chapter it is only meta-
phorically. Nor is there any accommodation for the spectators. It is true that booths are erected for the visitors, but
these are meant for shelter during the heat of the day, not
for grand-stands during the performance of the drama.
The spectators in fact cluster round the actors, and though
sometimes they do not display as keen and silent an interest
in the play as one would expect, their interest is, nevertheless, curiously sympathetic. When, e.g., the stage furniture
is brought on by the ballet, some of the spectators will lend
a hand to set it up. When the *binei* breaks his mock spear,
a spectator runs to supply him with another. Or you may
see a bystander offer his bamboo pipe to one of the players,
or spread a mat for the old woman when she is about to
lie down, or bring a fire-stick when she wishes to light the
fire. The actors, in fine, present their play not before the
spectators, but among them. It may be worth remarking,

incidentally, that the audience does not always thoroughly understand the action. I have been surprised at the diversity of interpretations placed upon one drama by different members of the audience. The plot was not divulged previously, and when the play had been performed those whom I questioned as to its story or meaning seemed somewhat mystified and, be it confessed, somewhat indifferent.

Disposal of Paraphernalia

Before attempting a general appreciation of the drama and the dance there still remains the last episode to describe, viz. the final disposal of the paraphernalia. This has been spoken of before as the last of the mortuary ceremonies (*vide* p. 224), and it usually follows the dance and drama, which constitute the penultimate ceremony, by a space of one or more months. A brief description of this rite will help us to understand the ceremonial significance of much that has been described in this chapter. Some time after the performance of a dance and play in the village of Horanada I received an invitation to witness the rite called *sirari*, lit. 'pushing away'. The *pipiga* costume of the *samuna*, his imitation spears, and his wooden phallus had been kept since the day of the drama. They were now placed on a raft with some cooked taro and pig, and a little boy (son of the deceased man for whom the dance and drama had been made) waded out pushing it before him into the current and there let it go. I was told that the *sovai* of the deceased, for whom the dance and drama had been celebrated, travelled on this raft.

On another occasion, which I did not witness, it appears that even the timbers of the men's house and all the *ando*, or costumes, of the dancers were put on rafts and sent down the river, the chief man crying out the names of the deceased for whom the dance had been held, and bidding them begone from the neighbourhood of the village. And obediently, I was informed, the *sovai* would go aboard the raft and drift down to the sea. It can hardly be doubted that there is some connexion between the paraphernalia of the dance and drama and the spirits of the dead for whom these ceremonies were performed.

Ceremonial Significance of Dance and Drama

It remains now to attempt an appreciation of the dance and drama in respect of their functions and value, to connect them with what has been described in the previous chapters, and to place them correctly in the life of the community.

The combined dance and drama of the Orokaiva have, I believe, less real value as ceremonial than as art or play. However, we may for a moment ignore this latter and more important aspect, and consider what meaning—latent or otherwise—they may possess as ritual.

In the last chapter I implied that the dance and drama constituted a mortuary rite. Earlier it was suggested that they were in some degree or in some instances an initiatory rite, taking the place among the Aiga and Binandele of the *embahi* ceremony among the southern tribes. It seems probable that the set performance, combining dance and drama, sometimes fulfils both these functions together.

We have seen that the occasion of it brings to an end the tabu on the village coco-nuts, which was instituted expressly because of the death of a villager. The *naterari*, or tabu post, may be presented with offerings of food at the feast which accompanies the dance and drama, and it is made clear that these offerings are to the dead whom the *naterari* apparently represents. Before the dance and feast begin, the *sovai* or *binei* are hailed and bidden to attend, though information has not been entirely consistent on this point, some saying that the words are addressed to the particular individuals for whom the tabu was instituted and the feast is now being made, others that an invitation is offered to the spirits at large. In more than one straightforward instance, however, it appeared that the ceremony was definitely performed for one deceased individual; and in one of these instances it was affirmed that when the dancers began, the *sovai* of the deceased would 'get up and dance with them'. Again, while the ballet is going forward, the widows of the village wail and slash their cheeks, being reminded, it is said, of the time when their husbands danced and made merry. Lastly, when the performance is over, the para-

(*a*) Puppet used in the Drama at Poho

(*b*) The *Sirari* Ceremony

PLATE XXXIV

phèrnalia of the play are stacked together, and so await a last ritual disposal, when the *sovai* of the deceased is bidden farewell. These facts, then, should be enough to show that the dance and drama can be regarded as a mortuary rite.

The actual significance of the rite remains a matter for conjecture. The native informant will say that it is celebrated in honour of the dead, who is called upon to be present and witness it, and to partake of the feast. It is plainly in the nature of a placation, and when it is all over it is hoped that the spirit will take his departure for good.

One is inclined to think, however, that it is the feast rather than the accompanying dance and drama that is the real act of placation. If this be so, what is then the function or significance of the dance and drama? One or two points of evidence have hinted at a possible explanation. An informant once told me that the spirit of the dead man for whom the feast and dance were being held would be present and dance with the dancers. There is again the queer practice of the widows, who, when the dancers appear, may break forth into lamentation and slash their cheeks and foreheads with quartz. They are said to be reminded of their husbands. It is as if in the semi-disguised figures of the dancers they saw their own men-folk returned from the place of the spirits.

The rite called *sirari*, i.e. the ritual disposal of the costumes, &c., of the actors and sometimes of the dancers, is not out of keeping with this idea. What remains of the *samuna* or of the dancer, i.e. his costume and paraphernalia, is put aboard the raft and abandoned, and it is said at the same time that the *sovai* of the deceased travels aboard the raft. It is difficult not to associate the two, almost difficult not to identify them. It might well enough be that the *samuna*, grotesque and foolish as he is, was in some manner impersonating the deceased, and that now the disguise in which he did it is being mentally identified with him.

There is something, moreover, in the secrecy as to the identity of the dancers and in the more or less complete disguise they wear—matters which have been already referred to (*vide* p. 238). These, together with a point of similarity in costume, have suggested a possible affinity with the masked dance of the Western and Gulf Papuans, and the suggestion here put forward—be it remembered, in an entirely tentative manner—is that the performers in the Orokaiva dance and drama originally impersonate the spirits of the dead, who foregather to partake of the mortuary feast.

The feast is the real act of placation. It is provided for the spirits, and in order to make the donors of the feast feel more satisfied that it is accepted by them, the spirits are brought on to the scene in the persons of the disguised dancers and actors. It may be repeated that no native ever placed this interpretation on the dance and drama, and that, in the absence of more telling evidence than I have been able to supply, it is intended for nothing more than a conjecture.

We have next to consider the dance and drama as constituting a rite of initiation. I regret that during the whole of my stay among the Aiga and Binandele there was no opportunity of witnessing an initiation, so I can bring forward only verbal evidence that the *ehamei*, or 'new children', i.e. the initiates, make their appearance together with the dancers, and witness the performance of a play. I have also been told that in some cases the initiate bears a minor part in the play, viz. that of a *huvivi*. At any rate, however, it may be regarded as certain that the dance and drama form part of the cycle of puberty ceremonies among the Aiga and Binandele.

The question is whether they constitute the essence of the ceremony, i.e. whether they correspond to the meeting with the *embahi*, which is the essence of initiation among the southern Orokaiva. Here again it may be remembered that no native has ever spoken of the two rites as corresponding, and the suggestion that the dance and drama have some initiatory significance is my own. It is based upon the following facts: (1) The dance and drama always form part of the puberty cycle. (2) In the dance the performers are virtually disguised by their costumes, and their identity is meant to remain secret, just as it is with the *embahi*, who are supposedly irrecognizable to the initiates. (Further, as I have just indicated, one is tempted to conjecture that the disguised dancers among the Aiga and Binandele originally represented spirits of the dead.) (3) In the drama we find the same kind of secrecy. The identity of the actors is not revealed, and the plot of the play is not divulged before its performance, nor does any one care to pry into these matters. Furthermore, in the drama there always appears at least one *binei* or *sovai*, i.e. spirit of the dead.

The gist of initiation among the southern Orokaiva is to bring the candidate into contact with the supposed spirits of the dead, and make him acquainted with the bull-roarer and the flutes which are the voices of the spirits; whereas among the Aiga and Binandele, who know neither the bull-roarer nor the flute, the candidate is, nevertheless, brought into contact with the spirits of the dead in the drama and conceivably also in the dance which accompanies the drama.

This interpretation of the ceremony, viz. as a rite of initiation, may be thought unnecessary in view of the other, which gives it a mortuary significance. It will be noted, however, that the two are not incompatible if there be any truth in the theory that the dance and drama bring forth impersonators of the spirits. It may be noted that, since the confinement of a batch of youths and girls is a comparatively rare occurrence, the dance and drama appear usually in their mortuary guise alone.

In fine the combined dance and drama seem to me primarily of a mortuary nature, but this may make them all the more suitable for initiation, an essential idea of which is, apparently, to bring the initiate into contact with the supposed spirits of the dead. For the present, then, I shall set down only this much as a conclusion, viz. that the dance and drama (whatever their real significance) constitute a mortuary rite, and possibly also an initiatory one, and as for their significance it is suggested that the performers in the dance, and at least the main actors in the drama represent spirits of the dead.

Aesthetic and Recreative Value

So far I have spoken of the ceremonial functions of the dance and drama. I now wish to draw attention to their more real, 'live', functions, viz. the aesthetic and recreative.

The dance or ballet is one of swift, swinging, vigorous action. There is no place in it for cramped or stilted movement, and, although all figures are strictly regulated, they never lose a certain dash or impetuosity. At the same time the dancers must be intent on their work, for the figures are not without difficulty, and are only perfected after many rehearsals. But when their dance is in full swing it is obvious that the dancers take great pleasure in the successful performance of a difficult work of art. And this pleasure is, of course, intensified in each by the fact that all are acting in concert. The dance is a fine piece of 'team-work', conducted to a stirring rhythm which the dancers themselves create, for each holds and beats his own drum.

It goes without saying that every performer, brilliantly befeathered and draped with flowing garments of dyed grass, feels a delightful titivation of his self-regarding impulses. The folk-tales dwell upon the personal successes of dancers, and it is well known that young female spectators are sometimes ravished into matrimony.

Altogether it may be claimed that the Orokaiva ballet is a beautiful and valuable creation. No spectator could withhold his admiration for the brilliancy of its colour, for the charm of its figures, and for the grace and vim of its performers, while to the performers themselves it clearly means aesthetic satisfaction, *camaraderie*, and heightened self-esteem. If such a comment may be ventured in this report, I do not know of any more charming and admirable feature of native life than the Orokaiva dance, nor of any that is better worth preserving.

The drama, or dramatic interlude in the ballet, is of special interest. It may be that the faculty for dramatic representation is strongly developed in most primitive peoples, but comparatively few at the low cultural level of the Orokaiva have evolved a set form. Whatever may have been its original ritual significance (and I have suggested that it is a mortuary, and perhaps also an initiatory rite), it has practically reached the stage when it is an end in itself. Although seldom, if ever, performed without some ceremonial pretext, it nevertheless possesses an interest which is independent of any ceremonial purpose. Often tastefully performed it is definitely an activity which gives scope for the exercise of art and talent.

Its tastefulness, indeed, is very commonly marred by gross obscenity. But here, as in so many other instances, the European, who would appreciate native art, must wink at unpleasant accompaniments. And this broadness will be in some measure excused when we remember that the play is essentially comedy or farce, and the success of a performance is judged by the amount of laughter it causes. I cannot agree with one charge which has been levelled against the Orokaiva drama, viz. that its obscenity serves to arouse the passions of the spectators and prepare them for an orgy of immorality. I have no evidence that any such orgy takes place, and, furthermore, the obscenity of the play is far too gross and comical to have the effect ascribed to it. Some of the actors, those known as *huvivi*, play respectable parts, and their manners are as charming and their movements as graceful as native art can make them: the others, known as *samuna*, or 'the bad men', appear in the role of *sovai* or *binei*, and their behaviour and appearance are merely those of an inconceivably ragged circus clown. Both kinds of actors enjoy their own performance. One may be almost amused at the expression of complacence on the face of a dancing *huvivi*, and I have watched a *binei* helpless with laughter at his own antics. We have seen also that the audience finds pleasure in the performance and is in remarkable sympathy with the actors. On the whole, therefore, we may agree that the drama, like the dance, is a thing of charm in itself, and a valuable element of native culture. Quite apart from any ceremonial significance it may have, it is valuable as a source of pleasure and amusement, and as an art that is its own reward. Here, if anywhere, we have an instance of a purely native product which deserves to be perpetuated, and which contains seeds of development which are worth the tending.

XV

THE SPIRITUAL SUBSTITUTE

THE two following chapters, more than any others, show what difficulties may attend even a work of mere ethnography. When the observer is confronted by a mass of vague and very tangled beliefs, it becomes a rather delicate task to set them down in a manner that will be intelligible to the reader and yet have an honest regard to their limitations. The first difficulty arises in the fact that a native's beliefs are largely inexplicit; he has never tried to frame them in words, and thus one is sometimes compelled to fall back on inference. The next difficulty arises in the fact that of even the more explicit beliefs many turn out to be mutually irreconcilable. Whereas a modern educated mind must be continually raking over its beliefs and conscientiously casting out any inconsistencies, the mind of the native (like the mind of an uneducated modern—only more so) remains blissfully unaware of these inconsistencies. Thirdly, the native's beliefs are not always firmly held. There is no such thing as strict orthodoxy, and, indeed, it may be claimed that abstract belief, compared with practice and ritual, is to him of small account. Where we find uniformity of practice we may also find a variety of theoretical explanations, and the same informant may cheerfully switch from one explanation to another, or simply declare that 'he doesn't know'. In fine, natives are unable or reluctant to formulate their beliefs; the beliefs when formulated are often inconsistent with one another: and not less often they are light, inexact, variable things, qualified with a non-committal 'perhaps' or 'who knows?'

Those beliefs which relate to the spiritual and the supernatural are probably hazier and more confused than any other. It is the business of these chapters to set them down as far as possible systematically, yet resisting the temptation to manipulate or trim them, or to force them into a system that may be intelligible to the reader but does not necessarily exist in the mind of the native. More specifically our subjects are the beliefs concerning what may loosely be called the spirits of the living and the spirits of the dead. Out of the confused mass of evidence we may extricate two propositions, and set them down definitely as a ground-work. (1) Of every creature and thing there is a 'spirit' or immaterial counterpart called *asisi*. (2) Every human being survives death, and the entity which thus survives, whatever its form, is called a *sovai*.[1] These two propositions are matters respectively of native philosophy and religion. We shall continue here to discuss the first, and shall reserve the second until the next chapter.

The Meanings of Asisi

The word *asisi* [2] is, I believe, in general use. One hesi-tates to lay down its literal meaning, but it is used for 'shadow', and for 'reflection', and these are the simplest of its meanings and probably fundamental. There is thus far no psychic implication in the word. Shadows and reflections are ordinary phenomena to the Orokaiva, which he observes and accepts without beating his brains for an explanation. But there are other manifestations which take a rather more psychic turn. Such are the appearance of human and other beings in dreams and visions, and to these the name *asisi* is extended without, of course, implying that they are identical with shadow or reflection. In this connexion *asisi* stands for the immaterial counterpart which is visible. In so far as the native bothers to form a theory of dreams (*eture*), he says that in his sleep he may be visited by *asisi*, or, on the other hand, that his own *asisi* may travel.[3] It is not necessary to give examples of dreams, but merely to repeat that in them the *asisi* is regarded as the immaterial but visible counterpart of the person or thing dreamt of.

But when, in the native's dream theory, the *asisi* of the

[1] For other dialectal forms see p. 267.
[2] In the 'Taro Cult' (Report No. 6 in *Orokaiva Magic*), which dealt with a move-ment originating among the Binandele, the Binandele form *atiti* was used through-out. *Asisi*, in accordance with the rule adopted in this book, is the Aiga form.
[3] It is also said that a man's *eye* travels as he dreams, though there is, of course, no notion of a material eye-ball passing through the air.

dreamer travels, it is not necessarily implied that it is visible, and this brings us to another meaning of the word, and necessitates a widening of definition. We may say that the *asisi* is an immaterial entity, not necessarily visualized, but identified with, or acting as substitute for, some person, in this case the dreamer. Thus when Dasiga, the visionary of Manau,[1] received his commandments, it was his *asisi* that went up into the sky and saw God, and such a use of the word is not due to any external suggestion, as, e.g. of Christianity, but is typical of Orokaiva usage. Dasiga does not have a cut-and-dried theory for a 'soul' which leaves his body for the time being as a mere inanimate clod while it travels the skies; he believes that he himself ascended in immaterial form. His *asisi* is merely a substitute for himself in Dasiga's own mind; for he has never thrashed the matter out and formulated a definite theory of body, soul, and spirit. Such a conception is not limited in reference to human beings. Animals and inanimate objects may also have their *asisi*. When, for instance, a hunting magician feels a certain sensation in his right side, 'like the kicking of an unborn puppy in its mother's belly', he says that it is the *asisi* of a pig which has entered him. We must not press him too closely for a definition of the form of *asisi*. He has not thought this out and he cannot explain. He thinks that the pig has come to him in some form or other, altogether immaterial unless it be for that slight throbbing in his side. Again, when a mourner declares that the *asisi* of the dead is immanent in the mourning jacket of *baja* (Job's Tears), he has no definite idea of how it got there or of what form it takes, except that it is obviously both immaterial and invisible.

The best example of the reference of *asisi* to inanimate nature is found in the doctrines of the Taro Cult, whose originators were possessed by the *asisi* of the *ba*, or taro, itself. And it is instructive to note, as illustrating the confused conception of the form of the *asisi*, that the originator of the cult saw the spirits of the actual taro plants in the shape of young men who danced before him.

[1] See 'Taro Cult' in *Orokaiva Magic*, pp. 74 ff.

In short, we see that *asisi* is a loose word covering a variety of conceptions, and we must seek a correspondingly wide definition.

The Asisi as Spiritual Substitute

Now, for the time being, we may dismiss the idea of an *asisi* or 'spirit', and view certain native beliefs apart from any ulterior, i. e. spiritual, explanation. It would, then, seem as if the native believed that persons and things could on occasion act, exist, or be present to consciousness in a manner independently of their concrete selves. To take the last of the above-mentioned examples, for instance, it would seem that in native belief the taro plant could influence the human being although he had no contact whatever with the actual vegetable.

For this proposition in general there is a mass of evidence —dream appearances, trance journeys, spirit possession, the action of charms and medicines, &c., all of which are familiar to anthropology. A few concrete examples from the Orokaiva, however, may be added. A man has eaten sugar-cane, which is for some reason unwholesome or harmful. So long as the wind does not blow he is comfortable, but when it rises and sways the sugar-cane in the garden it sets up a synchronous disturbance in the victim's stomach and makes him ill. Again a man attributes his cold in the nose to the numerous unripe bread-fruit. Why? According to his own explanation they are as yet of a watery consistency, and so by their mere presence make him rheumy, inclined to spit and snivel. A youth, having offered a cigarette to his sweetheart, pokes the butt into a nest of ants. The ants bite the cigarette, and the girl is stimulated into loving him. A woman has eaten of a pig whose flesh is for some reason harmful. Her child falls ill and is supposed to have imbibed the cause of its sickness together with its mother's milk. Two women live in parts of the same house. One of them has eaten carpet-snake, cooking it in a pot over the fire. Subsequently the other woman cooks some taro in the ashes of the same fire and gives them to her husband. He falls ill and ascribes his sickness to the unwholesome carpet-snake.

When Buninia, the originator of the Taro Cult, was preaching his doctrines the people would lean on him, embrace him, and rub their axes and digging sticks over his body, so that the taro which was influencing him should also influence them and their gardens.

Now it is not our business here to determine the real psychological basis of such beliefs (though I cannot imagine that the native looks at every-day things through a haze of mystic potentialities as some psychologists would have it; rather would I adhere to the older idea that he feels there is some physical interaction between things that he associates in his mind). The question is merely that of his own explanation, the scientific worthlessness of which need not concern us.

Now here, as in so many other cases, the native is inclined to take matters for granted. This thing, he feels, has an influence on that thing, or this process over that process; and he does not usually bother his head about an explanation. But when for some reason or other he pauses to think the matter out, what explanation is he to put on it? I believe his stock explanation is that when one thing acts on another, exists, or is present to consciousness, apart from its concrete self, it does so by means of its *asisi*; though, to repeat, this is commonly a forced explanation, for he usually takes the matter simply for granted. It is the *asisi* of the taro plant which enters Buninia and which is in turn passed on to the bodies and the garden implements of those who embrace him; and, if we tax the native hard enough, he will probably tell us that it is the *asisi* of the carpet-snake, which passing in some manner from the pot into the ashes of the fire, and thence through the taro into the body of the man, causes his sickness.

When anything (person, creature, or object) functions, apart from its concrete self, he feels that it does so by means of a second self which is identified with, but for the time being separated from, the concrete. We might call this a spiritual manifestation of the concrete thing, or an immaterial self which co-exists with the material self; but in more general terms it is simply the native's undefined mental substitute for the concrete thing. Perhaps the phrase 'spiritual substitute' would make the best definition. Whenever the native thinks of this spiritual substitute in the abstract and feels it necessary to give it a name, he, very naturally and suitably, extends to it the word *asisi*, which means 'shadow' or 'reflection', and thus affords a very close parallel.

Elsewhere, particularly in the Taro Cult, I have translated *asisi* by 'spirit' (as I have translated *sovai* by 'spirit of the dead'). This is only, of course, an approximation, and the word has been used, at the sacrifice of some accuracy, simply to make the subject more readable. That is the only defence I can offer for the use of a term, which in our language is so fluid and ill-defined. And it may be as well to emphasize at this point that some of the accepted implications of 'spirit' do not belong to the concept of an *asisi*. I cannot, for instance, discover from my informants that the *asisi* is regarded as an entity separate from but residing in the body to which it belongs. It is not a 'breath of life', a vital principle, or an animating essence. Such ideas are, I believe, in advance of Orokaiva philosophy as we find it. Accordingly I have avoided the word 'soul' as being rather more unsuitable for a translation than 'spirit'. No informant has ever given me a theory of survival after death other than this, that the *embo be*, 'real man', becomes a *sovai*. At any rate it may be confidently stated that there is no conception of a vital principle or 'soul' which inhabits the body but survives it; and such a meaning cannot be attached to the word *asisi*.

To repeat a conclusion, therefore, the *asisi* is the native's name for a spiritual manifestation of anything; or for an immaterial self which co-exists with but is separable from the concrete self; or, in other words, whenever anything functions apart from its concrete self, it does so by means of a spiritual substitute which is called its *asisi*.

Asisi of the Dead

The word *asisi*, which is thus seen to be of very wide meaning, may stand not only for a manifestation of the living, but also for a manifestation of the dead, i.e. a ghost, visible or invisible. But it must be made clear that in proper usage *asisi* is not wholly synonymous with the being that survives death, viz. the *sovai*, though there is some confusion between the two words. Such confusion is largely due to the recent movement known as the Taro Cult which has been dealt with at length in another report.[1] The movement originated on the River Mambare, where its founders believed themselves, or affected to be, possessed by the *asisi* of the actual taro plant. It is not necessary here to describe the ritual, doctrines, and physical manifestations of the cult, but merely to draw attention to the significant change which it has undergone in the course of its dissemination, and the bearing which this change has had on the meaning of the word *asisi*. Near what we may call the dispersion centre of the cult, viz. the neighbourhood of the Mambare mouth, its exponents still affect to be possessed by the taro *asisi*. On the other hand, in the great majority of the whole division through which the cult has spread, its exponents say they are possessed by the spirits of the dead. This is quite in keeping with old belief, and merely indicates that a new and somewhat outlandish cult has relapsed into a form more acceptable to the old-established beliefs of the Orokaiva. But together with other features of ritual the Taro Cult has spread abroad a certain distinctive vocabulary of terms; and among these terms is *asisi*. The consequence is that *asisi* is now frequently used as synonymous with the spirits of the dead by whom the majority of Taro Men think they are possessed. I have been assured by reliable witnesses, however, that this general and regular application of the word *asisi* to the beings who survive death is new-fangled and attributable to the Taro Cult. The old word is *sovai*, which, in the taro jargon, has been supplanted by *asisi*. It is not to be assumed that *asisi* was never used formerly for the spirit of the dead as well as the spirit of the living, but it was not wholly synonymous with the beings who survived death. A fundamental difference exists between the two words. *Asisi* normally stands for an image of or substitute for some other and more concrete reality; whereas a *sovai*, whatever ¹ts form, does not represent anything; it exists by itself.

[1] 'Taro Cult' in *Orokaiva Magic*.

XVI

SURVIVAL AFTER DEATH

NATIVE ideas regarding the life after death, although involved in great confusion, are, nevertheless, easier to deal with than those which concern the *asisi*; for despite many inconsistencies they come near to being explicit, and there is less of inference required in their description.

The 'Sovai', or Being who Survives Death

It will be understood that the living man possesses an *asisi*; he neither is nor possesses a *sovai*, but when he dies he *becomes* a *sovai*. That is to say *sovai* means 'the being who survives death', or 'the living form into which death converts a human being'. In accordance with the general rule of this book the forms of the Aiga dialect have been used. The being who survives death is known by a variety of names:

Aiga	.	.	.	.	*Sovai*
Binandele .		.	.	.	*Binei*
Wasida	.	.	.	.	*Embahi*
Hunjara	.	.	.	.	*Siango*

but although there is continual diversity of belief regarding details, the main concepts, as far as they can be abstracted, remain constant throughout the tribes. In order to avoid confusion, therefore, the word *sovai* will be used exclusively in this chapter.

The *sovai* will be found to take a variety of forms, including those of fiends or hobgoblins, which probably have their origin merely in fear and imagination but are nevertheless classed in native terminology with *sovai*, or spirits of the dead. Such characters, besides existing vaguely in the imagination, are constantly told of in Orokaiva legends, and it appears that some of these 'legendary' *sovai* may be conceived of as still existing and retaining their personality and attributes. Cases of legendary or personal *sovai* are, however, so few as to be almost negligible.

Apart from the very faint hint which these last may give us there is nothing to suggest a deity or any supernatural being of independent existence, least of all a high-god. I do not know of any cosmogony, and there is no attribution of divine powers to the phenomena of nature. On the whole it will be found that Orokaiva religion concerns itself primarily with the spirits of the dead.

In any one tribe the beliefs regarding the *sovai* are found to be confused and conflicting to the last degree, and it will be as well for the sake of clarity to set down several conceptions immediately.

(1) The *sovai* is sometimes conceived of as immaterial but retaining human characteristics. (2) It is also conceived of as taking the concrete form of beast, bird, reptile, or fish. (3) It is also conceived of as a semi-human monster of altogether frightful disposition inhabiting the bush; or in this case it might be nearer the truth to say that there are imaginary monsters (fiends, hobgoblins) to whom the name *sovai* is extended, and who are thus identified with spirits of the dead. (4) Fourthly, there are a few instances in which the *sovai* are known by personal names and, apart from their constant appearance in legends, are thought of as still actually existing.

No native, I fancy, would fail to endorse any of the above propositions, nor does he find any difficulty in holding all these beliefs simultaneously. He pictures the *sovai* as ghost, animal, or hobgoblin, and it depends entirely upon his mood or the subject of the conversation which of the three pictures will be on view. It is not to be supposed that he would make a rigorous choice and so definitely and permanently make up his mind as to the real nature of the *sovai*. His conception of it is as kaleidoscopic as his emotions, and changes form and colour as he ranges between affection, distaste, and fear.

Transition from Living Man to 'Sovai'

It is definitely asserted that a man becomes a *sovai* at death, but there seems to be no satisfactory theory regarding the transition. It is very tempting for a European to put a construction on the matter and say that the native must suppose the *asisi* of the living man to leave his body at death and survive in the form of a *sovai*. But, unfortunately, I have never heard such an interpretation from a native, nor do I feel confident that his conception of an *asisi* would allow of it. Save for one or two fanciful explanations which I have heard from isolated witnesses and which will be mentioned presently, we must allow that the native simply takes the transition for granted, as he does so many other abstruse happenings.

On cessation of breathing (*heh*)—about which the native holds no psychic theory—the man is dead, and his *sovai* is hovering somewhere in the environs of the village. It is interesting to note that in native belief a man may die and come to life again. Upon the appearance of coma, which is interpreted as death, the friends and relatives set up a very noisy lamentation. The *sovai* is lurking on the outskirts of the village, but may be so affected by compassion as to return; whereupon the corpse is reanimated. In such a case I have heard the *sovai* spoken of as *sovai isapo*, 'the small *sovai*', but no explanation was offered of how it departed and returned.

To show how singularly confused and, in a sense, ill-made are the beliefs regarding the transition from living man to *sovai*, I quote a case which, despite its rather fabulous complexion, purports, nevertheless, to be true. A man named Hosisi (an exceptionally good informant who told me this story himself) was going to fish in the river. Meanwhile a very old man named Divinopa lay sick in the village. On the way Hosisi saw a cuscus which he immediately realized was the *sovai* of Divinopa, recognizing it, as he explained, by the whiteness of its fur which so resembled the white hair of the old man. Hosisi called the latter's son to his assistance, and together they succeeded in catching the cuscus. They addressed it affectionately as 'grandfather' or 'old man', and took it with them to the village, where they induced it to eat for the next two days. Meanwhile they watched Divinopa, feeling that the appearance of the *sovai* cuscus was a sign that his end was close at hand. On the

third day both he and the animal died, and were buried
together. In response to a question my informant said that
Divinopa's *sovai* still existed as a cuscus. A case such as this
can hardly be made to square with the general belief that
the living man becomes a *sovai* at death. One can only lay
down the generally accepted doctrine and dismiss a case of
this sort as a cheerful aberration.

The two ensuing theories are somewhat isolated, i. e. they
were not sufficiently verified by being repeated at other times
and in other places, so that they probably do not amount to
general beliefs. The corpse of an Orokaiva is wrapped in
a mat and laid in a coffin-like structure of wood, to which a
number of sticks laid crosswise and lengthwise constitute
a lid. According to a group of informants on the River Gira
these parts of the 'coffin' (*detemba*) are in some manner
animated by the stench (*opu*) of the corpse as it decomposes
in the grave, and the mat becomes a cuscus, the framework
of the coffin becomes a crocodile, the cross-sticks of the lid
become a pig, and the long sticks become snakes. It is
worth noting that these informants gave 'one man, one *sovai*'
as a rule—with which their theory seems hardly in accord.

The other theory has already been mentioned in another
connexion (p. 216). It is that the maggots, which appear
somewhat inexplicably from the corpse and disappear just
as mysteriously, have turned into the *sovai*. (In the one or
two cases where this theory was put forward it appeared
that the *sovai* took the form of a certain bird, though I do
not know whether this latter point is essential to the theory.)
How widely the belief itself may be held I am unable to say,
though it cannot be denied that there is a certain amount
of plausibility and even ingenuity about it.

Except for such somewhat fanciful theories we can only
say that the native simply believes that the *sovai* comes into
existence on the death of a human being, and that he is
content to leave the method of transition unexplained.

The Forms of 'Sovai'

When a man dies his *sovai*, as we have seen, is thought to
be present in some form about the village. Thus it is that

the mourners at a funeral may be startled by any noise in the surrounding bush, the breaking of a twig for instance, which they will attribute to the *sovai* of the deceased. Approaching a village where a death had occurred in the early morning, I once heard a hissing noise in the scrub close to the track. I imagined that it was probably the hissing of a snake, but when I asked the native who accompanied me he answered in rather matter-of-fact tones that it was the *sovai* of the man who had died that morning. When I told the villagers some time afterwards they immediately gave the same explanation, and that without any collusion. It seems, then, that the first idea of the *sovai* is of something quite ethereal and invisible which haunts the village and betrays its presence by movements or noises. And the *sovai* may long remain in this immaterial form. It is thought sometimes to haunt houses and afflict their inmates with sickness. It also visits the gardens, and both here and in the villages may be seen small platforms (*harau*) of food offerings, sometimes with miniature ladders of the most fragile construction to assist the *sovai* in climbing up (Plate XXXV*a*).

But the *sovai* may appear, more or less disembodied, in human form. When one evening my boys were telling each other spookish stories, one of them, an Orokaiva, suddenly scrambled across the hut and sat there trembling in every limb. He had looked out into the darkness and seen the figure of a man recently dead in the village: what first drew his attention, he said, was the smell of death which attached to the *sovai*. Such hallucinations are of common occurrence. One hears of a mother who was mourning the death of her daughter, when she looked up and beheld the girl dancing before her in all her finery. Following the girl, who danced backwards into the bush, she suddenly found herself surrounded by *sovai* in human form, whom she thought to be hostile warriors. In such cases, of course, the *sovai* is an apparition or ghost in the usual sense of the word. So also the dead constantly reappear to dreamers in their familiar living form. Again, in the legends the *sovai* are eminently human though sometimes betrayed by some small evidence of death; as when the youth slain in fight returned in *sovai* form to his sweetheart, but was detected by a trickle of blood from his ear; or when the *sovai* woman revisited her husband and would have passed off for living had he not noticed the earth caked in her nostrils, and so suspected that she had risen from the grave.

Leaving this conception of the *sovai* as a ghost, visible or invisible, we may pass on to another with which it seems completely at variance: the *sovai* is supposed to take the form of some creature of the bush or river. No native has ever maintained that this form is subsequent, i.e. that the *sovai* is first a ghost and afterwards an animal, bird, or reptile, though there is little doubt that the ghostly form is thought of first when an individual has recently died. The general fact is that a native sometimes pictures the *sovai* in one way and sometimes in another. A great variety of creatures may be *sovai*—wallabies, cuscus, pigs, snakes, crocodiles, lizards, frogs, eels, bats, birds, and fishes; but it will be understood that of these species many members are normal or ordinary animals and nothing more, while others are *sovai*. The latter are commonly detected by some queerness or abnormality. For instance, if a snake were very active and writhed over much it would be called a *sovai*, simply, of course, because its slayers were startled or horrified into thinking it such. A lean and ugly cuscus, or a bush-pig that looked unusually rakish would excite the abhorrence of its captors, and a careful man would refrain from eating it. Sometimes the classification as *sovai* is retrospective. When a man falls ill he looks about him for possible causes, and recollects that he recently ate a flying-fox: he draws the conclusion that the flying-fox was a *sovai*. In several instances that came to my notice it was some association with the deceased that had caused the creature to be classed as *sovai*: when for instance a snake had been seen emerging from the grave shelter of a woman recently dead.

There is very little to say about the behaviour of the *sovai* animal. I was once told that thievish men turned into thievish animals such as pigs, rats, and flying-foxes—in which, however, there was no hint of retributive reincarnation but merely an association of ideas. The *sovai* creature

(*a*) A *Harau* with Ladder for the *Sovai*

(*b*) The Pool Monoda

PLATE XXXV

is naturally regarded with fear and abhorrence: the case of the cuscus quoted above (p. 269) is one of the few in which it does not appear to possess a malignant and dangerous character. But it is not easily distinguished from the ordinary example of the same species, and it has often been killed and eaten before the difference is discovered.

This killing of the *sovai* animal raises the question of what we may call its constitution. It is obviously of a nature sufficiently corporeal to be killed and eaten. What is its relation to the deceased with whom it is identified? It would be tempting to suppose that the *sovai* in immaterial form possessed, or entered into, the animal as the evil spirits entered into the Gadarene swine. But I have never heard such an explanation from a native, and I do not know that we can infer that such a theory is in the back of his mind: on the other hand I have been assured that the animal *is* the *sovai*. Nevertheless, it survives what may be called the second death. A simple illustration of this belief is afforded by the following incident. A bush-pig found rooting a garden was speared and killed. That night the owner of the garden (who happened to be my informant) was visited in a dream by his deceased elder brother, who explained that the pig was himself: he had been hungry and had come to his brother's garden for food (by which news the owner was deeply affected and refrained from eating any of the pig).

The theory that best squares with this belief is not that the *sovai* is only an immaterial entity which can enter a concrete body, but that it is an entity of exceedingly variable nature, sometimes immaterial and sometimes material, which can change from a mere invisible breath to the solid body of a pig, or from that again to the appearance of a human being. Such a power of metamorphosis is often met with in the tales of *sovai*. When, for instance, a girl was supposedly kidnapped by *sovai*, her rescuers at length found her in the bush sitting amid a circle of them; when the rescuers made bold to approach, the *sovai* became birds and flew away. Or again, in one village the mourners found themselves after nightfall in the garden of the deceased and engaged in pitched battle with a large number of *sovai*; but whenever they brought down one of their opponents it would turn into a wallaby or a bird and make off.

One may mention at this point several variant forms of the *sovai*. The fire-fly (*uvi*) is very commonly regarded as a *sovai* form; sometimes more fancifully it is said that the fire-flies are the eyeballs of the dead. Again, the phosphorescent fungi *himbaja* may be *sovai*, though, of course, they are not always so, and little boys will play with them quite fearlessly, fixing them as luminous disks to their foreheads at night time. Again, the *sovai* may take the form of the *siriho*, i.e. the nest of the termite in a tree, which for some reason always has an uncanny suggestion to an Orokaiva. Again the meteor *hara* has been referred to in my hearing as a *sovai*, though I do not believe this to be an important or a general belief.

One variant, or rather specific, form of the *sovai* is, however, of great interest. When a man has been slain in fight he becomes a *diroga*, and although the actual form or forms of the *diroga* have never been accurately defined in my hearing, they all have this much in common that they are *i-sovai* —'upper' or 'on top' *sovai*—i.e. they do not belong to the earth or the stream, but flit about in the upper air, where they are sometimes heard to whistle as they pass. This singular, but apparently very general, belief has formed the groundwork of one of the variants of the Taro Cult, and a fuller description of the subject may be seen in the report on that movement.[1]

We may now pass to the third general form in which the *sovai* may appear, viz. that of a fiend or hobgoblin, or of any monstrous creature that inhabits the bush and is liable to attack the lonely wanderer. Various imaginative descriptions are given of the *sovai* in this character. They may have hairy bodies and long fangs; several have pictured them with eyes in the back of their heads; one informant who saw a *sovai* in his boyhood recalled with horror the unnatural skinniness of its arms and legs. It is in this form that the spirits of the dead are represented to the initiates among the

---

[1] 'The Taro Cult' in *Orokaiva Magic*, pp. 68–72.

southern Orokaiva (*vide* Chapter XII; among the southern tribes they are called *embahi* or *siango*). They are supposed to pursue their victims, biting and clawing them, and it is with threats of this kind that the initiates are supposedly reduced to terror.

As fiend or hobgoblin the *sovai* appears in a number of cases which deserve a fuller description than it is possible to give them here. They are cases in which an individual under the influence of some mental aberration 'takes to the bush' under the impression that he has been seized or kidnapped by a *sovai*. We have, for instance, the case of a youth who was missing during the day and found at evening with cuts on his cheek and hand and traces of earth on his face and body. He offered the explanation that he was taken by a *sovai* who caused the wounds by biting him. No one hesitated to believe him, though, as he was accustomed to fits of violence and was known to fall into the fire on occasion, we should probably be right in supposing him to be epileptic.

There is another case which may perhaps be diagnosed simply as one of sleep-walking. A man named Ogomeni was discovered to be missing one night, and a search party discovered him sitting on the branch of a tree whence he gave them muffled answers to their calls, and from which he was helped down in a half-awake condition. On another occasion the same man was spearing fish when suddenly the poised spear was snatched out of his hand from behind, and he was carried off in a swoon. A search party eventually found him lying covered with leaves, and not far from home. His explanation was that he had been seized by a *sovai*, and fully accepting this as a fact his rescuers tied a liana to his belt on the way home to prevent a repetition of the capture, and once safely in his house he allowed his wife to make him fast by means of the liana to one of the floor joists. Ogomeni seemed a perfectly rational man, and it should be emphasized that the precautions of his wife and friends were not meant to keep him in his place but were levelled against the *sovai*.

It is not necessary to multiply instances. It is true that

some of these disappearances come under suspicion of fake, some men pretending to have been in association with the *sovai* for the purposes of sorcery or magic, and one case that came to my notice seemed like deliberate kidnap and holding to ransom. But such examples of trickery are merely taking advantage of the popular belief that the bush is peopled by malignant creatures or fiends known as *sovai*, who are always liable to seize and carry off the lonely wanderer.

It is at this stage that we may briefly consider certain beings who belong mainly to Orokaiva legends, but who, nevertheless, continue to have a vague existence in popular imagination. The legends (*hihi*; Binandele *kiki*) are full of characters known as *sovai*. These are commonly anthropomorphic, and although their dispositions vary, they are more often than not ridiculous or hateful. The Orokaiva, who possess a fine body of legends and fables, are quite alive to the difference between fact and fiction, or between their real beliefs and their fanciful stories, so that while one may quote a legend as illustrating any particular conception, it is, of course, not possible to assume that the legends always embody true belief. When, therefore, a native retells the tale of a well-known legendary character—Korevajà, Hovepakutota, Egovagova, to mention a few such—he does not necessarily believe that such a character ever existed except in fiction, much less that it is still in existence. In accordance with their general attributes he classifies these as *sovai*, and dismisses the matter from his mind.

Yet, despite this general attitude, we come upon sporadic instances in which these legendary *sovai* are spoken of as still existing. The instances that have come to my notice are so few that I will, as briefly as possible, set them all down.

(1) Totoima was the man-monster who formerly decimated the Orokaiva and remained invincible until two youths obtained possession of his detachable tusks, and thus having him at their mercy killed him. He is commonly regarded as no more than legendary, or as an historical being who passed out of existence when the two youths killed him. Yet a man of the River Gira (with which Totoima is specially associated) assured me that it was the custom for

a warlike party to call upon Totoima (as a mighty slayer) to precede them, and fall upon their foes in spirit (*asisi*), after which they would go and deliver their own attack in the flesh.

(2) Jappi Jappi Tururu is the subject of a long tale in which, although an old hag of particularly odious habits, she figures as an invariably successful huntress. A pig-hunting magician who is possessed of certain medicines and who receives visits from the *asisi* of bush-pigs, is in the habit of calling on Jappi in terms which may be translated as follows: 'O Jappi, I go forth into the bush to spear a pig; grant me a pig and make it come near me; I go now in search of one, and having found it I will soon return.' The man who originated this ritual gave it out that Jappi once conducted his spirit into the bush where she gave him the pig medicine, and instructed him how to proceed.

(3) Moraralau was accredited with the origin of the taro. He lived alone, and was eyeless, earless, noseless—in fact devoid of any bodily orifice or member—until visited by a woman who obtained the taro from him and at the same time made a man of him. After this Moraralau fled to a cave where he baffled every attempt at capture. My informants said that his *asisi* still dwelt in the cave. When a man plants taro he may ejaculate 'Moraralau!' (though it was not stated that this was an appeal to him to make the plant grow).

(4) Kokowaio is identified with the 'floating island' on lake Embi, i.e. with the cohering mass of water plants which is sometimes to be seen floating on the surface of the lake. The legend is, that Kokowaio (sometimes represented as female, sometimes as male) rescued, by taking on to her back, a boy and girl, the sole survivors of a flood which led to the formation of lake Embi. Now Kokowaio exercises some sort of control over the lake, which is generally regarded as a place full of danger, except for men of the Umondaha clan, to which it belongs. When, in company with Mr. Ashton, the Assistant Resident Magistrate of the district, I voyaged across the waters to visit the floating island on an extempore raft, our escort was apprehensive of the wind

which Kokowaio might send if he were displeased, and continually hailed him with assurances that our intentions were harmless, as if to ask for consideration. Mr. Wurth, the Resident Magistrate, had a similar experience, and his attendant explained that 'he was telling the waters of Embi not to be wild as he was only taking his master to see the island. . . . Had he not done so the canoe would have capsized '.[1] It remains very uncertain what form Kokowaio takes in native imagination beyond his association with the floating island.

Mr. Leo Flint, who in the course of magisterial work has given a good deal of study to the Orokaiva, names several of these personal *sovai*. He writes:

'The Bines, who are alleged to have the greatest powers are—Koi, who informs the people of the name of the necromancer who caused the death of a certain person; the Umbubuka, who walks the road at night; the Owadegoiari, who controls the spirit of children who die in infancy. Owadegoiari is credited with having a tail, and lives in the sago swamp. The legend of the tail is that it has grown from the umbilical cord of infants who have died shortly after birth, or in the uterus.' [2]

I have met with only the last mentioned in my own inquiries, and the version which I received being somewhat different, is worth recording. *Hovatu-koiari* (to use the Aiga form) does not stand in this version for a single personal *sovai* who controls the spirits of children dying in infancy, but for the spirits of the children themselves. The word means literally 'after birth (*hovatu*)—bury (*koiari*)', and the spirit of the still-born or aborted child survives as a little creature inhabiting the sago swamp. It is a foot or so high, and has a long tail which, as Mr. Flint was told, originates from the navel string. When the *hovatu-koiari* walk the tail drags behind, but when the little creatures sit down to scrape sago it is thrown over the shoulder and hangs in front. They are to be seen and heard occasionally singing a plaintive song in time to the beat of their sago-scrapers. 'Why did our mothers throw us away?', they say.

[1] *Annual Report*, 1922–3, p. 25.   [2] *Ibid.*, 1920–1, p. 49.

'Had they but kept us we might have been good children who could work and make sago for them.'

Destination of Sovai

Where beliefs as to the nature of *sovai* are so confused and indefinite we need not expect to find a carefully formulated doctrine as to their habitat or destination. Nightbound in a lonely place, a native would feel positive that the *sovai* were ubiquitous, and if they abounded in one place more than another it would be in his own vicinity. But when his fears were calmed, he could expound some more specific theories, albeit not entirely consistent.

In the first place the *sovai* are felt to haunt the village they lived in as men. I have already given evidence of this belief in relation to the ghostly form of the *sovai* (*vide* pp. 270–2), and it appears that this haunting may be more than merely temporary. There is a custom called *peni*, i.e. 'gift-offering', in which a number of young men do a round of the village carrying a pig on a pole or some cooked food on a dish. Beating their drums as they go, they pause at every house and lay the pig for a moment on the verandah platform, or leave there a morsel of cooked food. This ceremony is a placation of the *sovai* which are thought to haunt the houses. Sometimes it is not the actual village, but the neighbouring bush that is inhabited by the *sovai*. Of this idea the most interesting illustration is the custom of *jage* or hailing, in which the *sovai*, being called by name, gives answer in a long-drawn inarticulate cry from the concealment of the forest.

It seems that in the main, however, it is the *sovai* of the more recently dead who are thought of as frequenting the village. The mortuary ceremonies are at least in part intended as placations of them; and when all due honours have been paid, the final ceremony, viz. *sirari* (*vide* p. 253), is apparently a means of getting rid of the *sovai*, or inducing it to leave the village for good and all. Thus, for example, at the conclusion of a cycle of mortuary ceremonies in the village of Suporosusu certain paraphernalia of the dance were placed on the raft and floated down the river

Opi, and the chief man of the village cried out the names of those deceased for whom the ceremonies had been performed, and bade them go right down to the sea and there turn into *sovai* creatures, naming crocodiles, sharks, and water-snakes. After this, he said, the *sovai* would be 'afraid' to remain in the neighbourhood of Suporosusu.

It does not appear that the sea or the sea-shore is commonly regarded as the destination of the *sovai*, but there are, on the other hand, a number of definite localities belonging (sentimentally if not actually) to the various clans, whither their people are supposed to repair after death. Such localities are called *sovai-ta-na* or '*sovai* villages', and almost every one of the clans of the Aiga tribe could name its own. They take the form of some well-defined feature such as a hill, rock, or pool. The *sovai-ta-na* of the Samanahu clan, for instance, is a cluster of large rocks which constitute a small island midstream in the Kumusi. It is worth recording an incident associated with this place. A man was fishing nearby; when he looked up he saw the figure of a woman on the steep bank opposite standing in the conventional posture with staff held in both hands and resting on the head. He cried out to her, but she merely turned aside her head and remained silent. When he had repeated his call with the same result, he suddenly felt that the situation was an uncanny one, and returned precipitately to his village, where he found that a woman had died. No one questions that the man actually saw the woman's *sovai* (it is doubtful, indeed, whether an Orokaiva recognizes the possibility of delusion), and the incident verifies the character of the place. I may note in passing that when I visited these rocks the men who accompanied me showed no reluctance to land on them.

Another example of a *sovai-ta-na* is to be seen in the pool Monoda, which belongs to the clan Eugahu. In reality a stagnant backwater of the Kumusi, Monoda lies secluded amid heavy, dank forest, and is certainly dismal enough for a place of the dead. Natives would not approach the pool too closely, and when we disturbed a snake at our feet they would not interfere with it, but watched it glide rapidly down and disappear in the waters of Monoda itself. Even such an incident as this, no doubt, does something to enhance the reputation of a *sovai* village.

It is sometimes thought that the *sovai* foregather in these places (which, of course, have no resemblance whatever to the villages of living humans). There is a *sovai-ta-na* not far from the village of Bologasusu named Henjauti, consisting of a large isolated rock some twenty-five or thirty feet in height. When a young man named Patuna, small and not of a very courageous aspect, was recently returning home at dusk, his way took him past Henjauti, where he was horrified to hear the rustling and whispering of *sovai*. The sounds now came from every direction, and Patuna realized that he was surrounded by the *sovai* who inhabited the place, so he made such speed as he could to climb a tree and shouted for help. A body of villagers armed with torches rescued him from what every one thought a very serious predicament; and Patuna subsequently showed me with some pride the tree—about thirty yards distant from the rock—in which he had taken refuge. Some people have actually witnessed or overheard the union of the new *sovai* with the old. It is thought—or we should say sometimes thought—that the *sovai* of those formerly deceased assemble to receive the new *sovai* and bear him away with them. In the valedictory address at the grave he is told to make himself known to them, and to offer them gifts in order to make sure of a cordial welcome (see p. 215). It would seem that the *sovai* is sometimes reluctant to leave the life on earth. Thus listeners at Henjauti have heard the *sovai* of the newly dead weeping; and when a man hidden under a pile of pig-nets heard the *sovai* passing by on their way to Monoda, the new-comer whom they were conducting to the *sovai-ta-na* was protesting and wrangling with his escort. (It may be unnecessary to explain that the man under the pig-nets was a diviner who made a practice of overhearing the conversation of the *sovai* on such occasions in order to discover the identity of the sorcerer who was responsible for the death. He merely imposes on popular belief.)

The Orokaiva does not think of a happy home for the departed. It is true that at the graveside the *sovai* is bidden

to go to some place of sunshine where there are neither
march-flies nor mosquitoes to bother him, but there is no
definite idea of where this place is nor of what manner of
life the *sovai* may lead there; and the description as far as it
goes does not seem to suit the tangible examples of *sovai-
ta-na* which I have seen. There are one or two tales of
sky-dwellers but no hint of a heaven (though there is the
extremely vague belief that some *sovai* go aloft, and are
accordingly known as *i-sovai* or 'upper' *sovai*. Among these
are the *diroga* or spirits of those slain in fight. It was never
suggested, by the way, that these *i-sovai* were in any sense
superior to the others.) There is also an interesting tale of
the underworld into which a man follows his deceased wife,
and finds there a very large population of *sovai*, including
some of his relatives. But this, as the native often says, is
hihi—'only a fairy-tale'.

In short, the only places of the departed which Orokaiva
doctrine has definitely formulated are the *sovai-ta-na*; and
these are natural features—hills, pools, and the like—which
are associated with the several clans. In almost every case
they are situated on the land belonging to the clan, and
where this is not so it appears probably that they are situated
on land which formerly did belong to the clan.

Attitude of Sovai toward the Living

We must lastly consider the mental and moral attitude of
the living toward the dead. This will naturally depend upon
the attitude which the dead are supposed to hold toward the
living, and from what has gone before it will be seen that
this latter attitude is of a mixed nature. It is alternately
benign and malign, though there is little doubt that the latter
is felt to predominate.

I shall first recall evidence that the *sovai* may be well disposed toward the living. The most striking instances are
found in their association with magicians, weather experts,
and the like. The report on the Taro Cult will be found full
of such evidence. The Taro man, who is in effect a spiritual-
horticultural expert, most commonly attributes his special
powers to one of the dead, who has visited him probably

in a dream and bequeathed him some instructions or a tangible 'medicine'. Sometimes the healer is in like manner indebted for his gift to a benevolent *sovai*; or the hunting magician may receive from a *sovai* the intelligence that a pig is waiting to be caught.

But apart from the favours which the *sovai* are supposed to bestow on specialists, we find that every gardener and hunter feels that the dead may send him success. It is true that the negative side of this proposition is more often in evidence, i.e. he is more prone to attribute failure to the displeasure of the *sovai* than success to their favour, but there is, nevertheless, the belief that they are able to make the gardens flourish and to drive the pigs into the pig-nets, and this is proved by the custom of adjuring the *sovai* to do so in the farewell address at the grave.

Even in the legends, where the *sovai* usually plays a very villainous part, we occasionally meet with one that is grateful or well disposed to the living. There is, for example, the case of the grateful warrior whose younger brother cared for his children after he had been killed, and who subsequently, in the form of a bird, warned this younger brother of an approaching raid. Nor did his gratitude stop at this, for abandoning his bird-shape he assumed that of a warrior, and held a large number of raiders at bay while his younger brother ran for help.

But such benevolent conduct on the part of the *sovai* is to say the least unusual, and it must be confessed that on the whole the Orokaiva regards his relatives and friends after their death as enemies. Any failure of the crops may be attributed to them; they may baffle the hunters; they may send the pigs to break through the fences and despoil the gardens. Sickness is perhaps ascribed more often to the malevolence of *sovai* than to any other cause. It is sometimes believed that the *sovai* enter the body in immaterial form, and sometimes that they may cause disease by a mere evil influence, e.g. by touching food. If they are eaten in their animal form sickness invariably follows. We have seen that they have more direct ways of wreaking their ill feelings, and in the guise of monsters they pursue, capture, and maltreat their victims. Even general calamities may be ascribed to their malignancy: an earthquake, for instance, is caused by *sovai* travelling underground and presages a general sickness. One may quote the particular instance of Unina. This village used to stand on a flat hill-top, but for many years its inhabitants have been watching the ground crumble away till now their very building-room is threatened. This unfortunate process they ascribe to the malice or vengeance of the *sovai*, with whom they were once unwise enough to do battle in the neighbourhood. The fact that the process of detrition has apparently stopped for the present is said to be due to the intercession of one particular *sovai* who has taken pity on his old village.

It may be granted, then, that the attitude of the *sovai* toward the living is conceived on the whole to be one of malignancy; or it may be more correct to say that the *sovai* are thought of as intensely dangerous, and that besides having powers for good they have also powers for evil, which they are constantly ready to use. What then is the counter attitude of the living toward the *sovai*?

Attitude of the Living toward the Sovai

We must not underestimate the intensity of sorrow which an Orokaiva feels at the death of his relative or friend, and we cannot but suppose that towards the being which he believes so confidently to survive death he still continues to have some feeling of affection. When, for example, the small fragments of tobacco or betel-nut are set on the platform as an offering, or when the *sovai* are called upon to be present and witness the dance, it is not necessary to suppose that those who perform these rites are devoid of any tender feeling for those in whose behalf they are made. But how long such feelings last is another question. The Orokaiva inherits a body of beliefs regarding the *sovai* which picture them in a variety of horrible and dangerous forms, so that he cannot help regarding them with aversion, and especially with fear. His feelings are, therefore, ambivalent, and according to circumstances first one aspect and then the other will take his attention.

In his general conduct the less kindly emotions are often in evidence. Sometimes they find expression in open hostility, and we find the villagers defying and actually doing battle at night with a host of imaginary foes. Usually, however, it is the anxious endeavour of the living to placate the dead. Therefore we find the offerings of food in the village and in the gardens, and witness the performance of a mortuary ceremony which seems in the main of a placatory nature. Besides these we see the presentation of formal gifts, a handful of costly ornaments offered to the departing *sovai* at the grave-side, or suspended before the door of a house of sickness to induce the *sovai* to discontinue his persecution.

While it is certain that the Orokaiva goes in real fear of the power of the *sovai*, the means of placation often seem peculiarly off-hand. All gifts, as far as I know, are given only to be taken back, or at the most they fall into the hands of the magician or healer who acts, so to speak, as intermediary, and, if the patient recovers, annexes the presents which were ostensibly meant to buy off the *sovai*. There is seldom any deliberate sacrifice of real valuables, as, e.g., by burying them. I may quote what purports to be the true case of an old man who was unable to recall his dog from a hole in which it had pursued some animal. Concluding the dog must have been seized by a *sovai* who lived in the hole, he placed some ornaments at the entrance by way of a bribe, but no sooner did his dog reappear than he snatched up the ornaments and ran for dear life to the safety of his village, the more speedily because he was convinced that he heard the pursuing footsteps of the *sovai*. It is difficult to reconcile such hocus-pocus with the genuine fear of the *sovai* which motivates so much of an Orokaiva's conduct; but whatever form it may take, the act of placation is felt to be necessary and is constantly performed.

Besides the placation of the *sovai* by ceremonial gifts we find some traces of direct appeal or prayer.[1] I do not feel justified in applying this word to the *kasamba*, i.e. the concerted singing of the Taro men (which is described in the 'Taro Cult', pp. 37 ff.), though there is good reason to

[1] *Vide* further *Orokaiva Magic*, p. 207.

suppose that the now somewhat garbled songs are in origin hortatory. The exhortation, however, is addressed rather to the taro itself or the spirit (*asisi*) of the taro, and I have no definite instance in which the song is addressed to the *sovai*. But the definite instances are not wanting elsewhere. We need go no further than the grave-side address, to which reference has been made so often, where the *sovai* is requested to send pigs to the hunters and prosper the gardens. Again, apart from the ritual *kasamba*, the Taro Cult provides examples of what we may call genuine prayer, when the Taro man in the act of planting calls on the *sovai* of his mother, father, and grandfather to make his taro flourish.

But the most interesting examples are perhaps those connected with hunting. The Aiga villager says that the new moon is the time to set up his *bage*, or pig-trap, and then after dusk he will cry, *sostenuto*, into the darkness of the bush:

> *Hariga, Hoindapa, Bavari . . . &c.*
> Moon, Hoindapa, Bavari . . .
> *Bage etenavara, Hambuto hatijo araikai.*
> A trap I have set, go, leap on it and break it.

How the moon comes into the prayer I cannot say, for there is nothing in the least resembling a moon cult among the Orokaiva; but the names Hoindapa, Bavari, and the string of place-names that follow are of *sovai-ta-na*, and it is explained that the prayer is addressed to the spirits of the dead who inhabit them. The ensuing words are of course addressed to the pig, telling it to enter the trap to its destruction, and they are no more than an elementary spell in which the hunter utters in words what he wants to happen in fact.

Mr. Flint gives the following account of the same practice as carried out by a hunting party. One of their number is requested to hail the spirits.

'He does so by tapping his throat lightly, and warbling simultaneously. Having aroused the spirits, he calls out vociferously, "We come with our dogs or nets, you send plenty of pigs straight to us." As I was very interested in this alleged communication, I asked my informants if the spirits listened to their talk. I was informed, "Oh, yes, if he did not listen, we would catch no pigs".' [1]

[1] *Annual Report*, 1924–5, p. 48.

Lastly, there are the sporadic instances of the personal and semi-legendary *sovai*, who may be hailed and exhorted to grant a favour or pardon an intrusion. But such direct appeals are of relatively small importance. The aim of the Orokaiva is to appease or to win the favour of the *sovai*, and his regular methods are those of placation by gifts and ritual.

I may now repeat what was written towards the beginning of this chapter, viz. that on the whole Orokaiva religion concerns itself primarily with the spirits of the dead. The *sovai* are viewed as beings both powerful and dangerous, and it behoves the living to keep on the right side of them. It is not to be supposed that an all-embracing philosophy regards the *sovai* as the guiding and controlling spirits of all nature. The native is not urged on by a philosophic inquisitiveness which demands an interpretation for everything. The phenomena of nature are largely taken for granted, and when things are going well he is content to ask no questions. He does not theorize upon the movements of the sun, for instance, and postulate some personal entity—*sovai* or any other—that makes it rise and set. But in the face of calamity or sickness, or any hitch in the course of nature, he may cast about for a cause, some one or something on which to fix the responsibility, and perhaps his favourite scapegoat is the *sovai*. The *sovai*, therefore, are not conceived of as invariably presiding over the course of nature, but rather as being able to influence the course of nature for or against living humans. Further, because of their somewhat malevolent disposition, they are exceedingly prone to the latter kind of interference, so that it is the very essence of Orokaiva religion to placate them.

XVII

MEDICINE AND MAGIC

WE have seen that in the easy-going philosophy of the Orokaiva the course of nature is largely taken for granted. All the things and processes of the world exist or happen *per se*; they are not under any omnipotent control nor do they submit to continual regulation by any personal powers. But we have also seen that they may be *influenced* for good or evil by the *sovai*, i.e. those beings who survive death.

Now it appears that the *sovai* are not the only agencies by which nature may be mysteriously influenced in one direction or the other. There is in Orokaiva philosophy a second kind of agency, equally occult, by which the normal happenings of nature may be interfered with: this is the power of magic and sorcery. Magic and sorcery have been dealt with at length in another report,[1] so that it is not my purpose here to describe their general methods, much less to elaborate the theory which was attempted in that essay. The present chapter will deal with a single subject—fairly well defined— that of diseases, their putative causes and treatment, and it will touch upon the magical aspect of these treatments only in passing.

Causes of Disease

The native, while believing that the *sovai* and the living magician or sorcerer can influence nature both for good and evil, is yet more impressed by misfortune than by ordinary success, so that it is especially in the face of calamity or failure that his thoughts turn to occult explanations. Since no misfortune, perhaps, impresses him so frequently or forcibly as that of sickness or disease, we shall not be surprised to find the responsibility for this, which seems like an interference with the normal course of nature, fixed sometimes upon the *sovai* and sometimes upon the sorcerer.

[1] *Orokaiva Magic.*

Native ideas on the subject of disease, therefore, while possessing an intrinsic interest and, indeed, revealing a certain amount of straightforward good sense, will also serve to illustrate the attitude toward both the spirits of the dead and the power of living magic; and, further, they will incidentally exemplify the actual procedure of magic.

Classification.

As the result of a good deal of questioning on this subject I feel justified in reducing diseases, according to their putative causes, to the following classification: (1) *Casual Diseases*: the result, e.g., of accident, of weather conditions, of over-exertion, &c., or of chance contact with some harmful substance or thing which often appears in one form or another to enter the body. All these afflictions, which I have lumped together under the not wholly satisfactory expression Casual Diseases, are distinguished from the two classes which follow in that they are not due to any personal agency, but to causes which the native regards as natural. They are misfortunes, not inflictions. (2) *Sovai Diseases*: i.e. those caused by the attack of the *sovai*, and in many instances by its immanence in the body. (3) *Sorcery Diseases*: i.e. those which are brought about by black magic.

It is necessary to add that the most prevalent native conception of disease is that of an intrusive element. One cannot say that this is invariable. It does not appear to cover all natural diseases nor all *sovai* diseases, and, as far as I am aware, it does not apply to any sorcery diseases; but it is, nevertheless, the usual native theory, and will be found to account for a large number of treatments. The word for sickness is *ambu.* I dare not attempt to define its applications, but, since sickness as an intrusive element takes so many varying forms in native imagination, some of them apparently quite immaterial, one will not be far wrong in saying that *ambu* may be regarded, like 'sickness', as an abstraction. The native will say that the *ambu* enters the body, leaves it, passes from one to another, &c., without having any set idea that it possesses form or consistency of any sort.

It is not to be supposed that a native will always be able to set down his ideas of disease and its causes under logical headings, but I have often enough found the above three-fold classification implied and sometimes expressed. One man, for instance, who practised as a healer or expeller of diseases, classified the causes as follows: (1) heat, strain, cold, and the like, where a man is said to sicken *'teho'*, i.e. 'by himself' or 'for nothing'; (2) the entry of injurious substances; (3) the attack of *sovai*; and (4) the use of *inja*, i.e. the sorcerer's specific. His first two divisions will, in the main, coincide with our first class, viz. casual diseases.

Casual Diseases.

Orokaiva natives, like others in the Territory, probably suffer to some considerable extent from malaria. They are certainly afflicted by headaches and attacks of fever. When the colder winds from the south-east, called *pishi*, spring up, they learn to expect these attacks. They call them *ambu isapo*, or 'small sickness', and usually regard them as natural occurrences with no ulterior causes, such as that of a visitation from the *sovai*, or the malice of a sorcerer. So again we find a doctor attributing a man's sickness to a drenching from the rain; or in another case to working in his garden through the hottest part of the day; in another to over-exerting himself by carrying two small pigs tied to a pole across his shoulder. Such straightforward ailments, besides being called *ambu isapo*, 'small sicknesses', are sometimes spoken of as *memei*, which means 'ache' or 'pain'; and in the generality of cases they are accepted without question as natural phenomena, the transient ills to which all flesh is heir.

It is interesting to note that in the last instance quoted a doctor discovered (by means of a method of extraction to be described presently) several fragments of a pig's larger intestine in the patient's body. This affords an example of the very common view which has been referred to already, viz. that disease or sickness is an intrusive element. It is true that the doctor in question subsequently discovered a variety of other tell-tale fragments and offered a number of diagnoses of what must have been a very complicated disease; but, in so far as the disease was due to the strain of carrying the pigs it was *present in* the man's body, evidenced by the pig's intestine. On one occasion my cook-boy, who suffered from headaches, took it upon himself to consult a *bara* woman, i.e. one who practises extraction. She succeeded in removing from his forehead a small piece of trade twist: his complaint had been due to over-smoking. The same woman treated a man with a pain in his foot. It appeared that in fording a stream he had struck his foot against a boulder, and the *bara* woman contrived to extract a small pebble from his instep. This, the man himself told me, must have got into his foot as he crossed the stream. It will be seen presently that there is some doubt whether such material objects are always believed to be actually present in the patient's body. But in the cases where they are not believed to be so present, they are at least allowed to stand in imagination for the sickness, and are thus in keeping with the idea of the sickness as a foreign presence which has intruded itself into the body.

This assimilation or absorption of a sickness mostly comes about by eating, and the diagnosis is, of course, retrospective. A man with a pain in any part of his body—though, we may suppose, usually in the region of his stomach—remembers what he ate, and not unnaturally makes it bear the blame. Any kind of food—bananas, sugar-cane, e.g.—may be intrinsically bad, and the victim still unable to explain why it should be so. Very often, as we shall see, its injurious properties are due to the presence of or contamination by a *sovai*, but this is not invariable. I have known a man profess to abstain from eating snake because he could not bear the thought of the reptile writhing in his stomach, and another who would not eat flying-fox for fear of the internal flapping and fluttering.

All these are examples of casual diseases. They are acquired in the course of daily experience, and they are acquired directly, i.e. not through any personal agency such as that of *sovai* or sorcerer. It seems that we must place in the same category those diseases which were specially treated by the Taro men. According to the doctrines of their cult certain species of the taro plant were regarded as *koropa*, or 'strong'. To eat them caused illness, and this illness was supposedly due to the presence in the victim's body of the *asisi* of the taro. Nor was it only by eating that the taro *asisi* could be absorbed. If, for example, a man pulled taro from the gardens without first having consulted the *ba-embo*, or Taro man, then the *asisi* of the aggrieved plant would enter into the offender and make him sick. It was then the opportunity of the *ba-embo* in his capacity of doctor to entice the *asisi* back from the patient's body, and so put an end to his sickness.

Sovai Diseases.

It will be remembered that among the great majority of the followers of the Taro Cult it was toward the spirit of the dead rather than the spirits of the actual taro plant that all ritual was directed; and accordingly we find that sickness is with them very commonly attributed to the *sovai*. In this the Taro Cult (i.e. the popular form of it) was wholly in keeping with former belief. No agency is more readily made responsible for human illness than are the *sovai*, who are so often regarded as dangerous and spiteful. Remarkable as it may seem, it is especially the *sovai* of close relatives who are blamed for sickness, and they are sometimes thought to enter the bodies of their victims at the actual funeral, when the mourners indulge in the habit of embracing and mauling the corpse. If after such demonstrations—which are in fact inspired by affection—the mourner eats with unwashed hands, or goes to sleep with his hands under his ear for a pillow, he is likely to be entered by the *sovai* and laid up with a sickness. There are many ways—some of them very vaguely conceived—in which the *sovai* may inflict the living with sickness. We hear, for instance, of a man with a swollen jaw who had been 'struck on the mouth' by a *sovai*; another merely ate food which had been cooked over the same fire as the flesh of a *sovai* animal; but in most cases sickness is due to eating the *sovai* in animal or reptile form.

It has been explained that the spirit of the dead may

assume such a form, viz. that of some creature of the forest or stream (*vide* pp. 269, 272), so that whoever eats snake, cuscus, lizard, and so forth—even bush-pig—does so at a certain risk. The creature may be an ordinary specimen of its kind, or it may be a *sovai*. In the latter event the man who eats it is in all probability stricken down with illness. The exponents of the *Baigona*, or 'snake cult', which had a vogue in the Northern Division some fifteen years ago, made great play with this belief in animal reincarnation. Not only snakes but a great variety of animals and reptiles were held sacred, and fundamentally their sacred character was due to the fact that they were reincarnations of the dead. Any one, therefore, who killed and ate, or even offended one of these creatures, e.g. by neglecting to hail it respectfully, would incur the anger of the *sovai* which it embodied, and fall sick in consequence. Such cases constituted the peculiar province of the *Baigona* healers, who professed to be able to entice the *sovai* out of the sufferer's body. It is not altogether remarkable that although the *Baigona* was practically stamped out as a cult more than ten years ago there should still be practitioners (some of them actually retaining the title of *Baigona*-men) who continue to make use of methods and theories which are so firmly founded on old belief.

Sorcery Diseases.

From diseases caused by malevolent *sovai* we may turn to the last category, viz. that of diseases caused by sorcery.

It cannot be said that there is anything essentially distinctive in the symptoms of sorcery disease, though one may go so far as to say that it is the more mysterious and inexplicable of symptoms which call for this interpretation; and while it is true that when a native's anger or suspicion is aroused he is liable to strike out with a charge of sorcery for even the most trivial affliction, it remains the general rule to impute this cause only for the more serious complaints. Further than this, it is imputed as cause especially for those complaints which cannot be cured. Thus when a doctor has tried his methods on a patient without success he is likely to set the case down as a hopeless one of sorcery and discontinue his treatment; and, indeed, if he be astute enough, he may decide to have no truck with any case that seems too far gone. For it is generally held that sorcery sickness cannot be cured by the ordinary methods of the healer. Failing other explanations, therefore, he adopts this most pessimistic one. Sorcery is, in fact, the native's exegetical last card.

It is not my intention to deal with the methods of the sorcerer further than to say that (*a*) they follow the characteristic procedure in which some symbol of the victim is subjected to a treatment representing in symbolic form the sickness which it is hoped may afflict him; and that (*b*) this process is thought to be made infallible, i.e. the hoped-for result of it inevitable, by the addition of some element of a supernatural character which is known only to the sorcerer. Examples of their methods have been supplied in the essay on Orokaiva Magic, to which the reader is referred. At any rate they need not enter into the subject of the present chapter; for what concerns us here is not the actual practice of black magic, but that entirely disproportionate belief in its practice which has so often supplied a diagnosis of disease.

Common-sense Treatments

We may now turn our attention to native methods of treating disease. These may be considered under three heads: (i) Common-sense, (ii) Expulsive, and (iii) Placatory (which, by the way, are not meant to correspond with the three heads under which were classified the causes of disease).

To the first division there belong a number of treatments which, whatever their degree of futility, seem nevertheless to be straightforward and 'common-sense'. Wounds, for instance, are washed and subjected to a treatment of hot air, blown through a tube of heated bark or banana stalk. After that they may be given a hot compress of leaves. For snake-bite the treatment, I am told, is to cut about the bite and let the blood flow. For headache there is the old remedy of blood-letting from the forehead (by means of a series of small cuts). For the open sores (*kini*) or ulcers, which so commonly afflict the natives, there are a number of remedies in the form of applications. One consists of the scrapings of the bark of the Goru palm mixed with dry coco-nut; another of the green fruit of the tree *Puga* (which contains a poison) mixed with ashes; another of a paste of lime and the scrapings of a bark called *Popo*. These are only examples. The different treatments are innumerable, and it does not appear that they are widely known, for inquiry will always discover new methods in new places. Nor can it be said that they are very efficacious, or even that they are often employed. I have seen a man wearing a very neat bandage of leaf on his heel tied about his foot: it covered an application of *gamboja*, a kind of phosphorescent fungus, which he said generated heat. But sores are commonest on children, and as it appears that some of the remedies are painful the children refuse to endure them and soon tear off the bandages. In most cases, therefore, the sores are left to look after themselves.

For the skin disease, *tinea imbricata*, commonly known in Papua as *simpoma*, the natives have a number of remedies which, as far as I know, are all ineffective. I can cite a kind of astringent fig juice, scraped yam, and wallaby blood. The last may seem to us magic pure and simple, though it is, no doubt, as much common-sense to the native as our own idea that mutton fat is good for the complexion is common-sense to us.

In ordinary indisposition a man lies down as close as he can to the fire and is nursed by his wife, who will support his head in her lap. He often removes his *bo* and goes completely naked, though I do not know of any reason except that it makes him feel more comfortable. A sick man often moves with his wife to a garden house or some other secluded place in order to secure peace and quiet. That is the ostensible reason for what is quite a voluntary isolation; though I have known a sick man to vacate his house because he suspected the presence of a *sovai*, so that maybe when the patient retires into isolation it is more than the mere noise and bustle of the village that he means to leave behind him.

Sometimes the position is reversed, and unaffected men and women will leave the village for the bush in order to escape an epidemic (*tauni*) which has seized on its inhabitants. In this case there is no doubt as to their motive: they leave the village to escape the *sovai* who have caused the *tauni*.

The few examples I have given, however, will show that the native possesses a certain number of methods in the treatment of sickness which, however wide of the mark they appear to us, are yet in a manner reasonable. They are common knowledge and, to the native at least, common-sense. They are his household remedies.

Expulsive Treatments

From these we may turn to the characteristic kind of treatment which I have called expulsive. There are many varieties of expulsive methods, and they are all based on the very prevalent idea of disease as an intrusive element in the body; furthermore, they call for special powers in those who practise them, so that whereas common-sense treatments are known to any one and every one, expulsive treatments are usually carried out by 'doctors'. This word will stand for those individuals who make a special practice of curing and who are thought to possess powers and medicines (*sivo*) which make their methods effective. The word *sivo* also requires explanation. It stands for good 'medicine', i.e. for any substance (usually a leaf) which possesses a mysterious potency for good; and it applies equally to, e.g., a medicine planted with the taro to make it grow, a medicine given to a sick man to make him well, and a medicine used by a magician to make his methods, the mere routine of magic, have their desired effect.

It is with one general class of *sivo* that I may introduce the subject of expulsive treatments, though it is to be noted that this class (contrary to the general rule of expulsive treatments) consists mostly of home remedies which are not administered by a doctor. In many cases it is impossible to get at the *modus operandi* of the *sivo*, because its use may be traditional and the user may be as ignorant of the way it acts as the ordinary layman is ignorant of the action of *nux*

(*a*) The *Jura* Treatment

(*b*) The *Jura* Treatment

PLATE XXXVI

vomica. But in not a few cases it appears that the potency of the medicine consists in its smell. Thus we find a man suffering from a severe cold who is taking as medicine a bark called *Siganapa.* This, which is strongly scented, is boiled and the decoction added to a stew which the patient eats. According to the explanation, the sickness inside the man's stomach will smell the *Siganapa* and go away; so that in such a case we may regard the *sivo* as typically expulsive. Such a remedy need not be taken internally; it is enough to smell it in one's nostrils. So a man smells scented leaves for stomach-ache ; and I have seen another garlanded about his shoulders and waist with strands of a creeper called *Toiho,* which gave out an abominable smell, resembling that of tree-bugs. Its virtue consisted in its smell (*mune*), by which the sickness was 'frightened away'. Another effective remedy is the fragrant lemon-grass (*Dariva*).

The same idea—that of driving out the sickness by smell —is at the bottom of a process called *jura,* which consists of fumigating the sick (*vide* also pp. 200–1). In one case which I saw the subject had been suffering with headache and general pains. His friends prepared a mixture in which seven kinds of leaf or bark were added to coco-nut milk in a *teva* or wooden dish. The patient descends from his house and squats over the *teva* dish; a hot stone has been held ready in a coco-nut husk and is now dropped into the mixture; a pandanus mat is thrown over all and the patient remains underneath enveloped in steam. Principal among the seven ingredients was *Toiho,* the extremely evil-smelling creeper mentioned above, and all the remaining six had a more or less decided odour.[1]

The commonest and simplest of expulsive treatments is one of a very different kind, known as *humbari,* 'taking away'. One or more doctors operate on the patient, who lies on his

[1] In another case of this fumigating process, the technique was the same, but the principle apparently quite different. If a man's sickness were diagnosed as the result of eating a 'bad' snake, some snake bones would be put into the *teva* with water and the hot stone added. The patient would sit in the rising steam, and, if the diagnosis were correct, the treatment would be effective. If the sickness were due to eating a 'bad' banana, then banana skins would take the place of snake bones. I did not see this process, nor any similar in principle, carried out, so the information may not be wholly reliable. No satisfactory explanation was offered.

back. They massage his limbs and body, pinching the flesh very hard. The rubbing proceeds usually towards the extremities, and the operator, continually removing his hands from the patient's body with what resembles a plucking motion, affects to be throwing something away. The principle of *humbari* is to locate the sickness or cause of the sickness in some portion of the sufferer's body, to work it towards the extremities, and there to cast it out.

In conjunction with *humbari* we often find the treatment known as *kavo*, or 'blowing'. The operator (known as *kavo-embo*, or 'blower') pauses every now and then to blow into the patient's ears, or his nostrils; sometimes into his hair, and very commonly into his fingers and toes. I have watched a dying infant subjected to the treatment of the *kavo-embo*, and whenever the child opened its mouth in a convulsive yawn the doctor would seize the opportunity of blowing into what he found a convenient aperture. It does not appear certain that *kavo* is an expulsive method, and its significance remains doubtful. No informant ever offered a rationale for the process, so that one is justified in forming an inference. This might be that the blowing into the orifices and extremities of the body was meant to set the disease in motion, and finally to blow it out of the body altogether; but one is inclined to give it a different meaning. The *humbari* doctors chew a medicine, or *sivo*, before they begin work, and it is this that imparts to them the necessary power to cast out. They chew while they work, and occasionally they spit on to the patient's body; and not only do they blow into his ears, finger-tips, &c., but into their own closed fists. It seems likely, therefore, that the ordinary *kavo*, like the spitting and blowing into the fist, is a means of in-breathing the powerful influence of the *sivo* into the material they are working on and the instruments they are working with.[1]

Perhaps the most interesting of all expulsive treatments is

---

[1] I find, however, that Mr. Flint, in giving a description of this treatment (together with *humbari*) under the name of *gau-o* (the Binandele form of *kavo*), does not hesitate to regard it as expulsive. An old woman blew into the ears and mouth of the patient, and Mr. Flint writes, 'This was done to drive out the demon who was keeping the patient ill'. He does not expressly state that this is a native explanation.

the time-honoured practice of extracting the sickness from the patient's body in some tangible form. Among the Orokaiva this is called *bara*, a word which appears to stand as well for the practice as for the practitioner. To cite an example: a man suffering from temporary lameness called in a *bara* specialist to treat him. The *bara*, having chewed the medicine on which he relies for power, together with some betel-nut, sucked at the patient's leg and finally spat out a mass of chewed betel in which was found a small fragment of wallaby bone. It transpired that the patient had eaten wallaby flesh some time before, and it was assumed that this was the cause of his sickness. In one remarkable instance of this treatment a woman pressed a handful of leaves about a sick infant's neck, coming near to strangling it in the process, and then withdrawing her hand and opening the leaves disclosed a red mass of chewed betel and a huge boar's tusk. It appeared that the mother had eaten a *sovai* pig, and in suckling her child had passed on to it the penalty of sickness.

In the practice of *bara* there is, of course, a great deal of charlatanry, and although the specialist is clever in sleight of hand it is not difficult to see where his opportunities for trickery are taken. In one case where a husband and wife practised in partnership, the former sat on the ground chewing betel and the appropriate medicines, the latter half in and half out of her doorway, and the patient on the platform between the two. The husband having chewed the betel and medicine spits it on to a leaf and hands it up to his wife; she puts it into her own mouth and continues to chew, meanwhile feeling the patient about the body, massaging and squeezing; then she takes the twice-chewed mixture from her mouth and returns it to her husband, who probes it with a small stick and discovers various scraps or objects which purport to have come out of the patient's body into that of the woman. This operation continued for some time with fresh mouthfuls of betel, and the husband succeeded in discovering altogether two fragments of native tobacco leaf, two of pig's intestine, a piece of rat's tail, some human hair, some pandanus seed, and part of a mango leaf—for all of which he had a ready explanation. It will be seen that there are here many opportunities for introducing foreign substances into the chewed mixture—particularly when the wife takes it from her husband, for she puts it down inside her doorway before putting it into her own mouth. We may also note that there are several methods of *bara*: sometimes the object is sucked out of the patient's body; sometimes it passes up the specialist's arm into her mouth; sometimes it is found actually in her hand.

It is important to note that *bara* is practised by specialists (mostly women in my experience) and that the specialist commonly, if not invariably, takes some medicine (*sivo*) before operating. Thus while the procedure, the mere technique of the process, is common knowledge, yet (in native belief) it is not every one who could succeed in really performing the act. It is certainly remarkable that sick natives readily submit to this treatment and that they apparently place considerable faith in it, often, no doubt, experiencing a certain amount of relief when they see it used on themselves. This confidence, I believe, is mainly due to the belief in the magical, i.e. supernatural, powers of the operator, either intrinsic or acquired by the chewing of a medicine. The doctor—or as we might call him the manipulative surgeon—whether he practise *humbari* or *bara*, begins by himself taking the medicine, which I have elsewhere called more definitely a 'Specific'.[1] This he chews with betel-nut, and it appears to be an essential factor in the cure. The habit of spitting on the patient, and perhaps also that of *kavo*, or blowing, appears to be merely a means of using the medicine on the body of the subject and thus expediting or facilitating the process of casting out or drawing out his disease. It must be borne in mind that the medicine is essential to success.

Expulsive Treatments as Magic

Now in certain of these expulsive treatments we may, I think, find a good illustration of the methods of magic. Sickness being often conceived of as an intrusive element in the body, it is the desire of the patient to have it expelled,

[1] *Vide Orokaiva Magic*, pp. 173, 200 ff.

and of the doctor to expel it. The doctor, accordingly, employs a method which is essentially that of magic: the whole gist of his treatment is to get rid of the disease in make-believe. He hopes to see it go, and therefore he pretends it is going and gone. He plucks it out and throws it away as in *humbari*; or, as in *bara*, he takes it clean out of the body in symbolic form—the pig's tusk for the disease caused by eating a *sovai* pig, or the fragment of tobacco for the head-ache caused by over-smoking. One does not attempt to deny that on the part of the doctor there is often deliberate fraud: he may pretend to extract a wallaby bone simply to gull his patient and perhaps earn a fee. But there is quite another way of looking at the matter. The doctor may be in earnest. He is trying to get the disease out of his patient, so he takes it out in make-believe and in symbolic form. Just as the sorcerer, intent on destroying his victim, makes believe to roast him, so the doctor, intent on curing his patient, makes believe to drag the cause of disease out of his body. He is still pretending, but he enters into the pretence himself; if he is practising deception it is at least half self-deception; he is not bluffing his patient, rather he is entering into a sort of collusion with him, and trying to rid him of the disease in a way which both believe will be effectual. Viewed in this light *bara* is not a piece of chicanery or deception in which the doctor bluffs the patient that he has cured him, but an attempt of a magician to put certain supernatural powers to their proper use. We may even call it an honest attempt.

A good deal hinges on the aetiology of the case. Either the doctor is unaware of any imputed cause before he operates (in which event he would presumably extract any object he pleased and invent a cause in keeping with it) or, on the other hand, he is previously acquainted with the imputed cause (in which event he would extract some object in keeping with or symbolizing that cause). I regret to say that in no case did I make sure of this point, though I should be prepared to guess from general impressions that very frequently, if not usually, the latter event is what we should meet with: the doctor would learn from conversation with the patient and his friends what was suspected to be the cause of the illness. When, for example, my cook-boy, who suffered from headaches, had a fragment of tobacco drawn from his forehead, or when the man, who struck his foot against a rock in the stream, had a pebble sucked out of his instep, I think it probable that the *bara* woman who performed these operations knew the circumstances of the cases before she began work. I cannot say, to repeat, how often this foreknowledge influences the case, but if and when it does, we may be justified in putting on the act of *bara* this more generous construction, viz. that it is a genuine effort, in the manner which is thoroughly typical of magic, to draw the disease out of the body. It is a symbolic representation of the wished-for result, and by virtue of the special powers of the *bara*, and the medicine which he chews, this representation is felt to assist in bringing about that result.

What we really have to account for is the belief, both on the part of the doctor and patient, that the *bara* treatment can cure. I will not attempt to deny that there may be among *bara* specialists many sheer impostors who wilfully gull their clients and realize that their treatment can do them no good. But I am confident, on the other hand, that many *bara* specialists do believe that they can cure their patients; for the *bara* man commonly feels confidence in his own powers, either intrinsic or acquired from his medicine or specific. What then is his attitude towards his technique, towards the procedure of extracting an object from the patient's body? Of course, he must know that he does not do it in actuality, for he deliberately secretes the object in his hand or mouth. But he makes believe to do so, and he makes the simulation as near reality as possible by tricks of concealment

Regarding the patient we can say with confidence that he believes the *bara* treatment to be able to cure him, otherwise he would not trouble to undergo it. What then is his attitude toward the apparent extraction of an object from his body? He may actually believe, as he sometimes declares he does, that the object is really taken out of his flesh and bone. I certainly cannot think that he always does so (though I do not remember hearing an Orokaiva admit a doubt); but if and when he does disbelieve, he enters fully into the pretence of the doctor in whom he places so much confidence. Then not only is the doctor pretending to suck out the wallaby bone, but the patient is also pretending that he sucks it out. To put it shortly, the doctor makes-believe, and the patient either actually believes, or in lieu of that, makes-believe with the doctor, and both of them are confident that the thing works.

After this digression, which is the attempted application of a theory of magic to a special case, we may return to the classification of treatments. Hitherto I have spoken of ex-pulsive treatments mainly in reference to the casual diseases, and the thing expelled is the disease in the abstract, or else some tangible object representing the cause of the disease. But expulsive treatments go further than this: the same principle often applies to the *sovai* diseases, with the differ-ence that now it is the *sovai* itself which is being cast out or enticed out of the sick body. The majority of Taro men (who were credited with powers of healing) proceeded on the assumption that disease was due to a visitation from the *sovai*, and their methods are characteristically expulsive. One, for instance, is to beat drums about the patient. A number of Taro men, like a consultation of doctors, may assemble to treat one man. They sit about him in a circle and beat their drums 'to scare away the *sovai*'. Another idea was to hold the mouth of the drum close to the patient's body, so that the spirit should pass from one into the other, whence it could be expelled by beating in the gardens.[1]

The doctors of the *Baigona* cult were specially qualified to deal with diseases caused by *sovai* in their animal form, e.g. those which a patient usually contracted by eating a *sovai* animal. Their methods accordingly amounted to a casting out of the *sovai* animal which had invaded the body in immaterial form. Thus we see a Baigona man practising *humbari* and, at the same time, ejaculating *Oro! Baigona!*

[1] It happens that on the only occasion when this method was actually explained to me, it was the *ba asisi*, or spirit of the actual taro plant, which was thought to be causing the disease; but I have no doubt that a similar explanation would be used for the far more numerous cases in which disease is attributed to the spirits of the dead.

Ena saireri! which are the proper expressions used in hailing the *sovai* animal and are in this instance addressed to the *sovai* which the operator hopes to cast out of his patient. In other cases the Baigona doctor would simply place his lime-gourd and coco-nut-leaf basket one on either side of the sick man so that they might attract the disease (i.e. the *sovai*) out of his body into themselves. Again, in the most typical of expulsive treatments, viz. that of *bara*, it may be the *sovai* which is removed from the patient, symbolized, e.g. by a tuft of the dead man's hair. It is not necessary to give further examples to show that *sovai* diseases as well as casual diseases are amenable to the expulsive method.

Placatory Treatments

There is, however, another method which is applicable to the former and not the latter. This is the method of placation, which to the native is as much a treatment of disease as is the use of the knife or the draught of medicine. The method is best exemplified by the practice of making offerings to the *sovai* in order to induce it to leave the sufferer. Thus we find sets of feathers or ornaments suspended in the village: they are meant for the *sovai* in general, or for some particular *sovai*—probably that of some recently deceased relative of the sick man. It is seldom that such offerings are actually abandoned to the *sovai*: it appears that they usually fall into the hands of the doctor who is attending the case. Natives are very reticent on this subject because they realize that the acceptance of payment for their cures is not always looked on with favour by the Government (the good reason being that, as the characters of the healer and the sorcerer are so mixed together, the acceptance of fees may degenerate into extortion). We may perhaps accept what is often enough stated to be the rule, viz. that the doctor retains payment only if the patient recovers.[1] So we come

---

[1] The Rev. Copland King relates a corroborative incident. He had allowed a Baigona healer to try his methods on a mission boy who was dying of consumption. 'Eroro visited Frank every day to see what effect the treatment had. When he found it had done no good, he brought back the pay which had been given, and said that it was a sickness that Frank had brought from the white man's country, and his charms were of no avail. He replaced all but the tobacco, which had been already smoked, and gave necklaces to make up the value.' *Annual Report*, 1912–13, p. 154.

upon a doctor carrying a bunch of valuable ornaments to his house. They have been handed to him by the husband of a woman who is apparently dying. He explains that he is about to hang them up on his house verandah as an offering to the *sovai* of a man not long deceased, who is supposed to be afflicting the sick woman. If this *sovai* wishes the woman to recover he will accept the presents (which means that they will remain in the possession of the doctor); if he allows the woman to die, then the doctor will return them to her husband, for they have not achieved their purpose.[1]

Apart, however, from these eleventh-hour acts of placation, there are the daily observances which have been constantly referred to in earlier chapters, and these may be regarded as in some degree a prophylactic placation; for they are not meant only to ensure general prosperity, but especially to ward off the sickness which *sovai* malignancy is so fond of inflicting.

In so far as sorcery disease admits of any cure, that cure also is a matter of placation. It is a case of 'squaring' the sorcerer. I have already pointed out that the doctor—whatever his speciality, be it *humbari*, *bara*, or any other—acknowledges his inability to deal with a case that he diagnoses as sorcery; and it has been seen that it is just then, when his stock remedies have been applied without success, that he falls back on this diagnosis. I have seen a Baigona man, celebrated as he was for his powers, stand aside assuming an air of complete indifference while a dying patient was surrounded with wailers. He had tried his own methods without avail, therefore he did not hesitate to say that the

[1] The doctor's responsibilities were indeed sometimes rather severe. I have myself been privately requested to hale one of them before the magistrate for his refusal or inability to effect a cure, and Mr. A. E. Oelrichs, a former Resident Magistrate of the Northern Division, gives the following extreme instance. A man had undertaken to cure a sick woman, and had received from her son-in-law as payment for his 'few passes' a dog and a pig as well as some native ornaments. 'Unfortunately, he returned next day, and, while in the village, the woman died. Her son-in-law then went up to the "doctor" saying, "You did not cure the woman, and, as I have paid you, I am going to kill you." The deceased admitted the fact, but did not attempt to run away. The three prisoners, all of whom were present during the interview, then went to their respective houses, obtained weapons, and, while the son-in-law speared the sorcerer, the other two hit him on the head with stone clubs.' *Annual Report*, 1910–11, p. 132.

case was due to some one's sorcery, and to acknowledge that he was incompetent to deal with it.

Such being the common attitude, we do not find any one attempting to make counter-magic. The only acknowledged method is to go to the imputed sorcerer and ask him to relent; and even this last resort is a matter of theory rather than of practice. For there is first of all the difficulty of discovering the sorcerer, and then there is the practical certainty that the accused man will deny the charge. Were he from any motive to acknowledge it, he would *ipso facto* assume the power of restoring his victim to, health; for it is only necessary for the sorcerer to undo his work, to cease subjecting the symbol of the victim to its symbolic suffering (whatever form either of these may take), and the patient will recover. Assuming this power the sorcerer may accept a bribe and consent to neutralize his magic. But if the man succumbs, the acknowledged sorcerer lays himself open to revenge. On the whole I am prepared to believe that the man who is accused of sorcery usually hastens quite truthfully to deny it. And further, I am prepared to believe, despite perfectly authentic instances, that charges of sorcery and requests to relent are not made very frequently before the patient dies. A sick man, or one of his friends, may discover the guilty party in a dream, or may draw his own conclusions from a grudge, but as a rule the patient dies first and then, when it is too late, his relatives may place the guilt and begin to think of revenge. While, therefore, the only remedy for sorcery sickness is to placate the sorcerer, it seems that this treatment is one of theory rather than of practice. Sorcery is the stock explanation of a hopeless case, or of a death, and it is always ready for the baffled doctor to save his face, and for the aggrieved relatives to give them grounds for a revenge.

In conclusion, I may shortly reconsider the native's ideas of disease in relation to his general philosophy. That philosophy, as we have seen, is only fragmentary. Much is taken for granted. Ordinary phenomena, things that are 'going well', simply explain themselves; but whatever is extraordinary, particularly what is unfortunate, puzzles and annoys and calls for explanation. Just as the wonderful may remind a Christian of his God, or calamity jog the most forgetful worshipper into remembering his prayers, so will extraordinary or unfortunate happenings rouse the *insouciant* native to summon up his own ideas of what is occult or supernatural. He has two funds to draw upon for explanation: they are essentially distinct and more or less alternative, for he sometimes uses the one and sometimes the other, viz. (1) the *sovai*, and (2) the living magician. Exactly how these two kinds of forces operate remains, as we should expect, unformulated. The power of the *sovai* is intrinsic, that of the magician commonly rests upon the use of some secret, usually a 'medicine' or specific; but it is enough, I imagine, for the native to believe that each of them possesses a mysterious power, without trying to define that power or track it to a further source.

Disease, illness, accident—all bodily ailments—being in more or less degree both mysterious and troublesome, admit of either of these explanations. But ailments of the commonest kind, and those which entail no great suffering, are likely to be accepted without further investigation or conjecture as to their cause; they are 'all in a day's work' in fact; part of nature itself; normal incidents in the life of the body. It is only the more inexplicable and the more serious complaints that call for explanation, in that they appear as interruptions in the routine of nature, in the course of wellbeing. Then the native feels he must put the blame on something or somebody, and there are ready to hand those two agencies whom he has credited with a not-understood power for good and evil, the *sovai* and the living magician.

XVIII

MORALITY

IN discussing the question of morality it must be realized that we deal with responsible adults. One still repeatedly hears that 'the native is nothing but a grown-up child'; but in this sententious comparison the fallacy is now well enough recognized. It is indeed only in respect of education that the comparison might be said to hold good, and even so, we are probably guilty of underestimating the extent of tribal knowledge, which remains almost as much an undiscovered country to us as does our culture to the untutored savage. Still, granting as we must his cultural backwardness, he is in all essentials of character a grown man, and if any readers are disposed to doubt this view, they should search the faces shown in the earlier part of this book for any signs of puerility. The comparison of full-grown native with European child is on the whole misleading. Despite the obvious difference in cultural levels, he can only be fitly compared with the European adult; for the truth probably is that in all fundamentals he resembles us as closely in mind as he does in body, where the differences, however striking, are merely minute variations from a common pattern.

Granted this degree of mental approximation, we shall expect to find in the adult native the same groundwork of passions as in the European; and further, from the misdirection of those passions, anger, lust, greed, and the rest, into anti-social channels, we may expect to find the same major tendencies toward crime. And yet despite these full-blooded passions we do not find licence and anarchy. There is nothing to resemble the lawless savagery which popular imagination clothes with fur, and arms with the club of a 'cave-man'; on the contrary we find everywhere comparatively well-ordered, law-abiding and peaceful communities, whose internal life is possibly freer from strife than our own.

To what is this condition due? We shall have to deal in this chapter with native morality and the rudiments of law; and our subject may be divided roughly into two parts. There are first the norms, the ideals, the theoretical standards of morality, which, however dimly formulated in the native mind, are nevertheless to be discovered by observation of his conduct. These standards define the kinds of behaviour which, in relation to the society which has evolved them, are satisfactory, i.e. the kinds of behaviour which have been found to *work*. Selected by generations, they have been unconsciously designed to suit the narrow needs of family, clan, or tribal unit; they are essentially social norms, and they are meant to ensure the smooth running and happiness of social life. It is our first business then to formulate these standards—a work in which unfortunately we may look for little direct assistance from the native himself, who is not a preacher or a moralist. Now these standards, although there is no central authority to enforce them, are nevertheless observed with a large measure of fidelity; for the individual is so sunk in the social unit that he obeys its laws for the most part automatically. But no Orokaiva is perfect, nor is he absolutely under the thumb of the society he lives in, so that there is inevitably a falling-short of the standards; and our second task is therefore to discover what means Orokaiva society has of ensuring a fair degree of good conduct, of keeping the individual up to the scratch; in short what are the sanctions of Orokaiva morality.

The Sympathy Group

The primitive ideal of conduct divides itself immediately and emphatically into two. There is first the question of proper conduct towards one's fellows within the group, and second the question of proper conduct towards those outside the group; or in a phrase there are the standards of *intra-group* and *extra-group* morality. These two—divergent as they are in civilized society—are found to be almost antithetical in primitive society. It might fairly be maintained that the sphere, i.e. the actual size of the group, within which the former standard holds good should constitute a fair criterion of moral advancement. It is true there are those who (with more or less sincerity) feel themselves members

of a world-brotherhood, and with such the distinction between intra-group and extra-group morality fades out of
sight—theoretically. But in practice there are units of every
degree, from nations down to families, to which the individual feels he owes allegiance; he gives them his sympathy,
and from them he expects to receive sympathy; and their
limits are the limits of his intra-group morality. For convenience this unit may be called the *sympathy-group*.

In terms of the above criterion, the smaller the group the
more primitive the society, or vice versa. In the case of
the Orokaiva I have already dwelt on the character of the
clan. In the typical instance clan and village coincide, and
this clan-village unit is the one which, more decidedly than
any other, encloses the intra-group morality of the individual. But the unit is not hard and fast: it may fluctuate with
circumstances. Sometimes the group dwindles, and a man
finds himself taking sides with more immediate relatives
against the other members of the clan-village unit (though
it is safe to say that in the primitive society of the Orokaiva
this does not happen very often). On the other hand the
sympathy-group will sometimes embrace a number of clan-
village units, as indeed it does (1) with the clan, which is
sometimes widely scattered, (2) with the locality group,
which takes in a number of villages, and (3) with the tribe
as a whole. But, while civilized man may sacrifice the
interests of the smaller and more immediate sympathy-
group to those of the comprehensive body of which the
former is merely a component, we do not find any such
sacrifice among the primitive; and when, as it is sometimes
bound to do, discord enters, it is followed by disintegra-
tion; the circle of the individual's fellows immediately con-
tracts, and we find once more the elementary small sym-
pathy-groups.

It is not necessary, then, to define strictly the scope of
the sympathy-group, which is a fluctuating thing; though
among the Orokaiva, as before stated, it is seen most typically in the clan-village unit. Whatever its size, however,
it is always in existence, and proper conduct within and
proper conduct without that group are very different things.

The distinction is simply between fellow men and men who are not fellows.

Extra-Group Morality

Since the interest of this chapter will be principally with intra-group morality we may dismiss the other side of the question rather briefly. We have seen that the Orokaiva tribe lived in a state of ever-recurring warfare with some or other of its neighbours. There were peace-makings or truces, but the truce was always a fragile one, and no village lived in permanent security. The Orokaiva achieved and probably deserved a warlike reputation, and in such conditions it is not surprising that they should set some store upon the virtue of bravery—though it does not seem to take the foremost place that we might expect. A brave warrior was called *koropa-embo*, a 'spearman', or *ivu-embu*, a 'manly man', *ivu* being the word for husband or a fully matured man. Another term is *sarika*, which is perhaps best translated 'formidable', and connotes not only fierceness but size and strength. (By way of example one of the late magistrates of the Division was called *sarika* on account of stature, and another on account of his severity.) A coward is called *atoha-embo* or *jouro-huso*, and of course there are to be found some cowards among a generally brave race. Some of my informants in one village named a few men as *atoha* (and it is interesting to note in passing that, like true native gentlemen, they named them in whispers for fear the men in question should overhear and have their feelings hurt).

But more striking than any bravery is the sheer bloodthirstiness which seems actually to be raised to the status of a virtue. It is not for fearlessness that the insignia called *esa* or *otohu* (p. 177) are bestowed, but for the mere taking of human life. Many an old warrior, counting over his victims, will show as great a pride in the slaughter of women and children as in a man-to-man victory; and indeed the majority of Orokaiva victims have met their end in surprise and massacre rather than in fair fight. While I have found no evidence to show that the Orokaiva was expected sometime during his career to take a human life, as if this were a social imperative, it is not too much to say that every individual aspired to be a man-slayer, and that his success brought him a great deal of honour.

There can be no doubt, however, that revenge was regarded as an obligation, though the obligation might be fulfilled by any one of the victim's group, just as the vengeance itself might fall upon any one of the slayer's group, and not of necessity on the guilty man himself. Vengeance with its expressive name *diroga-mine* [1]—'an exchange of the spirits of the slain'—may have had a supernatural sanction behind it, viz. the possible anger of the unavenged *diroga*, though I have never heard such an explanation expressed; but at any rate the unpaid debt of blood probably entailed a painful sense of inferiority which could only be removed by the satisfaction of killing one of the aggressors.

Needless to say there were no conventions of war, no gratuitous mercy, and no sportingness. Men—young or old —were killed; old women were killed; young women might be raped and killed or borne off to become captive wives; children were killed or made prisoners. Though, on the other hand, there was no gratuitous cruelty, the victims were not tortured; and captive women and children were treated with kindness.

Treachery, of which one or two examples have been given (pp. 166–7), was not regarded as contemptible, and according to Beaver, as we have seen, one kind of homicidal emblem was specially assigned to the slayer of a peace emissary. Towards all outsiders the correct attitude was one of suspicion if not always of hostility; a complete stranger wandering alone would be regarded both as potential enemy and good meat; and when visitors came in friendship, as at a feast, there was never any lack of warlike readiness on either side. The very cries of welcome which are so characteristic of the Orokaiva are possibly a sign of the dormant hostility between guest and host, being recognizable in one case at least as meant for reassurance of the former regarding the intentions of the latter.

[1] See p. 170.

One feature—almost amusing—in the attitude toward outsiders is a propensity for objurgation—though one does not imply that the Orokaiva swear more ardently than other natives. But the gravest and sternest of men may work himself into a hoarse frenzy, and caper and gesticulate in a perfect abandonment of abuse when he is addressing the enemy on the opposite bank of the river; and strange to say (and here we see a complete contrast with intra-group morality) it is the 'strong-man' who swears the loudest and hurls defiance in the most boastful and abusive terms. The Aiga tribe are not ashamed but proud of their legendary reputation as ' strong-talkers' (p. 158).

Along with this hostility toward outsiders goes an intense pride in the group itself. This, in times of peace as well as war, finds expression in boasting and display. At the *esu*, which is a kind of mock warfare, the fierce harangues of the principals are composed of bragging and derision. They dwell continually on their prowess as fighters, on their mere strength of numbers, and on their material wealth. So much store is set upon the last-mentioned that it must be one of the highest satisfactions in the Orokaiva's life to set forth a great display of garden food and a number of fat pigs before the guests. Accordingly we must allow a place among the extra-group virtues to liberality, albeit by no means free from the taint of self-display. Moreover, one may always perceive a formal courtesy and an observance of all the somewhat noisy rites of hospitality when the guests arrive at a public function, although the several parties may be like tinder awaiting the spark. On the part of the guests themselves there is an almost impressive assumption of gravity while they file in amid the din of welcome, wearing expressions that may vary between complete indifference and a somewhat fierce sternness, but must never betray a glimmer of excitement, least of all a flattered smile. It is their way under the circumstances of evincing their corporate pride and dignity; so they maintain a reserve even in the face of hospitality, as if they almost grudged acknowledgement. But these milder virtues of extra-group morality are unsteady things. Let there be some cause of offence and they will vanish in a moment, giving place to open hostility and the conduct which that condition demands.

Before leaving this subject of extra-group morality it is worth while quoting some opinions of those who in the early dangerous days had to face the Orokaiva as enemies. Sir Wm. MacGregor, after many and various meetings with hostile tribes from end to end of Papua, wrote (of the Mambare people): 'It is very clear that these natives are more warlike, pugnacious, and cunning than any we have had to deal with hitherto.'[1] W. E. Armit, the resident magistrate, who in the days of the gold-rush had as wide a fighting experience of them as any other, wrote (of the Papangi): 'They are certainly not destitute of courage, but, on the other hand, they are treacherous, truculent, aggressive, cruel, and cunning. . . . They fight treacherously and lie abominably'; and of the people about Wasida he records a very nasty first impression: 'The men have villainous faces, coupled to a peculiar cunning leer which imparts a diabolical look to their countenances.'[2] These natives of Wasida are later spoken of as the 'most rampant and obstinate of savages' who 'persistently attacked every Government party which went near them'.[3] It is pleasing to add that under different circumstances, viz. those of service with the Armed Constabulary, the character of the Orokaiva appears more favourably. Speaking as Commandant, Capt. Barton said that the Mambare police were 'brave to a fault';[4] later as Administrator he said, of the police recruited from the Northern and North-Eastern Divisions at large, that they have 'stronger characters than is the case in the majority of Papuans, and are also physically sturdy and alert';[5] and H. J. Ryan, a true soldier himself, found that the Northern men in his detachment at Kikori performed their allotted tasks cheerfully and willingly, and when on patrol were most zealous to distinguish themselves, especially when facing hostile natives.[6]

[1] *Annual Report*, 1896–7, p. 28.
[3] *Ibid.*, 1904–5, p. 14.
[5] *Ibid.*, 1903–4, p. 13.
[2] *Ibid.*, 1899–1900, p. 98.
[4] *Ibid.*, 1900–1, p. 87.
[6] *Ibid.*, 1912–13, p. 78.

Intra-Group Morality

When we turn to the consideration of intra-group morality the contrast is almost surprising. Here the ideal is one of concord and restfulness. Village life runs like a simple engine freely oiled; not called upon to achieve any complicated result, but fulfilling its routine work with a great deal of efficiency and a minimum of friction. While we may stand aghast at the quarrelsomeness of the Orokaiva group in its external relations, we cannot but admire the degree of peace and good fellowship that prevails within its circumference. This is not to say that discord never breaks the serenity of village life: for, quite apart from the raids and affrays which caused the Government most of their trouble before the tribes were pacified, there is still no lack of 'cases' of a more domestic kind. Nevertheless, one may risk the statement that, in its freedom from quarrels and ill-feeling, the group life of the Orokaiva compares by no means unfavourably with our own.

Those who administer justice and those who have consulted the records of justice among the Orokaiva may be disposed to disagree with this view as over-lenient, citing as their argument the number of crimes of violence that come before the magistrate. But it must be borne in mind that I am speaking of intra-group morality alone, and that fact immediately cuts out a very large proportion of these crimes; further, that the savage resorts to violence of a serious kind—spear-work and club-work—more readily than the member of a civilized community, and such violence, if it lead to bodily harm, can hardly escape the eye of the magistrate. It is no doubt true that a greater proportion of quarrels have a violent issue among the Orokaiva than among ourselves; but what I desire to emphasize is the relative freedom within the primitive group from the quarrels themselves.

In dealing with the standards of intra-group morality I shall first draw attention to a number of detailed points and then try to sum them up in broader terms. What follows is a rather sketchy list of Orokaiva virtues, on which we may begin with the more positive or active.

Perhaps the most characteristic of them all is *liberality*. The liberal man is *handembo*, the word *hande* meaning distribution, or especially the sharing out of food. It is easy to understand how this should be a popular virtue, for the Orokaiva, like other natives, are much addicted to the making of feasts—and not because of a merely gluttonous appetite, as some who know least about natives have supposed, but more because of the glamour and the excitement of a social gathering. It is true we cannot acquit the *handembo* of a certain motive of self-display; for there is nothing, not valour in war nor prowess in the chase, that brings an Orokaiva so prominently into the public eye as the providing of a big feast. Yet no one could deny the existence of true generosity. This is shown in countless details of daily life. The paddler pauses to refresh himself with cold cooked taro; he wrenches a mouthful with his strong teeth and hands the lump without a word to the man behind him, as a boy might give his chum a bite out of the apple. Or when the carriers halt for a 'smokeoh' and receive their stick of tobacco, there is never one of them but has a puff or two; and when they push on again with their loads, a man will place a half-finished cigarette on a stump by the track, and another coming behind will hastily snatch it, take a few draws, and leave it once more on another stump fifty yards farther on for the next man.

Although there is no systematic sharing of food supplies, yet the constant gifts and the feasts large and small achieve in the long run what amounts to equal distribution. As we have seen, the family is a self-supporting unit and garden produce is privately owned; further, since every man and woman works hard enough for the supply of immediate wants, there is no scarcity (except in a hard season when all may suffer alike). Therefore we may take it that in common daily life the consumption of food is fairly equal all round, and when a man with his family and dependants have a surplus, that surplus will not be devoted to private over-eating, but to a feast; and the succession of these feasts means in the long run that the fairly equal distribution of food is maintained. To give freely of one's food is regarded as the proper thing to do; it is an elementary virtue in respect of which there are few failures. Of actual greed it is hard to find any evidence: informants quite understand what is meant by the word, yet I never persuaded them to name a man with a reputation for it. No man, I am told, would hesitate to ask for food among his own people, nor for betel and tobacco among outsiders—though to speak truth the asking would probably never be needed; but it appears there are some who go beyond proper bounds and are inclined to impose on hospitality. Such individuals are called *hasiri*, though I do not believe there are many of them; indeed, it was stoutly affirmed in one quarter that there were none except for children, who had a right to be *hasiri*.

For his liberality a man receives a reward of honour; but beyond that—and this should not be thought to disqualify it entirely as a virtue—he constantly looks for an equal return in kind. This is one of the striking features of primitive economics—the return of gift for gift, the maintaining of a balance. The return may be made long subsequently, but it may be called a matter of honour to equal or exceed the original gift; just as it is a matter of disgrace and lowered self-esteem to fail. There can be no question that self-display enters into the primitive virtue of liberality, and it is in respect of worldly wealth that the individual seeks most to display himself. One might almost say that the native made a virtue of wealth and that liberality was compounded of two things—mere wealth and true generosity.

There are many observers of Papuan natives who will be amused at the inclusion of *industry* with the other Orokaiva virtues. While having no practical interest in the amount of work a native does, I cannot in my own judgement absolve him from the charge of laziness; but nevertheless, allowing a relative value to the term, industry is regarded in native eyes as deserving of commendation. The industrious man is *pure-huso*, which means simply expert in or given to gardening, for *pure*, the garden, is the usual scene of Orokaiva labour. A lazy man, in the native sense, is *pure-ambo*, literally one who is not a gardener, and of course the term applies as well to the other branches of work. It is perhaps as a necessary condition to wealth and the opportunity for display that industry is regarded as worth while. Otherwise the native, who enjoys *peogo* (rest or leisure) more than work for its own sake, might be disposed to discount it altogether. But the fact is that he does not. While loafing occupies a good deal of the Orokaiva day, we do not find any who neglect their work to an extent which in native eyes would be culpable (unless it be a wife in the eyes of her husband); and on the other hand a man who works harder than most is admired for it.

While the Orokaiva family is obliged to support itself, and is in the ordinary round of life a working unit, we find numerous instances of a wider co-operation. Such co-operation is seen especially in the earlier stages of gardening, in fencing, in sago-making, and in the hunting or fishing expedition; and the point that claims our attention is that among those who are expected to participate in such undertakings there are commonly no defaulters. I have asked often enough what would happen to a hypothetical defaulter, but such questions seldom meet with a satisfactory answer because one's informants seem almost unable to visualize an unusual situation. It is answered simply that all the able-bodied who should take part will take part; nor can I recall any concrete case of a man deliberately shirking his duty in any major enterprise of the group. This willingness to co-operate or assist is a sufficiently striking native trait which we may call simply *helpfulness*. It is seen most strongly perhaps in war or in minor quarrels, where the native is always too ready to take up the cudgels in behalf of his people or his friend: it is the active aspect of clannishness. One of the reasons why a village is sometimes almost depleted of its young men because they all elect to 'sign-on' for labour in a batch is simply this desire to stand by one another. 'What will happen to our brother', they say, 'when he is set upon by a mob of stalwart Kiwais, if we are not there to help him?' But in all the incidents of daily life the same spirit of helpfulness is apparent: a man is lost, and there is a great turn-out to find him; if he is ill or in distress he is never neglected; if he cries 'Help!' there is an excited

rushing to the scene. On the whole we may say that the
Orokaiva seldom fails in this duty of helping the members
of his group.

A passive virtue, yet one which possibly ranks first in
Orokaiva estimation, is that of *good temper*. I find no specific
term for it, but the good-tempered man is called simply
javo-embo, or 'good man'. A squabbler, a vituperator, or a
bully is strongly disliked, and since it is these very pro-
pensities—even that of mere vituperation—which bring
credit to a man when he directs them against the outsider,
we see at once a contrast between intra-group and extra-
group morality. A man of anger is *tumo-huso*, which could
be said to mean literally 'liverish', but which in actuality
implies something more fiery than mere crabbiness. A man
is *jujuno-huso* if he is given to verbal quarrelling, and *embogi-
huso* if he be an actual brawler. Such a one was Buninia,
who some fifteen years ago was a noted warrior among the
Aiga. With his great size and prowess a fierce temper combined to make him almost a terror to the neighbourhood.
As a warrior he was named as particularly *sarika*; but his
offensives were not always directed towards the legitimate
enemy. He had stolen pigs and fought with neighbours in
near-by villages, so that he is nowadays remembered as a
strong man but a bad one. But usually there is very little
that resembles bullying in a native village. To force a man
to do one's will by personal violence is a thing that hardly
enters the native's mind; and when a fisticuffs occur—which
in fact is seldom—one ventures to believe it is only in the
heat of anger. Between husband and wife it is somewhat
different: a man may thrash a neglectful spouse in order to
give her a better idea of her duties, though the corrective
aspect is probably not very prominent when a man is be-
labouring his woman in a rage. All informants have agreed
upon the justifiability of wife-beating, but they have all
agreed that there are proper limits, and an habitual wife-
beater has a bad name. I have seen children smacked, but
never chastised, and would venture to say that when children are beaten it is only in anger and not with any cool
intention of punishing them or improving them. I remem-

D d

ber noting the fondness of one man for his son, an attractive boy of six or seven years. Asked whether he ever beat the child he said, 'No; his first son had gone to work on a plantation and had died there. How could he beat his second son?' On the whole it may be said that the Orokaiva hold up good temper and kindness as a virtue, a thing which society demands from the individual; and on the whole, again, they carry out that ideal to a greater extent than is popularly supposed.

Along with this ideal goes that of *dignity* or weight, very much akin to the classical *gravitas*. A man is admired if he can make his personality felt, but in so doing he must not make a nuisance of himself. He may fulminate against the enemy, and will even be praised for it; but at home he does better to play the role of strong silent man. Such characters are undoubtedly admired, though one cannot profess to discover any consistent expression of the ideal. The gravest *paterfamilias* will on occasion cast aside restraint and become a ranter, and does so, too, without losing his dignity in the eyes of the village. But a chatterbox, or one who reveals his excitability too frequently, is under ordinary circumstances regarded as a bore.

Another ideal is that of *courtesy*, and by this I mean something wider than mere politeness. Indeed, of formal politeness as we know it ourselves there is rather a conspicuous absence. The Orokaiva is off-hand when he does a kindness, and apparently indifferent when he receives one. He does not offer his friend a betel-nut with a bow and a smile, but throws it surlily across; and the friend does not say thank you, but picks it up and tears the husk off with his teeth, vouchsafing neither word nor even look to the man who gave it. But—and this is the best thing we can say of the native—there is a very high and constant regard for others' feelings. Towards the enemy you may point the fingers and twist or screw the hand in the infamous gesture called *gingi gongo*, and call him the child of a devil-devil, or even tell him he has a scraggy neck; but it is only in the extremity of rage that a man would insult his clansman or fellow villager. To point at a man is out of taste; to swear at him would be to provoke an open breach; to gibe at his personal deformity would be the last blow. Baldness, for instance, is regarded as unseemly and ridiculous; but there are no Elishas and no mocking children. It is not of course to be supposed that men of the same group never bandy words, yet rudeness and abuse are always deprecated. Ordinarily the native, who is keenly enough alive to the peculiarities of his fellow, will only refer to them behind his back, and this for no other reason than to avoid doing injury to his feelings. Roughness or rudeness is said to produce in its victim that emotion, or complex of emotions, called *meh*, which we usually and somewhat inadequately translate 'shame', and it is regarded as a serious thing; so much so that if a man commits an unjustifiable affront, not only does the victim suffer, but the culprit's fellows, who feel they share his responsibility, will be positively covered with vicarious *meh*.

We may now turn to the consideration of *practical honesty*. One cannot claim that there is here any high abstract ideal. The native certainly feels no moral obligation to tell the truth in all circumstances—as who should know better than one who spends his time in questioning them? But honesty is a virtue at least in the limited and practical sense of respect for property. Petty thieving is common enough and is treated with a good deal of tolerance, though, considering the absolutely unguarded condition in which property is commonly left, the general honesty of a native village may impress one rather favourably, and would certainly bear comparison with that of a civilized community. It is probably true that as European influence first extends among a primitive people, the decrease in crimes of violence is more than countered by an increase in thieving and other crimes of stealth, and whatever the cause of this latter condition, it implies the decay of one primitive virtue. It is at any rate the common experience of Europeans that the more sophisticated natives are more inclined to steal.

Lastly, we may refer briefly to *married chastity*. Among the Orokaiva a woman is expected to be faithful, even during long absences of her husband. There is no bartering or lending of wives, and the only exception is during the ceremonial licence that follows an initiation ceremony (p. 192). The question of how far this rule of chastity is regarded or disregarded in practice does not concern us for the moment; the fact of interest is that adultery is considered an offence; so that those, particularly women, who are known to commit the offence habitually are generally despised and compared to dogs. There is, of course, no such restriction upon the unmarried, though it has been observed elsewhere that young people do not give their passions an entirely free rein. As for continence in itself, I cannot find that it is ever regarded as virtuous in any degree, unless it be enjoined by some ceremonial necessity.

Summary of Intra-Group Morality

The foregoing does not claim to be more than a fragmentary list of native virtues. However, it covers enough ground to allow us to see the general trend of Orokaiva ethics. The group, as we have seen, lives within itself a peaceful and contented life. It cherishes no distant and ambitious ideal of progress, but contents itself with two main requirements—(1) material plenty, and (2) internal concord. The individual must fit himself into this scheme, for the virtues enumerated above are essentially social. There is little, if any, idea of a self-centred righteousness. On the contrary, each virtue implies agent and reagent. Not incontinence, for instance, but adultery is condemned, because a right of possession has been infringed; not gluttony, but greed, because others must suffer by it. In fact the norms of individual conduct have been evolved to meet the needs of society, to satisfy its ideal of a somewhat passive well-being. The moral factors in this ideal are, on the positive side, Liberality, Industry, and Helpfulness; on the negative, Good Temper, Dignity, Courtesy, Practical Honesty, and Married Chastity. They might be summed up in two terms, if we allow them their widest meaning, viz. (1) co-operation and (2) self-restraint, which are the two main moral requirements that correspond with the two main social requirements of material plenty and internal concord.

Attempts at Standardization

Native morality is for the most part inexplicit; we do not expect to find an established code, and it is mainly by observing conduct and its apparent reaction on the public mind that we arrive at any general principles. But it is worth mentioning the few incipient traces of standardization. The foregoing list of virtues will call to mind the *otohu* ideal, the character of the *otohu-embo*, and the instructions which are given to the youth or girl who receives the emblem (pp. 191, 204, 205). Apart from being urged on to deeds of valour, the recipient was enjoined, with more insistence perhaps, to observe the milder social virtues which would make him an amenable or respectable member of the group. Such versions as I heard of the moral instruction given at the *otohu* ceremony were possibly somewhat abbreviated, but their tone was consistent, and it is fair to say that the *otohu* injunctions are a brief *précis* of social morality, and would thus constitute a standardization, albeit only transmissible by word of mouth.

There is a word *igege* (Binandele *yege*) which may be translated 'moral law', or perhaps, since the examples are all negative, 'moral prohibition'. The examples were such as the following: not to steal a man's vegetables, canoes, spears, &c.; not to usurp his fishing rights; not to take his dog to hunt, but to drive it back if it followed the hunter of its own accord; not to commit adultery; not to beat one's wife overmuch; not to commit assault on another man. These *igege* were for adults; they did not apply to children, who had to be treated with so much indulgence; still less to dogs, whose nature it was to steal on sight. While not implying standardization, the mere existence of the word hints at a definite conception of right and wrong.

With respect to property it is worth noting under this head the various tangible protection marks. Whatever their sanctions they have no real value as physical barriers to trespass or appropriation.

(1) The commonest is *papara* or *ese*, the frond of coco-nut palm tied about the butt, which means that no one is to

climb for nuts. (2) The *heri* is a strip of bark or a liana tied to uprights and encircling a house or some forbidden ground. (3) A *harihari* is some object, usually leaf or twig, placed in the cleft of a split stick and set up, e.g., at the mouth of a creek as a sign of a fishing right. (4) *Inja* is simply a few handfuls of grass laid across a track to bar the passage. We might include (5) the *naterari* and *pamba* (p. 226), which serve to mark a village tabu on the coconuts, and (6) logically enough the ordinary garden boundary, *tani*, which consists merely of a series of tree-trunks or branches laid on the ground between adjacent plots. These are all regarded quite strictly: no man would step over an *inja* or take a short cut across an area enclosed by a *heri*. Less regular marks which may serve as reminders for some casual rule are observed with equal stringency. For instance, I have seen an eight of diamonds wedged in a split stick and set up in a village to forbid the playing of cards; it had been erected by a man of influence who has somehow acquired conscientious scruples regarding the forbidden game. The sanctions for the strict observance of these marks will be discussed presently; the signs themselves are described here merely to show the existence of tangible safeguards, principally, but not always, of the law of property.

Education

We have discussed at length the theoretical standard or ideal of morality; but performance naturally falls short of the ideal, and we have now to consider the means by which Orokaiva society seeks to prevent that falling-short. It is not necessary to dwell upon the customary sanction, which is as obvious here as in other primitive societies. Suffice it to say that the almost automatic obedience of the native to the customs of his people and his almost unfailing concurrence in social desires go a long way to account for the law-abidingness which we have seen to be characteristic of the Orokaiva group. Nor is it necessary to treat at length of direct training as a means of ensuring morality, viz. the means of education. Education in the broader sense of the word is as much a means toward morality with natives as with ourselves; but it is difficult at the primitive stage to separate it from custom; for of education in the narrower sense, viz. that of formal training, there is practically none except for the rather scanty instructions given at the *otohu* ceremony. A native's education consists in the gradual and effortless assimilation of the customs and manners of his people; and there is no school save that of daily contact with his elders, whose example is merely the reproduction of a previous example set to them.

Absence of Central Authority

Our interest centres rather upon the indirect means of ensuring morality, i.e. upon the means of preventing shortcomings or offences; and here our subject becomes more than ever mixed up with that of primitive law. We shall do well to bear in mind the distinction between criminal and civil offences, though no attempt will be made to deal with them separately in respect of their sanctions. In an Orokaiva group the former, viz. those of an individual against the group as a whole, seem to be relatively uncommon, and this because the individual's interests are so bound up with those of his group that he does not very often find himself at variance with his fellows. As examples, however, one may quote the breach of a coco-nut tabu, the defilement of a water-supply, the betrayal of a raiding party, and malicious weather-magic, all of which are cases that have come to my notice. Civil offences, on the other hand, are common, though, as I have implied before, it is a question whether theft, adultery, assault, &c., are more prevalent in Orokaiva society than in our own.

But how are these offences prevented, or how punished? It will be understood that there is no such thing as a central authority to enforce the law. Orokaiva chieftainship (to risk the use of the word) is of the most elementary kind (p. 104), and certainly involves no power of inflicting punishment, nor even any means of maintaining order except by the exercise of purely personal influence. I have heard of a man of importance—and the Orokaiva 'chief' is really no more than that—who interfered to prevent his son from beating his (the son's) wife. The chief's daughter (who related the incident), now intervened between father and son, and said that she got a thrashing for her pains. But this is the only concrete instance which I can quote, and it is obviously one of domestic rather than judicial authority. Nor, again, is there any other judicial mechanism. It is popularly supposed that the 'elders' were in the habit of punishing offences: in the old predecadent days, it is said, they would punish with death the infringement of certain tabus. Without attempting a wholesale denial of such a condition in Papua, I must confess I have met with no trace of it in my own researches; and among the Orokaiva at any rate it is needless to say that the system did not exist. On the whole, one is struck by the high degree of personal freedom. For, apart from the restrictive power of custom and tradition, the native is left to do a good deal as he likes; so much so that one man, whatever his status, is reluctant to answer for another, to lay down what he will do or should do. 'He himself', he will say, with a certain inflection of the voice that dismisses all responsibility. At all events there are in Orokaiva society certainly no personal guardians of the law. This being the case with criminal offences, it is more than ever so with regard to civil offences. Natives are found somewhat disinclined to meddle in the affairs or quarrels of individuals, unless it be with merely pacificatory intentions or else in active partisanship. In these two ways interference is met with frequently enough. A number of bystanders will sometimes combine to separate and appease two men who are actually fighting or who (as sometimes appears) are mutually bluffing and suffer themselves rather willingly to be drawn apart. This is an amorphous kind of control, and the interference is merely in the interests of peace and quiet. On the other hand, the two disputants may be respectively joined by their immediate relatives and friends, when, so far from adjudication and the restraint or punishment of the offender, we get only an extension of the quarrel. Such partisanship is so characteristic that it is difficult to picture a situation, whether relating to criminal or civil offence, in which the group as a whole would actually punish one of its members. I have no concrete instance of this kind, and it seems likely that, as far as the Orokaiva are concerned, the offender would always find some supporters, and the result would be two parties confronting one another.

The Sanctions of Morality

It is clear that the sanctions of Orokaiva morality are something less solid than legal authority, and that there are virtually no guardians of the law. We may look for a super-natural guardian, i.e. for a supernatural sanction; but except within a limited field of conduct we should look in vain. By the supernatural sanction I mean the desire to please or the fear of offending any of those occult beings which are felt to possess more than human powers; and in Orokaiva religion, as we have seen, such beings are first and foremost, indeed almost exclusively, identified with the spirits of the dead, of whom the living stand in very real fear. The super-natural sanction, however, may be very briefly dismissed, for except in relation to semi-religious observances it cannot be said to exercise much influence. Though if we allowed a place in our list of native virtues to filial piety, even limited to piety of the posthumous kind, we should be dealing with what is truly one of the most important obligations in native conduct and one which is to a great extent dependent on the supernatural sanction. But this hardly comes within the scope of our present subject.

As for the sanctions which govern ordinary conduct, the relevant data point to a threefold division, viz. (1) the fear of retaliation, (2) the fear of public reprobation, and (3) the sympathetic sanction. These will be dealt with in turn, the last-mentioned obviously requiring some ex-planation.

Retaliation. This sanction naturally operates in regard to civil rather than criminal offences. Generally speaking, the retaliation will take either of two forms—direct violence or the more subtle method of sorcery; or, more correctly, retaliation is envisaged in either of these forms (for with physical retaliation no less than magical, the dread of it is out of all proportion to the actual practice of it). There is no lack of instances of retaliatory violence, however. In cases of adultery it was recognized as an ordinary thing; so much so that informants have reckoned the Government punishment of gaol as but a poor substitute for the old-fashioned use of spear and stone club. Not only was the co-respondent formerly liable to attack from the husband, but I have a case in which a husband, finding his wife *in delicto*, killed the woman while her lover made good his escape. Ordinary theft might lead to the same violent redress. A man, finding a woman stealing in his garden, immediately struck her on the back with a pineapple club; another, under similar provocation, entered the thief's house and hit him on the head with a stone. Interference with garden boundaries has been a fruitful cause of actual fighting, and informants have related how they fought one another with spears, clubs, and shields over this matter, though always, it has appeared, without fatal results. In another case the cause was a usurpation of fishing rights. Except for a complete absence of any formality or any rules of combat, these fights might be spoken of as duels. But it seems that the combatants are not bent on killing, nor are they altogether reluctant to be separated; and the most striking feature of such engagements is that they commonly end in a mutual exchange of gifts—pigs or dogs—by way of peace-making. In one or two cases the culprit has made no show of fight, but, very possibly from a sense of guilt and deserts received, has 'taken his medicine'. In certain of these private quarrels, again, the rest of the group have abstained from taking any part whatever, as if they approved of the act of vengeance; in which we may perhaps see one of the earliest steps toward legal punishment, i.e. the countenancing of the retaliatory act which eventually becomes the legalization of it.

The second kind of retaliation, viz. sorcery, exercises a still more important influence on conduct. The threats of it, which are not uncommon, and the dread of it which is ever-present, together make one of the most powerful deterrents against wrongdoing. A simple instance is seen in the protection marks described on pp. 323–4. It is true that these signs are often regarded or obeyed automatically

and without any reflection or motive; again, they may be
regarded out of pure consideration for the man—neighbour, relative, or friend—who has set them up; but there
is an additional sanction, simply that of sorcery. The very
name, *inja*, of one of these conventional signs is that of black
magic, and if a native pauses to explain why he avoids tres-
passing beyond a *heri* or an *inja*, he will have but one explanation—the danger of sorcery. But sorcery is not merely a
protector of property; it operates in all walks of life, a man
will hesitate to wrong another in any way if he thinks of
the crippled leg or the crop of boils which vengeance armed
with magic may give him in return. In short, it is not worth
elaborating what has been often enough observed, viz. that
sorcery, despite being in itself the most hated of crimes, is
undoubtedly, by reason of the superstitious fear it inspires,
a stalwart guardian of individual rights.

Public Reprobation. Perhaps more important than the foregoing is the fear of public reprobation, which certainly does
much to keep offenders in check, and that quite independently of any power of concrete punishment. The native is
proverbially susceptible to the opinions of others, and Orokaiva feelings are no less tender than we might expect.
Certain it is that the disapproval of his fellows—whether it
take the form of anger, disgust, or ridicule—makes him
extremely uncomfortable. Without insisting on the emo-
tional instability which is probably a character of primitive
minds, we may say with confidence of the Orokaiva that
when his *ego* is exalted he is happy and contented; and that
when it is thrust down he is miserable and certainly penitent.
One may occasionally hear the evening harangues, in which
some grievance is aired and recriminations are poured upon
the wrongdoer. Since among primitives there are usually
two sides (in the sense of mere numbers) to every question,
it is usual to hear excited answers from more than one individual; but at other times the culprit must endure in shamefaced silence. There are times, I am assured, when the
perpetrator of some wrong remains undiscovered and the
victims do not know upon whom to vent their indignation.
Then the proper object of it may hide his guilt and even

add his voice to the uproar, saying, 'What scoundrel could have stolen your taro?' But it is perhaps more usual for him to own up and reinstate himself in public favour by a gift in conciliation. There are other ways of expressing public disapproval or of punishing the offender by holding him up to ridicule. When a man finds his coco-nuts stolen he may tie a fragment of husk to a stick and set it up on the track near his palms: then every one will see that a theft has been committed, and the thief, even though his identity remain unknown, will feel a pang of shame whenever he passes the spot. Similarly, the owner of a ravaged garden will affix a taro leaf to a coco-nut palm in the midst of the village for all to see and for the special discomfort of the culprit. These devices, like the wearing of the *heratu* in the armlet (p. 116), are a means of advertising a wrong and thereby of striking shame into the heart of the man who has committed it.

It is this sanction of public reprobation that reacts especially upon the more ideal virtues such as liberality, dignity, helpfulness, and the rest, where sins of omission are not liable to any concrete punishment.

The Sympathetic Sanction. There remains one highly important sanction. The wrongdoer, as we have seen, cannot endure the bad opinion of his fellows at large, but neither can he endure to see the pain or feel the anger and enmity of the man he has wronged. This in itself is quite irrespective of public opinion, though of course a personal wrong, if discovered, will bring down the weight of public censure as well as the enmity of the victim upon its perpetrator. To be short, I believe that this last sanction is simply the fear of hurting the feelings of one's fellow man, i.e. of one's fellow man in the limited native sense of a member of the sympathy-group. It is, in fact, what has been noted by other observers as an amiable native trait, viz. a natural consideration for others' feelings.[1] It goes hand in hand with a desire

---

[1] 'Intellectually the Papuan is not nearly so far inferior to ourselves as many people suppose him to be; and in manners he is often our superior. "It is a common experience among travellers that many, if not all, savages are gentlemen." I am quoting from Dr. Haddon's Conway Memorial Lecture on "The Practical Value of Ethnology", and, if by the word "gentleman" is meant a man who has a regard

to keep on friendly terms with the other members of the sympathy-group, and I shall refer to it as the Sympathetic Sanction. This considerateness is constantly evinced in daily life, e.g. by a reticence regarding the peculiarities of one's neighbours, by an absence of any cruel competitive spirit by which one man seeks profit at another's expense, even by the reluctance to exercise compulsion on another individual; and I believe that the common regard for property rights is supported by this sanction more strongly than by the fear of retaliation or of public censure, which are rather in the nature of reinforcements; for Orokaiva property, for instance, is nearly always safe from the thief even when he is absolutely free from the risk of detection, and I believe he respects it primarily out of consideration for its owner.

But it is from the negative instances that we may most safely deduce the value of the sympathetic sanction; that is to say, when the sanction has failed to work and some personal offence has been committed, we may observe the psychological effect upon the offender. In such an event the offender is amply punished by being thoroughly sorry for his victim and thoroughly ashamed of himself. We may consider a simple instance (though in our eyes a somewhat extraordinary one), viz. when a man inadvertently uses the name of his brother-in-law, which the Orokaiva regards as a very grave insult. The unfortunate offender will throw his hands up with a despairing gesture and hang his head in shame and confusion which are truly comical to behold; while the brother-in-law, if he chance to have overheard, will be deeply offended and, strangely enough, covered with equal shame. The matter can only be mended by a gift.

The conciliatory gift is a characteristic way of compensating for personal wrong. In a case previously referred to (p. 186), where a man had given a youth some feathers to wear before his formal investiture with the *kokumbari*, and

for the feelings of others, I think that the statement is generally true of the Papuan' (Sir Hubert Murray, *Papua of To-day*, p. 223). Upon looking up this passage I was so struck by its appositeness to the present chapter, that I suspect it must have had something to do with shaping the general views expressed therein, more indeed than I realized when writing.

by so doing had offended the boy's relatives, he immediately sought to make amends. He left the village, but presently came striding back with a half-grown pig across his shoulders; holding the animal by the hind legs he swung it round and dashed its head against the butt of a coco-nut palm, and then flung it dead at the feet of the man he had offended. Not many moments after, I saw one of the latter's brothers enter the village with a fine dog on his shoulders and go through precisely the same performance, killing it against the same tree and offering it as a return present. The pay-back of the conciliatory gift is indeed almost the regular thing: there are numerous instances of quarrels and fights over such matters as theft or interference with garden boundaries, which have been settled eventually by an exchange of pigs, not only the offender but the victim also showing a genuine desire to resume friendly relations. It is not to be supposed, of course, that the sympathetic sanction is infallible. The man who does wrong to another no doubt often 'gets away with it', remaining undetected and perhaps suffering few regrets; but there is no question that he is often exceedingly contrite. It would almost seem that the victim plays upon the feelings of the offender to secure this result, though it would not do invariably to attribute any such definite intention to a man who is deeply affected by a sense of wrong. But the Orokaiva can on occasion be very sorry for himself, and it would seem that he wants others to be sorry for him, and particularly the man who has wronged him. His attitude is not so much 'I'll make you sorry for what you have done' as 'I'll make you sorry for me'; and so he takes 'the revenge of being injured'. Accordingly we find a person under a sense of wrong going to extraordinary lengths of self-castigation, from merely fasting or running away from home for a while, to delivering himself up to an enemy tribe or hanging himself from a tree. I have seen a dozen water-melons hacked into fragments and strewn upon the track. Their owner, finding one of them stolen, had demolished the whole crop and carried them to the path where the thief, whose identity he did not know, would pass and realize what he had done. Similarly I have seen a young man return home at evening and find one of his spears taken from his verandah; when his inquiries failed to trace his spear he took an axe and razed his house to the ground before the eyes of the whole village. Such an attitude of mind has a definite name, *sisira*, and is indeed very often to be met with. Composed, I imagine, largely of anger and self-pity, it does not fail to excite a response in the impressionable heart of the man whose offence has caused it. He is affected with *meh*, that complex state of mind which, following the lead of pidgin English, I have elsewhere translated 'shame'. But whereas in the *meh* caused by public reprobation the predominant emotion is self-abasement, there is in the *meh* that results from a sense of having wronged a fellow man a definite admixture of pity. However, the culprit is very effectively 'put to shame', and very unpleasant he finds it.

The sympathetic sanction is therefore no more than the fear of injuring the feelings of any member of the sympathy-group; and I cannot but regard this as a fundamental motive. In fact there would appear to be a very definite *sentiment of friendliness* toward all members of the group, as on the other hand there is a definite *sentiment of enmity* toward all those who are outside its pale. I will not venture to debate the question of the instinctive bases of these two opposite sentiments, nor the question of whether they may not be instinctive reactions in themselves. But for the present discussion it seems that the sentiment of friendliness is fundamental, requiring no ulterior explanation, and that it is a natural guarantee of morality because it implies a desire not to hurt the feelings of those to whom it extends, i.e. it provides the sympathetic sanction.

The Moral Sense

Lastly there arises the question whether our native may be said to have a moral sense. Naturally he possesses no idea of morality in the abstract; he does not set up good conduct as an ideal, and is certainly free from any charge of priggishness. On the contrary, his good conduct is for the most part unreflective, a matter of routine; so that every native usually and easily does what in native eyes is the right thing. It is probably true that he has a clearer sense of wrong than of right; for while happily free from any objectionable pride in himself for doing right, he is most unpleasantly affected when, as occasionally happens, he does wrong; and it is then, if ever, that he becomes for the moment aware of morality.

What we have seen regarding the sympathetic sanction may justify the conclusion that when a native hurts one of his fellows he feels in himself that he has done wrong; and that emotionally he finds himself just in that state which we describe by the word 'conscience-stricken'. It would seem then that we may credit him with a moral sense to this extent, viz. a deep-seated, if not actually innate, tendency to avoid injuring his fellows, which in conflict with his other selfish or anti-social tendencies, acts as a natural guardian of morality.

It appears, therefore, that what has been called the sympathetic sanction might with fairness have been called the moral sanction, and there is no doubt that, whatever name we give it, it is no less effective than either the fear of retaliation or the fear of public reprobation in keeping the individual from doing wrong. On the whole we are in danger of underestimating the scope of native morality. Being in certain respects so different from our own, it has been by some too freely discounted or even entirely ignored. But all genuine inquiries, however backward they may find the native in respect of our own standards, must forbid us to excuse or brand him as 'unmoral'.

The foregoing estimate is perhaps more generous than some others who know the Orokaiva well might be inclined to make, but it is perhaps nearer the truth, because the writer has been fortunately placed in a position, as it were, of complete neutrality. For to one who has lived for some time in close association with the villager, and who, by not requiring any unwonted service, does not have to contend with sullenness or disobedience or laziness; and who, by being under no obligation to teach a higher morality, is free from any disappointment in what must seem at times an incorrigible wickedness—to one so placed an impartial view of native virtues and failings will come more easily. And in conclusion one may promise that such an impartial view will discover less to despise or pity in the native's character and much more to admire. But all who know the Orokaiva best will share the writer's opinion that on the whole they are what we should call a very good lot.

NOTE ON ORTHOGRAPHY

Vowel sounds have been recorded as follows throughout the book.

A =	same vowel sound as in				'part',	e.g. *ābo*
or	,,	,,	,,	,, ,,	'pat',	,, *ăsănga*
E =	,,	,,	,,	,, ,,	'*père*'	,, *ēti*
or	,,	,,	,,	,, ,,	'pet'	,, *ĕmbo*
I =	,,	,,	,,	,, ,,	'peat',	,, *īna*
or	,,	,,	,,	,, ,,	'pit'	,, *ĭnja*
O =	,,	,,	,,	,, ,,	'port',	,, evo*bo*
U =	,,	,,	,,	,, ,,	'pool',	,, agŭ*ma*
or	,,	,,	,,	,, ,,	'put',	,, hŭ*mbari*
AI =	,,	,,	,,	,, ,,	'pipe',	,, i*ai*
AU =	,,	,,	,,	,, ,,	'powder',	,, a*ute*
EI =	,,	,,	,,	,, ,,	'pate',	,, bin*ei*
OI =	,,	,,	,,	,, ,,	'poison',	,, o*i*vo
OU =	,,	,,	,,	,, ,,	'potent',	,, Dir*ou* Tribe

A, E, I, and U are either long or short. Quantities have not been marked.

O is usually rather long. This vowel sound (viz. that of 'port') occurs so frequently in the language that the letter O has been adopted for it instead of AW. This English O (which has been recorded as OU) is comparatively rare.

Similarly the letter E has been adopted for the vowel sound of *père*, which is very common in the language.

GLOSSARY

(The meaning of most of the native words used is explained as they occur in the text.)

Abo, tail; fundamental orifice.
a-dorobu, bride-price.
aguma, warrior who bestows the *otohu*.
aha, mother (*hunjara*).
ahije, grandparents; grandchildren; sister's children (see p. 109).
ai, wife (see p. 109).
aja, mother (see p. 108).
ajimo, tree yielding bark-cloth.
ando, frayed palm-leaf worn as costume in dances.
araha, village clearing; clan.
arijo, men's house; a kind of dance.
asanga, ceremony of welcome to bride.
asisi, shadow; spirit; spiritual substitute.
asora, a contrivance for catching bats.
ate-ate, demonstration; a rite of purification.
atovo, father-in-law (see p. 109).
aute, bush, forest.
autembo, people of bush or forest.

Ba, taro.
bage, log-trap for pigs, &c.
bahari, laying-out platform for corpse.
baigona, former snake cult.
baja, Job's Tears; jacket of same.
bara, symbolic extraction of disease.
bate, dog's teeth.
bi, penis.
bi-dorobu, 'bridegroom-price'.
binei, spirit of dead; fiend, 'devil-devil'; clown in drama.
biteambo, younger brother (see p. 109).
bitepemi, elder brother (see p. 109).
bo, bark-cloth; perineal band of; skirt of.
bubuko, see *pupuho*.

Dera, sword-fish.
diriu, blue pigeon.
diroga, spirit of slain enemy; a variant of the Taro cult.
dorobu, price or compensation.
doru, widow.
du, sister (see p. 109).

Ehamei, 'New child', initiate.
embahi, spirit of dead; fiend, 'devil-devil'.
embo, man; men.
embogi, inter-clan fighting.
enga, raft.
epe, maternal uncle (Wasida dialect).
erumo, ovulum shell; ornament of same.
esa, homicidal emblem.
esu, sham fight.
eti, large string bag.
eva, sea; coast.
evobo, ancestor.

Gaga, platform; floor of house.
gana, an ornament of boars' tusks, seeds, &c.
gorukari, emergence of widow from seclusion.

Hahari, upper floor or platform of house.
hajai, self-imposed mourning tabu.
hajojo, Flying 'squirrel'; a kind of tree; native tobacco.
hambo, ornaments.
harasi, yam-house.
heratu, plant emblem.
hetava, small string bag.
hihi, legend, fable.
hono, an ornament of boars' tusks and shell.
hoto, pit-trap for pigs, &c.
hovatu, sister-in-law (see p. 109).
huave, a kind of shell ornament.
hui, trumpet (shell or wood).
humbari, 'taking away'; massage treatment.
hute, a bird net; a fish net.
huvivi, actor in drama (with a graceful role).

Iai, daughter (see p. 109).
imboti, mother-in-law (see p. 109).
imi, son-in-law (see p. 109).
ina, an edible andropogon.
inja, a tabu mark; a kind of sorcery.
ino, dog; the large drum
isoro, inter-tribal raid.

Jage, ceremony of hailing the dead.
java, dance.
javo, name.
jura, treatment of sickness by fumigation.

Kaiva kuku, masked dance of Gulf Division Papuans.
kananga, large lime pot.
kasamba, concerted singing.
kavo, blowing; a treatment of disease.
kenatu, see *heratu*.
kerari, child betrothal.
ki, spear.
kigi, clandestine love making.
kiki, see *hihi*.
kisa, belonging to dead (of garden).
kitoho, enemy.
kokumbari, to decorate; feather head-dresses; ceremony of bestowing
    same.
koni pamoni, a whistle made from the hollow shell of the *Puga* nut.
koropa, the black palm; adj., strong.
kotopu, see *otohu*.
kuku, tobacco (native or European); tattoo on drums.

Mama, father (see p. 108).
mei, son (see p. 109).
mine, exchange.
monga, pig-net.

Nabori, brother-in-law (see p. 109).
nobo, maternal uncle (see p. 109).
naterari, village tabu post.

O, lime.
obu, clay pot.
ohi, pandanus-leaf mat.
ohu, platform for food, &c., at feast.
oivo, miniature pit-trap.
ori, oblong shell slabs.
oro, men's house.
otavo, friend, mate.
otohu, ceremonial and honorific ornament; adj., of character appro-
    priate to same.

Pako, melon shell; ornament of same.
pamba, a kind of soft-wood.
pauri, cuscus; fur of same.
paruka, a kind of dance.
peka, peace.
pereho, adj., bush or inland (e.g. men or pigs).
peremo, hornbill; beak of same.
pipiga, a rough kind of bark-cloth.

pohu, bark-cloth hat or cowl.
pono, see *hono*.
pore, shell disks (*sapsap*).
puga, a fruit-bearing tree; a kind of dance.
pupuho, keloids.

Sa, betel.
saima, small white shells.
sama, seclusion enclosure.
samemi, pearl-shell armlets.
samuna, the 'bad' actor, or clown, in the drama.
saunda, small drum; a kind of dance.
savai, tree-house.
si, a kind of dance.
siango, spirit of dead; fiend, 'devil-devil'.
simbo, cross-cousin (see p. 109).
sirari, 'pushing away'; the ceremonial disposal of drama costumes, &c.
sivo, medicine.
sovai, spirit of dead; fiend, 'devil-devil'.
sovai-ta-na, villages of *sovai*, i.e. supposed abodes of dead.
su, ground compartment of house.
suna, purificatory stew.
supi, banana seeds.

Tata, paternal aunt (see p. 109).
tato, god-parent; god-child.
tauga, *okari* nut.
tekahoka, dependants; retinue.
tere, coco-nut leaf mat.
teva, wooden bowl or dish.
tunga, neck.

Uhu, trunk of a tree.

Yako, fish-net on triangular frame.

INDEX